Burning Books

Burning Books

HAIG BOSMAJIAN

McFarland & Company, Inc., Publishers

Jefferson, North Carolina, and London

ALSO BY HAIG BOSMAJIAN

The Freedom Not to Speak (1999)
Metaphor and Reason in Judicial Opinions (1992)
The Language of Oppression (1983)

LIBRARY OF CONGRESS CATALOGUING-IN-PUBLICATION DATA

Bosmajian, Haig A.
Burning books / Haig Bosmajian.
p.   cm.
Includes bibliographical references and index.

ISBN-13: 978-0-7864-2208-1
ISBN-10: 0-7864-2208-4 (illustrated case binding : 50# alkaline paper) ∞

1. Book burning — History.   I. Title.
Z659B67   2006   098'.109 — dc22   2005035201

British Library cataloguing data are available

On the cover: Nazi book burning bonfire in 1933 (*National Archives*);
background imagery ©2006 PhotoSpin

Manufactured in the United States of America

*McFarland & Company, Inc., Publishers
Box 611, Jefferson, North Carolina 28640
www.mcfarlandpub.com*

CONTENTS

To Hamida — for half a century
my wife and best friend

PREFACE

As I completed work on the manuscript for *Burning Books*, the fiftieth anniversary of Ray Bradbury's *Fahrenheit 451* was being commemorated. At the same time, however, as we honored Bradbury's foreboding novel warning against thought control, conformity, and book burning, literary, religious, and political books continued to be set afire from Indonesia to the Ivory Coast, from China to Nigeria, from India to the United States. It is no coincidence that the same year *Fahrenheit 451* was published, President Eisenhower delivered a speech at Dartmouth College in which he warned: "Don't join the book burners." By the time these warnings were expressed in 1953, the twentieth century had witnessed book burners around the world reducing to ashes millions of subversive-obscene-blasphemous books, some of them great works of literature.

Even though books were burned worldwide all through the twentieth century, as they had been through previous centuries, two very reputable sources pointed out, in 1988, that there was a "dearth of intensive historical investigation" in the problem of book burnings, and, in 1997, that "a contemporary survey of book burning as a form of censorship remains to be written." As I looked into this absence of publications focusing on book burnings, it became clear that while there were several good books on book *banning* there were none on book *burning* that provided a survey and examination of this particular form of ultimate censorship around the world. I found no book available focusing on the auto-da-fé, ancient and modern, involving not only the burning of books, but also the punishing, burning, and elimination of their authors. Further, as I did the research for the book, it became clear that many of the books burned, and their authors, seldom, if ever, appeared in works dealing generally with book banning.

It is my hope that, if nothing else, the reader will now recognize some of the books and their authors that paid the ultimate price and yet have remained neglected as victims. As I traced and examined the history of the "killing and massacre" of books and their "funerals," it was somewhat despairing to find that the book burners' atavism, fanaticism, inhumanity, and malice had not been identified and revealed in any one work dealing with the subject.

While I see it important to bring to the reader's attention books and authors that have hitherto remained relatively obscure, it is equally important to recognize the universality and timelessness of book burnings and to be aware of the condemnatory figurative language accompanying the fiery rituals. When books are persistently being condemned as "pestilence, poison, vermin, cancer, and virus" they are being prepared for elimination, probably by fire. The horrific history of exterminating books, sometimes exterminating the authors at the same time, is as much a part of current history as it was of earlier times. Decade after decade, century after century, the book burners have lit the fearful, powerful, magical fire to reduce to ashes the fearful, powerful, magical books.

If one considers that with the writing and publication of a book there occurs a conflation of book and author, then more than letters imprinted on paper pages have been eliminated. There is something frightful, dismaying and tragic when crowds of human beings stand in awe, celebrating a bonfire of condemned books going up in smoke and reduced to ashes. I hope the following pages contribute to an awareness of the magnitude of that historical and universal tragedy and inhumanity.

INTRODUCTION

For over two thousand years, book burners have set ablaze millions of books condemned as either religiously heretical, blasphemous, immoral, obscene, politically subversive or seditious. The book burning rituals have taken a variety of forms. Books have been attached to the bodies of heretics as they were set afire at the stake. Books have been burned to ashes in the bonfire of vanities. Books have been burned in church yards, college yards, school furnaces, and in city streets. Books were ordered burned by the hand of the "common hangman" in the public square. The image of the thousands of "un–German" books being cast into the bonfires throughout Nazi Germany in May 1933 still conveys the atavism and horrors of the fiery public ritual of the destruction and obliteration of literary, political, and scientific works. Up into the latter half of the twentieth century, books were being set afire around the world, from Argentina to Vietnam, from Turkey to Chile, from Brazil to China, from Spain to the United States.

The book burnings have continued through the centuries despite the continued warnings of the folly and evils of book burning. In his 1644 attack on governmental licensing and censorship, John Milton warned in *Areopagitica* of the dangers and perniciousness of the destruction of books. In reference to the burning of the books of philosopher and rhetorician Protagoras in fifth century Athens, Milton wrote: "In Athens, where books and wits were ever busier than in any other part of Greece, I find but only two sorts of writings which the magistrate cared to take notice of: those either blasphemous and atheistical, or libelous. Thus the books of Protagoras were by the judges of Areopagus commanded to be burnt, and himself banished the territory, for a discourse begun with his confessing not to know 'whether there were gods or whether not'" (1951 7). At the outset of *Areopagitica*, Milton personified the book: "[U]nless wariness be used, as good almost kill a man as kill a good book: who kills a man kills a reasonable creature, God's image; but he who destroys a good book, kills reason itself, kills the image of God, as it were in the eye" (1951 6). Both homicide and bibliocide are reprehensible. Sixteen years after *Areopagitica* was published, two of Milton's books containing treasonable passages were "killed" by order of the King's Proclamation to be "publicly burnt by the hand of the hangman" (1848 xxxviii).

In 1882, Heinrich Heine had one of the characters in the drama *Almansor*, Hassan, warn that "where men burn books, they will burn people in the end" (187). Prior centuries had provided sufficient evidence to support this nexus between book burning and the destruction, the burning, of human beings. If read literally or figuratively, Heine's "where men burn books, they will burn people in the end" has tragically turned out to be an insightful, accurate observation.

In 1943, United States Supreme Court Justice Robert Jackson warned in the Court's *West Virginia State Board of Education v. Barnette* opinion in favor of the Jehovah's Witness students who had refused to salute the flag: "Those who begin coercive elimination of dissent soon find themselves exterminating dissenters. Compulsory unification of opinion achieves only the unanimity of the graveyard" (641). Exactly one decade earlier, thousands of "un–German" books had been removed from the libraries in Nazi Germany, thrown onto flaming pyres, and reduced to ashes; within ten years, Jews, Communists, Jehovah's Witnesses, homosexuals, gypsies, and other "enemies" of the Nazi state were sent off to be killed in the concentration and extermination camps.

On June 14, 1953, President Dwight Eisenhower found it necessary to tell his audience at Dartmouth College: "Don't join the book burners" (Leviero 1). Eisenhower's comments were partly in response to Senator Joseph McCarthy's efforts to cleanse U.S. State Department overseas libraries of "un–American" books, especially those written by authors who had refused to testify before un–American activities committees about alleged Communist affiliations. The cleansing of the libraries involved the banning or burning of the "un–American" publications of such writers as Dashiell Hammett, Langston Hughes, Herbert Aptheker, Howard Fast, Alan Barth, and Lillian Hellman.

When in 1973, after the school committee in Drake, North Dakota, had copies of Kurt Vonnegut's classic novel *Slaughterhouse-Five* burning in the school furnace, Vonnegut admonished the school board: "Perhaps you will learn from this [national negative reactions to the book burning] that books are sacred to free men for very good reasons, and that wars have been fought against nations which hate books and burn them" (Vonnegut E19).

Despite such warnings and denunciations of book burning, the bibliocausts have continued decade after decade, century after century. In some cases books were burned, but the authors survived. In other cases, books were burned prior to the author being sent to the stake or books were burned after their authors had been condemned to death. And then there was the case of book burner Girolamo Savonarola whose "bonfire of the vanities" in 1498 set ablaze tapestries, perfumes, veils, and pictures portraying nudity, but also "books in Latin and also Italian, containing indecent and lustful poems." Several months after the "bonfire of vanities," Savonarola, by now condemned for preaching "heretical and perverse doctrines," was hanged and burned on the same Piazza della Signoria in Florence where he had set afire books by Boccaccio, Plato, and Dante (Erlanger 173).

And the case of John Wycliffe took still another turn; Wycliffe, a vocal critic of the Pope and Church, did die a natural death in 1384 and was buried in his own parish at Lutterworth; however, years later, in 1403 and 1410, his books were condemned by Church authorities and were burned. Still later, the Church decided that Wycliffe was himself a heretic and the 1425 Decree of Synod of Constance declared: "This synod also decreeth and ordaineth, that the body and bones of the said John Wickliff, if it might be discerned and known from the bodies of other faithful people, should be taken out of the ground, and thrown away far from the burial of any church, according to the canon laws and decrees" (Foxe 3 95). The Church "ungraved" Wycliffe, as John Foxe wrote, "and turned him from earth to ashes; which ashes they also took and threw into the river. And so was he resolved into three elements, earth, fire, and water" (Foxe 3 96).

As the fires have consumed the books through the centuries, book burners have attempted to extirpate history, to intimidate, to stamp out opposition, to create solidarity, to cleanse the land of "pestilence and disease," to purify. The promise of the book burner often has been that the phoenix will rise from the ashes of the burned books. During the book burnings in Nazi Germany on May 10, 1933, Propaganda Minister Joseph Goebbels declared the book burnings meant that the "German nation had cleansed itself internally and externally" through the destruction of books written by "degenerate and Jewish authors," including the works of Thomas Mann, Upton Sinclair, Jack London, Karl Marx, Helen Keller, Eric Maria Remarque, Albert Einstein, and Sigmund Freud. As the fires consumed the books, Goebbels orated: "These flames do not only illuminate the final end of the old era, they also light up the new. Never before have the young men had so good right to clean up the debris of the past.... The old goes up in flames, the new shall be fashioned from the flame in our hearts" (Birchall 12).

This atavistic, centuries-old ritual of book burning has, surprisingly and unfortunately, remained essentially unrecorded and unexamined in any single work. In a paper presented in Berlin "marking the passage of fifty years since the Nazi book burnings in 1933," Leo Lowenthal presented a brief review of book burnings and then stated in the 1988 publication of his paper: "One would accordingly assume that the burning of books is an important subject for research in history and political science. Astonishingly, however, this is not the case; there is a dearth of intensive historical investigation into this problem" (8). Ten years later, in 1997, the three volume reference source titled *Censorship* observed that "a contemporary survey of book burning as a form of censorship remains to be written" (*Censorship* 1 84).

There is a paucity of works devoted exclusively to the subject of book burning and the only two books in English that entirely focus on the subject are limited to book burnings in Great Britain. At the outset of his 1892 work *Books Condemned to Be Burnt*, James A. Farrer writes that his book "is confined to books so condemned in the United Kingdom" (2). Charles R. Gillett states in the Foreword to his 1932 *Burned Books: Neglected Chapters in British History and Literature:* "The following pages present the story of the burned books, principally in Great Britain" (viii).

A few books include pages or paragraphs devoted to book burning, along with a general treatment of censorship and bibliophobia. W.H. Hart's 1872 *Index Expurgatorius Anglicanus* is "a descriptive catalogue of the principal books printed or published in England, which have been suppressed, or burnt by the common hangman, or censured, or for which the authors, printers, or publishers have been prosecuted" (1); this work is limited to seventeenth century English book bannings and burnings. William Blades' 1888 *The Enemies of Books* includes a brief chapter dealing with books destroyed by fire, with chapters devoted to the destruction of books by water, dust, and vermin. Holbrook Jackson's 1932 *The Fear of Books* contains a few pages dealing with book burning. Marc Drogin's 1989 *Biblioclasm* includes a chapter titled "Up in Smoke: From Well Intentioned Book Burnings to Wanton Conflagration." Rebecca Knuth's *Libricide* (2003) presents five case studies of the destruction of books in twentieth century Germany, Bosnia, Kuwait, China and Tibet. Matthew Battles' *Library: An Unquiet History* (2003) includes a chapter titled "Knowledge on Fire," focusing on twentieth century destruction of European libraries.

In light of this background indicating the absence of a single contemporary book devoted entirely to the subject of worldwide book burnings through the centuries, I have attempted to fill this void with this work devoted exclusively to book burning and not with a publication covering the subject of censorship generally. "Book burning" is to be taken literally here, not figuratively. Often, "book burning" is used figuratively by authors to mean book banning. There have appeared articles that are headlined with "book burnings," but a close reading of the articles reveals that they are about book bannings, not book burnings. Further, I have omitted inclusion of books that were said to be "destroyed" or "confiscated" because such terms did not directly indicate they were actually burned.

Hence, the purpose of this work is to identify the book burners and the works they purposely set afire over the centuries and to examine the persistent use of metaphoric language "justifying" the fiery destruction of the heretical, seditious, and obscene books and some-times their authors.

What becomes evident as one traces the history of book burnings is the heavy reliance on condemnatory, figurative language, transforming the books into "tares," "pestilence," "plague," "cancer," and "poison"—all inviting extermination. The persistent use of such metaphoric language contributing to reducing books to ashes cannot be underestimated. As Beardsley has warned: "The trouble with metaphors is that they have a strong pull on our fancy. They tend to run away from us. Then we find that our thinking is directed not by the force of argument at hand, but at the interest of the image in our mind" (245). Similarly, Shibles has warned: "Without being conscious of metaphor and one's metaphors, one becomes their captive" (27). Or as one of George Eliot's characters in *Middlemarch* declares: "We all of us, grave or light get our thoughts entangled in metaphors and act fatally on the strength of them" (63).

One of the most devastating examples of a people having their "thoughts entangled in metaphors" and acting "fatally on the strength of them" is provided by Thomas Friedman in his discussion of the Nazis' redefinition of Jews into "vermin," "bacilli," and "lice":

> [I]n an act that might be considered almost poetic were it not so horrifying and grotesque, the Nazi administrative captured the spirit of the metaphor its propagandists had devised. It contacted the chemical industries of the *Reich*, specifically the firms that specialized in "combatting vermin." Simply, it requested that these manufacturers of insecticides produce another delousing agent, one a bit stronger than the produce used for household ticks and flies, but one that would be used for essentially the same purpose. The companies complied. Thus was *Zyklon B* created. The gas, used in milder form for occasionally fumigating the disease-ridden barracks where other victims were penned, killed millions of men, women, and children. Obscenely clinging to the metaphor they had accepted, the Nazis herded their Jewish victims into gas chambers of death that were disguised as "showers" and "disinfectant centers." What the bureaucrats accomplished, the propagandists had made psychologically possible [254–255].

The insidiousness and danger of the "virus," "cancer," "bacillus" metaphors, as Lowenthal and Guterman have explained, is that "the micro-organism seems to combine all the various enemy qualities in the highest degree. It is ubiquitous, close, deadly, insidious, it invites the idea of extermination, and, most important, it is invisible to the naked eye—the agitator expert is required to detect its presence" (55). If such dehumanizing, condemnatory metaphors have contributed to the burning of human beings, we should not be surprised to hear similar metaphors being used to "justify" burning the book labeled "pestilent," "filthy," "cancerous," or "poisonous."

The book burner is not only ridding the land of "tares" and "pests," but is also symbolically eradicating the condemned author. What becomes evident as one traces the history of book burnings is that the book burners have not hesitated, in fact have encouraged, conducting the bibliocaust in public view with the citizens watching the destruction of what the minds of the authors of the condemned books had produced. The author's words on the printed page, the book created by the author, being publicly destroyed in the fire became a symbolic destruction of the author; in effect, the author was being reduced to ashes. As the books go up in flames, the book burner exclaims and the newspapers report that Remarque, Marx, Freud, and Mann went up in flames. The metonymy is at work here, the metonymy being like a metaphor, a figure of speech, but in this instance the author standing for the book. Something more than inked marks in paper books went up in flames when Voltaire, Rousseau, Defoe, Steinbeck, and Einstein were tossed into the bonfires.

As Margaronis has observed, "A book, like a human being, is mind incomprehensibly contained in matter, the word made flesh" (148). She cites both *Don Quixote* and *Areopagitica* to illustrate; from Don Quixote: "'Here master licentiate,' cries Quixote's housekeeper, rushing out with a bowl of water, 'pray take and sprinkle the closet, lest some one of the many enchanters contained in these books, should exercise his art upon us, as punishment for our burning, and banishing them from the fact of the earth.'" In his *Areopagitica* John Milton saw book burning as a "kind of homicide": "We should be wary ... what persecution we raise against the living labors of public men, how we spill that seasoned life of man, preserved and stored up in books; since we see a kind of homicide may be thus committed, sometimes a martyrdom."

When in 1919–1920 issues of the literary journal *The Little Review* were burned by the U.S. Post Office because of the inclusion of episodes from James Joyce's *Ulysses*, journal editor Margaret Anderson stated: "It was like burning at the stake as far as I was concerned" (Lidderdale and Nicholson 167). The public bibliocaust was a dramatic, fearful reminder to the citizenry of what happens to those who express impious, obscene, heretical, and seditious views. The destruction of the books was usually not enough; the bibliocide implied a homicide to be viewed, to be experienced, by the public. The fiery public ritual was an atavistic expression of intimidation and terror, less likely to be achieved if the books were simply collected and destroyed out of sight of the populace.

When Protagoras was charged with impiety and atheism in the fifth century B.C.E., his book *On the Gods* was publicly burned in the agora, according to some classical scholars. In the twelfth century, heretic Peter Abelard's *On the Unity and Trinity of God* was ordered by the Church to be burned "in sight of all"; Abelard was ordered to throw his own book into the flames and watch his work burn to ashes.

In the thirteenth and fourteenth centuries, thousands of copies of the Talmud were publicly set afire in France, Italy, and Spain. In 1319, "at the requisition and mandate of Bernard Guy [Inquisitor of Toulouse], two large waggon-loads of Hebrew books, being as many as could be found in searching the houses of the Jews, were drawn through the streets of Toulouse, with a procession of servants of the royal court, and a crier going before, who proclaimed with a loud voice that the books, said to be copies of the Talmud, contained blasphemies against Christianity, and, having been examined by persons learned in the language, were to be burnt; and they were burnt accordingly. Gregory IX., a zealous persecutor of Jews, had commanded the Talmud to be burnt, which was done by the Chancellor of Paris in the year 1230, before an assemblage of clergy and people" (Rule 55). In 1321, Pope John XXII ordered the destruction of the Talmud in Rome, and "when in Rome volumes of the Talmud were thrown into the flames a fitting background was given to the scene by the Roman mob, which terrified the Jews by robbery and murder" (Popper 17). The Talmud achieved the distinction of being the only book that was consistently burned for nine consecutive centuries, from the thirteenth to the twentieth century.

In the fifteenth century, Inquisitor General Torquemada "celebrated a number of burning festivals, especially of Hebrew Bibles and, after final defeat of the Moors in Grenada in 1492, of Arabic books also" (Longhurst 78). When in 1409 the books of condemned heretic John Wycliffe were burned, "the burning of the books was accompanied by the ringing of all the bells of Prague and the solemn chanting of the *Te Deum*" (Spinka 97). At the end of the fifteenth century, the Archbishop of Toledo, Spain, "collected five thousand Arabic books, many of them splendidly ornamented and illuminated, and in spite of the entreaty of friends who begged of him the priceless MSS., he burnt them all on the public square, except those on medicine, which he reserved and finally deposited in his University of Alcala" (Lea 1967 21). The burning of books as a public ritual, a public "festival,"

Saint Dominic and the Books of the Heretics, a painting by Pietro Damini. (Cameraphoto Arte, Venice/Art Resource, NY.)

with the ringing of the bells in the public square, was firmly established by the fifteenth century. As Lea has indicated, "At the height of its power the Inquisition spared no labor or expense to lend impressiveness to the *auto publico general*, as a demonstration of its authority and of the success with which it performed its functions" (Lea 1988 209).

In 1546, French scholar and printer Etienne Dolet was arrested and imprisoned for authoring and printing books condemned as blasphemous and seditious. It was ordered that he be taken in a cart from the prison to the Place Maubert in Paris "where a gallows was to be erected in the most convenient and suitable place, around which was to be made a great fire, into which, after having been hung on the said gallows, his body was to be thrown with his books, and burnt to ashes" (Christie 470).

In the sixteenth century, Spanish scholar and physician Michael Servetus had the "honor" of being burned in effigy and a few months later being sent to the stake, along with his books. In June 1553, Servetus was found guilty of heresy for, among other things, the views he expressed about the Trinity in his book *Cristianismi restitutio*. The imprisoned Servetus escaped and was publicly burned in effigy, along with five hundred copies of his book (Fulton 35). His effigy was "paraded through the streets of Vienne [France], brought to the place of public execution, hanged upon a gibbet erected for the purpose, and finally set fire to, and with the five bales [of books] burned to ashes" (Willis 275). Several months later, on October 27, 1553, Servetus was again found guilty of various charges: "First: with having, between twenty-three and twenty-four years ago, caused to be printed at Hage-nau, Germany, a book against the Holy Trinity, full of blasphemies, to the great scandal of the Churches of Germany, the book having been condemned by all their doctors, and he, the writer, forced to fly that country.... Item: with having in said book called all who believe in a Trinity, tritheists, and even Atheists, and the Trinity itself a daemon or monster hav-ing three heads.... Item: with declaring the Baptism of Infants to be sorcery and a diabol-ical invention..." (Willis 480–481).

The court condemning Servetus then declared: "[W]e now pronounce our final sen-tence and condemn thee, Michael Servetus, to be bound and taken to Champel, and there being fastened to a stake, to be burned alive, along with thy books, printed as well as writ-ten by thy hand, until thy body be reduced to ashes" (Willis 483). In a procession through the streets, Servetus was taken to the site of the burning and a crowd watched as his body was chained to the stake: "Around his waist were tied a large bundle of manuscript and a thick octavor printed book. The torch was applied, and as the flames spread to the straw and sulphur and flashed in his eyes, there was a piercing cry that struck terror into the hearts of the bystanders" (Fulton 25).

Early in the seventeenth century, the Church ordered that the books of heretic Gior-dano Bruno, who refused to recant and was excommunicated, "should be publicly burnt." In July 1656, two Quaker women, Mary Fischer and Ann Austin, arrived in Boston harbor from Barbados and were immediately jailed until they were shipped back five weeks later to Barbados. Their baggage had been searched by Massachusetts' authorities and one hun-dred books and pamphlets were confiscated. "The women were ordered held prisoners aboard, and the 'corrupt books' by order of Council were burned in the market-place by the hangman" (Blumenthal 14).

In England, the University of Oxford *Judgment and Decree* of July 21, 1683, declared on the title page that the judgment and decree had been passed "against certain Pernicious Books and Damnable Doctrines Destructive to the Sacred Persons of Princes, their State and Government and of all Humane Society." After listing the objectionable propositions advanced in various books, the *Decree* stated: "We decree, judge and declare all and every of these Propositions to be false, seditious and impious, and most of them to be also Hereti-cal and Blasphemous, infamous to Christian Religion and destructive of all Government in Church and State" (7). The provision for a public burning was also included in the *Decree*: "We also order the before recited books to be publicly burnt, by the hand of our marshal in the court of our Scholes" (7). Included in the list of "pernicious" books con-demned to be burned was Thomas Hobbes' *Leviathan*.

While the "impious, obscene and seditious" books of Voltaire, Rousseau, Servetus, Hobbes, and other Europeans were being burned in Europe in the eighteenth century, "trea-sonable and seditious" books, along with woodblocks, were being set afire in China. Luther Goodrich has identified eight "tests" seemingly used by the Chinese "to determine a book's fitness to exist" (44). Three of the more important tests were: (1) "Was it anti-dynastic or rebellious?"; (2) "Did it insult previous dynasties which were, in a sense, ancestral to the Ch'ing?"; (3) "Did it concern the northern and northwestern frontiers and military or naval defense?" (Goodrich 44–48). Hence, the 1779 "Report of the Grand Secretary San-Pao, Governor-General of Fukien, Regarding the Search for Books of a Seditious Nature" read: "While at my former posts as governor of Chekian and governor-general of Hukuang I was constantly pressing my subordinates to look for seditious books.... Formerly occupants of my present office have on six occasions made deliveries to the capital of seditious works. Now I am again sending books that ought to be burned, to the number of 113 items.... I have annotated them all and find every one seditious and worthy of destruction. They are being sent up with a list through the Grand Council for that body to examine and destroy by fire" (Goodrich 184).

In 1781, an official "Edict on the Books of Yin Chia-ch'uan," an author and governmental officer who offended the Emperor, was issued ordering the burning of his seditious works: "I now have the report of Ying Lien and Yuan Shou-t'ung. They have checked the books of Yin Chia-ch'uan at his Peking residence, including those written by himself. These last contained many false and rebellious passages. None may be saved, and I have already ordered their burning. The seditious works of Yin were very numerous.... Let Yuan Shou-t'ung seek these out, and cause these books and woodblocks to be carefully assembled and delivered, and not one be hidden. Each one is to be brought to Peking to be destroyed by fire" (Goodrich 203–204).

In 1695, a warrant was issued in Massachusetts to search out copies of Thomas Maule's *Truth held forth and maintained & etc.* and the Council ordered "that the said bookes now under seizure both at Boston and Salem be publicly burnt here and there" (Duniway 72). Five years later, in 1700, Robert Calef published *More Wonders of the Invisible World* in which he criticized the manner in which the Salem witch trials were conducted and in which he attacked Increase Mather and Cotton Mather and other Boston ministers. The book so enraged Increase Mather that he publicly burned the book in the Harvard College grounds (Poole 170). A half century later, in October 1754, the Massachusetts House of Representatives ordered the burning of an anonymous satirical pamphlet titled *The Monster of Monsters* which the House concluded affronted the representatives in that the publication was "a false, scandalous libel, reflecting upon the proceedings of the House in general and on the members in particular. The hangmen was ordered to burn it in King Street below the courthouse, and the messenger was required to see that the order carried out" (Duniway 115).

In the eighteenth century, it was in France that much more book burning was taking place. The works of Jean Jacques Rousseau and François Voltaire especially were reduced to ashes. As Farrer has indicated, "no other writer, indeed, of the eighteenth century contributed so many books to the flames as Voltaire" (15). In 1734, Voltaire's *Lettres philosophiques* was condemned in Paris "to be publicly burned as scandalous and contrary to religion, morality, and the respect due the authorities" (Orieux 107). Voltaire's *The Story of Dr. Akakia* and *The Native of St. Malo* "were burned by the hangman at street corners of Berlin, and before the house in Taubenstrasse, in which Voltaire lived" (Brandes 72). *Candide* was publicly burned in Paris in 1759 and his *Dictionnaire philosophique* was burned in Geneva, Paris, and Rome (*Censorship* 3 842).

The books of Voltaire's antagonist, Jean Jacques Rousseau, were also being reduced to ashes in the middle of the eighteenth century. Rousseau's *Emile* was condemned as a work "which dares deny the truth and prophecies of the Bible and wishes to set aside the evidence of miracles recounted in holy books" (Brandes 2 92). The Parlement de Paris ordered the book to be "torn and burnt at the foot of its great staircase" (Farrer 13). In 1762, Rousseau's *The Social Contract* was set ablaze in Geneva along with *Emile* (Handel 2 255). His *Lettres de la Montagne* was publicly burned in Switzerland and Holland (Brandes 2 101) Rousseau died on July 2, 1778, a month after Voltaire's death. While during their lifetimes there was much hostility between the two great authors who shared the experience of seeing their books burned, in death they shared, according to some biographers, the same fate together. According to Huizinga, Rousseau's remains were placed in "the Pantheon, where Voltaire himself was laid to rest. And how dizzily the Grand Old Man must have spun, his teeth rattling in his skull, as he found himself compelled to spend eternity under the same vaulted roof with, of all people, the detested Jean-Jacques.... As things turned out their cohabitation lasted only a few years at the end of which persons unknown, who held timid peace-loving Jean-Jacques responsible for the sanguinary excesses of the Revolution, broke open his tomb and scattered its contents to the winds" (252). Similarly, Tallentyre has Voltaire and Rousseau meeting the same fate, both have their remains placed in the Pantheon in Paris and then "with the connivance of the [Bourbon] ministry, the tombs of both Voltaire and Rousseau were violated, their bones removed in a sack at night to a waste place outside the city and emptied into a pit filled with quicklime" (565–566).

Across the Atlantic, the first half of the nineteenth century brought book burnings to the United States in the form of fiery destructions of anti-slavery writings. For example, in 1860, a non-slaveholder southerner, Hinton Helper, published *The Impending Crisis of the South* in which he presented his "scheme for the abolition of slavery in the Southern States." Helper's 410-page book was seen by southern slaveowners as a threat and "at High Point, North Carolina, ten copies were publicly burned in the civic center" (Blumenthal 18). While Helper argued for the demise of slavery in the South, his goal was to improve the lot of white southerners, he said, by ridding the land of degrading and uneconomical slavery. Helper had little sympathy for the slaves and was critical of attempts to bring about equal treatment of the races. Even though Helper shared the racism of the slaveowners, his advocacy of ridding the South of slavery was not to be tolerated and hence the burning of his book.

In 1909, Helper committed suicide in Washington, D.C., and *The Literary Digest*, in reporting his death, referred to the significance of *The Impending Crisis in the South*: "Recently an old, destitute, and friendless man died by his own hand in a Washington garret. Some fifty years ago he wrote a book which eventually had almost as much influence on the slavery agitation of the day as did 'Uncle Tom's Cabin' or 'John Brown's Raid.' His book also became a real factor in promoting the election of Lincoln" ("A Forgotten Hero of Slavery Days" 569).

The nineteenth century also saw book burnings in Germany where, in October 1817, hundreds of students and others gathered at the Warburg Festival to celebrate the "three hundredth anniversary of Luther's promulgation of the Ninety-Five Theses and the fourth anniversary of the Leipzig Battle of the Nations, Napoleon's last fight on German soil" (Snyder 154). A torchlight procession took place and then "a great bonfire was kindled, and the books of 'anti-student' and 'reactionary' tendency were cast into the flames, along with a bagwig, a pair of guardman's stays, and a corporal's cane — symbols of the military authoritarian state" (Snyder 154). Leo Lowenthal has referred to the similarities between the 1817 Warburg Festival auto-da-fé and the 1933 Nazi book burnings: "The rituals of book-burning, accompanied by anti–Semitic outbreaks, the screaming student choirs, the infamous participation of university professors who aided in inciting this ill deed at the Warburg Festival as well as in German university towns in 1933, are expressive of the similarities between 1817 and 1933" (Lowenthal 16).

Late in the nineteenth century, when Anthony Comstock helped establish the New York Society for the Suppression of Vice, the organization created its own seal that appeared on its stationery and elsewhere; on one half of the seal was a picture of a police officer placing a purveyor of vice into the jail cell and the other half pictures a man in a high hat casting some books into a heap of books ablaze. Encircling these two pictures were the words: "THE NEW YORK SOCIETY FOR THE SUPPRESSION OF VICE." Two years before he died, Comstock proudly spoke of the number of people he was instrumental in convicting and of the huge amount of obscene materials he had destroyed: "In the forty-one years I have been here I have convicted persons enough to fill a passenger train of sixty-one coaches, sixty coaches containing sixty passengers each and the sixty-first almost full. I have destroyed 160 tons of obscene literature" (Brown and Leech 15–16).

One would have assumed that with the coming of the twentieth century, modern civilized societies had moved beyond the atavistic, irrational appeals of book burnings. However, the twentieth century book burners were not to be outdone by their predecessors in searching for heresies, obscenity, impiety, and subversion. The twentieth century book burners continued to rely on the "argument by force"; as Charles Gillett wrote in describing the sixteenth-eighteenth century civil and ecclesiastical book burners, "The fiery trial was quicker than the course of protracted debate, and in controversy there is always the danger of defeat.... Fire was their last argument, and it was used in cases not a few" (Gillett I 4). This "last argument," the reduction of books to ashes, was relied on just as often and universally as it had been prior to the twentieth century.

Two of the first victims to the torch at the outset of the twentieth century were James Joyce's *The Dubliners* and *Ulysses*. In a letter dated September 11, 1912, Joyce wrote: "The 1000 copies of *Dubliners* which are printed are to be destroyed by fire this morning" (Ellmann 319). Several days later, in a letter to W.B. Yeats, Joyce said: "I suppose you will have heard the fate of my book *Dubliners*. Roberts refused to publish it and finally agreed to sell me the first edition for 30 so that I might publish it myself. Then the printer refused to hand over the 1000 copies which he had printed either to me or to anyone else and actually broke up the type and burned the whole first edition" (Gilbert 71–72). Several years later, Joyce again referred to the burning of *The Dubliners* in a letter dated December 19, 1919: "For the publication of *Dubliners* I had to struggle for ten years. The whole first edition of 1000 copies was burnt at Dublin by fraud" (Gilbert 132). Of this book burning incident Joyce scholar Richard Ellmann has written: "On September 11 the sheets [for *Dubliners*] were destroyed. Joyce said by fire, Roberts [the publisher], stickling for accuracy in his later accounts, insisted they were destroyed by guillotining and pulping. Burnt or dismembered in effigy, Joyce had no further business in Dublin, and he left with Nora and the children that same night" (346).

Joyce's *Ulysses* began appearing serialized in the American literary journal *The Little Review* in March 1918. Finding Joyce's writing "obscene, lewd, lascivious, filthy, indecent and

Logo of the New York Society for the Suppression of Vice. (Negative #77508d. Collection of the New-York Historical Society.)

disgusting," the U.S. Post Office seized and burned some issues of the journal in 1919–1920 (Johnson xli). In a February 25, 1920, letter, Joyce wrote: "This is the second time I have had the pleasure of being burned while on earth so that I hope I shall pass through the fires of purgatory as quickly as my patron S. Aloysius" (Gilbert 137).

When *Ulysses* finally appeared in book form in 1922, the U.S. Post Office confiscated and burned 400–500 copies of the book. Irish, Canadian, and English authorities also ordered that *Ulysses* be burned. In 1923, 500 copies of *Ulysses*, published in Paris, were seized by the Customs at Folkestone, England, and after Harriet Weaver, the publisher, decided not to challenge the seizure, "customs proceeded to the next stage: the destruction of the books by burning" (Lidderdale and Nicholson 217).

About the same time that Joyce's work was being burned, D.H. Lawrence's *The Rainbow* was being denounced in England as "utter filth" and was publicly destroyed by fire, as legend would have it. *The Times* reported on November 15, 1915, in an item titled "The Rainbow. Destruction of a Novel": "At Bow-street Police Court on Saturday, Messrs. Methuen and Co. (Limited), publishers Essex-street, Strand, were summoned before Sir John Dickinson to show cause why 1,011 copies of Mr. D.H. Lawrence's novel *The Rainbow* should not be destroyed. The defendants expressed regret that the book should have been published, and the magistrate ordered that the copies should be destroyed and that the defendants should pay 10.10s costs" (Draper 102). Writing in *New Statesman* on November 20, 1915, critic J.C. Squire reported: "Last Saturday, at Bow Street, Mr. D.H. Lawrence's new novel *The Rainbow* was brought before the bench and sentenced to death" (Draper 104). Copies of the "bawdy" and "disgusting" *The Rainbow* were, according to legend, "burnt by the public handman outside the Royal Exchange" (Sagar 90).

While the "filthy" *Ulysses* was being burned in the United States and the "disgusting" *The Rainbow* was being destroyed in England, "trashy" literature was being burned in Germany. In June 1922, *The New York Times Current History* published an article by Lillian Eagle in which she sympathetically described the "moral crusade" of the "youthful reformers" of the German *Jugendbewegung* (youth movement): "The great revolution that followed the World War, instead of proving a cleansing storm, has developed more and more into an economic struggle, and as there is no one to protect the young from post-war vices and evils they are determined to do it themselves. Smoking and drinking are tabooed. Shops with unclean postcards and books are boycotted. Flaming protests against immoral performances in the theatres and cinemas are posted in all public places.... Even if these efforts have until now remained abortive, they are in a right direction" (Eagle 450–451). The article was illustrated with a photograph of "Berlin police burning wagon loads of trashy juvenile fiction which school teachers have collected in an effort to suppress the evils of bad literature" (Eagle 451).

With the rise of Nazism in the 1920s and 1930s came the massive book burnings throughout Germany on May 10, 1933, in Berlin, Munich, Breslau, Kiel, Heidelberg, Frankfurt-am-Main. On May 11, 1933, Fredrick T. Birchall reported in *The New York Times* on the previous night's burning of "un–German" books:

> More than 20,000 books were on the pile that students of the University of Berlin ignited in the Opera square tonight.
>
> * * * *
>
> A hundred massively bound volumes — the works of "un–German" writers — were public burned in the Koenigsplatz [in Munich] tonight after a picturesque torchlight parade of students.
>
> All the books destroyed came from the university library, but they were consigned to the flames lit by the students' inquisitorial tribunal because of their "disintegrating influence" [12].

A few days later, more books were set ablaze in Heidelberg: "The books burned numbered several thousand, extracted mainly from public libraries. The huge pile was covered with Communist flags before it was lighted and a cap from the uniform of the outlawed Reichsbanner was put on top, the assembled studenthood cheering frantically. The burning was preceded by a torchlight procession through the town in which Nazi storm troopers and Stahlhelm members were supported by the students dueling corps in full regalia, booted and sword-belted" (*The New York Times* May 19, 1933 9).

While the use of fire in Germany to destroy condemned writings was, of course, nothing new — Luther's 1520 burning of Papal Bull and books, the 1817 Warburg Festival book burnings, the burnings of "trashy and smutty" books in the 1920s — what was new was the emphasis on the widespread use of fire in the Nazi persuasion. Torchlight parades, S.A. men sitting around bonfires eerily lighting up the sky, bowls of fire as part of mass meetings, the Reichstag fire — the magic and power of these fires appealed to the atavistic side of the participants and views, as did the book burnings. Referring to the 1933 book burnings, Stieg has observed: "The literary world has few dramas that can compare: flames against the dark night from a ring of torches surrounding the victims, inspiring oratory, the chanting of aroused participants, and finally — the focus and culmination — a gigantic funeral pyre of the intellect" (91). The Nazis' book burning ritual, states Stieg, was "mainly designed as an act by which the past and its false values were rejected. Not only was the impact of the book burnings intended to be symbolic, the proceedings themselves were rife with symbolism. Fire, for example, has been associated with purification rites. Use of the term auto-da-fé linked the book burnings with such historic conflagrations as Savanarola's Burning of the Vanities, many of which were expressions of religious zeal" (94).

One year after the 1933 book burnings in Nazi Germany, Chiang-Kai-shek was ordering the burning of "proletarian literature" in China, including books by Maxim Gorky, Upton Sinclair, Bertrand Russell and others whose works had also been reduced to ashes in the Nazi bonfires (Hsu Ting 92–93). As the decade came to a close, books were being burned in Spain and the United States. By 1939, book burnings had become commonplace in General Francisco Franco's Spain; when the Spanish Civil War ended in 1939, "virtually everything was forbidden. Many private libraries had been burnt and went on being burnt until long after" (Dieguez 91). Also in 1939, at the same time Americans were denouncing the Nazi book burnings, they were burning John Steinbeck's *Grapes of Wrath* in California, Illinois, and Oklahoma because it was "filthy," "vile propaganda," and "false sensationalism" (*Look* 15; *Publishers Weekly* CXL 21).

As the next decade began, Professor of Education Harold Rugg asked, "Book burning in 1940?" The reason he asked was that his *That Men May Understand* was set afire in Bradner, Ohio, because his social science books were "un–American," "anti–free enterprise," and giving the child "an unbiased viewpoint instead of teaching him real Americanism" (Rugg 3). The burning of "un–American" books also occurred in Oklahoma City in 1940 after a Father Webber announced over the radio that books purchased at the Progressive Bookstore were to be burned in the Oklahoma City Stadium" (*Publishers Weekly* CXL 21).

With World War II came the massive destruction and burning of books and libraries as a result of the indiscriminate bombings of cities in England, Germany, and other European countries. In 1941, the *American Library Association Bulletin* published an article by John R. Russell titled "Libraries Under Fire" in which he wrote of the destruction of English libraries from German air raids: "The library of University College, the University of London, is one that has suffered severe losses.... The library, first opened in 1829 with a collection of 6000 volumes, had become one of the great libraries of England, its more than

400,000 volumes including special collections of great importance. The librarian, Mr. John Wilks, reports that approximately 100,000 volumes have been lost" (277). Seven thousand volumes in the Great Hall of Bristol University were "completely destroyed by fire resulting from incendiary bombs. In addition to the destruction of university libraries, "public libraries in England have also been hit by bombs. The Minet Public Library, operated by the boroughs of Lambeth and Camberwell, was struck by fire bombs and burned to the ground in December...." (Russell 278). Further, "Coventry's central library was completely destroyed by fire; only 30,000 volumes from the Gulson Reference Library were salvaged from a total of about 170,000 volumes" (Russell 279).

According to the UNESCO publication *Memory of the World: Lost Memory — Libraries and Archives Destroyed in the Twentieth Century*, "It has been estimated that a third of all German books [in Germany] were destroyed during World War II." Also, "During the Sino-Japanese War, a great many libraries were destroyed." Further, "Heavy damage was done to Russian libraries. It has been estimated that more than 100 million books were destroyed, mainly from public libraries" (*Index on Censorship* 2 1999 166–167).

Such destruction and burning of books and libraries during air raids is not of direct interest in this work which deals with the intentional burning of books because of their suspected seditious, heretical or obscene content. Catastrophic as this massive destruction of libraries and burning of books was, the writings on the library shelves were not specifically targeted for devastation; while the Allies were firebombing Dresden, Breman, and Hamburg, the designated targets were not libraries. While German bombers dropped their incendiary bombs on London, day after day, night after night, German bombardiers were not zeroing in on public libraries to set afire the books in the stacks.

However, during the war, aside from the books destroyed in the air raids, there were books intentionally burned because they contained ideas unacceptable to the book burners. In Poland, "the Germans formed 'Brenn-Kommandos' (arson squads) to destroy Jewish synagogues and books. Thus the Great Talmudic Library of the Theological Seminary in Lublin was burned. On the eve of the German evacuation of Poland in January 1945, the main stacks of the Warsaw Public Library were burned" (*Index on Censorship* 2 1999 166). In the Baltic states, "After the occupation by Soviet troops an official list of Banned Books and Brochures was issued in Latvia in November 1940. With additional lists, over 4,000 titles were proscribed. In Latvia, as in Estonia and Lithuania, such books were removed from bookstores and libraries and, in many cases, publicly burned" (*Index on Censorship* 2 1999 166).

After the war, there was enough book banning and burning going on in the United States that President Eisenhower saw it necessary to declare in his June 14, 1953, Dartmouth College speech: "Don't join the book burners" (*The New York Times* June 15, 1953 10). That same year, as Blumenthal reported: "In June 1953, some 300 books by eighteen authors were 'purged' from U.S. Information Service Libraries abroad on order of the State Department, because they were alleged to be Communist propaganda or by suspect authors. A few were said to have been burned, but most were sold for pulping or otherwise destroyed" (18). Also in 1953, a Chicago mob "broke up a meeting of the Council of American-Soviet Friendship. More than one hundred books, including nineteen copies of Dr. Corliss Lamont's *Soviet Civilization* were burned or otherwise destroyed in the street" (Blumenthal 18). One month after Eisenhower's Dartmouth speech, police, firefighters, clergy, and civil leaders attended a auto-da-fé in Newark, New Jersey, witnessing the burning of "pornographic" books, films and photographs (*The New York Times* March 8, 1953 72). The combination of socialism and sex led to a book burning in Sapulpa, Oklahoma, in 1952, the book burners contending the school library books "approved" of socialism and "dealt too frankly with sex" (*The New York Times* February 12, 1952).

While Eisenhower was telling Americans not to "join the book burners," the United States was providing economic and political support to South American countries that were burning the works of Karl Marx, Frederick Engels, Gabriel García Márquez, Walt Whitman, John Steinbeck, Garcia Lorca, and Pablo Neruda. The military dictatorship of Guatemala was burning "subversive" books, such as *Les Misérables* and Miguel Ángel Asturias's *El Señor Presidente* and the Argentine government, as part of its widespread censorship, ordered the burning of "textbooks such as Marx and Engels" (Graham-Yooll 1973 43). After democratically elected President Salvador Allende was overthrown by Pinochet, the right-wing junta "broke into bookstores and libraries, seized thousands of books which they decided were Leftist in character and fed them to the flames" (Chavkin 218). In Uruguay, there occurred in 1973 a widespread dismissal of university professors and a "purifying" of the libraries of materials "of Marxist content or supposed sympathies," all ending up on "bonfires or in paper processing plants" (*Index on Censorship* Jan/Feb 1979 50).

In the Mideast, the American supported regime of the Shah of Iran instituted the policy of requiring bookstores to "record the names and addresses of everyone who buys books, so that, if a book is blacklisted after distribution, the government has access to the names and addresses of those who have bought copies. These can then be collected from their owners, burned or turned into pulp" (Baraheni 16). Then in 1989, the Khomeini authorities called for the assassination of Salmon Rushdie because of his "blasphemous" book *Satanic Verses* which was subsequently burned in Bradford, Birmingham, and other cities in the United Kingdom" (Noble 192–207). In response to the burnings of his book, Rushdie wrote in 1989: "The justification [for the condemnation of *Satanic Verses*] is that I have 'given offense.' But the giving of offense cannot be a basis for censorship, or freedom of expression would perish instantly. And many of us who were revolted by the Bradford flames will feel that the offense done to our principles is at least as great as any offense caused to those who burned my book" (25). *The Satanic Verses*, explained Rushdie, was not "an antireligious novel"; and "the saddest irony of all," he wrote, was that "I should see my book burned, largely unread, by the people it's about, people who might find some pleasure and much recognition in its pages" (26). Perhaps the most astute and distressing observation made by Rushdie in his one page essay "The Book Burning" was: "How fragile civilization is; how easily, how merrily a book burns!" (26).

While the books by John Steinbeck, Pablo Neruda, Walt Whitman, Karl Marx, Garcia Lorca, Jean-Paul Sartre, and others were being burned in the 1970s in such countries as Argentina, Chile, Turkey, Iran, and Uruguay, Kurt Vonnegut's *Slaughterhouse-Five* was being reduced to ashes in Drake, North Dakota, after the school board decided that the book was, among other things, "dirty" (*Chicago Sun-Times* 40). Four years later, a group of senior citizens in Warsaw, Indiana, set fire to copies of the controversial high school textbook *Values Clarification*, the book burners objecting to the book's downplaying of absolute principles and emphasizing moral relativity. As Jenkinson reported, "On December 15, 1977, the [Warsaw] *Times-Union* published a photograph of a group of senior citizens burning forty copies of *Values Clarification* " (5). The Warsaw school board's removal of *Values Clarification* and other books from the school library and classrooms was challenged in court by a student and when the case reached the United States Court of Appeals, the court, while vacating the District Court's judgment and remanding with instructions, in a footnote criticized the fiery destruction of the books: "This contemptible ceremony, which has greatly animated the discussion of this case by *amici curiae*, took place in December, 1977.

No self-respecting citizen with a knowledge of history can look upon this incident with equanimity" (*Zykan v. Warsaw Community School Corp.* 1302).

"Contemptible" as the book burning ceremony may have been to the U.S. Court of Appeals in 1980, the book burners around the world continued their fiery destruction of what they condemned as objectionable literary, political, and religious works. While Salmon Rushdie's *Satanic Verses* was set ablaze in 1989 because it was "blasphemous," videotapes and records were being burned in 1987 in Oklahoma because they were "ungodly." A bonfire of vanities, reminiscent of Savonarola's fifteenth century blaze consuming "indecent and lustful" books, pictures, perfumes, masks, etc., was ignited in Seminole, Oklahoma, where "a pentecostal preacher and his congregation at the Temple of Praise church in Seminole burned rock n' roll records and cassettes, videotapes, cosmetics, and revealing clothes August 10 to cleanse themselves of items they said are ungodly" (*Newsletter on Intellectual Freedom* November 1987 228).

In March 1990, the *Index on Censorship* reported that "since the start of the Intifada on 9 December 1987, the Israeli government has denied Palestinians and their institutions the right to freedom of expression and information as part of its campaign to put down the Palestinian uprising." Book burning was part of the widespread censorship: "On 1 May 1989, Israeli soldiers raided the Dar al-Khadra press and translation office in Nablus, where they searched, confiscated material, and threw books and magazines out the window. They then burned the books in the street" (*Index on Censorship* March 1990 26–28).

In the last year of the twentieth century, books were being burned in China, just as they had been burned in China in the ninth century when the scholar Han Yu wrote: "Now if this is the situation, what should be done to bring about a proper state of affairs? I say: If we do not stop [Buddhism and Taoism], [Confucianism] will not spread; if we do not halt [the former], [the true way] Will not develop. Let us man their sectaries, let us burn their books, let us secularize their temples" (Goodrich 3). As Luther C. Goodrich has indicated in his *The Literary Inquisition of Ch'ien-Lunq*, "No action was taken at the time, but a generation later, in 843 A.D., in connection with the proscription of the Manichean religion the order went out for 'the officials ... to collect the books and images of the Manicheans and burn them in the public thoroughfares'" (3). A thousand years later, in 1999, the Chinese government conducted a crackdown on the Falun Gong "spiritual movement." While *The New York Times* reported on July 30, 1999, that "books on the Falun Gong movement were thrown into a pulping machine in Shanghai," on August 6 it published a photograph of a bonfire of books and pictures with the caption: "Books and other materials relating to the Falun Gong sect were set afire in the Chinese city of Shouguang, on Wednesday. Though propaganda against the sect is intense, most followers detained are quickly released" (Faison A8).

Whether the books were being burned in ancient Athens and Rome or in fifteenth century Seville, in sixteenth century Paris or seventeenth century Boston, in eighteenth century Vienna or nineteenth century Charleston, in twentieth century Berlin, Santiago, Istanbul, Shouguang or Drake, North Dakota — the book burners participated in a kind of primeval ceremony which involved a fiery magic reducing to ashes authors and their words.

Despite the centuries old condemnations of book burning, the bibliocausts have continued in public ceremonies, in the streets and squares, with no effort to hide the bibliocide from the citizenry. Instead of displaying shame and regret, the book burners flaunt their fiery destructions, demonstrating publicly that they can kill a book, "kill" an author. There is an escape from rational argument and ideas into the world of violence and exorcism. Almost invariably, the book burnings have been accompanied with various degrees of punishments and atrocities; if the condemned authors and their adherents have not been imprisoned, exiled, tortured, hanged, or burned, they have been censured, censored or blacklisted. In 213 B.C.E., the Chinese Emperor Shih Huang Ti ordered that all history and literary works, excluding books on medicine, divination, and horticulture, be burned; the following year, four hundred and sixty nonconformist literati were buried alive for "treasonable language." In the twelfth century, Abelard's books were burned at the same time he was excommunicated and "detained."

In the sixteenth century, Franciscans were burning Mayan books in the "new world" and at the same time killing the indigenous population. In the eighteenth century, while Daniel Defoe's "seditious" *The Shortest Way with the Dissenters* was burned in London, Defoe was pilloried and imprisoned. In the twentieth century, the 1933 book burnings in Nazi Germany foreshadowed the mass killings in the Nazi concentration and extermination camps. In the 1950s, with McCarthyism came blacklisting, censorship, jailings, and book burnings. In the 1970s, with Pinochetism in Chile came the imprisonment, torture, murder, and disappearance of hundreds of thousands of authors, journalists, socialists, and other "enemies" of the state — all this inhumane treatment accompanied the book burnings in Chile. At the same time the book burnings were occurring in Iran under the Shah, "subversive" writers were tortured, imprisoned or liquidated. To paraphrase Heine, where men burn books, they will, in the end, blacklist, jail, torture, pillory, excommunicate, liquidate, or burn people.

The primeval pull of the fiery book burning ritual is always there; as the books are consumed by fire all the senses are brought into play: sight, smell, touch, sound, and kinetic. What becomes evident is that invariably the book burning ritual comes with totalitarian religious and political groups and regimes. In more democratic institutions and governments, while book burnings that occur may be looked upon with some suspicion, there always lies below the surface individuals and groups waiting for the opportune time to set fire to the books metaphorized into "poison," "disease," "pestilence," "filth," or "plague," some of the same metaphors used in the attempt to justify the killing and eradication of "enemy" human beings (Bosmajian 20–26). Alluring in its simplicity and efficiency, the magic surrounding the book burning ritual is ever present, waiting to be used; the book and its author are reduced to ashes with the light of a match. The discursive world of discussion, debate, and diversity gives way to the magical world of uniformity and bibliocide in which the archaic call is: When all else fails, burn the books!

1

THE MAGIC OF BOOKS AND FIRE

Books and fire — both have been endowed with magic and power. When books are set ablaze in the book burning ritual the result is an interaction between two potent forces. On the one hand, as Michael Olmert has pointed out, "The magical properties of books are universal.... The power — and thus, implicitly, the threat — of books has always been recognized" (23–24). At the same time, as Mardiros Ananikian has indicated, "Fire was and still is the most potent means of driving the evil spirits away.... Not only evil spirits but also diseases, often ascribed to demonic influences, cannot endure the sight of fire, but must flee before this mighty deity" (54–55).

While separated by centuries, the sixteenth century burning of Michael Servetus at the stake along with his books because his writings were "poison," "venom," and "infectious" and the twentieth century burning by the Nazis of the works of Freud, Marx, and Mann because they represented the "disease," "demonic," and "debris of the past" — these burnings, before and after, reflected the magic and power in books and the book burning ritual.

This magic and power attributed to writing and books has a long history. Of the timelessness and universality of the magic of books, I.J. Gelb wrote in 1952: "The concept of the divine origin and character of writing is found everywhere, in both ancient and modern times, among civilized as well as among primitive peoples. In the main it is due to a widespread belief in the magic powers of writing" (230). Similarly, Walter J. Ong has referred to the magic and power of the written word and books: "Writing is often regarded at first as an instrument of secret and magic power.... Some societies of limited literacy have regarded writing as dangerous to the unwary reader.... Texts can be felt to have intrinsic religious value: illiterates profit from rubbing the book on their foreheads, or from whirling prayer-wheels bearing texts they cannot read" (93).

The magic, mystery, and awe of the book has existed through the ages for both the literate and illiterate: "The veneration of books is of great antiquity.... Manuscripts were expensive and slow to make, and the materials were costly. A book can have an almost magical or spiritual quality as the conveyor of a text. To a literate person, a manuscript was a precious link with the words of a long dead writer; but to someone who could not read, a book was invested with mystery and awe" (Olmert 9).

The magic of the book was preceded by the magic of writing, whether on animal skins, bones, stone, wood, leaves, bamboo, or shells. Edward Clodd, relating the story of the alphabet, refers to the "widespread belief in the efficacy of written characters to work black and white magic, to effect cures, and otherwise act as charms — a belief largely derived from the legends which ascribe the origin of writing to the gods — legends themselves the product of Ignorance, the mother of Mystery" (15)

In his discussion of "incantations & incidental marvels attributed to letters & words," Drogin has observed that it was believed that God or the Gods invented the alphabet and hence the letters were holy. And "since it was letters that formed words, the words were equally holy. In a time when what was holy was born of the miraculous and when the fine line between miracle and magic was difficult to discern, the three terms could be easily interchanged. Letters and words were miraculous in origin and therefore the stuff of magic. And with the stuff of magic one could *produce* magic" (33). Drogin provides the following example of letters and words being seen as alive:

> The Egyptians' hieroglyphic writing system was a combination of pictographic and ideographic symbols along with a few that were alphabetical. Among the symbols or "letters" were those in the shape of an eagle, chick, owl, crane, lion, dog, snail, frog, fish, snake, and so on. The Egyptian belief in the inherent magic in these letters was not obscured by the mists of time. It was clearly expressed, for example, in the hieroglyphs of the pyramid of Princess Neferuptah. The daughter of Pharaoh Amenemhet III (who ruled 1842–1797 B.C.), she lay in state in a room one of whose walls was covered with the customary description of the importance of the deceased royal person. Archaeologists who first came upon these writings were surprised to discover that, of the letters forming the testimonial, all those represented by creatures were mutilated, lacking appropriate limbs, wings, or tails.... The Egyptians fear that, when all the people had left the pyramid and the doors were sealed, the letters would come to life and the fish swim, the birds fly, the animals run, and the text be lost. The text had been too important to the princess and to posterity for any chance to be taken. They crippled them all so none would escape and the text would remain forever intact [33–34].

This association of writing with magic and divinities has appeared in various cultures and religions. In China, Ts'ang Chieh was the god of writing. In Indian legend, the god Ganesh was believed to be the inventor of writing. In northern Europe, the Norse god Odin was believed to be the inventor of the runes. In the New Testament it is written that "in the beginning was the Word, and the Word was with God, and the Word was God" (John 1). With this nexus between writing, the word, and the gods came the magic of the divinities and the power of the gods.

"Everywhere," says Gelb, "in the East as well as in the West, the origin of writing is ascribed to a divinity." Referring to the "widespread use of the magic effect in writing" in modern times, he continues: "Here we may mention the phylacteries with sacred writings which the Jews wear during prayer, and the inscriptions on the doorposts of Jewish houses which are supposed to protect the inhabitants from harm. The Mohammedans carry amulets with enclosed verses from the Koran. Among Christians we find the custom of fanning a sick person with leaves of the Bible, or having him swallow a pellet of paper with a prayer written on it" (233).

Historically, the written word and the book have not only been "eaten" and "drunk," but they have also been given the power to "talk" and to "see." In 1968, Jack Goody wrote of "drinking the word": "[I]n early pen-and-paper cultures, the 'drinking of the word' is often found in connection with curses, oaths and ordeals, since once again it intensified oral communication.... As writing turns speech into a material object, words can be more readily manipulated.... The practice of 'drinking the word' is widespread today in those parts of West Africa that have been influenced by Islam." Goody reports that he was "offered the blackened water at ceremonies of Gonja, and from Senegal to Hausaland it is reported that the blessing of the Holy Word of the Qur'an can be most fully absorbed in just this manner" (230).

Turning from Islam's "drinking the word" to Christianity's "eating the book," we read in Revelation: "Then I [John] heard the voice I had heard from heaven speaking to me again. 'Go,' it said 'and take that open scroll out of the hand of the angel standing on sea and land.' I went to the angel and asked him to give me the small scroll, and he said, 'Take it and eat it; it will turn your stomach sour, but in your mouth it will taste as sweet as honey.' So I took it out of the angel's hand, and swallowed it; it was as sweet as honey in my mouth, but when I had eaten it my stomach turned sour. Then I was told, 'You are to prophesy again, this time about many different nations and countries and languages and emperors'" (Rev. 10:8–11).

Poetically, Emily Dickinson writes of words being eaten and drunk:

> He ate and drank the precious Words—
> His Spirit grew robust —
> He knew no more than he was poor,
> Nor that his frame was Dust —
>
> He danced along the dingy Days,
> And this Bequest of Wings
> Was but a Book — What Liberty
> A loosened spirit brings—[Dickinson 658].

Books are still "consumed" and some books are not appropriate for child "consumption." When in 1976, the Island Trees Union Free School District Board of Education attempted to ban several books from the school libraries, including *Slaughterhouse-Five*, *Black Boy*, *Soul on Ice*, *Go Ask Alice*, and *The Naked Ape*, it issued a press release in which it declared that school board members were not "book banners or book burners," but they said, "This stuff is too strong for adult viewers, but some of our educators feel it is appropriate for child consumption" (*Pico* 391).

The belief that the written word could "speak" is exemplified in the experience of Ibo captive Olaudah Equiano who was taken to England, where he made his first close acquaintance with literacy in the shape of books that apparently "talked": "I had often seen my master and Dick employed in reading, and I had a great curiosity to talk to the books as I thought they did, and so to learn how all things had a beginning; for that purpose I have often taken up a book and have talked to it and then put my ears to it, when alone, in hopes it would answer me: and I have been very much concerned when I found it remained silent" (Goody 206).

Another human attribute and power attributed to the written word is the ability of the word to "see." In prefacing an example of the "seeing word," Gelb has written: "Among primitives writing and books are the subject of astonishment and speculation. To them books are instruments of divination.... The primitive fears the magic power of its 'words.'... A written message is a mysterious being which has the power to see things." Gelb then relates the story about "an Indian who was sent by a missionary to a colleague with four loaves of bread and a letter stating their number. The Indian ate one of the loaves and was, of course, found out. Later he was sent on a similar errand and repeated the theft, but took the precaution, while he was eating the bread, to hide the letter under a stone so that it might not see him" (232).

Olmert presents a similar tale told by English prelate and scientist John Wilkins in 1641; in this version the thief eats some figs, not a loaf of bread, the theft being revealed by the "seeing letter":

An Indian slave was once sent to deliver a basket of figs. He ate several of them along the way and when he arrived at this destination he was accused of stealing. His accuser: a letter that accompanied the delivery, stating the exact number of figs dispatched. Wilkins continues the story: "After this, being sent again with the like Carriage, and a Letter expressing the just Number of Figs, that were to be delivered, as he did again, according to his former Practice, devour a great Part of them by the Way; but before he meddled with any (to prevent all following Accusations) he first took the Letter, and hid that under a great stone, assuring himself that if it did not see him eating the Figs, it could never tell of him; but being now more strongly accused than before, he confesses the Fault, admiring the Divinity of the Paper, and for the future does promise his best Fidelity in every Employment" [27].

In still another version of the "seeing letter" a native Australian "who had stolen some tobacco from a package with an accompanying letter was astonished that the white man was able to find him out in spite of the fact that he had hidden the letter in a trunk of a tree. He vented his wrath upon the letter by beating it furiously" (Gelb 232).

Through the personification of the inanimate words on the inanimate page, the paper and ink take on the power of life to talk and to see. Hence, as the book burners set fire to the books it is not just the paper and ink that must be destroyed; the "life" in the book must be "killed."

Like live animals, books have been given the ability to "bark" and "howl" and like humans, books have been "hanged." When the Emperor of China in 1778 "fulminated" a Decree related to the seditious book *I Chu Lou Shih* by Hsu Shu-k'uei, he denounced not only Hsu (long dead), but also his son (also deceased) who had published the work and others who "have been captured and brought to the capital and are to be interrogated with great severity. The corpses of father and son must be dug up and mangled. The books of [Hsu Shu-k'uei] have been printed and have spread throughout the provinces. Let a table of them be drawn up and despatched to the high officials everywhere" (Goodrich 170). The Emperor then metaphorized and personified the condemned books: "Let all the books and woodblocks be found and sent up; so that these dog barks and wolf howls may be silenced for the sake of keeping straight the hearts of men" (Goodrich 170). The "dog barks and wolf howls" were silenced: "Eighteen books by Hsu were found and burned together with 385 woodblocks of the *I Chu Lou Shih*" (Goodrich 171).

A few years later, a book was "hanged" before it was burned. In 1782 Rabbi Hartwig Wessely's *Divrei Shalom V'Emet* was published in Berlin and was condemned by various Jewish scholars because Wessely supported the concept, proclaimed by Emperor Joseph II of Austria, that Jews establish "schools where various trades would be taught and where the language of instruction would be in German" (Carmilly-Weinberger 111). Rabbis who were critical of Wessely asserted that what he advocated would lead to assimilation which would be a threat to Jewish survival. Wessely's book was banned and burned in Vilna and Brody: "In Vilna the book *Diverei Shalom V'Emet* was 'hanged' in an iron band in the synagogue courtyard before it was incinerated" (Carmilly-Weinberger 111).

The personification of books has not been limited to book burners who condemn the works to the fire. In emphasizing the value of books and the authors' presence in it bibliophiles have instilled life into the book. As John Milton put it: "[F]or books are not absolutely dead things, but do contain a potency of life in them to be as active as that soul was whose progeny they are; nay, they do preserve as in a vial the purest efficacy and extraction of that living intellect that bred them" (5). Then, in condemning the Church's destruction of books, Milton wrote: "Till then books were ever as freely admitted into the world as any other birth; the issue of the brain was no more stifled than the issue of the womb" (5). The book becomes a person, a "progeny," a "birth."

Such personifications of the book imbue the paper and ink with a life the bibliophile insists on preserving and the bibliophobic book burner demands destroyed.

The merger, the union, between book and human being becomes even more evident and pronounced when we use metonymic expressions that substitute the author with the book: "We need to get rid of all the Voltaires and Rousseaus in the library." "Marx and Freud were thrown into the bonfires." In his 1942 radio dramatization *They Burned the Books*, Stephen Vincent Benét portrays the Nazi book burnings:

NAZI VOICE: The books of the Jew, Albert Einstein — to the flames!
OTHER VOICES: Sieg Heil!
NARRATOR: Einstein, the scientist, Who thought in universes. Einstein, the man we honor in our land.
NAZI VOICE: To the flames with him — to the flames!
VOICES: Sieg Heil!
NAZI VOICE: The books of Sigmund Freud — to the flames!
[Noise of flames]
NARRATOR: Freud, prober of the riddles of man's mind, World-known, world famous.
[Noise of flames]
NAZI VOICE: To the flames — the flames! Burn them — we don't want thought — we don't want mind. We want one will, one leader and one folk!
HEINE'S VOICE [cutting in]: One vast, inexorable stupidity!
NAZI VOICE: Who said that? Gag him — burn him — to the flames! To the flames with Heinrich Mann and Thomas Mann, Gorki the Russian, Schnitzler the Austrian, Hemingway, Dreiser, the Americans, And now, to the flames with this! [Benét 8–9]

This metonymic connection, along with the personification of books, when carried to the ultimate tragedy, sent authors to the stake with their books wrapped around their bodies; author and book went up in flames together. In death, author and book became one.

In 1328, heretic Cecco d'Ascoli was condemned by the Inquisition in Rome to be burned together with his offending work *De Sphaera*; also in 1328, Pope John XXII condemned and ordered destroyed "the writings of the Minorite Petrus Johannes Oliva, which had been examined and reported upon by nine theologians. The bones of Oliva were disinterred and were burned with copies of his books" (Putnam 1906 1 68). In 1639, Francisco Maldonado de Silva was sent to the stake in Lima, along with his books tied around him neck: "He was led to his auto da fe in Lima (January 1639) at the age of forty-nine; a friar describes his last moments as follows: 'Frail, gray-haired, long-bearded, and with the books he had written tied around his neck, when led to the fire the wind had ripped off the curtain behind the podium; seeing this, he exclaimed: "This has been so arranged by the Lord of Israel as to see me face to face from heaven"'" (Lazar 179).

In 1624, Marco Antonio de Dominis was condemned by the Inquisition for his criticisms and attacks on some practices of the Church and it was ordered "to deprive him all his honour, benefit or dignity; to confiscate his goods; and give him over to the secular powers, as *de facto*. They then gave him over, that he and his picture, together with a little sack full of bookes he had printed, should be burned" (Gillett 1932 119–120). On December 21, 1624, de Dominis, his picture and books were burned at Campo di Fiori in Rome.

All condemned authors, of course, have not been burned at the stake with their books attached to their bodies to be reduced to ashes. Other forms of punishment have been imposed on authors whose books were ordered to be set afire. Instead of being consigned to the same flames that consumed their books, authors and printers have been imprisoned, sent into exile, hanged and quartered, pilloried, and had their hands and ears cut off.

William Thomas was "hanged and quartered, and his head set upon London Bridge, May 18, 1554" after his book *A Historie of Italie* was burned because of its anti–Catholicism which displeased Queen Mary (Gillett 1932 31). Twenty-five years later, Queen Elizabeth ordered the burning of John Stubbs' book *Discoverie of a Gaping Gulph whereinto*

England is like to be swallowed by another French Marriage, if the Lord forbid not the Banes by letting her Majestie see the Sin a Punishment thereof, "calling it a lewd, seditious Book ... bolstered up with manifest lies" (Gillett 83). While Stubbs was not burned at the stake nor hanged and quartered, his right hand was cut off as punishment.

When in the seventeenth century William Prynne's *Histrio-Mastix* was ordered by English authorities to be burned because of its attack on stage-plays, the attack interpreted as a criticism of the Queen, the punishment imposed on Prynne included the cutting off of his ears, standing in the pillory, and imprisonment. In May 1634, "a warrant was issued to collect all the copies of the 'Histriomastix' that had been sold or were still in stock. Oxford University and Lincoln's Inn hastened to strike the name of Prynne from off their rolls. On the seventh of May he stood in the pillory at Westminster and there suffered the loss of one ear. On the tenth he stood in the pillory in Cheapside, and there lost the other ear. There, too, the copies of his book, so far as they could be collected, were burnt by the hangman in his presence, and so near that he was almost suffocated by the smoke. He was then remanded to the Tower for perpetual imprisonment" (Lounsbury 802). Eventually, Prynne was released from prison, was elected to Parliament, and died on October 24, 1669.

The fires that burned the books during the third century B.C. in China; the fires that burned English Bibles in the sixteenth century; the fires that Martin Luther lit to burn the Papal decrees; the Catholic Church's burning of Luther's works; the fires that reduced to ashes the books of Voltaire, Steinbeck, Marx, Rousseau, Hus, Abelard, Bruno, Servetus, and thousands of others—those fires were still burning the printed word at the end of the twentieth century. As indicated in the previous chapter and in subsequent chapters, while blasphemy was not the prevalent charge against books set afire in the twentieth century, books denounced as subversive, seditious, and obscene were burned and the authors were penalized by being blacklisted, imprisoned or condemned to death, whether in Argentina, Chile, China, Germany, Iran, Spain, Turkey or the United States.

Through the centuries the magic and power of the written word, the book, have been challenged by the magic and power of the fire and too often fire has prevailed. In his *The Enemies of Books* William Blades discusses the various forces of nature — water, dust, bookworm, etc.— that destroy books and he asserts at the outset of this 1888 work: "There are many of the forces of Nature which tend to injure Books; but among them all not one has been half so destructive as Fire" (1).

The public ritual of burning the books has been especially important to book burners. It is not enough to merely destroy the books; they must be set afire, usually in a public place. There are, of course, other ways to deny people access to the condemned books: bury the books; rip them up; pulp them; throw them into a body of water; store them in warehouses out of sight of the public; or burn the books in private.

The allure, the magic and power of the public fiery ritual is much more gratifying to the book burner who is interested in displaying the utter destruction of the book and author. The book burning ritual provides an archaic, communal experience as one watches the fire and smoke rising while the book is reduced to ashes. The book burner looks in awe as the powerful, magical, mysterious, fearful words are being completely and wondrously consumed by the more powerful fire. The book burnings are a form of regression, providing a catharsis that other methods of destroying the book would not provide. Even a child is attracted to the flame, aware that something fearful and dangerous, something enticing is taking place with finality.

For centuries the alluring, terrifying, purifying, magical, and powerful fire has been part of the mythologies and religions of the world. The myths of ancient Greece and Rome include, among others, Hephaestus the Olympian god of fire and Vulcan the Roman god of fire. Ra was the Egyptian fire god and Atar was the Zoroastrian fire god. Angi was the Hindu fire god and Kagutsuchi the Japanese. Xiuhtecuhtli was the Aztec fire god and amongst the Chinese fire gods were Ho Shen, Hui Lu, and Chu Jung (Leach 295–303).

Again and again, the Old and New Testaments contain passages that invoke fire to be used to purify, to inflict revenge, to impose penalties. Jeremiah 36:22–23 — "It was the ninth month, and the king was sitting in the winter house and there was a fire burning in the brazier before him. As Jehu'di read three or four columns, the king would cut them off with a penknife and throw them into the fire in the brazier, until the entire scroll was consumed in the fire that was in the brazier." John 15:4–6 — "Abide in me, and I in you. As the branch cannot bear fruit by itself, unless it abides in the vine, neither can you, unless you abide in me. I am the vine, you are the branches. He who abides in me, and I in him, he it is that bears much fruit, for apart from me you can do nothing. If a man does not abide in me, he is cast forth as a branch and withers; and the branches are gathered, thrown into fire and burned." Revelation 21:6–8 — "I am the Alpha and the Omega, the beginning and the end. To the thirsty I will give from the fountain of water of life without payment. He who conquers shall have this heritage, and I will be his God and he shall be my son. But as for the cowardly, the faithless, the polluted, as for murderers, fornicators, sorcerers, idolaters, and all liars, their lot shall be in the lake that burns with fire and sulphur, which is the second death." Hebrews 10:26–27 — "If, after we have been given knowledge of the truth, we should deliberately commit any sins, then there is no longer any sacrifice for them. There will be left only the dreadful prospect of judgment and of the raging fire that is to burn rebels."

These beliefs in the power, magic, and fear of fire, its power to destroy evils and to purify, appear in various forms in later centuries. James Frazer has provided us with innumerable historical examples of the magical, purifying, destructive powers of fire. At the outset of his extended discussion of "The Fire Festivals of Europe," Frazer wrote: "All over Europe the peasants have been accustomed from time immemorial to kindle bonfires on certain days of the year, and to dance round or leap over them. Customs of this kind can be traced back on historical evidence to the Middle Ages, and their analogy to similar customs observed in antiquity goes with strong internal evidence to prove that their origin must be sought in a period long prior to the spread of Christianity.... Not uncommonly effigies are burned in these fires, or a pretence is made of burning a living person in them; and there are grounds for believing that anciently human beings were actually burned on these occasions" (10 106).

In *The Golden Bough* Frazer argued that the "true explanation of the [fire] festivals" was "that they are purifactory in intention" (10 vii). Farmers and peasants ignited the fires to rid the land of disease, vermin, witches, and Judas. The fire festivals were used as a "cleansing agent, which purifies men, animal, and the plants by burning up and consuming noxious elements whether material or spiritual, which menace all living things with disease and death" (10 341). In Normandy, "men and women, and children run wildly through the fields with lighted torches, which they wave about the branches and dash against the trunks of the fruit-trees for the sake of burning the moss and driving away the moles and field mice.

They believe that the ceremony fulfills the double object of exorcising the vermin whose multiplication would be a real calamity, and of importing fecundity to the trees, the fields, and even the cattle; and they imagine that the more the ceremony is prolonged the greater will be the crop of fruit next autumn" (Frazer 10 340). In Silesia "a very powerful means of keeping witches at bay are the Walpurgis [April 13] bonfires, which are still kindled in the Hoyerswerda district and the Iser Mountains.... About Hoyerswerda they call these fires, as usual, 'Burning the Witches'" (Frazer 9 163).

The fire festivals were not only an attempt to rid the land of witches, pestilence, and vermin, but also to destroy the Judas. The public burning of Judas was a world-wide spectacle, from Greece to Peru, from Italy to Jerusalem. "In Brazil the mourning for the death of Christ ceases at noon on Easter Saturday and gives place to an extravagant burst of joy at his resurrection. Shots are fired everywhere, and effigies of Judas are hung on trees or dragged about the streets, to be finally burned or otherwise destroyed" (Frazer 10 128). Dancing, shouting, and rejoicing accompanied the burning of Judas. In Upper Bavaria, "on the afternoon of Easter Saturday the lads collected wood, which they piled in a cornfield, while in the middle of the pile they set up a tall wooden cross all swathed in straw.... The first to arrive set fire to the heap. No woman or girl might come near the bonfire, but they were allowed to watch it from a distance. As the flames rose the men and lads rejoiced and made merry, shouting, 'We are burning the Judas'" (Frazer 10 143).

Just as the fires were lit to rid the land of pestilence, moles, vermin, tares, and demons, the fires were ignited to cleanse the land of pestilent and demonic books, and finally the fires were used to eradicate the plague by burning the pestilent and poisonous Jews. A fourteenth century chronicle by a Franciscan friar recorded the burning of Jews as a means of protecting the populace from the plague: "In 1347 there was such a great pestilence and mortality throughout almost the whole world that in the opinion of well-informed men scarcely a tenth of mankind survived.... In the cities of Bologna, Venice, Montpellier, Avignon, Marseilles and Toulouse alike, a thousand people died in one day, and it still rages in France, Normandy, England and Ireland. Some say that it was brought about by the corruption of the air; others that the Jews planned to wipe out all the Christians with poison and had poisoned wells and springs everywhere" (Horrox 207). The rumors identifying the Jews with poisons and the plague led to their being burned all across Europe:

> The persecution of the Jews began in November 1348, and the first outbreak in Germany was at Solden, where all the Jews were burnt on the strength of a rumour that they had poisoned wells and rivers.... During December they were burnt and killed on the feast of St. Nicholas [6 December] in Lindau, on 8 December in Reutlingen, on 13 December in Haigerloch, and on 20 December in Horw they were burnt in a pit.... Once started, the burning of the Jews went on increasing.... On 4 January [1349] the people of Constance shut up the Jews in two of their own houses, and then burnt 330 of them in the fields at sunset on 3 March [Horrox 208–209].

The "Black Death," as Mullett has observed, "produced the most diverse effects.... Diabolism flourished as persons paid homage to the devil, and sorcerers abounded.... Jews, as might be expected, were brutally massacred when charges of ritual murder and the deliberate distribution of a plague poison gained wholesale credence" (15).

In Normandy, on the Eve of the Twelfth Night, during the ceremony of the "Moles and Field-Mice," bonfires and torches were used by adults and youngsters screaming curses to rid the land of pestilence: "They bid the moles and field-mice to depart from their orchards, threatening to break their bones and burn their beards if they tarry.... Customs of the same sort used to be observed on the same day (the Eve of Epiphany, the fifth of January) in the Ardennes. People ran about with burning torches, commanding the moles and field-mice to go forth. Then they threw the torches on the ground, and believed that by this proceeding they purified the earth and made it fruitful" (Frazer 9 317).

The same fire that exorcised the vermin, drove away the moles, destroyed the noxious elements, rid the farms and communities of witches and the Judas, was used to cleanse the land of demonic, pestilent, blasphemous, seditious, obscene books. The argument to use fire to eliminate heretical, seditious works was heavily based on Biblical passages such as John 15:6 and Acts 19:19. While there was no doubt on the part of authorities that it was appropriate and necessary to put heretics to death and destroy their poisonous, demonic writings, "there have been differences of opinion on the subject of the means by which this should be done. The scholiast is entirely on the side of the large majority that considers fire the proper instrument, and actually cites the Saviour's own authority for this: 'If a man abide not in me, he is cast forth as a branch that is withered; and men gather them, and cast them into the fire, and they are burned' (John 15:6)'" (Sabatini 222). *The Jewish Encyclopedia*, in its summary of the "uses of fire," refers to Old Testament references to fire as a means of eradicating enemy "idols," "obnoxious books," "garments infected with leprosy," and "animal refuse and stubble": "Idols especially were destroyed by fire (Deut. vii. 5; II Kings xix. 18).... Books of an obnoxious character were thrown into the fire (Jer. xxxvi. 23).... Garments infected with leprosy were consigned to the flames (Lev. xiii 52. 57). Animal refuse and stubble were burned (Lev. iv. 12. vi. 30; Isa. v. 24)" (292).

In their attempts to justify book burnings both Catholics and Protestants resorted to citing the Biblical passage Acts 19:19 which reads: "Some believers, too came forward to admit in detail how they had used spells and a number of them who had practiced magic collected their books and made a bonfire of them in public. The value of these calculated to be fifty thousand pieces of silver." Both Protestant Martin Luther and Catholic Inquisitor-General Matthieu Ory turned to Acts 19:19 to justify the burning of their opponents' "poisonous evil books." In 1520, the Papal Bull *Exsurge Domine*, "threatening Luther with excommunication, also included a demand to burn his books. The official publication of the Bull in Rome on June 15, 1520, was accompanied by the burning of Luther's books" (Luther 31 381). Luther responded with his own book burning. In Wittenberg, on December 1, 1520, "Luther cast into the fire volumes of the canon law, the papal decretals, and scholastic philosophy. Then Luther, deeply agitated, stepped from the crowd and consigned a small document to the mounting flames, the papal bull threatening him with excommunication" (Luther 31 381). Within a few days, Luther attempted to explain and justify the burning of the Catholic books and documents by writing and publishing his "Why the Books of the Pope and His Disciples Were Burned": "In the first place," he wrote, "it is an ancient traditional practice to burn poisonous evil books, as we read in chapter nineteen of the Acts of the Apostles. There they burned books for five thousand pennies [fifty thousand pieces of silver], according to the account of St. Paul [Acts 19:19]" (Luther 31 381).

Three decades later, the same Biblical passage was relied upon by the Catholic Inquisitor-General in France, Matthieu Ory, who conducted the trials of such heretics as Spanish physician Michael Servetus who was condemned as a heretic because of his writings related to baptism, the Trinity, pantheism, and the immortality of the soul. The verdict of the Inquisition concluded: "[S]peaking in the name of the Father, Son and Holy Spirit, we now in writing give final sentence and condemn you, Michael Servetus, to be bound and taken to Champel and there attached to a stake and burned with your book to ashes" (Bainton 209). After referring to Acts 19:19, Inquisitor-General Ory argued that if "dead books may be committed to the flames, how much more live books, that is to say, men? Scripture says that a witch should not be allowed to live and heretics are spiritual witches" (Bainton 80).

Both books and their authors became the fiery victims of the notorious auto-da-fé (act of faith), a term that came to be applied to not only the burning of heretics at the stake, but also to the book burnings. In discussion of the twenty-four cartloads of the Talmud in

1424, Graetz writes: "Filled with hatred against the rabbis and the Talmud, the apostate [Donin] determined to revenge himself on both [Jews and Christians]. Probably urged on by the clergy, he became the instigator of the great auto-da-fé of the Jews and their writings, and it was he that occasioned the bloody persecution in Poitou" (573). Again, in 1306, "copies of the Talmud were once more delivered up to the auto-da-fé" (Graetz 50).

Referring to the burning of Wycliffe's books in Prague in 1410, Johann Loserth wrote: "This auto-da-fé was carried into effect in the court of the archiepiscopal palace on the Hradschin, in the presence of the Cathedral chapter and a great multitude of priests. More than two hundred MSS. were consumed, containing the works of Wiclif" (116).

When the Inquisition came to the Portuguese colony of Goa in the middle of the sixteenth century, "all books written in Sanskrit and Marathi, whatever their subject matter, were seized by the Inquisition and burnt on the suspicion that they might deal with idolatry" (Priolkar 176). The Church ordered that books brought to Goa in Dutch or English ships, in whatever language, be turned over to the Church's "Board of the Holy Office for executing the order concerning forbidden books." The "boxes containing Prohibited Books were carried in procession during Auto da Fe and burnt" (Priolkar 177). At the same time the books were being reduced to ashes, heretics and "New Christians" (Jews who had converted to Christianity and reverted to Judaism) were also burned: "Then they cause all these poor culprits to march together in shirts steeped in sulphur and painted with flames of fire; the difference between those that have to die and the rest being that their flames were turned upwards and others downwards. They are led straight to the great church or *A See* which is hard by the prison, and are there during the mass and the sermon, wherein they receive the most strenuous remonstrances. Thereafter they are conducted to the *Campo Sancto Lazaro*, where the condemned are burned in the presence of the rest, who look on" (Priolkar 29–30).

Books and heretics were "executed" together at the ceremonial auto-da-fé. In 1512, the Inquisition in the Netherlands condemned "as a heretic Magistrate Hermann of Ryswick, who is burned at The Hague together with his books" (Putnam 1906 2 81). In 1590, when the editor of an Index to Books to be Expurgated was condemned for including "erroneous and heretical passages," he was "brought to the stake at Salamanca as a heretic. Llorente states that at the same auto de fe, Torquemada caused to be burned many Hebrew Bibles and six thousand other volumes" (Putnam 1906 1 68).

In his discussion of the mistreatment of the Yucatán people during the Inquisition, Leo Deuel writes of the 1562 "auto-da-fe of Mani, at which Mayans of the old faith were burnt, together with some five thousand idols and the priceless native picture books that had been sedulously rounded up by the inquisitors." Deuel cites Franciscan Diego de Landa who had written of the burning of the Mayan writings: "These people also made use of certain characters or letters, with which they wrote in their books their ancient affairs and their sciences, and with these and drawings and with certain signs in these drawings, they understood their affairs and made others understand them and taught them.... We found a great number of books in these characters, and, as they contained nothing in which there was not to be seen superstition and lies of the devil, we burned them all, which they regretted to an amazing degree and caused them affliction" (381–382).

The burning of heretics and books at the autos-da-fé became a public ritual attracting throngs of Church officials and people of the community. Henry Kamen provides in his *Inquisition and Society in Spain in the Sixteenth and Seventeenth Centuries* some details dealing with the auto-da-fé and the public nature of the event: "Among native Spaniards it began its career as a religious act of penitence and justice, and ended it as a public festivity rather like bullfighting or fireworks.... Whatever the modern verdict, there is no doubt that autos were popular. Accounts, engravings and paintings show us that every function of this sort always had a maximum audience up to the beginning of the eighteenth century. Visitors would throng in from outlying districts when it was announced that an auto would be held, and the scene would invariably be set in the biggest square or public place available" (Kamen 190).

In 1415, after John Hus was put through the degradation ceremony and after a procession composed of various officials and armed men, followed by an "immense multitude," passed by a pile of Hus's burning books, Hus was paraded to the stake: "As the procession passed on, they reached a bridge at which it was necessary to pause. It was not considered safe for the whole multitude to pass over it at once. The armed escort first proceeded, one by one, and then the crowd of citizens followed" (Gillett *Life* 67).

In his biography of Torquemada, Rafael Sabatini refers to the auto-da-fé as "the greatest horror that was sprung from the womb of Christianity." He cites Voltaire who had written: "An Asiastic arriving in Madrid on the day of an Auto da Fe, would doubt whether there was a festival, a religious celebration, a sacrifice, or a massacre. It is all of these. They reproach Montezuma with sacrificing human captives to God. What would he have said had he witnessed an Auto da Fe?" (216).

As seen by the inquisitors, the auto-da-fé was a public ritual to be witnessed by a wide audience: "It was good for the people to see what happened to those who sinned against the laws of the Holy Church; it filled them with fear and determination that they would not stand among those wretched men and women. It was looked upon as a rehearsal for Judgment Day" (Plaidy 1969 148). The words "auto-da-fé," observes Plaidy, "must have caused a thrill of horror, yet hideous fascination, even among the most insensitive" (155).

The public that was exposed to the auto-da-fé was not limited to those who were actually in attendance; a report, a *Relación*, was circulated for those who did not attend. In his "Auto-da-fe and Jews," E.N. Adler reports on the circulation of news of the autos-da-fé: "The Object of such a *Relación* was twofold — external and internal. Its external object was to benefit the public, as being calculated to promote religious conformity, and perhaps also by way of pandering to the sensational appetites of the thousands who had witnessed, and the tens of thousands who would have liked to witness, the solemn and exciting 'act of faith'" (394).

Centuries later, it was still "good for the people to see what happened to those who sinned against the laws of Holy Church," but in the twentieth century the Holy Church had been replaced by the Holy State Authorities. When in 1933 the Nazis committed to the flames the books of Marx, Freud, Mann, Remarque, and others, "the whole nation had to be made aware of the significance of this gesture and to this end radio, film, sound recordings and all the propaganda resources of the modern communications media were employed so that those not actually present could hear over and over again the announcer's voice, the recitation of the authors' names, and the reason for the commitment of their books to the fire" (Ritchie 69). As in earlier centuries, there was no hesitancy to expose the book burnings to as wide an audience as possible.

In 1976, when the military rector of the University of the Cuyo in Argentina had the homes of lecturers and students searched for "subversive" materials, "some 10,000 books were seized, which the colonel displayed at a press conference." As reported by Nick Caistor, "In Cordoba on 3 April 1976 the local commander carried out a great book-burning that was shown on television, and claimed that he was destroying the pernicious texts of Marx, Che Guevara, Castro, etc." (20). The military officer announced that the books were burned "to avoid Argentinian youth being led into error over what our true patrimony is, namely our national symbols, our family, our church, and our cultural heritage founded on God, the homeland, and the hearth" (Caistor 20).

While the punishments imposed on authors of condemned books in the twentieth century may no longer have included burning at the stake, the books continued to be set afire. The practice of burning authors at the stake was replaced with the imprisonment, torture, exile, or blacklisting of the "seditious" and "obscene" writers. In 1933, Sigmund Freud wrote in a letter: "What progress we are making. In the Middle Ages they would have burnt me; nowadays they are content with burning my books" (Jones 182). However, what Freud did not foresee was that had he not fled to England in 1938 he indeed would have been imprisoned or burned in one of the ovens in the Nazi extermination camps. As Freud scholar Ernest Jones has stated, referring to Freud's letter: "He was never to know that even that was only an illusory progress, that ten years later they would have burned his body as well" (182). Freud died in England in 1939 just as the Nazis began constructing the ovens to rid the land of the Jewish bacillus, plague, vermin, demon, the Nazis applying the same metaphors as had been used centuries earlier when heretics and their books were set ablaze.

All through the centuries the metaphoric, infectious, poisonous, demonic, dirty books invited a fiery destruction. In his sermons against the heretical Cathars the Abbot Eckbert of Schonau had defined and labeled their blasphemous beliefs as Satan-like, foul poison, and infections, while at the same time defining the heretics themselves as apes, wolves, and Judas. Referring to the heretics, Eckbert declared in 1163: "They have secretly corrupted the Christian faith of many foolish and simple men, so that they have multiplied in every land and the Church is now greatly endangered by the foul poison which flows against it on every side. Their message crawls like the crab, runs far and wide like infectious leprosy, infecting the limbs of Christ as it goes" (Moore 1975 90). Not only was the Cathar's message crab-like and a "foul poison," the Cathars were "little foxes who are destroying the vineyards of the Lord of Sabaoth." Further, the heretical Manichees were "children of the devil" (Moore 1975 92–93).

The poison, germ and plague metaphors were applied in 1163 to the sect referred to as Publicani "who undoubtedly originated in Germany from an unknown founder and who have spread the poison of their wickedness through many lands. Indeed so many are said to have been infected by this plague throughout France, Spain, Italy and Germany, that they seem, as the prophet says, to have 'multiplied beyond number.' Wherever the leaders of the Church and secular princes treat them with too much laxity in their provinces these treacherous foxes emerge from their holes" (Moore 1975 83). In 1199, Master John of Orvieto described the heretics as seeming "to be sheep though in reality they were wolves," and then mixing his metaphors he wrote: "So, as beloved enemies or highly virulent germs these snakes in the grass drew many men and women into the labyrinth of their heresy under the pretext of piety" (Moore 1975 128).

In his 1543 publication *On the Jews and Their Lies* Martin Luther recommended setting fire to the synagogues at a time when all across Europe Jews and the Talmud were being set ablaze. Relying heavily on the same dehumanizing metaphors used by the Catholic Church in defining "heretics," Luther warned: "[B]e on your guard against the Jews, knowing that wherever they have their synagogues, nothing is found but a den of devils in which sheer self-glory, conceit, lies, blasphemy, and defaming of God and men are practiced most maliciously and vehemently, just as the devils themselves do. And where you see or hear a Jew teaching, remember that you are hearing nothing but a venomous basilisk who poisons and kills people merely by fastening his eyes on them" (Luther 47 172). "What shall we Christians do with this rejected and condemned people, the Jews?" asks Luther. He answers:

> First to set fire to their synagogues or schools and to bury and cover with dirt whatever will not burn.... Second, I advise that their houses also be razed and destroyed.... Third, I advise that all their prayer books and Talmudic writings, in which such idolatry, lies, cursing, and blasphemy are taught, be taken from them.... Fourth, I advise that their rabbis be forbidden to teach henceforth on pain of life and limb.... They wantonly employ the poor people's obedience contrary to the law of the Lord and infuse them with this poison, cursing, and blasphemy [Luther 47 268].

While Luther was advising that synagogues be set afire and that Talmudic writings be confiscated, the Inquisition, at the same time it was burning Luther's works, was burning the Talmud. In the middle of the sixteenth century, the "poisonous," "blasphemous" Talmud was being reduced to ashes in Spain, Italy, France, and elsewhere.

In the seventeenth and eighteenth centuries the book burners increasingly set fire to condemned works identified and labelled as seditious, sometimes blasphemous *and* seditious. Since fire was the power that could cleanse the farms and communities of their witches, moles, vermin, disease, and pestilence, and since heretical, blasphemous infections, plagues, and poisons could be destroyed through book burnings, the cleansing, purifying, dreadful, magical fire was also ignited to rid the land of seditious and impure obscene works. In 1703, Daniel Defoe's *The Shortest Way With the Dissenters* was condemned to the flames by the House of Commons which had asserted that the work was "full of false and scandalous Reflections upon this Parliament" and tended to "promote Sedition." Eight years later, two books by Matthew Tindal, *The Rights of the Christian Church Asserted Against the Romish*, and *A Defence of the Rights of the Christian Church, In Two Parts* were ordered by the House of Commons to be burned because the books were "scandalous, seditious, and blasphemous libels, highly reflecting upon the Christian Religion, and the Church of England, and tend to promote immorality and Atheism, and to create Divisions, Schisms, and Factions, among her Majesty's subjects" (Gillett 1932 613).

In the United States, with its commitment to the separation of church and state, the U.S. Supreme Court asserted in 1872 that the "law knows no heresy" (*Watson v. Jones* 728) and in 1952 the High Court declared that a state may not ban a film on the basis of a censor's conclusions that it is 'sacrilegious'" (*Burstyn v. Wilson* 506).

At the same time that there was diminishing interest in punishing heretical speech, there was an increased effort to destroy obscene and subversive works. For centuries, the church and state had given higher priority to punishing blasphemous-heretical expression than to obscene speech. As Ernst has observed, "[F]or the Church the index of the good life was freedom from heresy and not from obscenity" (142). Once obscenity became the target of the censors, the language used to condemn blasphemous and seditious works was applied in condemnations of obscene books: poison, pollution, filth, vermin, Satanic. Armed with these metaphors, the book banners and book burners denounced the obscene and proceeded to destroy by fire such works as James Joyce's *Ulysses*, D.H. Lawrence's *The Rainbow*, John Steinbeck's *Grapes of Wrath*, and Kurt Vonnegut's *Slaughterhouse Five*. The public burning of obscene books was provided for in Missouri's Revised Statutes, §542.420: "If the judge or magistrate hearing such cause shall determine that the property or articles are of the kind mentioned in section 542.380 [dealing with obscenity], he shall cause the same to be publicly destroyed, by burning or otherwise." On December 12, 1957, a circuit judge in Missouri "filed an unreported opinion in which he overruled the several motions [to quash the search warrants, etc.] and found that 100 of the 280 seized items were obscene.

A judgment thereupon issued directing that the 100 items, and all copies thereof, 'shall be retained by the Sheriff of Jackson County ... as necessary evidence for the purpose of possible criminal prosecution or prosecutions, and when such necessity no longer exists, said Sheriff ... shall publicly destroy the same by burning within thirty days thereafter'" (*Marcus v. Search Warrant* 724).

Obscene books, like blasphemous-heretical writings, were transformed into subversive threats to the purity, welfare, and stability of the nation. The seditious-subversive books, some of them including obscenities, continued to burn around the world well into the twentieth century and the beginning of the twenty-first. Victor Hugo's *Les Misérables* and Dostoyevsky novels were burned in Guatemala in the 1950s. After the Pinochet regime took over Chile in 1973, books were taken from university libraries and burned in order for "the university to recover its purity." In 1975, communist officials in Vietnam burned books to eliminate "the decadent culture of the south." In 2001, forty thousand copies of Wei Hui's novel *Shanghai Baby* were burned in China, with Hui denounced as "decadent, debauched and a slave to Western culture." In 2001, Hindus were burning Muslim writings, Muslims were burning Marxist books, and Christians were burning Muslim works.

Through the centuries, the magical fire that had purified the farm lands of pestilence, vermin, tares, and witches was used to eradicate the magical, poisonous, cancerous, filthy words on the page in the book, whether the book was blasphemous, seditious, or obscene. As the books have gone up in flames, the book burners have attempted to eradicate history, "to switch off the national memory," whether in the third century C.E. in China or in the nations around the world in the twentieth century. With the magical, fearful fires the book burners reduce to ashes the magical, fearful words on the page. The live words and the live books, the book burner fearfully hopes, will no longer see us or talk to us.

2

BURNING BLASPHEMOUS-
HERETICAL BOOKS

Antiquity Through the Fifteenth Century

"As to the gods, I have no means of knowing either that they exist or that they do not exist. For many are the obstacles that impede knowledge, both the obscurity of the question and the shortness of human life," wrote the influential Greek sophist Protagoras in his *On the Gods* which was condemned for impiety and, according to some authorities, burned in the agora in Athens in 415 B.C.E.

Various philosophers and historians have identified the burning of *On the Gods* as the first incident of setting a book afire because it was condemned as impious. Writing in the first century B.C.E., Cicero referred to the importance of Protagoras and to the book burning: "As for Protagoras of Abdera, whom you have just mentioned and who was quite the most important sophist of his day, he prefaced his book with the words 'I cannot say whether gods exist or not,' and by order of the Athenians he was banished from their city and territory, and had his books publicly burnt" (Cicero 24–25). The third century historian Diogenes Laertius wrote in his *Lives of Eminent Philosophers* that as a result of Protagoras expressing his view that there was no way of knowing whether the gods exist, he was expelled by the Athenians and "they burnt his works in the market-place after sending around a herald to collect them all who had copies in their possession" (465).

Centuries later, John Milton also referred to the burning of the Protagoras book in his 1644 classic work attacking censorship, *Areopagitica:* "In Athens, where books and wits were ever busier than in any other part of Greece, I find but two sorts of writings which the magistrate cared to take notice of: those either blasphemous and atheistical, or libelous. Thus the books of Protagoras were by the judges of Areopagus commanded to be burnt, and himself banished the territory, for a discourse begun with his confessing not to know 'whether there were gods or whether not'" (7).

Later scholars, while agreeing that copies of Protagoras' work had been set afire, have not always been in agreement as to whether the book was burned because it was "impious," or "atheistical," or "blasphemous." Writing in his 1936 article titled "Books for the Burning," Clarence A. Forbes says of the first book burnings: "It was not many centuries after the first books were made that some writers stirred men's anger to the burning point. The first cause ever alleged for condemning books to the fire was atheism. This was the violet-crowned, glorious city of Athens, in the fifth century B.C." Forbes then refers to *On the Gods* for which Protagoras "was condemned to exile, and all copies of his book were collected by the public crier and burned in the agora" (117).

After identifying Protagoras as one of the greatest of the Sophists," J.B. Bury wrote in

1952: "A charge of blasphemy was lodged against him and he fled from Athens.... Copies of the work of Protagoras were collected and burned, but the book of Anaxagoras setting forth the view for which he had been condemned was for sale on the Athenian book-stalls at a popular price" (18). Mario Untersteiner, writing about the Sophists, saw Protagoras being condemned for "impiety" and either avoiding the trial by fleeing or being banished and condemned to exile (5). "Subversive writing" has also been used to describe the Protagoras work; Wilhelm Schmid, referring to burning of the Protagoras books, wrote in 1940: "He was exiled and his subversive writing, as far as they were in the possession of Athenians, were gathered and burnt under pronouncement by the herald. During the journey to Sicily, where he had been before, he suffered shipwreck and drowned" (1).

A contemporary of Protagoras (492–421 B.C.E.), Anaxagoras (500–428 B.C.E.), was also charged with impiety and, according to some authorities, also had his books burned by Athenian officials. Charles Gillett has observed that Anaxagoras "produced results in physical research which were regarded as derogatory to the gods, so that his books were burned as impious and he was exiled" (5). Anaxagoras had denied that the sun and moon were divine beings and contended that "the sun, instead of being a god, was an intensely hot mass of molten rock and was larger than the peloponnesus" (Wheelwright 154).

Anaxagoras, writes Levy, "was the first philosopher to reside in Athens and probably the first freethinker to be condemned for his beliefs.... He regarded the conventional gods as mythic abstractions endowed with anthropomorphic attributes" (Levy 1993 4). Further, Gershenson and Greenberg describe Anaxagoras as "the first thinker of repute who was a scientist in the sense in which we use the term today" (xiii).

Both Axagagoras and Protagoras were influential in the life of Pericles. Burnet states that "Anaxagoras is said to have been the teacher of Perikles, and the fact is placed beyond the reach of doubt by the testimony of Plato" and "so too Isokrates says that Perikles was the pupil of two 'sophists,' Anaxagoras and Damon" (254). In about 438 B.C.E., a decree provided that one should "denounce those who do not believe in the divine beings (*la theia*) or teach doctrines about things in the sky" (Burkert 316). Commenting on this decree and its relationship between Anaxagoras and Pericles, Burkert points out: "It was known that this [decree] was directed against Anaxagoras and was meant to harm Pericles. Anaxagoras' most famous assertion was that Helios [sun], like other heavenly bodies, is a glowing lump of metal, as the fall of a meteorite in 456 had proved to him. Now such doctrines were forbidden by the state. Anaxagoras had been teaching in Athens for 30 years; he now left the city. Thereafter, as far as we know, the decree was no longer used, and seems to have passed into oblivion. But the conflict between piety and natural science, and indeed wisdom of all kinds, had come to stay; it re-echoes in the *Clouds* of Aristophanes as it does in Euripides" (316).

While scholars agree on the importance and influence of Anaxagoras and Protagoras, they have continued to disagree on how they and their works were treated by Athenian authorities. On the one hand, *The Oxford History of Western Philosophy* (1994) states that both Socrates and Protagoras "offended powerful parties, and were respectively killed and banished by the city of Athens (as was Anaxagoras of Clazomenae [500–428 B.C.], nicknamed the Mind, who first suggested that Reason, despite appearance, ruled the world, and that the sun was a heated lump of metal, not a god)" (21). On the other hand, the *Encyclopedia of Classical Philosophy* asserts: "Some sources tell us that Protagoras was tried in Athens and condemned for impiety, but scholars usually reject this on the basis of Plato's testimony that Protagoras was honored to the end of his nearly seventy years.... He was evidently an original thinker, known in antiquity for his claim that 'a human being is the measure of all things,' for his agnosticism about the gods, and for his method of teaching opposed speeches" (Zeyl 455).

On the one hand, Leonard Levy writes in his *Treason Against God* (1981): "That the Athens of the fifth century B.C. could drive Socrates, Phidias, and Protagoras to their deaths and drive away Anaxagoras, Alcibiades, and Diagoras proved rather early in the history of the West that religion when supported by the state can be hostile to enlightenment and personal liberty" (14). On the other hand, I.F. Stone argues in his *The Trial of Socrates* (1988) that the stories about Anaxagoras and Protagoras being tried for impiety and their subsequent banishment are "fables" and "melodramatic" (237–239). Stone rejects E.R. Dodds' position that men like Anaxagoras, Protagoras and Socrates were victims of heresy trials. Dodds had written in his 1951 work *The Greeks and the Irrational:* "About 432 B.C. or a year or two later, disbelief in the supernatural and the teaching of astronomy were made indictable offences. The next thirty-odd years witnessed a series of heresy trials which is unique in Athenian history. The victims included most of the leaders of progressive thought at Athens— Anaxagoras, Diagoras, Socrates, almost certainly Protagoras also, and possibly Euripides.... [T]he evidence we have is more than enough to prove that the Great Greek Enlightenment was also, like our own, an Age of Persecution — banishment of scholars, blinkering of thought and even (if we can believe the tradition about Protagoras) burning of books" (189).

The evidence in support of the persecutions of Anaxagoras and Protagoras, according to Edward Schiappa, is unconvincing; Schiappa writes in his 1991 work *Protagoras and Logos: A Study in Greek Philosophy and Rhetoric:* "It is significant that Diogenes Laertius also reported that Protagoras' books were ordered burned.... Such an unprecedented and unparalleled action would surely have been discussed by at least one fifth- or fourth-century source, but it was not.... The origin of the whole trial story is impossible to determine, but it is plausible that — like the story of Anaxagoras's persecution — it was an attractive myth since it served as an antecedent to Socrates' trial" (145). Schiappa's position closely reflects that of Daniel Gershenson and Daniel Greenberg who wrote in 1964 in their *Anaxagoras and the Birth of Physics:* "The trial of Anaxagoras is a persistent historical myth based on plausible reconstruction, which because of its spectacular nature in posing him as the earliest martyr of science, and as the forerunner of Socrates, has appeared in almost every biography of Anaxagoras written since the third century B.C.E." (348).

Historian Will Durant, in his *The Life of Greece,* described Protagoras as "the most renowned of the Sophists" and after citing Protagoras's famous lines "With regard to the gods I know not whether they exist or not...," Durant states: "The Athenian Assembly, frightened by that ominous prelude, banished Protagoras, ordered all Athenians to surrender any copies they might have of his writings, and burned the books in the market place. Protagoras fled to Sicily, and, story tells us, was drowned on the way" (360).

Whichever side one takes in the debate about the burning of the works of Anaxagoras and Protagoras, or even if we could actually determine whether the books were burned, we still might have difficulty determining whether the books were set afire because of impiety or because of sedition. On the surface, the books were burned because they were impious, but while the official charges were impiety and blasphemy, the books and their authors were considered as undermining government and society. W.K.C. Guthrie has observed that there was more than "impiety" involved in the persecution of Anaxagoras: "Plutarch and Diodorus agree that the persecution of Anaxagoras for impiety was at least partly due to the desire of Pericles's political opponents to attack him through his friendship with the atheistic scientist" (268).

Further, as I.F. Stone has recognized, there was a nexus between impiety-blasphemy and disloyalty-sedition: "In the Greek city-states, as in the Roman, not to recognize the city's gods was to be disloyal to the city" (203). J.B. Bury, writing about Anaxagoras, Protagoras, and other Greek rhetoricians and philosophers, asserts in his discussion of Socrates that there can be "little doubt that the motives of the accusation were political" (21). Referring to Socrates, Protagoras, Anaxagoras, and other Athenians who were either condemned to death or sent into exile, Levy also recognizes the political aspects of the trials: "The record does not show that any of the victims reviled the deities. The cases tended to be as much political as religious in character. Treason against the gods was close to treason against the state, but Athens could accept a charge of impiety more easily than it could a political charge" (1993 7).

Being charged with *asebeia* (impiety), Protagoras, Anaxagoras, and Socrates were, in effect, being tried because their religious *asebeia* had political implications. As H.D. Rankin has explained: "City states depended upon the good will of the gods, and if these gods were ignored, misdefined or reinterpreted, the safety of the city was placed in danger.... If he [Athenian] openly denied the gods or suggested they were other in their nature than they were generally supposed to be, he became liable to prosecution for *asebeia* or impiety, and the penalty could be very heavy.... Consequently, overt expression of doubt or published criticism of the gods or doubt of their existence was dangerous" (136).

As will become apparent in subsequent centuries, impiety and blasphemy became seditious because, as English Jurist Windham said in 1661, "The Ecclesiastick is the prime part of the Government of England," and hence a blasphemous work could be condemned to the fire by secular authorities, for "to reproach the Christian religion is to speak in subversion of the law" (Nokes 48).

In addition to the problems of determining whether the Anaxagoras and Protagoras books were actually burned and of determining whether they were actually burned because of religious or political reasons, we are further confronted with the problem of the careless use of the terms "impiety," "blasphemy," "heresy," and "irreligion"— terms that have been invoked when books, and sometimes their authors, have been set afire. Often the terms have been used interchangeably; sometimes authors and their books have been condemned as being both heretical and blasphemous. As Levy has indicated, "At various times in the past blasphemy was nearly indistinguishable from the crimes of idolatry, sacrilege, heresy, obscenity, profanity, sedition, treason, and breach of the peace" (1993 570).

While one author states that "the last of the Pericleans to be tried for blasphemy was Socrates" (Levy), another writes of the "impiety charge" against Socrates (Stone 199). Where one author refers to the "accusation of impiety" against Protagoras (Untersteiner 5), another declares that the charge against Protagoras was "blasphemy" (Melchinger 32) and still another source, *The Cambridge Ancient History,* has Protagoras being indicted "for irreligion, on account of his treatise *On the Gods* " (384). James Farrer identifies Protagoras as the "first avowed Agnostic, for he wrote a work on the gods, of which the very first remark was that the existence of gods at all he could not himself either affirm or deny. For this offensive sentiment his book was publicly burnt" (Farrer 3). And finally, Rudolf Pfeiffer, in his *History of Classical Scholarship* (1968) refers to Protagoras as being accused of "atheism" (31).

While half way around the world Lord Shang Yang (390–338 B.C.E.) was recommending book burnings in China as a means of eradicating history, followed by the burnings of several classic Chinese writings in 213 B.C.E. (see Chapter 3), in Rome in the same year books dealing with religious matters, with prophesies, superstitions, and divinities were being set ablaze. Writing of the book burnings of 213 B.C.E., Livy stated in his *History of Rome:* "How often, in the ages of our fathers, was it given in charge to the magistrates, to prohibit the performance of any foreign religious rites; to banish strolling sacrificers and soothsayers from the forum, the circus, and the city; to search for, and burn, books of divination; and to abolish every mode of sacrificing that was not conformable to the Roman practice?" (Livy XXXIX. 16).

Referring to the edict ordering the collection of the condemned books, Livy observed: "The evil now appearing too powerful to be checked by the efforts of the inferior magistrates, the senate gave a charge to Marcus Atilius, praetor of the city, to free the public from those superstitious nuisances. For this purpose, he read their decree in a general assembly: and, at the same time, gave notice, that whosoever had any books of divination, and forms of prayer used on such occasions, or the art of sacrificing in writing, should bring all such books and writings to him before the calends of April, and that no person should in any place, either public or consecrated, perform sacrifice in any new or foreign mode" (Livy XXV. 1).

Emperor Augustus, in 12 B.C.E., ordered condemned books dealing with "prophesies and destinies" collected and burned. As MacMullen has observed: "As Augustus pointed the way for the control of divination, so did he for prophecy, confiscating and burning in 12 B.C. more than two thousand books on the subject, Greek and Latin (Suet. Aug. 31. 1). Henceforth their private ownership was forbidden (Tac., Ann. 6. 12)" (130). Suetonius had referred in his *History of Twelve Caesars* to the book burnings that occurred during the reign of Augustus: "Finally, on assuming the office of Chief Pontiff vacated by the death of Marcus Lepidus—he could not bring himself to divest his former colleague of it, even though he were an exile—Augustus collected all the copies of Greek and Latin prophetic verse then current, the work of either anonymous or little-known authors, and burned more than two thousand" (Suet. Aug. 31. 1).

The book burnings increased with the destruction of the Christian Holy Scriptures, books and Christian martyrs set afire together. Accompanying the burning of the Christian books and churches were the demands to sacrifice and those who refused faced execution or forced labor. Referring to the February 303 Diocletian edict ordering the burning of the Scriptures, Lactantius wrote: "When that day [Feb. 23, 303] dawned, in the eighth consulship of Diocletian and seventh of Maximianus, suddenly, while it was hardly light, the prefect, together with the chief commanders, tribunes, and officers of the treasury, came to the church [in Nicomedia], and when the gates had been forced open they sought for an image of God. The books of the Holy Scriptures were found and burnt; the spoil was given to all" (Ayer 259).

In his *Ecclesiastical History,* Eusebius, reporting on the "great persecution" of the Christians, records that in 303 "all things in truth were fulfilled in our day, when we saw with our very eyes the houses of prayer cast down to their foundations from top to bottom, and the inspired and sacred Scriptures committed to the flames in the midst of the market-place, and the pastors of the churches some shamefully hiding themselves there, while others were ignominiously captured and made a mockery by their enemies" (VIII. 1. 9–11.1).

Within a few years, it was the Christians who were ordering and carrying out the book burnings after the Roman Emperor Constantine converted to Christianity and began the persecution of pagans and critics of his new-found religion. As Levy has indicated, "Religious intolerance soon became a Christian principle, contrary to the Scriptures.... By 435, there were sixty-six laws against Christian heretics plus many others against pagans" (1993 44).

In decree after decree, the expulsion of heretics and the elimination of heresies relied on figurative language dehumanizing the enemies into pestilence, poisons, and polluted contagions. For example, in 381 it was decreed that "the contamination of the Photinian pestilence, the poison of the Arian sacrilege, the crime of the Eunomian perfidy, and the sectarian monstrosities, abominable because of the ill-omened names of their authors, shall be abolished even from the hearing of men" (Pharr 451). A Church command of 408 identified the Jews with heretics and the condemned Donatists and then identified all of them with "a pestilence and a contagion" (Pharr 458).

After the Greek scholar and philosopher Porphyry (234–302) wrote his *Against the Christians* in which he rejected the Christian conception of God and the idea that Jesus saved souls and in which he ridiculed Jesus' parables and contended that "the Incarnation was a logical impossibility," Constantine ordered in 324 that "all copies of *Against the Christians* to be burned, prescribing the death penalty for any who furtively retained the work" (Barnes 211). A century later, *Against the Christians* was burned by emperors Valaentinian II and Theodosius II. What these Christian book burners found objectionable, as Barnes reports, was that "Porphyry, like other Platonists of the period, objected to the elevation of faith above reason. He rejected both the Christian conception of God and the Christian interpretation of history. If God were omnipotent (he argued), then God could lie — which is absurd.... More fundamentally still, Porphyry contended that the Incarnation was a logical impossibility" (Barnes 176). Henceforth, the person labeled a Porphyrian was condemned as an enemy of Christianity.

Referring to the censorship and burning of Porphyry's work, Croke has observed: "The third-century Neoplatonist Porphyry of Tyre was not a lucky man. His hard-headed attitude to the Christian scriptures and way of life was not appreciated at Caesarea where he was thoroughly beaten up by a Christian gang. Posterity did the same to his reputation. His works were outlawed by a newly Christianized imperial court in the earlier part of the fourth century and were still being ceremoniously burnt a century and a half later" (168).

Several illustrations of Porphyry's attacks on the Bible are provided by Anastos who has written, for example: (1) "Porphyry makes much of errors and contradictions he discovers in the Bible, and condemns the disciples of Jesus as ignorant men, unworthy of respect, who performed miracles by magical arts and thereby persuaded wealthy women to give them their property." (2) "Porphyry had no respect for either Peter or Paul, and ascribes the conflict between them ... to Paul's jealousy of Peter." (3) "Porphyry's most telling blows were struck at the doctrine of immortality of the body and the Gospel account of Christ's crucifixion and resurrection" (421–449). Porphyry, Anastos has written, was "One of the most formidable of the pagan opponents of Christianity on the threshold of the Middles Ages.... He wrote an erudite and caustic polemic against Christianity in fifteen books. Unfortunately, this work, entitled *Against the Christians...*, which is of inestimable value in appraising the nature of the pagan criticism of Christian doctrine, was systematically destroyed in accordance with an edict of the Emperor Constantine I in 325, after the Council of Nicaea, and again in 448 by order of the Emperors Valentinian III and Theodorius II" (423). The burning and destruction of Porphyry's *Against the Christians* was "so effective that only a scant 105 fragments now remain" (Anastos 423).

In 333, Constantine condemned Alexandrian priest Arius (250–336) as a Porphyrian, as "a mouthpiece of Satan," and ordered the burning of Arius' writings. The edict ordering the burning read, in part: "[I]t is, now, my decision that Arius and such as have opinions similar to his should be called Porphyrians in order that they may have the name of those whose way of life they imitate. In addition to this, if any treatise composed by Arius is found, let it be put into the fire, in order not only that his defective doctrinal works may be destroyed, but also that no reminder at all should remain with him.... I order that if anyone is detected in concealing anything composed by Arius, and not giving it up instantly for feeding it to the fire, his penalty shall be death" (Keresztes 350).

Some of the objectionable blasphemous ideas proposed by Arius included: "God was not always the Father, but there was a period when God was not the Father. The Word of God did not always exist, but came into existence out of nothing. For God, who existed, made him who did not exist out of what did not previously exist. Hence, too, there was a time when he was not. For the Son is a creature and an object. He is neither like the Father in substance, nor the true and natural Word of the Father, nor his true Wisdom, but one of the created objects, and he is improperly called Word and Wisdom, since he himself came into being by the proper Word of God and the Wisdom of God, in which God made both everything and him. Hence he is both mutable and changeable by nature, as are all rational creatures" (Barnes 203).

By burning these blasphemies, as Constantine asserted in his edict, the "defective doctrinal works may be destroyed"; but the Christians were not satisfied with the destruction of Arius' "defective works." In Constantine's words, let the Arius treatise "be put into the fire" also so that "no reminder at all should remain with him [Arius]." The purpose of burning Arius' writings was, in part, to send him into oblivion. Arius was excommunicated and banished from Alexandria, allowed to return for a brief time before he died in 336.

The Christians' book burning rituals that were to last for several centuries were well on their way in the fourth and fifth centuries, with both Church and state involved in the fiery extermination of blasphemous, heretical books and their authors. As Edward Peters has observed, "By the last decade of the fourth century, the now-Christianized Roman Empire began to attack religious dissidents as it treated political dissidents and criminals, with legal means" (1980 42). The religious blasphemy and heresy became a political sedition. Writing of the persecution of the heretical Donatists, Maureen Tilley states: "The most important factor in evaluating religious persecution in the Roman Empire, whether of Donatists or others, is the degree to which Church and State were entwined. Roman religion presumed that the people of a state and the local worshipping community were for all intents and purposes indistinguishable" (xxiii).

The Theodosian Code commanded that the books containing the doctrines of the "Eunomian and Montanist [heretical] superstitions" were to be sought out and "be consumed with fire immediately under the supervision of the judges" (Pharr 456). A 409 decree of the Code provided that the books of astrologers were to be burned and that "astrologers shall be banned not only from the City of Rome but also from all municipalities, unless, after the book of their false doctrine have been consumed in flames under the eyes of the bishop, they are prepared to transfer their faith to the practice of the Catholic religion and never return to their former false doctrine" (Pharr 239). Sixteen years later, it was commanded that "the Manichaeans, heretics, schismatics, astrologers, and every sect inimical to the Catholics shall be banished from the very sight of the City of Rome, in order that it may not be contaminated by the contagious presence of the criminals" (Pharr 462). In 435, Nestorius was condemned as "the author of a monstrous superstition" and it was decreed that his books be "diligently and zealously sought out and publicly burned" (Pharr 463).

Decree after decree ordered that "the madness of the heretics must be suppressed," that "crowds shall be kept away from the unlawful congregations of all heretics.... The contamination of the Photinian pestilence, the poison of the Arian sacrilege, the crime of the Eunomian perfidy, and the sectarian monstrosities, abominable because of the ill-omened names of their authors shall be abolished even from the hearing of men" (Pharr 451). Banishment or death awaited the heretics who did not comply. The actions taken against the Montanists have been summarized by Christine Trevett: "Life had become harder for such heretics (which Montanists now were) since the reign of Constantine. The story was one of proscription and banishment, book-burning and heresy-hunting, confiscation of churches by the catholics, capital offenses and legal impediments. The death-knell probably sounded between 527 and 531 C.E. Justinian promulgated laws against heretics and the *enforced* conversion of pagans was made explicitly legal." Montanists were "forbidden to assemble, baptise, share common meals, be in receipt of welfare or buy slaves. Even the power of making a will was denied them." As Trevett concludes: "[H]eresy was politicized. It had come to be seen as treason, as failure to be at one with the welfare of the State. To deprive heretics of leadership there were penalties for creating Montanist clergy. Montanist books were burnt, with threat of execution for anyone found hiding such books" (228–229).

The politicization of religious heresy during the reign of Constantine and the accompanying book burnings has been referred to by Harold O.J. Brown in his work titled *Heresies*: "Constantine ordered the burning of Arius' writings and immediately began to take repressive measures against his supporters. It was the Emperor, not the orthodox bishops, who ordered the repression of the Arian party, but the orthodox welcomed his action. The mutual persecution of Christians by Christians, using the power of the state, had begun" (118).

The preoccupation of the Church with "filthy," "poisonous" sects and heresies was reflected in the several works devoted to listing and describing the condemned "foul and shameful" teachings and practices. The heretical books consigned to the fires were metaphorized into "deadly serpents," "pestilence," and "rot." In succeeding centuries this was the language used to define and label the heretics and their works as they were sent to the stake.

In his fourth century work titled *Panarion* Epiphanius of Salamis dealt with eighty heresies and sects that he condemned. *Panarion,* meaning "Medicine Chest," began with a Proem in which Epiphanius declared: "Since I shall be telling you the names of sects and exposing their unlawful deeds like poisons and toxic substances, matching the antidotes with them at the same time — cures for those who are already bitten, and preventatives for those who will have this experience — I am drafting this Preface here for the scholarly, to explain the 'Panarion,' or chest of remedies for the victims of wild beasts' bites. It is a work of three Volumes and contains eighty Sects, which stand symbolically for wild animals or snakes" (3). In writing against the second century Gnostic, Epiphanius relied heavily on the "scum" metaphor, emphasizing that "this scum spent his entire life in these places" and after summarizing the unacceptable ideas of Basilides, Epiphanius writes "Such are the recitals of the scum's invention." By the end of his "refutation" of Basilides, Epiphanius has transformed the "scum" into "a horned asp [that] lies buried in sand, but pokes up into air with its horn, and inflicts death on those who happen on it" (70–76).

In his attack on Arius, Epiphanius concludes his "refutation" with: "But let us pass him by too, as though we had squashed a dung or blister-beetle, or the bug we call a buprestis, [and], on the foundation of the church and with God's power, go on once more to the rest, calling on God for aid" (497). At which point he presents a sixty-nine page "refutation" against the Anomoeans and Aetius, the founder of the condemned sect, concluding: "This is [the] information I have [about] Aetius and his disciples, to whom some have given the name of Anomoean because he has come to an opinion still more frightful than the heresy of Arius. With God's help I have gone through his doctrines in detail as best I can, as though I had stamped on the serpent called the many-footed millipede, or wood-louse, with the foot of truth, and crushed it with the true confession of the Only-begotten" (Epiphanius 566).

The "poison," "venom," "viper" metaphors are applied in his denunciation of Montanus and the Montanists: "[I] feel that this here will be enough for this sect. I have crushed its poison, and the venom on its hooked fangs, with the cudgel of the truth of the cross. For it is like the viper of hemorrhage, whose mischief is to drain the blood from its victims' entire bodies and so cause their deaths" (Epiphanius II 21).

In his eighty-eight page "refutation" of the impieties of the Manichaeans, Epiphanius continued to draw on his venom-serpent metaphors and then identified the Manichaeans with the "astrologers" and their practices of "mumbo jumbo": "We have gone over a long road and many dangerous places, and [have] with difficulty [crushed the head] of this amphisbaena and venomous reptile, the cenchritis, which has coils of many illustrations for the deception of those who see it, and conceals beneath it the sting and poisonous source [of the lies of heathen mythology].... He [Mani] knows the lore of the magi and is involved with them, and he praises astrologers and practices their mumbo jumbo. He merely mouths the name of Christ, as the cenchritis too conceals its poison" (Epiphanius II 307).

Less than a century later, St. Augustine, in his own listing and treatment of the heresies, provided descriptions of the errors and practices of the heretics, especially the Manichees, Donatists, Arians, and Pelagians (Augustine 1990 34–60). Augustine concludes his treatment of eighty-three heresies with the poison metaphor: "We should, finally, inquire into what it is that makes one a heretic so that, in avoiding that with the Lord's help, we may avoid the poison of heresies, not only of those which we know, but also of those we do not know, whether they already actually exist or merely could exist" (1990 58).

All the while, the emperors commanded that "Manichaeans, heretics, schismatics, astrologers, and every sect inimical to the Catholics shall be banished from the very sight of the City of Rome, in order that it may not be contaminated by the contagious presence of the criminals" (Pharr 462). Under the reign of Constantine, "the story was one of proscription and banishment, book-burning and heresy-hunting, confiscation of churches by the catholics, capital offenses and legal impediments" (Trevett 227). Amongst the books that were set afire were the works of Arius, Nestorius, Donatus, and Montanus. Arius was excommunicated; Nestorius was exiled; Donatus was exiled; Priscillian was executed.

In the last century of the first millennium, Radulphus Glaber, also known as Ralph the Bad, condemned the heretical Vilgard of Ravenna who was accused of being a "ciceronian" and not a Christian and being corrupted by the writings of Virgil, Horace and Juvenal. In his denunciation of Vilgard, Glaber declared that many others who held Vilgard's "noxious doctrine" went to the island of Sardinia "to infect the people of Spain, but were exterminated by the Catholics." Glaber wrote of another heretic who when questioned the bishop concealed "the poison of his wickedness" (Wakefield and Evans 72–73).

As the first millennium came to a close, heretics had been defined as "poisons," "infectious," as "serpents," "tares, "ravening wolves," and as "bad trees that cannot bring good fruit." This language of the first millennium invited the burning of heretics and their writings was and largely based on the authority of the Bible in which there appeared the identical metaphorical language of condemnation. In Matthew 12:34 the blasphemers are a "brood of vipers"; in Matthew 7:15 false prophets are "ravenous wolves" and in Matthew 7:19 "every tree that does not bear good fruit is cut down and thrown into the fire." In 2 Chronicles 26:20–21 the leprous Uzzi'ah was cast out of the house of the Lord "because the Lord had smitten him" and he was a "leper to the day of his death, and being leper dwelt in a separate house, for he was excluded from the house of the Lord." According to Matthew 13:24–30, the "tares" are to be separated from the wheat and burned. Leviticus 13:45–52 asserted that the leper is "unclean" and if the priest finds "a leprous disease in a garment" it "shall be burned in the fire."

These biblical metaphors—lepers, wolves, serpents, vipers, tares—became institutionalized by the beginning of the new millennium in the Church's condemnation of heretics and their books. In his attack on the heretical Bogomils, Priest Cosmas relied on both the "ravening wolves" and "tares" metaphors, asserting in the tenth century: "Indeed externally the heretics appear as sheep: they are gentle and humble and quiet. They seem pale from their hypocritical fasts, they do not utter vain words, they do not laugh out loud, they do not show curiosity, they take care not to be noticeable and to do everything externally so that they may not be told apart from orthodox Christians. Inside they are ravening wolves, as the Lord said [Matt. 7. 15].... [W]hen they see anyone simple and ignorant, there they sow the tares of their doctrines and blaspheme the traditional teaching of the Holy Church (Hamilton 116). According to Priest Cosmas, the heretics are "worse than demons themselves, for the demons are afraid of the cross of Christ, while the heretics chop up crosses and make tools of them. The demons are afraid of the image of the Lord painted on a wooden panel, but the heretics do not venerate icons, but call them idols" (Hamilton 117). Relying heavily on passages from Matthew, Priest Cosmas warned that fire awaited the heretics:

> Scripture says, As Jesus sat on the Mount of Olives, the disciples came to him, saying, "Tell us, when will this be, and what will be the sign of your coming and of the close of the age?" The Lord answered them, "Take heed, for many will come in my name, saying 'I am the Christ' and they will lead many astray." But, he added, "You will recognize them by their fruits; a good tree cannot produce bad fruit, nor a bad tree good fruit. Men do not gather grapes from thorns, nor harvest figs from thistles" [Matt.7:16, 18]. All the same, you ought to recognize these men from their fruits; that is, their hypocrisy, their pride, their blasphemies: and when you have recognized them, avoid them, lest you share their condemnation. If a man who allies himself to the enemies of an earthy king does not even deserve to live, but is put to death along with them, how much more those who are enemies of the heavenly king; they will perish in the everlasting fire, as it is said, "Every tree that does not bear good fruit is cut down and cast into the fire" [Matt.3.10] [Hamilton: 116–117].

Just as the heretics were "bad trees" and "tares" to be destroyed by fire, so too were they metaphorized into "lepers." As R.I. Moore has indicated, "The analogy between heresy and leprosy is used with great regularity and in great detail by twelfth-century writers. Heresy spreads like leprosy, running far and wide, infecting the limbs of Christ as it goes.... Against so insidious an infection nothing less than fire was effective; when the leper died the hut in which he lived, and all his belongings were burned" (Moore 1987 63). During the 1130s, in his debate with the heretic Henry of Lausanne, the monk William of St. Thierry asserted: "You too are a leper, scarred by heresy, excluded from communion by the judgement of the priest, according to law, bare-headed, with ragged clothing, your body covered by an infected and filthy garment; it befits you to shout that you are a leper, a heretic and unclean, and must live alone, outside the camp, that is to say outside the Church" (Moore 1975 57). Heresy, declared the Church officials in the twelfth century, was both an "infectious pestilence" and an "infectious leprosy": "[T]he Cathars have multiplied in every land and the Church is now greatly endangered by the foul poison which flows against it on every side. Their message crawls like the crab, runs far and wide like infectious leprosy, infecting the limbs of Christ as it goes" (Moore 1975 90).

The association of fire with destroying pests, tares, leprosy, demons, etc. was established both through the biblical references and the traditional practices of using fire to rid the farms of pestilence, weeds, and demons. Put into syllogistic form, the reasoning went thus:

First premise: If one is confronted with the presence and spread of pestilence, disease, tares, and the demonic, the effective remedy is to set fire to them (as Biblical passages and traditional farmers' practices indicate).

Second premise: We are confronted with the presence and spread of [heretical] pestilence, disease, tares, and the demonic.

Conclusion: Therefore, the effective remedy is to set fire to them [heretics and their writings].

If one accepts the premises as true and valid, the conclusion follows. However, the invalidity of the argument is exposed when one recognizes that (1) the truth of the first premise is questionable; (2) the analogy between the physical pestilence and the pestilence of ideas is a false analogy; and (3) equivocation has occurred when "pestilence," "disease," and "tares" are used in one sense in the first premise and a different sense in the second premise.

At the same time Christians were burning heretics and their writings in Europe, the Chinese were burning religious books and images and persecuting non–Confucian sects and religions. Luther C. Goodrich reports that "early in the ninth century the great scholar Han Yu wrote in his essay on the Origin of the Tao: 'Now if this is the situation, what should be done to bring about a proper state of affairs? I say: If we do not stop [Buddhism and Taoism], [Confucianism] will not spread; if we do not halt [the former], [the true way] will not develop. Let us man their sectaries, let us burn their books, let us secularize their temples.' No action was taken at the time, but a generation later, in 843 A.D., in connection with the proscription of the Manichean religion, the order went out for 'the officials ... to collect the books and images of the Manicheans and burn them in the public thoroughfares.' The great Buddhist persecution followed in 845" (3). The burning of Manichean books in the ninth century was accompanied with the burning of books of the Mo–ri, possibly a word representing Manicheism. The order was "to sequestrate the books of the Mo-ri, and burn them on the roads together with their images; and that all their goods and effects should be confiscated at the profit of the mandarinate" (Groot 60). In 1258, an edict was issued by Kublai Khan ordering the burning of Taoist books and woodblocks: "I command that honorable Chang proceed to the dispatch of emissaries who will search out everywhere and take the texts of the listed books as well as the woodblocks used to print them. Within two months the books are to be brought to Peking where they will be stacked and destroyed by fire"; and then twenty-three years later, Kublai Khan issued another edict "decreeing the further burning of Taoist works, with the exception of the *Tao Teh Ching* and woodblocks and texts of diverse non-canonical writings, or books of medicine, pharmacy, etc." (Goodrich 4).

With the beginning of the new millennium there was a significant increase in the burning of books by authors whose works were condemned as either (1) blasphemous or (2) heretical, the former term being applied especially to Hebrew books as they were set afire. As Levy has indicated: "Beginning in the thirteenth century, popes habitually described Jews as blasphemers. The church identified Jesus Christ as God. No greater blasphemy existed than rejecting him, except the greatest blasphemy of all, deicide. The Jews were considered guilty of both" (1993 53). In its efforts to suppress "Jewish blasphemies," the Church ordered the burnings of the Talmud: "Gregory IX ordered the Talmud to be burned throughout Christendom for its alleged blasphemies against Christ and Mary. Tens of thousands of copies of the Talmud and other rabbinic writings were burned, especially in France" (Levy 1993 54).

In the eleventh and twelfth centuries, the Christian crusaders marching through Europe to the Holy Land killed Jews along the way and destroyed their writings. As Popper has pointed out: "Already in the XI century, the Crusaders in their march through Germany had left to mark the path behind them, beside the bodies of murdered Jewish children, heaps of burning Hebrew books" (6). The dehumanizing language against the Jews had already been established by the time the Crusaders attacked them and their writings in 1096. As Gilchrist has observed: "The Christian perception of the Jewish minority had become markedly hostile, preparing the way for future persecutions. However, the theoretical underpinnings of this new attitude were already in place well before 1096. In particular, by no later than the first decade of the eleventh century, ecclesiastical authorities had codified a pervasive body of legislation that cast the Jews in a negative light" (9).

At the outset of his *The Popes and the Jews in the Middle Ages,* Synan notes that the burning of the Torah scrolls and the Talmud manuscripts were part of the persecution, terrorizing and killing of Jews: "The medieval Jew went in fear of mob violence, a threat often tolerated and, at times, incited by the authorities responsible for public order. Badge and ghetto sealed with humiliation a systematic drive to degrade the whole Jewish community. Obscurantist zeal led Christians to burn cartloads of precious Torah scrolls and manuscript copies of the Talmud" (1).

The burning of the Talmud was suggested by Peter the Venerable when he declared: "I would justly condemn it [the Talmud] and its authors to eternal fire." Yvonne Friedman has written of this declaration: "This angry outburst was written by the so-called humanistic Peter the Venerable between 1144–1147. It was voiced about exactly a century before the actual condemnation of the Talmud to the flames in Paris" (171). In June 1239, Pope Gregory IX, in an order to Church officials, declared: "[We, through Apostolic Letters, order Your Discretion to have the Jews who live in the Kingdoms of France, England, Aragon, Navarre, Castile, Leon and Portugal, forced by the secular arm to give up their books. Those books, in which you will find errors of this sort, you shall cause to be burned at the stake. By Apostolic Power, and through use of ecclesiastical censure, you will silence all opponents" (Grayzel 243).

Five years later, Pope Innocent IV, writing to the King of France in May 1244, denounced the "wicked perfidy of the Jews" and the Talmud in which, he said, "are found blasphemies against God and His Christ, and obviously entangled fables about the Blessed Virgin, and abusive errors, and unheard of follies." After referring to Pope Gregory's decree ordering the burning of the *Talmud,* Innocent IV reiterated the need to burn the Jewish works: "[B]ecause the blasphemous abuse of these Jews has not yet ceased ... we ask your Royal Highness and we beseech you in the name of the Lord Jesus Christ, to strike down with merited severity all the detestable and heinous excesses of this sort which they have committed in insult of the Creator and to the injury of the Christian name, and which you have with laudable piety begun to prosecute. Also the above-mentioned books ... should at your order, be burned by fire wherever they can be found throughout your kingdom" (Grayzel 251). In describing the 1244 burning of the Talmud, Popper has written: "[F]inally the confiscation was carried out, and on a certain day, fourteen wagon loads (consisting of 12,000 volumes) of the Talmud and similar works, collected by force from the Jews of France, were delivered in Paris. When, on another day, six more wagon loads had been added, Donin's [a disgruntled Jew converted to Catholicism] desire was publicly fulfilled in Paris (Friday, June 17, 1244)" (11).

In May 1255, a command from the Provincial Council of Beziers declared: "The Talmud, as well as other books in which blasphemies are found, shall be burned. The Jews who refuse to obey this shall be expelled, and transgressors shall suffer punishment according to law" (Grayzel 337). The fiery destruction of the Talmud was supported and ordered by the Church because, among other reasons, it was contended that the Talmud distorted "the meaning of certain biblical passages," taught "unworthy conceptions of God," and the Talmud "was esteemed by the Rabbis as of more value than the Bible," and "above all, that in many of the passages abusive language is used in speaking of Jesus and Mary" (Popper 8). These charges against the Talmud persisted for the next eight centuries as hundreds of thousands of copies of the Talmud were set afire. Once the Inquisition was established by the Church, the number of burnings significantly increased.

The thirteenth century controversy amongst the Jews regarding rabbi-philosopher Maimonides and his *Sefer HaMadda* (*Book of Knowledge*) and *Moreh Nevukhim* (*Code for the Perplexed*) spilled over into the Catholic Church's search for heretical beliefs. As Joseph Sarachek has indicated, "Maimonides' philosophy created a sensational problem for the people of his day and succeeding ages. The *Guide for the Perplexed* ushered in a new epoch of Jewish history. It substituted an untraditional meaning for the literalness of scripture; it not only infused the Bible with philosophy, but held out to the Jew a new conception of God.... Although Maimonides retained the old nomenclature of Judaism, he seems to have understood the terms very differently. God, soul, God-given Torah, world to come, miracle, prophecy, angels and other terms meant one thing to the untutored Jew and another to Maimonides" (14). Traditional rabbinic scholars disapproved of Maimonides' books and "decreed that any person found reading them was to be banned and his property confiscated. In their indignation they turned to the church authorities, who, animated by anti–Aristotelian sentiment that was prevalent at that time in Paris, condemned the Maimonidean philosophic books to the flames" (Sarachek 86).

The burning of *Book of Knowledge* and *Code for the Perplexed* is described by Sarachek: "The light for the fire was obtained from the candelabra in the monastery. The Dominican priests kindled the fire and the burning took place in the market place before all the people.... [I]t should be remembered that the Guide had come into vogue among Christians and the scholastics refer at times to the Jewish heresies. In 1210, the Physics and Metaphysics of Aristotle had been ordered burnt by the Dominicans. The Talmud and other Hebrew books had been burnt by the Church. The Guide was only another book found objectionable for spreading Aristotelian ideas" (87).

There is some disagreement as to the site of the burning of Maimonides' books. "Abraham Maimoni gives the place as Montpellier, whereas Hillel of Verona, writing about 60 years later, lays the scene in Paris. Most historians today place the burning in Montpellier" (Sarachek 87–88). Carmilly-Weinberger has the book burnings taking place in both cities: "[C]opies of the *Sefer HaMadda* and *Moreh Nevukhim* were publicly burned in both Paris and Monpellier in 1233 by the Dominican friars.... In Paris, the burning of the Rambam's [Maimonides] books took place near the Cathedral of Notre Dame; the bonfire was lit with tapers from the altar. Only a year before (1232) Pope Gregory had sent his inquisitors to the Provence to suppress the heretical Albigenses. In this climate of intolerance, it was probably easy for such men as Rabbi Solomon ben Abraham ben Samuel of Montpellier and his associates to get the Dominican priests to burn the works of Maimonides too" (36).

The fiery destruction of Hebrew writings continued without letup into the immediately following centuries, the Talmud becoming the most burned book in history, century after century. In 1306, the king of Majorca commanded copies of the Talmud "delivered up to the auto-da-fé" (Graetz IV 60). The burning of the Talmud in 1322 is referred to by Foa in her *The Jews of Europe After the Black Plague*; she writes that Jewish chroniclers reported that "Pope John XXII, then residing in Avignon, decreed the expulsion of the Roman and Avignonese Jews and the burning of the Talmud. The episode was said to have taken place in 1322, contemporaneous with the slaughter of French lepers and Jews accused of poisoning wells. According to chronicles, the edict of expulsion, later rescinded by the pope, caused an outbreak of anti–Jewish violence in Rome, culminating in the public burning of the Talmud" (Foa 40).

In 1553, the Talmud was condemned to the fires because, among other things, it was "filled with blasphemies against God, Jesus and Mary." As Paul Grendler reports in his essay "The Destruction of Hebrew Books in Venice," "A papal order of August 12, 1553, condemned the Talmud and similar books to be burned.... On October 18, having heard from the report of the Esecutori contro la bestimmia [the civil tribunal charged with punishing blasphemy, moral offences, and violation of the civil press law] that the Talmud was filled with blasphemies against God, Jesus, and Mary, the Council of Ten (the supreme disciplinary organ to which the Esecutori were accountable) acted. It ordered the Esecutori to burn all copies of the Talmud collected to date, and authorized them to search in the ghetto and elsewhere, in the houses of Jews, Christians, and bookmen, for others" (106). When copies of the Talmud were burned on October 21, 1553, in Piazza San Marco, the nuncio declared that the burning was "a good fire." All across Italy the book burnings spread, reducing to ashes "possibly hundreds of thousands of books" (Grendler 106).

While the blasphemies in the Hebrew writings led to their fiery destruction, the Church was more concerned with the heretical writings of Christians. While there was widespread burnings of the Talmud and other Hebrew works beginning especially with the early centuries of the new millennium, there were more extensive burnings during this period of books written by heretical Christians. As Levy has indicated, "The preoccupying problem of the church was not abusive speech about religion but different interpretations of the faith" (Levy 1993 46). Or as Harold O. Brown has put it: "At an early date in the history of Christianity heresy became almost the worst offence in which a Christian could become involved; in the Middle Ages, heresy became a capital crime" (1).

In the same century the Christians were marching off in their Crusades to free the Holy Land from the Muslims, and setting fire to Jews and their books, heretics and their writings increasingly were being set afire. In 1050, theological writer Ratramnus of Corbu's *De Corpore et Sanguine Christi*, which had been written two centuries earlier, was condemned and burned because "in this work Ratramnus maintained that the eucharistic elements are not the actual body and blood of the Christ in history, but are mystic symbols of remembrance" (Hauck 402–403).

The teachings of Ratramnus influenced Berengar of Tours who in 1050 later was condemned by the Synod of Vercelli and excommunicated and later ordered to burn his treatise on the Lord's Supper (Putnam 1906 1 65). Berengar's emphasis on using philosophical theories to interpret matters of faith and his unacceptable views on the Eucharist could not be tolerated by the Church. As Gerard Verbeke has written: "Berengar likes dialectics, he speaks the language of Aristotle and Porphyry, even when he deals with the mystery of the Eucharist.... Berengar denies the doctrine of transsubstantiation, and emerges into a symbolic spiritualistic conception of the Eucharist: bread and wine are a symbol (figura) of the body of Christ and as such they may help to accomplish a spiritual union with the glorified Lord in heaven. [Archbishop] Lanfranc takes Berengar to task that instead of appealing to the sacred authorities, he relies on dialectical argument" (175–176).

After Berengar had "prostrated himself at the Lenten synod in Rome and confessed that he had hitherto been in error" and received a pardon on the condition that he remain silent, Archbishop Lanfranc wrote to Berengar: "Humbled in body but not humiliated in heart, in the presence of the holy council you lit a fire and tossed in the books containing the perverse doctrines while swearing ... to preserve the sacred faith transmitted [to us] by the fathers present at the council" (Fichtenau 287). This message to Berengar, provided in another translation, refers to the book burning thus: "Your works were examined and condemned at Rome by Nicholas of blessed memory, supreme pontiff of all Christendom, and by 113 bishops. So bowing low — yet with pride in your heart — you lit the fire and in full view of the council threw onto it your books of false doctrine and swore to the true faith" (Gibson 69).

Less than a century later after Berengar's works were condemned as heretical and burned, Peter Abelard's writings that reflected Beranger's views were set afire. The influence of Berengar has been recognized by Gerard Verbeke: "The main reproach made by [Abbot] Bernard of Clairvaux and William of St. Thierry against Peter Abelard, William of Conches and Arnold of Brescia is related to the same basic question, the use of dialectics for the purpose to explain the content of faith. Both Bernard of Clairvaux and William of St. Thierry are firmly convinced that all heretical doctrines of Abelard originate from his philosophical theories and excessive confidence in reason is the source of his heretical statements" (Verbeke 177–178). Similarly, Charles S. Clifton has written: "Together with such figures as Berengar of Tours and Arnold of Brescia, Abelard held up the value of the intellect as opposed to the value of dogma" (Clifton 4).

In 1121, Peter Abelard's treatise *On the Unity and Trinity of God* was condemned and he was ordered to burn his book. Leif Grane has written that "Abelard was sentenced [at the Synod of Soissons] to throw his book on the fire himself, and to permanent detention in the monastery of St. Medard.... The verdict was pronounced without Abelard's having an opportunity to defend himself" (76). Abelard himself wrote of the condemnation at the Synod of Soissons and the burning of his book: "He [the legate] agreed to condemn my book without any further inquiry, to burn it forthwith in the sight of all, and to confine me for a year in another monastery. The argument they used was that it sufficed for the condemnation of my book that I had presumed to read it in public without the approval either of the Roman pontiff or of the Church, and that furthermore, I had given it to many to be transcribed.... Straightway upon my summons I went to the council and there, without further examination or debate, did they compel me with my own hand to cast that memorable book of mine into the flames" (Peters 1980 85). Twenty years later, in 1140, Abelard was again condemned and his books were ordered to be burned. Bernard of Clairvaux had written to Pope Innocent II that Abelard must be excommunicated, referring to Abelard's writings as "poisonous pages," and to the heretics as "foxes which are laying waste the vineyard of the Lord": "Although I would that his [Abelard's] poisonous pages were still lying hid in bookcases and not read at the crossroads. His books fly abroad; and they who hate the light because they are evil have dashed themselves against the light, thinking light darkness. Over cities and castles is darkness cast instead of light; instead of honey, or rather in honey, his poison is on all sides eagerly drunk in" (Peters 1980 88). Bernard of Clairvaux then asks the Pope to "exterminate" the "foxes which are laying waste the vineyard of the Lord."

The Pope responded on July 16, 1140, with a first letter that imposed silence on Abelard and a second letter ordering him "to be confined and his books to be burned wherever they were to be found" (Flahiff 5). Abelard's books were burned at Rome and "Geoffrey of Auxerre writes that the pope himself set up a stake in St. Peter's for the burning of the books" (Grane 150). Two years later, after the pope asserted "we have imposed perpetual silence upon him as a heretic" and declared that the "followers and defenders of his error must be separated from the faithful and must be bound by the chain of excommunication," Abelard, who had been transferred to the Priory of St. Marcel, died on April 21, 1142 (Peters 1980 82).

While there is no question that Abelard's writings were set afire by the Church, there is disagreement as to whether the writings of his student Arnold of Brescia were also burned at the same time. Arnold, who was surnamed "Abelard's squire" (Gebhart 162), defended Abelard in 1140 at the Council of Sens and was accused by Bernard of Clairvaux of spreading the heretical doctrines of Abelard. Dahmus states that Pope Innocent II "ordered him [Arnold] exiled and his writings burned" (74) and Putnam writes that the Pope ordered the burning of the writings of Abelard and Arnold of Brescia (Putnam 1906 1 65).

However, Greenaway argues there is insufficient evidence to support the position that any Arnold writings were burned: "There is no clear evidence to warrant the assumption that Arnold ever at any time wrote books, and nearly all his biographers have answered the first part of the question [did he leave any writings?] in the negative. Guibal alone gives an affirmative answer, basing his opinion on Innocent II's rescript of 1141 condemning Abelard and Arnold, where 'the books containing their errors' (libros erroris eorum) were ordered to be burned. Yet it is not plain from the context any works other than those of Abelard are implied" (190). Earlier in his book, Greenaway, writing of Pope Innocent's letter condemning both Abelard and Arnold, states: "The second [letter] with a similar superscription, ordered both Abailard and Arnold of Brescia to be interned in separate monasteries and the book containing their errors to be confiscated and burned. In respect to this last provision the Pope himself set an example to the faithful by consigning to the flames such works of Abailard as were accessible in Rome" (80).

Just as it is not entirely clear whether Arnold's writings were actually set afire, there are differences of explanations of how he died in 1155, although there is agreement that his ashes were thrown into the Tiber. In the middle of the twelfth century, Otto of Freising, writing of Arnold's influence and death, states that Arnold "was held for trial by the prince and finally was brought to the pyre by the prefect of the city. After his corpse had been reduced to ashes in the fire, it was scattered on the Tiber, lest his body be held in veneration by the mad populace" (Moore 1975 66).

The *Encyclopædia Britannica* in its entry for Arnold reports: "He was seized by order of the emperor Frederick, then in Italy, and delivered to the prefect of Rome, by whom he was condemned to death. In June 1155 Arnold was hanged, his body burnt, and the ashes thrown into the Tiber" (422). Greenaway, in his description of Arnold's death, writes: "The extinction of the Republic was accompanied by the death of its most distinguished citizen. After being condemned by an ecclesiastical tribunal in accordance with canonical procedure Arnold was reserved to the judgment of the secular arm.... He was first hanged, his corpse being afterwards burnt and the ashes thrown into the Tiber" (157). Harold O.J. Brown writes of Arnold being beheaded, for "beheading was the penalty for rebellion, a criminal offense against the state, not for heresy" (259).

Just as there have been differences about whether Arnold's writings were actually burned and whether he was hanged or beheaded and then set afire, there have been differences as to whether he was charged with heresy or rebellion. Fichtenau has argued that Arnold "was never formally accused of heresy" and refers to "the predominantly political nature" of Arnold's activities (64). R.I. Moore also has alluded to Arnold being charged "with rebellion, not heresy" (Moore 1987 24). However, other sources have reported that

Arnold was excommunicated and hanged as a heretic." While there are these disagreements, there is no doubt that Arnold was condemned by the Church, excommunicated, and finally reduced to ashes, as had the writings of his teacher Abelard.

Like Berengar, Abelard, and Arnold of Brescia, philosopher and theologian David of Dinant was influenced by the works of Aristotle and like his predecessors his writings, *Quaternuli,* were ordered by the Church to be burned. In a 1210 decree of the Bishops of Sens, not only was it ordered that the body of pantheist Almaric (Amaury)of Bene be disinterred and burned, but it was also ordered that the writings of David of Dinant be burned: "Let the body of master Amaury be removed from the cemetery and cast into unconsecrated ground, and the same be excommunicated by all the churches of the entire province.... The writings of David of Dinant are to be brought to the bishop of Paris before the Nativity and burned" (Thorndike 2). The decree further provided that "neither the books of Aristotle on natural philosophy nor their commentaries are to be read at Paris in public or in secret, and this we forbid under penalty of excommunication. He in whose possession the writings of David of Dinant are found after the Nativity shall be considered a heretic" (Thorndike 2).

According to Lea, "When, in 1210, the University of Paris was agitated with the heresy of Amaury, the writings of his colleague, David de Dinant, together with the Physics and Metaphysics of Aristotle, to which it was attributed, were ordered to be burned" (1955 1 554). However, Leff interprets the above Sens decree to mean that while the order was to burn David's writings, the burning did not extend to Aristotle's works: "Aristotle's works were only one of the objects of anathema; they also included the heresies of Amaury of Bene and David of Dinant. Whereas the ban 'on the books of Aristotle on natural philosophy and their commentaries' only extended to their being 'read' at Paris in public or in secret, Amaury's body was to 'be exhumed and cast into unconsecrated ground,' and the writings of David of Dinant were to be burned; anyone found in possession of them after Christmas was to be considered a heretic" (Leff 1968 193).

The Amaury of Bene referred to above, also known as Amalric of Bena, was a philosopher whose pantheistic treatises were condemned as heretical by the Church which ordered the burning of his writings in 1210. Some of his followers were also set afire at the stake at the same time: "A number of Disciples of Amalric of Bena were burned in Paris in 1210 for teaching that God the Father was incarnate in the Old Testament patriarchs, that the Son became incarnate in Mary, and that the Holy Spirit was incarnate in them" (Brown 1984 274). Amalric died in c. 1206, four years before his writings were set aflame in 1210 at which time his body was disinterred and also burned (Clifton 12).

Amalric, like Abelard, Berengar of Tours, Arnold of Brescia, and David of Dinan, was influenced by Aristotelian philosophy and by ninth century philosopher Johannes Scotus Erigena, also known as John the Scot, whose writings were burned by the Church in 1225. Bett asserts that "it is beyond doubt that Berengar of Rours had read Erigena" (172) and that Abelard "also appears to have been influenced by the Scot" (173). At the same time he was influenced by Aristotle's works, David's philosophy and theology were a variation of Erigena's writings; Bett has written: "The little that we know of his teaching all seems to show that it was a reckless development of Erigena's doctrine" (178). As for Erigena's influence on Amalric, Hauck asserts: "There is no doubt that Amalric took up the teaching of Johannes Scotus Erigena, and developed it into a thoroughgoing pantheism" (146). Brown also has recognized Erigena's influence on Amalric and his followers: "Their views were apparently a kind of Neoplatonic pantheism dressed up in Christian terminology, inspired in part by the rediscovery of the work of the ninth-century philosopher John Scot

Erigena" (274). When in 1209 the heretical doctrines of Amalric were denounced, the condemnation charged that Amalric's doctrines were found in Erigena's *Periphysion:* "The dogma of the wicked Amalric is comprised in the book of the Master John the Scot which is called *periphysion* (i.e. De Natura), which the said Amalric followed ... and the said John in the same book cited the authority of a Greek Master named Maximum. In which book many heresies were contained ... of which three may suffice as examples. First and chief, that all things are God.... The second is that the primordial causes which are called ideas create and are created.... The third is that in the consummation of the ages there will be a union of the sexes, or there will be no distinction of sex, which union he says to have begun in Christ" (Gardner 136–137).

Erigena's *The Division of Nature* was condemned again in 1225 by Pope Honorius who "ordered that all persons possessing copies of the book must, under penalty of excommunication, deliver the same within fifteen days, to the ecclesiastical authorities for burning" (Putnam 1906 1 66). Erigena was denounced by the Archbishop of Sens as writing abominable blasphemies. The Pope asserted that the book was "swarming with worms of heretical perversity" and ordered that all copies be sent to Rome to be burned (John the Scot xiii). In his papal bull, the Pope in condemning Erigena's work, stated at the outset that "an enemy had been sowing tares among the wheat" (Gardner 139).

Up to the early thirteen century, heretics and their books were being burned on an *ad hoc* basis; as Peters has indicated: "As various forms of dealing with heresy on local ecclesiastical or lay levels came to be perceived as ineffective, the creation of specialist investigators empowered by the papacy as judges delegate came slowly to be considered a solution" (Peters 1988 54). As the twelfth century ended, "the official investigation (*inquisition*) of heresy was not as yet systematized. This task had long been left to the local bishops and ecclesiastical courts, but episcopal control was ineffective when heretics were numerous.... It remained for Pope Gregory IX (1227–1241) to establish a regular permanent institution chosen from the mendicant orders, chiefly the Dominicans— a body formed with very different aims. These inquisitors set up their own special courts and were practically exempt from local church authority" (Walker, Norris, Lotz, Handy 309). When the kings of Aragon were suppressing the Cathars early in the thirteenth century, Pope Gregory IX offered, in 1232, "the assistance of the Dominican Order to the Archbishop of Tarragona, and in 1233 both an episcopal and a secular inquisition was formed" (Peters 1988 76).

In a 1231 decretal, *Excommunicamus,* Pope Gregory IX declared: "We excommunicate and anathematize all heretics, Cathars, Patarines, the Poor of Lyons, the Passagians, the Josephites, Anroldists, Speronists, and other under whatever name they may be included, for although they may have different appearances, they are bound together the same at the tail, since by vanity they take pleasure in this" (Peters 1980 190). Further, in the same year, the Pope "issued the decretal *Ille humani generis,* written to the prior of the Dominican convent in Regensburg ... charging him with the organization of an inquisitional tribunal, with authority derived directly from the pope. This momentous act, the creation of a tribunal outside the normal procedure of the local bishop, was the birth of the papal Inquisition" (Peters 1980 191).

Early in the thirteenth century, the Church increased its attacks on and suppression of the Cathars whose beliefs were denounced as heretical for, as Lea has put it, Catharism "cast aside all the machinery of the Church. The Roman Church indeed was the synagogue of Satan, in which salvation was impossible. Consequently the sacraments, the sacrifices of the altar, the suffrages and interposition of the Virgin and saints, purgatory, relics, images, crosses, holy water, indulgences, and the other devices by which the priest procured salvation for

Saint Dominic and the Pyre of Heretical Books, a painting by Pedro Berruguete. (Scala/Art Resource, NY.)

the faithful were rejected, as well as the tithes and oblations which rendered the procuring of salvation so profitable" (Lea 1 1955 93).

The Cathars were searched out, tortured, and burned along with their books; as Denis de Rougemont has indicated, "The crusade against Catharism at the beginning of the 13th century 'resulted in the destruction of the towns inhabited by the Cathars, in the burning of their books, the slaughter and burning of the mass of people who loved them, and the violation of their sanctuaries and supreme High Place, the famous castle of Montsegur. The highly refined civilization of which they were the austere and secret spirit was brutally devastated'" (Lucas 1 429). The burning of heretical Cathars and their books was accompanied with the dehumanizing language that invited eradication and extinction.

As the Inquisition was being established early in the thirteenth century, the Cathars were metaphorized into disease, infection, plague, poison, tares, and leprosy. In a "Letter of Dedication to Pope Innocent III," a young monk Peter of les Vaux-de-Cernay condemned the heretical Cathars beginning the letter as follows: "In the first section of this work I will touch briefly on the heretical sects, and describe how the inhabitants of the South were infected by the leprosy of heresy for many years past" (Peter of Vaux-de-Cernay 6). In tracing the history of the Albigensian history, he wrote: "In the province of Narbonne, where once the true faith had flourished, the enemy of the faith began to sow tares" (7). A few sentences later, the "leprosy" and "tares" metaphors were augmented with still other more ominous metaphors inviting fiery destruction: "Two Cistercian monks ... — men fired with zeal for the true faith — were appointed legates by the authority of the Supreme Pontiff to fight against the plague of faithlessness. Determined to perform their mission with dedication and enthusiasm, they went to the city of Toulouse, the chief source of the poison of faithlessness which had infected the people" (8). The "detestable plague, the sin of heresy," the "poison of superstitious unbelief" had "so infected" the people of Toulouse with "this ancient filth" (10).

In his 1231 decretal *humani generis* Pope Gregory IX relied on similar dehumanizing metaphors in his attack on the heretics and their writings. After referring to the heretics who "have lain concealed for a long time, scuttling about in hiding like crabs" and "like little foxes, attempting to destroy the vineyard of the Lord of Hosts" and to the need to "do battle with these poisonous animals," Pope Gregory declares that "it is fitting that we rise up against them manfully, so that the faith of Christ may flourish and this heresy of theirs be confounded, and that a crown should be the reward of those who resist temptation. Since therefore, the faith has recently shown forth in Germany, and by it we desire to do battle with these poisonous animals, lest perhaps the simple be seduced by their artful deceptions" (Peters 1980 196).

This cleansing the land of parasites, disease, plague, and tares meant burning not only Hebrew writings and the works of heretics, but also the burning of the "Bible in the vernacular." In 1234, King Don Jayme I "drew up a series of laws instituting an episcopal Inquisition of severest character, to be supported by the Royal officials; in this appears for the first time a secular prohibition of the Bible in the vernacular. All possessing any books of the Old or New Testament, 'in Romancio,' are summoned to deliver them within eight days to their bishops to be burned, under pain of being suspect of heresy" (Lea 1 1955 324).

At the same time Christians were reducing the Hebrew "Bible" to ashes, they were setting afire the Christian Bible, centuries after the 1200s. As Laura Wild has indicated, "By 1401 English Bibles were ordered to be burned. By 1407 to possess a copy without a license was the first step to persecution" (45). Twelve years before the famous Torquemada set fire to thousands of Hebrew and Arabic works, along with books on magic, Bonifacio Ferrer's

1417 translation of the Scriptures into the Valencian or Catalonian dialect in Spain was ordered burned. M'Crie tells us that Ferrer's translation "was printed at Valencia in the year 1478.... But, although it was the production of a catholic author, and underwent the examination and correction of the inquisitor James Borrell, it had scarcely made its appearance when it was suppressed by the Inquisition, who ordered the whole impression to be devoured by flames. So strictly was this order carried into execution, that scarcely a single copy appears to have escaped. Long after the era of the Reformation, it was taken for granted by all true Spaniards, that their language had never been made the unhallowed instrument of exposing the Bible to vulgar eyes" (192).

The fourteenth century began with the continued burnings of the "blasphemous" Talmud and the "heretical" pestilent, diseased, and poisonous books condemned for their treatments of predestination, astrology, baptism, evangelical poverty, marriage, and challenges to Church authority. A thirteenth-fourteenth Christian sect that held "erroneous" positions on several of these matters was the Apostles of Christ, formed by Gerard Segarelli whose writings were burned and who himself was condemned as a heretic and burned alive in Parma on July 18, 1300. According to Putnam, Segarelli "was burned, together with such copies of his writings as had been collected" (1 67). Segarelli's Apostolic Brethren order was prohibited by the Church and members were condemned as heretics because, among other reasons, they refused to submit to ecclesiastical authority; Segarelli's "harangues against the hierarchical Church which he described as polluted and carnal, resulted in his temporary imprisonment by Honorius IV and Nicholas IV; in 1300 he was retired as a relapsed heretic, found guilty, and delivered to the secular authorities for execution" (O'Brien 1970 709).

Inquisitor Bernard Gui, in his famous manual for inquisitors, *Practica inquisitionis heretice pravitatis,* devoted a chapter to this "apostate and heretical sect" in which he describes their "errors." Gui points out that Apostles' initiation required the initiate to divest "himself of all his garments, in token of abnegation, and renounces all his property to symbolize the perfection of evangelical poverty. And from then on he may not accept money, possess or carry it, but must live on the charity offered him by others out of their own free will and accord, saving nothing for the morrow" (Wakefield and Evans 404). Among all their teachings and beliefs, according to Gui's 1324 manual, was included the declaration that they are "not bound to obey any man, the supreme pontiff or any other, inasmuch as their rule, which they claim directly from Christ, is one of freedom and of a most perfect life" (Wakefield and Evans 409).

After the burnings of Segarelli and his writings in 1300, the Church conducted crusades against the Apostles, resulting in tortures and burnings of thousands of Apostles who by the beginning of the fifteenth century had been exterminated. Lea, in writing about Segarelli and the Inquisition, has observed that "the harmless eccentricities of Segarelli were hardened and converted into a strongly antisacerdotal heresy" by the Inquisition, just as had been done with the "exaggerated asceticism of the Olivists": "There was much in common between the sects, for both drew their inspiration from the Everlasting Gospel. Like the Olivists, the Apostles held that Christ had withdrawn his authority from the Church of Rome on account of its wickedness.... Churches were useless; a man could better worship Christ in the woods, and prayer to God was as effective in a pigsty as in a consecrated building. Priests and prelates and monks were a detriment to the faith" (Lea 1955 3 120–121).

The Olivists referred to by Lea were the followers of Jean Olivi of the Franciscan Order who was commanded to burn his own writings by order of Nicholas IV (Lea 1955 3 43). Olivi died in 1298, formally accused of heresy, his body was disinterred and burnt. Thirty years after Olivi's death, Pope John XXII condemned and ordered destroyed "the writings of the Minorite Petrus Johannes Oliva, which had been examined and reported upon by nine theologians. The bones of Oliva were disinterred and were burned with copies of his books" (Putnam 1906 1 68) Those who refused to surrender for burning the writings of Olivi faced severe penalties. In one case, as Lea records, "Pons Botugati, a friar eminent for piety and eloquence, refused to surrender for burning some of the prohibited tracts, and was chained closely to the wall in a damp and fetid dungeon, where bread and water were sparingly flung to him, and where he soon rotted to death in filth, so that when his body was hastily thrust into an unconsecrated grave it was found that already the flesh was burrowed through with worms. A number of other recalcitrants were also imprisoned with almost equal harshness" (Lea 1955 3 47).

Among the reasons the Church ordered the burning of Olivi's books and the burning of his disinterred bones was his questioning of the concept of the Immaculate Conception. Church officials, David Burr has written in his *The Persecution of Peter Olivi*, "took issue with questions he [Olivi] had written on the Virgin Mary and submitted them to the minister general, Jerome of Ascoli, who in turn ordered them burned. Olivi's views on marriage were also challenged.... Olivi was particularly attacked for his denial of the sacramentality of marriage, his understanding of sacramental grace and the sacramental character, and his view of the relationship between the divine essence and the persons of the trinity" (1976 44). As the fourteenth century began, Franciscans sympathetic to some of Olivi's views were burned at the stake. As Burr indicates in another of his books dealing with Olivi, "On May 7, 1318, in the marketplace at Marseilles, four Franciscans were burned at the stake.... The four brothers at Marseilles went to the stake not because they were willing to die for a theoretical position on papal authority but because they were unwilling to obey a specific papal command. That command entailed compromising what they referred to as *usus pauper,* restricted use of goods, in specific areas such as food and clothing" (Burr 1989 ix–x). The burnings at the stake continued: "[I]n October 1319, the first lay supporters were burned. Others would follow" (Burr 1976 82).

While the Church was successful in burning Olivi's writings and his bones, ecclesiastical authorities were unsuccessful in retrieving Dante's bones for the purpose of burning them along with his writings. Dante's *De Monarchia,* however, did not escape the flames in 1329. Between 1310 and 1313, Dante Alighieri had written *De Monarchi* in which he criticized the popes and argued for a distinction between the powers and limitation of church and state. The book was burned in 1329 and eventually placed on the Church's *Index of Forbidden Books.* Boccaccio, in his *Vita di Dante,* indicates that Dante has divided his work into three parts: "In the first book he proves by argument of logic that the Empire is necessary for the well-being of the world.... In the second book, proceeding by arguments drawn from history, he shows that Rome rightly holds the title of the Empire.... In the third book by theological arguments he proves that the authority of the Empire proceeds directly from God, and not through the mediation of any vicar, as the clergy appear to maintain" (Boccaccio 69).

At the outset of Book Three Dante recognizes that what he is about to discuss would offend the Church authorities; he writes: "Now it remains to treat the third [question], whose true solution may bring upon me a certain amount of indignation on the part of those whom the bare truth will cause to blush.... The present question which we are about to examine divides two great luminaries, the Roman pontiff and the Roman prince. Does the authority of the Roman ruler, who, as we have shown in Book II, is the *de jure* ruler of the world, come directly from God or through some vicar or minister of God, I mean Peter's successor, who truly holds the keys to the kingdom of heaven?" (Dante 52–53). As Musa has explained, in *Monarchy* "the pope leads mankind to eternal life in accordance with revelation, while the emperor leads mankind to temporal happiness in accordance with philosophical teaching. The temporal monarch, who must devote his energies to providing freedom and peace for men as they pass through the 'testing time' of this world, receives his authority directly from God. Intellectual perfection, the happiness of the world, can therefore be attained without the Church.... Not surprisingly, the book was placed on the *Index of Forbidden Books*" (xxviii).

Boccaccio, in *Vita di Dante*, written in the 1350s, referred to the burning of *Monarchy*: "This book, several years after the death of its author, was condemned by Cardinal Belrando of Poggetto.... [who] seized the book and condemned it in public to the flames, charging that it contained heretical matters" (70). A century and a half later, both Boccaccio's and Dante's writings were set afire in Savonarola's "bonfire of the vanities."

Astrologers and their writings and practices also created problems for Church authorities seeking to maintain orthodoxy because on the one hand astrology was seen as providing "answers" to questions related to political events, scientific quandaries, and religious controversies and on the other hand astrology was "evil" and condemned. As Lea has written: "All astrologers ... practiced their profession under liability of being at any moment called to account by the Inquisition. That this did not occur more often may be attributed to the fact that all classes, in Church and State, from the lowest to the highest, believed in astrology and protected astrologers, and some special inducement or unusual indiscretion was required to set in motion the machinery of prosecution" (1955 3 440).

At the outset of Christianity, astrologers, soothsayers, and magicians were condemned and subject to harsh penalties. A section of the Theodosian Code, Title 16, was devoted to "Magicians, Astrologers and All Other Like Criminals." In 357, Emperor Constantius Augustus ordered that "no person shall consult a soothsayer, or an astrologer or a diviner. The wicked doctrines of augurs and seers shall become silent" and in 409 a decree ordered the banishment of astrologers and the burning of their books (Pharr 238–239).

Late in the fourth and early in the fifth centuries, St. Augustine, condemned in various works astrology to which he had been attracted in his earlier years. In his *Confessions*, Augustine writes of his repudiation of "the lying divination and impious absurdities of the astrologers" (1948 1 96). In one of his Sermons he warned: "[K]eep yourselves from detestable and corrupting practices, from going with detestable inquiries to astrologers, to soothsayers, to fortune-tellers, to augurs, to sacrilegious rites of divination" (1990 2 274). In his *The City of God*, Augustine concluded: "We have good reason to believe that, when the astrologers give very many wonderful answers, it is to be attributed to the occult inspiration of spirits not of the best kind, whose care it is to insinuate into the minds of men, and to confirm in them those false and noxious opinions concerning the fatal influence of the stars, and not to their marking and inspecting of horoscopes, according to some kind of art which in reality has no existence" (1948 2 62).

The fourteenth century inquisitor Nicolas Eymerich tells us, writes Lea, "that if a man was suspected of necromancy and was found to be an astrologer it went far to prove him a necromancer, for the two were almost always conjoined. Gerard Groot [fourteenth century theologian] denounced astrology as a science hostile to God and aiming to supersede his laws" (1995 3 444). Eymerich, reports James Given, "seems to have been a connoisseur of books of necromancy. In his *Directorium* he says that he had read two books of invocations of demons, one the 'Book of Solomon,' the other the *Thesaurus necromantiae*. After perusing these works, he burned them" (Given 50).

The astrological beliefs and practices of physician and astrologer Cecco d'Ascoli contributed to the burning of his writings and to his being burned at the stake in 1327. As Rule
reports, the Church officials in 1324 "compelled him to bring all his books of astrology to
be burnt, forbade him to lecture in Bologna or elsewhere anymore, either publicly or pri-
vately, deprived him of all magistracy or honour, and fined him seventy Bolognese pounds"
(2 154). Then in 1327, "The astrologer [Cecco] was openly condemned as a heretic in the
church of the Friars-Minors, and delivered over to the secular authority to be duly punished. A book he had written in verse, under the title of *Acerba,* was to be burnt at the same
time, and all who read it were to be excommunicated. On the same day the Governor's lieutenant 'forthwith sent Master Cecco in custody of his knight and servants, and in presence
of a great multitude of people, to be burnt; thus to signify the death eternal wherewith he
and all such will be punished'" (Rule 2 155).

In summarizing Cecco's ideas that would be "offensive to pious ears," Lea has written: "To illustrate his views he [Cecco] cast the horoscope of Christ, and showed how
Libra, ascending in the tenth degree, rendered his crucifixion inevitable; as Capricorn was
at the angle of the earth, he was necessarily born in a stable; as Scorpio was the second
degree, he was poor; while Mercury in his own house in the ninth section of the heavens
rendered his wisdom profound" (1955 3 443).

When Cecco was led to the stake to be set afire, "all Florence thronged to the place of
execution beyond the walls, many being anxious to see whether the famous astrologer would
merely burn like any ordinary man, or whether the evil spirits would come down to rescue and carry him off from their midst" (Baddeley 150). Cecco was "burned together with
his offending treatise, *de Sphaera*" (Putnam 1906 1 68).

The burning of books dealing with astrology, the occult, and magic continued into
the fifteenth century, even as religious and political leaders turned to astrologers for advice
and predictions. As Bernard Capp has indicated, "Throughout Europe monarchs, nobles
and indeed city councils competed to secure the services of the best-known astrologers....
Henry IV had an astrologer present at the birth of his son, the future Louis XIII; a generation later Louis in turn ordered the astrologer, Morin, to attend the birth of his son, the
future Louis XIV. Later still, Morin was concealed in the royal bedroom to record the precise moment when the young Louis XIV and his bride consummated their marriage, in order
to calculate the horoscope of the dauphin who would hopefully be conceived. A counselor
advised Philip II not to visit Mary Tudor in England in 1556 because of astrological prophecies that there would be a conspiracy against him there" (18).

At the same time religious leaders condemned astrology, some of them relied on
astrologers for guidance. Capp writes of popes who had more than a passing interest in
astrology: "Sixtus IV (1471–84) had been noted for his astrological prowess. Pius II imprisoned a man for predicting his death (correctly, as it turned out), but his successor allegedly
released and rewarded the captive. Paul of Middelburg, a noted astrologer of the late
fifteenth century, was made a bishop and designated cardinal. In the early sixteenth century the court of Paul III became a centre of astrological learning; Lucar Gaurico, who had
predicted Paul's accession, was rewarded with a bishopric. Gaurico was later invited to calculate the most propitious moment for work to begin on an important new building planned
by the pope" (17–18).

While churchmen and nobility did not hesitate relying on the prognostications of the
astrologers, and the almanacs which became so popular, some astrological works were
deemed dangerous and subversive and were set afire. As Lea reports, there was a public
burning in 1434 of "objectionable" books found in the library of the Marquis of Villena in

Spain, the marquis being a "man of learning and science [who] dabbled in occult arts and had earned the reputation of a skilful magician. At the command of King Juan II, his books were examined by the celebrated Lope de Arrientos, subsequently Bishop of Cuenca, who, by royal order, publicly burnt such as were deemed objectionable, for books on magic were always under the ban of the Church" (1967 18).

In 1494, the books in the library of astrologer and physician Simon de Phares were brought under scrutiny at the instigation of the archbishop of Lyons "who seized his library and sent its volumes for examination to the faculty of theology at the University of Paris. Simon was enjoined from practicing his art in the interim" (Graubard 105). The theology faculty concluded that the "arts mathematica or the divinatory arts are to be condemned. These arts involved horoscopes, nativities, interrogations and elections, but apparently excluded the annual predictions so popular at the time. Eleven of Simon's books, out of a total of two hundred confiscated, were ordered burned. These included treatises by Albumsar and Abraham Judacus, the Isagogue of John of Spain, a work by William of England explaining how to diagnose a patient's illness by reference to the stars without resorting to an examination of the urine, a Latin translation by Pietro d'Abano of a pseudo–Hippocrates on astrological prognostication from the moon, and finally a work by Firminus de Bellavalle on weather prediction" (Graubard 106).

As the fifteenth century came to a close, huge numbers of books on magic and sorcery were set afire in Spain, along with Hebrew writings, heretical works, and translated Bibles. Llorente reports that in 1490, "several Hebrew bibles and books written by Jews were burnt at Seville; at Salamanca more than six thousand volumes of magic and sorcery were committed to the flames" (100). While the prognostications of astrologers were invited by kings, princes and clergy, some predictions were seen as contributing to rebellion and subversion. As Capp has explained: "It was natural that early printed prognostications should contain much material of this kind [predictions of outcome of wars and rebellions]. Governments soon came to believe, however, that what was suitable for the eyes of the king was best concealed from his subjects. Speculation of upheavals in the state had an unsettling effect, and could easily give encouragement to potential rebels. The sixteenth century witnessed the gradual suppression of dangerous political material in almanacs through a combination of censorship, licensing and the self-restraint of timid compilers" (67).

Predictions of the death of kings, of wars and disasters, of uprisings and triumphs and downfalls of rulers, as Capp indicates, made it "not difficult to see why monarchs found political speculation offensive. A Scottish astrologer named Bruce was expelled for predicting the imminent death of James I's son and heir, Prince Henry, and his chief minister, Salisbury. Bruce was lucky to escape so lightly.... Speculation in print was far more guarded, but still dangerous. There was a risk that it might encourage rebellion and subversion by appearing to legitimize them" (69).

Meanwhile, books dealing with astrology and Taoism were being set afire in China. The Chinese emperor decreed in 1376: "All officials and commoners must deliver up all former books for the calculation of the seasons to be burned. Those who keep them and privily use them are to be beheaded" (Goodrich 4). An astrological work written by the emperor Hung-hsi who reigned in 1425 was ordered in the following decree of 1781 to be burned along with the woodblocks; the "Edict on Books Foretelling the Future" declared: "Among the works sent up to be burned by the province of Honan are two items: one written by the Ming emperor Jen-tsung, the *T'ien Yuan Yu Li Hsiang I Fu*; and another by an anonymous author, the *Ch'ien K'lun Pao Tien*. Both books senselessly foretell fortune and woe based on observation of the heavens, and are very likely to sway the minds of men.

Very probably the provinces have not wholly rid themselves of these works. I therefore issue this mandate for circulation to all governors-general and governors. Search everywhere for them, and for woodblocks too, and when found despatch them to Peking, that they may be utterly consumed by fire" (Goodrich 198).

During the Yuan or Mongol dynasty (1280–1368), Emperor Khubilai ordered the burning of all Taoist books. Charles Eliot writes of this edict: "Khubilai received complaints that the Taoists represented Buddhism as an offshoot of Taoism and that this objectionable perversion of truth and history was found in many of their books, particularly the Hua-Hu-Ching. An edict was issued ordering all Taoist books to be burnt with the sole exception of the Tao-Te-Ching but it does not appear that the sect was otherwise persecuted" (273). Late in the fifteenth century, more "Taoist books were collected and burnt" (Eliot 278).

While the Chinese were burning books on astrology and Taoism, the Koreans were setting fire to works by sorceresses and fortune-tellers. In 1413, Korean king T'a'jung ordered these writings delivered to the government so that they could be destroyed: "In 1413, the land suffered from a severe drought and the courtiers all advised that the monks and female exorcists and fortune-tellers be called upon to pray for rain; but the king replied, 'Buddhism is an empty religion and the exorcists and fortune-tellers are a worthless lot. If I were only a better ruler Heaven would not refuse us rain.' He thereupon ordered all the sorceresses, fortune-tellers, exorcists and geomancers to deliver up the books of their craft to the government and a great fire was made with them in front of the palace" (Hulbert 302).

The fifteenth century brought with it two important events that led to an extraordinary increase in book burnings—the introduction of the printing press and the onset of the Reformation.

In the middle of the fifteenth century Gutenberg's movable type resulted in its widespread use throughout Europe. In 1464, Caxton began printing in England; in 1470, the new book printing came to France and in 1489 to Copenhagen. While the Netherlands and France "were becoming acquainted with the art of printing it also spread to Spain and finally to North Germany" (Dahl 105). Putnam has observed that "the work of the printers was at first welcomed by the rulers of the Church. They convinced themselves that the Lord had placed at their disposal a valuable instrument for the spread of sound doctrine and for the enlightenment of believers and with this conviction they found funds for the support of a number of the early printers and kept their presses employed in the production of works of approved theological instruction" (Putnam 1906 1 2). But the printing press also introduced a means for spreading Protestant "heresies": "It was in fact not until nearly three fourths of a century after Gutenberg, when the leaders of the Reformation were utilizing the printing presses of Wittenberg for the spread of the Protestant heresies, that the ecclesiastics became aroused to the perils that the new art was bringing upon the true faith and upon the authority of the Church" (Putnam 1906 1 2). Thus the Church expanded its efforts at censorship; no books were to be printed before they had passed ecclesiastical censors; the Index was instituted to keep published works out of the hands of the faithful; and then there was the increase in book burnings as the ultimate censorship.

In 1501, Pope Alexander VI issued a bull in which he warned of the impact of printing on Catholic faith: "The art of printing can be of great service in so far as it furthers the circulation of useful and tested books; but it can bring about serious evils if it is permitted to widen the influence of pernicious works. It will, therefore, be necessary to maintain full control over the printers so that they may be prevented from bringing into print writings which are antagonistic to the Catholic faith, or which are likely to cause trouble to believers" (Putnam 1906 1 80).

With the printing press came the Church's fears of books being printed by, as one inquisitor put it, "moderns, full of a thousand innovations," with men exchanging "the ancient and secure doctrine of the virtuous doctors for the sophisticated and adulterated one of the moderns" (Crespo 175). The book, in the words of the Church censors, became "the silent heretic"; in this regard, Virgilio Pinto Crespo has written: "The religious conflicts of the sixteenth century aggravated the situation. The book, 'the silent heretic' as the censors liked to call it, allowed for the propagation of dissident thought. In this sense, even the manuscript book of a previous era had rendered an important service to heretics. The printed book, which could be produced at considerably less cost and with a speed almost infinitely greater than its predecessor, was far more effective" (175). In writing about "the impact of Protestantism in Spain," Jaime Contreras also refers to the Church's view that the book was "the silent heretic": "Everything was carefully reviewed, and almost everything was mutilated. A reign of fear had been imposed and orthodoxy rode on the croup of a politico-ecclesiastical ideal that sought to apply the most absolute authority. As a logical consequence the book, that 'silent heretic,' was from then on, at the mercy of the Inquisition" (54).

A century before Luther posted his "ninety-five theses" and burned the papal bull *Exsurge Domine* ordering Luther's excommunication and the burning of his books, the "perverse," "heretical" works of such "pernicious" men as John Wycliffe and John Hus were set afire early in 1410 and 1415, while Wycliffe was burned at the stake and Hus's bones were dug up years after his death, burned and the ashes "thrown to the four winds." Before Wycliffe's books were burned in 1410, Pope Gregory had written a letter "to the masters and chancellor of Oxford University censuring some of Wyclif's opinions" (Peters 1980 265) and in so doing the pope relied heavily on language that invited "extirpation," on metaphors that had by now become part of the language in denouncing the heretical "pests," "demons," "tares," and "disease." In his letter the pope admonished "the masters and chancellor" for not doing enough to eradicate the "tares": "That you through a certain sloth and neglect allow tares to spring up amidst the pure wheat in the fields of your glorious university aforesaid.... And you are quite careless, as has been reported to us, as to the extirpation of these tares.... And what pains us the more is that this increase of tares aforesaid is known in Rome before the remedy of extirpation has been applied in England where they sprang up" (Peters 1980 271). Having done with the "tares" metaphor in his condemnation of Wycliffe, the pope invoked the "pestilence," "infected," and "contagion" metaphors: "Wherefore, since we are not willing, nay, indeed, ought not to be willing, that so deadly a pestilence should continue to exist with our connivance, a pestilence which, if it is not opposed in its beginnings, and torn out by the roots in its entirety, will be reached too late by medicines when it has infected very many with its contagion" (Peters 1980 272).

As a major participant in the beginnings of the Reformation, Wycliffe became known as "the Morning Star of the Reformation"; in his *Wide as the Waters: The Story of the English Bible and the Revolution It Inspired,* Benson Bobrick titles the first chapter, devoted to Wycliffe, "The Morning Star." At the end of the chapter, Bobrick writes: "He [Wycliffe] was the moving force behind the first translation of the whole Bible into English; and for that, and the tenets of his theology, has justly been called the 'John the Baptist of the Reformation,' and its brightly shining 'Morning Star'" (75). Wycliffe as a forerunner of the sixteenth century Reformation was recognized by John Milton who had written: "Had it not been the obstinate perverseness of our prelates against the divine and admirable spirit of Wyclif, to suppress him as a schismatic and innovator, perhaps neither the Bohemians Hus and Jerome — no, nor the names of Luther or of Calvin — had ever been known: the glory of reforming all our neighbors had been completely ours" (Winn xii).

In denouncing Wycliffe, archbishop Arundel wrote in a letter to John XXIII: "that wretched and pestilent fellow, the son of the serpent, the herald and child of Antichrist, John Wyclif ... filling up the measure of his malice by devising the expedient of a new translation of Scripture into the mother tongue" (Workman 2 186). Some of the works by Wycliffe that were condemned included *On the Truth of Holy Scripture, On the Church, On Apostasy, On the Eucharist, On the Power of the Pope* and *On the Office of the King.* The ideas and practices that Wycliffe objected to are summarized by Bobrick: "Wycliffe could find no warrant in Scripture for the organization of the Church as a feudal hierarch, or for the rich endowments the Church enjoyed. From his study of the New Testament, he had concluded: First, that in the primitive Church or in the time of Paul, two orders of the clergy had been sufficient, that is, a priest and a deacon. All other degrees and orders ... had their origin in worldly pride. Second, that the legislative right claimed by popes, prelates, and councils, and the power of excommunication and absolution attributed to every member of the clergy, were impious invasions of the prerogatives of Christ." Further, Wycliffe "condemned the wealth and property the orders had amassed" and he "despised indulgences" (36–37).

Wycliffe was condemned a heretic in 1380; in 1410 his works were burnt at Prague and at Carfax, Oxford. Referring to this 1410 book burning, Johann Loserth wrote: "This auto-da-fe was carried into effect in the court of the archiepiscopal palace on the Hradschin, in the presence of the cathedral chapter and a great multitude of priests. More than two hundred MSS were consumed, containing the works of Wiclif" (Loserth 116). In 1412, a Church commission concluded that Wycliffe's teachings contained "errors, heresies, and sedition." As Spinka has indicated, the commission "declared that among his [Wycliffe's] books, both philosophical and theological, not one could be regarded free from errors, heresies, and sedition.... The teaching of Wyclif has spread not only throughout England, but to Bohemia and Portugal. The commission recommended that Wyclif's 'memory, doctrine, books and treatises' be condemned by both the Council and the pope. This recommendation was carried out to the letter. Wyclif's books were burned on February 10, 1413, in front of the basilica of St. Peter" (1966 136).

The Church, not satisfied with burning Wycliffe's books, disinterred his bones in 1428 and burned them. Seventeenth century preacher and theologian Thomas Fuller wrote of the disinterment and the burning of Wycliffe's bones: "Hitherto the corpse of John Wycliffe had quietly slept in his grave about one and forty years after his death, till his body was reduced to bones and his bones almost to dust.... But now such Spleen of the Council of Constance ... as they ordered ... to be taken out of the ground and thrown far off from any Christian burial." Church and government officials took "what was left out of the grave, and burnt them to ashes, and cast them into Swift a Neighboring Brook running hard by. Thus this Brook hath conveyed his Ashes into Avon; Avon into Severn; Severn into the narrow Seas; they, into the main Ocean. And thus the Ashes of Wicliff are the Emblem of his Doctrine, which now is dispersed all the World over" (Winn xix).

Within five years of the burning of Wycliffe's books, the Church ordered the burning of "Wyclifite" John Hus's writings. When Hus's books were sentenced to be burned, the sentence began with a denunciation of Wycliffe who, said the Church, "has begotten some sons of perdition, whom he has left behind him as successors in the inheritance of his perverse doctrine, against whom this holy council of Constance is compelled to rise up as against bastard and illegitimate sons, and cut off their errors as noxious tares from the garden of the Lord, by watchful care, and the knife of ecclesiastical authority, lest like a canker, they spread abroad to others' destruction" (Gillett 1864 2 56).

On July 6, 1415, two sentences were read condemning Hus and his books, one sentence "condemning the books of Hus to be burned, and the other requiring his degradation from the priesthood, in order that he might be given over to the secular arm" to be burned at the stake (Gillett 1864 2 56). Some of Hus's books and treatises, said the Church council, were "erroneous, some scandalous, others offensive to pious ears, many of them rash and seditious, and some notoriously heretical" and therefore it was decreed that his writings "shall be burned, solemnly and publicly, in the presence of the clergy and the people, in the city of Constance, and elsewhere" (Gillett 1864 II 58).

The second part of the sentence against Hus required that he be degraded and thus he was "defrocked" and a paper crown with demons painted on it was placed on his shaved head and he was led to the place of execution, followed by armed men, princes, and "an immense multitude, drawn by curiosity, interest and anxiety." "The procession, instead of taking the direct route thither, moved first in a nearly opposite direction, in order to pass upon the way the Episcopal palace, in front of which a pile of the prisoner's writings had been heaped up for the flames. They had been first condemned and were to be consumed" (Gillett 1864 II 66–67). After Hus refused, several times, to recant, he was bound to the stake and burned and "when every thing had been consumed, the ashes, and every fragment or memorial of the scene of martyrdom, were shoveled up and carried away, to be emptied into the Rhine" (Gillett 73).

While the books of Wycliffe and Hus were being burned in London, Prague and Rome, the books of Spanish poet and historian Don Enrique de Aragon (Marquis de Villena) were being set afire in Madrid. The Marquis had developed an interest in the occult and astrology and after his death in 1434 his objectionable books on magic were burned. In his description of the Marquis, Lea has written: "He was no vulgar magician. In his commentary on the *Æneid* he speaks of magic as a forbidden science, of whose forty different varieties he gives classification.... From his example it is easy to trace the evolution of the myths of Michael Scot, Roger Bacon, Albertus Magnus, Pietro d'Abano, Dr. Faustus, and other popular necromantic heroes" (1955 III 491).

Referring to the burning of the Marquis's books, M'Crie has pointed out that the "books were seized after his death, by the orders of Juan II, King of Castile, and sent for examination to Lope de Barrientos, a Dominican monk of considerable learning, and preceptor to the prince of Asturias. "Barrientos,' says a contemporary writer, 'liked better to walk with the prince than to revise necromancies, committed to the flames upwards of a hundred volumes, without having examined them any more than the King of Morocco, or understand a jot of their contents more than the dean of Ciudad Rodrigo'" (55).

While heretical and blasphemous books had been burning on continental Europe during these early centuries, Charles Gillett states at the outset of his 1932 *Burned Books,* devoted principally to the sixteenth and seventeenth century book burnings in England: "The first books to be burned for theological reasons were those of Reginald Pecock, Bishop, successively, at St. Asaph and Chichester (1440–1457)" (15). Pecock's books were burned at Oxford in 1457. However, Wycliffe's books had been burned at Oxford in 1410, almost a half century earlier. Obviously, Pecock's books were not the first books to be burned for theological reasons, even in England. The difficulty may lie in the "theological." But Pecock's books were set afire because they contained "pernicious doctrines, heresies, and errors." Similarly, Wycliffe's books were burned because they contained "errors, heresies, and sedition." Hence, "theological reasons" were involved in the burnings of both Pecock's and Wycliffe's books and therefore it would be more accurate to state that Wycliffe's writings were the first to be burned in England for theological reasons. Not only were Wycliffe's books burned at Oxford in 1410, in 1428 his bones were disinterred, burned and the ashes thrown into the English Avon river, twenty years before Pecock's books were reduced to ashes.

Further, Wycliffe's books were burned in 1410 at Oxford where Pecock was a student (Patrouch 18). Also, as Wendy Scase has indicated, "Pecock's earliest years in Oxford saw attempts by Thomas Arundel, Archbishop of Canterbury, to extirpate the Wycliffite heresy from the university and to exert jurisdiction over it" (18).

In 1457, Pecock had been charged with heresy, especially for his unorthodox views expressed in his *Book of Faith*. Among the views for which he was condemned were: "I. That it is not necessary to salvation to believe that our Lord Jesus Christ after his death descended into hell. II. That it is not necessary to salvation to believe in the Holy Ghost. III. That it is not necessary to salvation to believe in the Holy Catholic Church. IV. That it is not necessary for salvation to believe in the communion of saints. V. That the universal Church may err in those things which are of faith" (Patrouch 30–31).

In December 1457, Pecock knelt before Church officials and abjured, declaring the above beliefs were "errors and heresies." Then, after renouncing these beliefs, these "pernicious doctrines, heresies and errors," Pecock said: "I here openly assent that my said books, works, and writings, for consideration and cause above rehearsed, be deputed into the fire, and openly be burnt into the example and terror of all others" (Patrouch 42). This being done, "a fire was then kindled before the platform, and Pecock himself handed over three folios and eleven quartos of his works to be burned.... On December 17 all of his books to be found at Oxford were burnt. The rooting out and burning of Pecock's books continued into the following year, for as late as March, 1458, Archbishop Bourchier is sending letters to Kempe, Bishop of London, urging him to seek out and destroy Pecock's books" (Patrouch 42).

Pecock was punished by being sent to Thorney Abbey in Cambridgeshire and Abbot Lyles of Thorney was instructed to give Pecock "a secret close chamber (having a chimney) and convenience within the abbey, where he may have sight to some altar to hear mass; and that he pass not the said chamber. To have but one person that is sad and well disposed to make his bed, and to make his fire, as he shall need. That he have no books to look on, but only a breviary, a mass book, a psalter, a legend and a Bible. That he have nothing to write with; no stuff to write upon" (Green Bishop 64). While there is general agreement that Pecock died in 1460, where and how he died is in dispute. As Green has stated, "Although authorities differ, it is generally assumed, in absence of evidence to the contrary, that he died at Thorney somewhere about 1460–1" (65).

The year 1479 saw two heretics, one in Germany and one in Spain, charged with heresy, both having their books burned and both dying in 1481. In 1479, John von Ruchrath of Wesel (John of Wesel), a monk of the Augustinian order was charged with heresy; he "publicly recanted and abjured" in Worms, Germany, and his writings, reports Lea, "were burned before his face" (Lea 1955 II 422) The charges against him were that he condemned indulgences and rejected transubstantiation and original sin. Lea has described Ruchrath as "the true precursor" of Martin Luther, commencing "by an assault upon indulgences" and rejecting the "authority of tradition and the fathers, recurring to Scriptures as the sole basis of authority" (1955 II 420). While Ruchrath was not condemned to death, he was imprisoned for life and died in 1481.

In 1481, another heretic, Pedro Martínez de Osma, was condemned by the Inquisition and died after he was forced to recant in public. O'Callaghan writes that Martinez, "an erudite professor of theology at the University of Salmanca" was accused of "holding the view of John Wycliffe and John Hus concerning confession and indulgences; his book *De confessione* was burned, and he was compelled to make a public recantation" (O'Callaghan 634). Lea presents a similar account: "Pedro de Osma, a respected professor of Salamanca, who in 1479 was condemned by the Council of Alcala for heresies respecting confession and the papal power to remit the pains of purgatory," was required to "abjure in public, holding a lighted candle, and the book in which his errors were set forth was ordered to be burnt by the secular authorities, who promptly obeyed" (Lea 1967 18).

The most well known book burners of the late fifteenth century were, of course, Torquemada, Savonarola, and Ximenes. In fifteenth century Spain, the Inquisition that was burning *conversos* was also burning Hebrew and Arabic books. At the same time that he was overseeing the persecution and forced conversions of Jews and Muslims and ordering the imprisonments, expulsions, and burnings of conversos and heretics, Thomas de Torquemada was ordering the burning of books. As M'Crie reports: "In 1490, many copies of Hebrew Bibles were committed to the flames at Seville by order of Torquemada; and in an *auto-da-fe* celebrated soon after in Salamanca, six thousand volumes shared the same fate, under the pretext that they contained judaism, magic, and other illicit arts" (105). Arabic books were also set afire, as Longhurst indicates in his reference to Torquemada's 1492 book burnings: "To help guard against the spread of heresy Torquemada also celebrated a number of book-burning festivals, especially of Hebrew Bibles, and after the final defeat of the Moors in Granada in 1492, of Arabic books also" (78). Torquemada died in 1498 and was buried in the chapel of Saint Thomas at Avila. Three hundred thirty eight years later, according to Longhurst, "Liberal grave-robbers with an ironic sense of history broke open Torquemada's tomb at Avila. They took out his bones, burned them on the spot where his victims had perished before him, and cast his ashes to the winds" (142). Of the disinterring of Torquemada's remains, Plaidy writes that the bones were taken from "this resting place in 1836, when the tomb was rifled, and were then scattered. Thus Torquemada, who had caused suffering to so many, died in bodily misery; and he, who had caused many to be taken from their graves that their remains might be humiliated, had the same treatment accorded to his bones" (1969 28). Torquemada's legacy was that of a person who during his eighteen years as Inquisitor General was responsible for the deaths and burnings of thousands of books and heretics, conversos, and Moriscos.

Five years after the book burnings ordered by Torquemada, Italian "reformer" Girolamo Savonarola and his followers conducted their "burning of the vanities" in Florence on February 7, 1497. To cleanse the land of vices, paganism, obscenity, and some classic literature, Savonarola had his young followers search the city for the "vanities" to be set afire. As Hugh R. Williamson has written: "'Vanities' meant not only women's finery, make-up, powders and false hair and men's cards, dice and other means of gambling secured by the youthful militia using their sticks of office with the permission of the *Signoria* to use them but volumes of Petrarch and Boccaccio as well as classical authors, musical instruments and tapestries and exquisite paintings in which nudity occurred and jewels and gay frivolous masquing clothes" (256). Referring to the books that were set afire, Paul Grendler has observed that "At the 'burning of the vanities' in Florence on February 7, 1497, Savonarola's followers destroyed works of Boccaccio and Petrarch. Pulci's *Morgante* and other chivalric works, books of magic and superstition, and books containing obscene pictures" (67).

In her description of what was burned at the bonfire of the vanities, Rachel Erlanger lists: "Cards, dice, and gaming tables, chessboards, and ivory and alabaster chessmen; harps, guitars, and horns, books by Boccaccio, Plato, Luigi Pulci, and even Dante; carnival masks and costumes, terra-cotta Cupids and other 'indecent' statues; lascivious tapestries and paintings—all had to be given up. Even pictures of the Virgin were fair game if they did not meet the friar's standards" (173). "These trophies," writes Ralph Roeder, "were heaped on a wooden pyramid in the Piazza, filled with inflammable materials, and surmounted with a diabolical figure of King Carnival. On the appointed day, the children, preceded by an Infant Jesus and followed by a pious crowd, filed into the square and took up their positions under the Palace and the Loggia.... At a given signal, the trumpets rang out; the bells pealed; a dense acrid smoke rose from the pyre; and amid an overpowering roar of pious triumph, the sins of the city shot up in flame" (197–198).

Savonarola, who had claimed to have prophetic powers and to have divine revelations, was asked by Pope Alexander VI in 1495 to come to Rome to explain these powers and revelations. Savonarola refused the invitation and subsequently the Pope ordered him to stop preaching. Despite the papal prohibition, Savonarola continued preaching and in 1497 he was excommunicated; he was pronounced a heretic, imprisoned and tortured to elicit a confession of his errors and in 1498 he was hanged and burned near the "very spot where the pyramid of vanities had twice stood" (Erlanger 285) in the Piazza della Signoria at Florence. After making sure that Savonarola's remains were totally consumed by the fire, the ashes were thrown into the Arno River.

This last decade of the fifteenth century saw not only Torquemada's burning of Hebrew works and books on magic and Savonarola's burning of the works of Boccaccio and Petrarch, but also saw Inquisitor Francisco Ximenez de Cisneros' burning of the theological books of the Moors, including copies of the Koran. Ximenez conducted his book burnings in Granada in 1499 in efforts, as Walter Starkie has explained, "to sweep away all traces of the teaching of Islam, so that Granada might completely become Christian. With this object in view, he ordered the *alfaquies* [who ministered to the Moriscos] to hand over all the Korans, commentaries and theological books they could find, and make a huge funeral pyre with them in the centre of the Bibarrambla" (258).

Lea puts the number of books burned at five thousand: "[H]e [Ximenez] summoned the alfaquies to surrender all their religious books, of which five thousand — many of them priceless specimens of art — were publicly burnt" (Lea 1988 320). However, as Starkie points out: "The authorities differ as to the number of volumes burnt. Gomez, who is generally careful in his estimates, says it was 5,000; Conde, the authority on Arabic learning, says it was 80,000. Marmol, another chronicler, places the figure as high as a million. When the mountainous pile of religious books was complete, Ximenez gave order to apply torches to it, and in a few moments the gigantic bonfire blazed, and crackled, and lit up the crowded Bibarrambia with its glow" (258).

Writing of this massive burning of Moorish books, E.H. Lindo has observed: "Cardinal Ximenes issued the barbarous decree, that deprived the lovers of the sciences of those precious volumes. He ordered all to be burnt except about three hundred on philosophy and medicine, which he sent to his college at Alcala, 'without permitting (as his historian states) that the gold and pearl clasps and bindings should be taken from them although they entreated, and would have paid the 10,000 ducats at which they had been valued; he did not permit it, because they had been instruments of that accursed race'" (42).

Ximenes died in November 1517 after a long illness and was buried in the College of St. Ildefonso at Alcala. He was praised by some for his devotion to the Church and for his administrative abilities; the *New Catholic Encyclopedia* asserts that "his burning of the Korans, which was approved by almost all his contemporaries, has been condemned by many modern critics who do not understand the circumstances of the time." The Ximenes entry in the *New Catholic Encyclopedia* concludes: "Although accused of excessive severity, he was one of Spain's great political geniuses, and in the field of religion he is rightly regarded as the reformer and renewer of the Spanish Church before the Council of Trent" (XV 1063).

However, Plaidy, in her work on the Spanish Inquisition, is less enthusiastic: "He is praised by many who declare him worthy of sainthood. But reflect for a moment on an account of the numbers of his victims: 3,564 burnt at the stake: 1,232 burnt in effigy; and penitents who suffered from confiscation of worldly goods and other punishments, 48,059.... Fifty-two-thousand people is a large number; one can be sure that everyone of these would be very doubtful of the claim of Ximenes' admirers that the latter was a saint" (1969 91). "What can we really know of this man?" asks Plaidy and answers: "Not a great deal. We can though be sure of this: under his guidance the Inquisition firmly planted by Torquemada became that sturdy growth which was so firmly rooted in Spanish soil that it was able to exist through the seventeenth and eighteenth centuries and into the nineteenth" (1969 91).

In his *History of the Reign of Ferdinand and Isabella,* William Prescott devotes a chapter to "Ximenes in Granada — Persecution, Insurrection, and Conversion of the Moors" in which he says of the 1499 book burning by Ximenes: "This melancholy *auto da fe,* it will be recollected, was celebrated, not by an unlettered barbarian, but by a cultivated prelate.... It took place, not in the darkness of the Middle Ages, but in the dawn of the sixteenth century, in the midst of an enlightened nation, deeply indebted for its own progress to these very stores of Arabian wisdom" (413–414).

The Sixteenth and Seventeenth Centuries — A Significant Increase in Book Burnings

The fires reducing books to ashes increased significantly in the sixteenth century with more edicts, proclamations, bulls, manifestoes, sermons, and decrees from church and state ordering the burnings. The wider use of the printing press, the increased activities of the Inquisition in Europe and the "new world" colonies, the Reformation of the sixteenth century, the greater interest in eradicating seditious literature, the increase in literacy — these and other factors contributed to the significant increase, over the previous century, in book burnings.

In his discussion of the impact of printing in the sixteenth century, Maurice Rowdon identifies printing as "the factor which more than any other, more even than voyages of discovery, separated the Middle Ages from modern society" and he states that "printing diminished the influence of Latin, hitherto the shared and basically ecclesiastic language. Out of the 15,000,000 or 20,000,000 books printed before 1500 at least 12,000,000 had been in Latin. By 1530 books printed in the vernacular exceeded those in Latin by far. Thinking and writing in the vernacular encouraged men to identify themselves with those who spoke the same language and not with distant Rome, or distant Brussels. Nationalism was born" (81).

With the "twin forces of printing and Protestantism" the Bible became "a layman's book," writes Anthony Kenny who then cites from a poem by John Dryden:

> The book thus put in every vulgar hand
> Which each presumed he best could understand,
> The common rule was made the common prey,
> At the mercy of the rabble lay....
> While crowds unlearned, with rude devotion warm,
> About the sacred viands buzz and swarm,

> The fly-blown text creates a crawling brood,
> And turns to maggots that was meant for food.
> A thousand daily sects rise up and die;
> A thousand more the perished race supply [Kenny 4].

Of the impact of the "mechanical mass replication of texts," Kimberly Van Kampen has written: "Even the most cursory examination of a catalogue of early printed books for a given country displays a pattern of gradual progression — more vernacular books, more secular, classical and literary books, and a relatively higher percentage of contemporary texts (as opposed to those which had circulated for generations in manuscript). Printing nourished the popularization of literacy and education, and was essential to the propagation of Renaissance values and the success of the Reformation" (79).

Writing of the censorship and eradication of books in the sixteenth century, Philip Hughes has emphasized the breadth of the destruction: "Thousands of books, whole libraries were destroyed at Oxford in 1535, and again in 1550. Tens of thousands went when the seven or eight hundred monasteries were dissolved. There was still more destruction in Elizabeth's reign and raids, now, on private homes all over the country to search out and destroy. One authority has estimated that in all something like a quarter of a million liturgical books alone were made away with during this century" (96).

Francisco Penna, a Dominican defender of the Spanish Inquisition, complained: "Ever since they began to practice this perverse excess of printing books the church has been greatly damaged and every day it is confronted by greater and more obvious perils as men exchange the ancient and secure doctrine of the virtuous doctors for the sophisticated and adulterated one of the moderns" (Crespo 174). The printed book came to be viewed as "the silent heretic," as Crespo has indicated: "The book, 'the silent heretic' as the censors liked to call it, allowed for the propagation of dissident thought.... The printed book, which could be produced at considerably less cost and with a speed almost infinitely greater than its predecessor, was far more effective.... The battle against religious dissidence came to be seen, at least in part, as the battle of the book" (175).

Book burnings occurred in every decade of the sixteenth century and these fires included not only heretical and blasphemous works but now also treasonous and seditious books (the latter are dealt with in Chapter 3). With the Spanish colonization of the "new world" came the burning of the works of the indigenous populations, in an effort to eradicate their past. The book burnings were accompanied with the continued burning of heretics at the stake, the tortures inflicted to encourage recanting and conversions, the forced exiles.

In 1502, Queen Isabella, in giving the Moors in Spain the choice between conversion to Catholicism or exile, ordered at the same time burning of Arabic books. As Lea reports: "The conversos were allowed to retain all Arabic books on medicine, philosophy and history, and were ordered to surrender everything else. This command was but partially obeyed and in 1511 Ferdinand issued a decree requiring them within fifty days to present for examination all Arabic books in their possession, under pain of confiscation and arbitrary personal punishment; the books on the excepted subjects were to be returned to them, and all the rest were to be burnt" (1967 23).

The continual burning of books in Spain during the sixteenth century is referred to by Henry Kamen in his work on the Spanish Inquisition: "A royal decree of October 1501 ordered Arabic books to be burnt in Granada, and a huge bonfire was held under the auspices of Cisneros. From March 1552 the Inquisition ordered that heretical books be burnt publicly. Some twenty-seven books were ordered to be burnt at a ceremony in Villadolid in January 1558. In mid-century the Spaniards probably resorted to burning because it seemed the simplest way to get rid of offending material. Very many books perished 'on seven or eight occasions we have burnt mountains of books here in our college,' a Jesuit working for the Barcelona Holy Office reported in 1559" (1998 112).

In 1512, the Inquisition in the Netherlands condemned Hermann of Ryswick as a heretic and he was burned at the Hague "together with his books" (Putnam 1906 81). As Lea has indicated, Hermann of Ryswick had been condemned for teaching materialistic doctrines, including "that matter is uncreated and has existed with God from the beginning, that the soul dies with the body, and that angels, whether good or bad. are not created by God. He abjured and was sentenced to perpetual imprisonment, but escaped and persisted in propagating his errors. When again apprehended in 1512, the inquisitor at The Hague had no hesitation in handing him over as a relapsed to the secular arm, and he was duly burned" (1955 III 565).

The *New Schaff-Herzog Encyclopedia of Religious Knowledge* lists Hermann's heresies as follows: "The assertion that the world exists from eternity; there are neither good nor bad angels; there is no hell and no personal continuance after this life; Aristotle and his commentator Averroes, approached truth most closely; Jesus was a fool and miserable dreamer, a seducer of simple men; he spoiled the whole world and saved nobody, and it is lamentable that so many have been murdered for his sake and for the sake of his foolish Gospel; everything he did is in contradiction with human nature and pure reason, he is not the son of almighty God" (V 239). The entry reports that Hermann was tried in 1512 and admitted that he had written numerous heretical books; he was tried and burned. As to the burning of his books, "It is said that his books were burned with him" (V 239).

Two years later, German humanist and lawyer Johannes Reuchlin, who had publicly criticized the burning of Jewish books, saw his own work *Augenspiegel* condemned and burned by the Church in Cologne. Years before *Augenspiegel* was set afire by the Inquisition, John Pfefferkorn, a Jew from Cologne who had converted to Catholicism, proposed, as Lilly indicates, "the destruction of all Hebrew books, except the Old Testament. The Dominican Inquisitors approved of the proposal. Reuchlin, a man of high standing, and a distinguished scholar, specifically versed in Hebrew, wrote vigorously in opposition to this insane obscurantism" (150). In 1511, Reuchlin had published his *Recommendation Whether to Confiscate, Destroy and Burn all Jewish Books* in which he argued against the burning of Jewish works; at the same time he responded to the question of burning "slanderous and blasphemous language to speak of our beloved Lord and God, Jesus Christ, his venerable mother, and also the apostles and saints," Reuchlin stated that "if such a book is found among the holdings of a Jew who knowingly harbors it, a book that expressly and clearly heaps scorn, offense and dishonor upon our sacred Lord Jesus, his venerable mother, the saints of the Christian order, then one would have the right by Imperial mandate to tear it up, burn it or otherwise dispose of it" (Lilly 35). As Lilly has pointed out, "[I]n *Augenspiegel* Reuchlin seeks to reduce the difference between himself and his opponents to this: that they desired to destroy Hebrew book unconditionally, while he would destroy only such of them as were tainted with heretical sentiment" (200). Toward the end of his *Recommendation,* Reuchlin wrote of the importance of books to the Jews and of the coercion involved in the destruction of writings: "[W]e may conclude that we ... may not take their books away from them against their will, for books are as dear to some as their children. Do we not in our common usage follow the parlance of the poets, for whom the books they write are in a manner of speaking children of the soul! Here too, we must bear in mind: If our purpose in confiscating a Jew's books is precisely to bring him over to the Christian faith, then such an action would be tantamount to force" (Lilly 85–86).

After the publication of Reuchlin's *Augenspiegel,* "Reuchlin was branded a heretic by his opponents, and a torrent of controversial pamphlets and tracts were unleashed by each side. The controversy raged for a decade. In 1513, Jacob Hoogstraeten, head of the Inquisition in Cologne, began inquisitorial proceedings against Reuchlin's opinions. By 1514 he succeeded in doing to Reuchlin's writings what he had not succeeded in doing to Jewish books—they were condemned to be burned at the stake" (Lilly 22).

A year after the burning of Reuchlin's book, a papal bull issued in which Pope Leo X expressed concern about "book-printing," ordered that works not examined by the Church be seized and publicly burned. That section of the papal bull devoted to the printing of books warned against works that contained "error opposed to the faith as well as pernicious views contrary to the Christian religion and to the reputation of prominent persons of rank"; hence, "to prevent what has been a healthy discovery for the glory of God, the advance of faith, and the propagation of good skills, from being misused for the opposite purposes and becoming an obstacle to the salvation of Christians, we have judged that our care must be exercised over the printing of books, precisely so that thorns do not grow up with the good seed or poisons become mixed with medicines." The "thorns" and "poisons" to which the Pope and his council refer must, of course, be dealt with and the answer, asserts the document, is to impose censorship, and if that fails, the condemned books must be "seized and burnt." And finally, he who does not comply will be "punished with all the sanctions of the law ... in such a way that others will have no incentive to try to follow his example" which implied everything from imprisonment, exile, torture, and burning at the stake.

Before the end of the decade, the works of Martin Luther were being set afire. In 1517, Luther had posted on the Castle Church door at the University of Wittenberg his ninety-five theses in which he declared his differences with the Church on matters such as indulgences, penance, purgatory, and other Church policies and practices. Three years later, on June 15, 1520, Pope Leo's bull *Exsurge Domine* was issued, threatening, among other things, Luther's excommunication if he did not recant within sixty days. The papal bull ordered that Luther's books "be burned publicly and solemnly in the presence of the clerics and people." In ordering the burning of Luther's books, *Exsurge Domine* asserted:

> Moreover, because the preceding errors and many others are contained in the books or writings of Martin Luther, we likewise condemn, reprobate, and reject completely the books and all the writings and sermons of the said Martin, whether in Latin or any other language, containing the said errors or anyone of them; and we wish them to be regarded as utterly condemned, reprobated, and rejected. We forbid each and everyone of the faithful of either sex, in virtue of holy obedience and under the above penalties to be incurred automatically, to read, assert, preach, praise, print, publish, or defend them. They will incur these penalties if they presume to uphold them in any way, personally or through another or others, directly or indirectly, tacitly or explicitly, publicly or through their own homes or in other public or private places. Indeed immediately after the publication of this letter these works, wherever they may be, shall be sought out carefully by the ordinaries and others [ecclesiastics and regulars], and under each and every one of the above penalties shall be burned publicly and solemnly in the presence of the clerics and people.

From beginning to end, the papal bull is permeated with the metaphoric language inviting extermination. Immediately, in the first paragraph, the pope asserts: "Arise, O Lord, and judge Your own cause. Remember your reproaches to those who are filled with foolishness all through the day. Listen to our prayers, for foxes have arisen to destroy the vineyard whose winepress you alone have trod. When you were about to ascend to Your

Father, You committed the care, rule, and administration of the vineyard, an image of the triumphant church, to Peter, as the head and Your vicar and his successors. The wild boar from the forest seeks to destroy it and every wild beast feeds upon it." The "tongues" of the "lying teachers" are "fire, a restless evil, full of deadly poison." Luther's errors are a "pernicious poison." After presenting forty-one of these errors, the papal bull defines them as a "plague," "cancerous disease," and "harmful thorn bushes." Once the books had been identified with foxes, wild boars, deadly poisons, plague, cancerous disease, and harmful thorn bushes, the metaphors invited the next step which was, of course, to see them destroyed, preferably to be "burned publicly."

Six months later, on the morning of December 1, 1520, Luther's fellow reformer Melanchthon posted the following announcement on the University of Wittenberg bulletin board: "All friends of evangelical truth are invited to assemble, about nine o'clock, at the church of the Holy Cross, beyond the city wall. There, according to ancient, apostolic usage, the godless books of the papal constitutions and the scholastic theology will be burned inasmuch as the presumption of the enemies of the Gospel has advanced to such a degree that they have cast the godly, evangelical books of Luther into the fire. Let all earnest students, therefore, appear at the spectacle; for it is now the time when Antichrist must be exposed" (Manschreck 60). Students, doctors, and masters gathered at the Holy Cross outside of town, writes Manschreck, "where cattle were sometimes butchered and infected clothing burned. When the bonfire was lighted, Melanchthon watched his colleague [Luther] throw volumes of the Canon Law and various theological writings along with the *Exsurge, Domine* into the flames. After singing *Te Deum* and *De profundis,* the faculty returned to the university and the students riotously celebrated-parading, burning the pope in effigy, and conducting a funeral for a six-foot copy of the bull" (61).

In his *The Life and Letters of Martin Luther,* Preserved Smith describes the December 10, 1520, burning somewhat similarly: "[T]he students built a pyre, a certain 'master,' probably Melanchthon, lighted it, and Luther threw on the whole Canon Law with the last bull of Leo X, whom he apostrophized in these solemn words: 'Because thou hast brought down the truth of God, he also brings thee down unto this fire to-day. Amen.' Others threw on works of the schoolmen and some of Eck and Emser [Catholic theologians and professors]. After the professors had gone home, the students sang funeral songs and disported themselves at the Pope's expense" (101). Luther's burning of the papal works on December 10, 1520, writes Scott Hendrix, "was the unmistakable sign of his refusal to comply with the terms of *Exsurge Domine.* On that same day, his period of grace ran out and he was excommunicated from the Roman Church by Pope Leo on January 3, 1521" (123).

Within a half year of Luther's excommunication, the Edict of Worms was issued which as De Lamar Jensen has indicated "reemphasized the danger of heresies and false doctrines leading the faithful followers of Christ into error and the nations into schism. It recounted the steps taken by the papacy and by the emperor to bring Martin Luther back to repentance and obedience. His many errors were enumerated, from disturbing and condemning the sacraments to attacking the authority of the general councils and the pope. Such a rebellious and evil man, continued the edict, was not worthy to be considered or treated as a Christian.... His books were not to be bought, sold, kept, or read by anyone; and all existing copies were to be burned" (65–66). Emperor Charles V signed the document in May 1521 and by the middle of June the Edict of Worms was translated into German, French, and Flemish and published and circulated throughout Europe.

The section of the Edict devoted to the burning of Luther's books appeared at the end of the document, complete with the metaphoric "moral pestilence," "poison," "infection," and "contagion." That section of the Edict ordering the burning of the books warrants extended citation here:

> We order, upon the penalties contained herein, that the contents of this edict be kept and observed in their entirety; and we forbid anyone, regardless of his authority or privilege, to dare to buy, sell, keep, read, write, or have somebody write, print or have printed, or affirm or defend the books, writings, or opinions of the said Martin Luther, or anything contained in these books and writings, whether in German, Latin, Flemish, or any other language. This applies also to all those writings condemned by our Holy Father the pope and to any other book written by Luther or any of his disciples, in whatever manner, even if there is Catholic doctrine mixed in to deceive the common people. For this reason we want all of Luther's books to be universally prohibited and forbidden, and we also want them to be burned.

The Edict then points out that in the past good Christians burned the works of heretics and argues by analogy by invoking the poison metaphor:

> We execute the sentence of the Holy Apostolic See, and we follow the very praiseworthy ordinance and custom of the good Christians of old who had the books of heretics like the Arians, Priscillians, Nestorians, Eutychians, and others burned and annihilated, even everything that was contained in these books, whether good or bad. This is well done, since if we are not allowed to eat meat containing just one drop of poison because of the danger of bodily infection, then we surely should leave out every doctrine (even if it is good) which has in it the poison of heresy and error, which infects and corrupts and destroys under the cover of charity everything that is good, to the great peril of the soul.
>
> Therefore, we ask you who are in charge of judicial administration to have all of Luther's books and writings burned and destroyed in public, whether these writings are in German, Flemish, Latin, or in any other written language and whether they are written by himself, his disciples, or the imitators of his false and heretical doctrines, which are the source of all perversity and iniquity. Moreover, we ask you to help and assist the messengers of our Holy Pope. In their absence you will have all those books publicly burned and execute all the things mentioned above.
>
> [T]o kill this mortal pestilence, we ask and require that no one dare to compose, write, print, paint, sell, buy, or have printed, written, sold, or painted, from now on in whatever manner such pernicious articles so much against the holy orthodox faith and against that which the Catholic Apostolic Church has kept and observed to this day. We likewise condemn anything that speaks against the Holy Father, against the prelates of the Church, and against the secular princes, the general schools and their faculties, and all other honest people, whether in positions of authority or not. And in the same manner we condemn everything that is contrary to the good, moral character of the people, to the Holy Roman Church, and to the Christian public good [Jensen 105].

Having covered all the bases by condemning just about any general criticism, the Edict then covers all the bases regarding punishment of the critics: "We ask you to be diligent in apprehending and confiscating all the belongings of those who seem rebellious to the ordinance herein mentioned and to punish them according to the penalties set out by law — divine, canon, and civil.... Furthermore, we declare in this ordinance that if anyone, whatever his social status may be, dares directly or indirectly to oppose this decree — whether concerning Luther's matter, his defamatory books or their printings, or whatever has been ordered by us— these transgressors in so doing will be guilty of the crime of *lese majeste* and will incur our grave indignation as well as each of the punishments mentioned above.... Given in our city of Worms on the eighth day of May in the year of our Lord one thousand five hundred twenty-one. Signed Charles of Germany" (Jensen 111).

While Luther had denounced the Church for burning his works and then as he set fire to Catholic writings, he later advocated in his virulent anti–Semitic *On the Jews and Their*

Lies setting fire to Jewish homes and synagogues and taking from the Jews "all their books—their prayer books, their Talmudic writings, also the entire Bible." After many pages condemning the Jews as "liars," "venomous," "blasphemous," "mad," "devilish," and a "miserable and accursed people" involved in "poisonous activities," Luther presented his advice as to what must be done:

> Accordingly, it must and dare not be considered a trifling matter but a most serious one to seek counsel against this and to save our souls from the Jews, that is, from the devil and from eternal death. My advice, as I said earlier, is:
> First that their synagogues be burned down, and that all who are able toss in sulfur and pitch; it would be good if someone could also throw in some hellfire....
> Second, that all their books—their prayer books, their Talmudic writings, also the entire Bible—be taken from them, not leaving them one leaf....
> Third, that they be forbidden on pain of death to praise God, to give thanks, to pray, and to teach publicly among us and in our country....
> Fourth, that they be forbidden to utter the name of God within our hearing....

Luther then asks: "But what will happen if we do burn down the Jews' synagogues and forbid them publicly to praise God, to pray, to teach, to utter God's name? They will still keep doing it in secret.... So let us beware. In my opinion the problem must be resolved thus: If we wish to wash our hands of the Jews' blasphemy and not share in their guilt, we have to part company with them. They must be driven from our country" (Luther XLVII 285–288). While Luther urged that all books be taken from the Jews, the holy scrolls, the Torah, prayer books, manuscripts and other writings within the synagogues were being reduced to ashes as the buildings were set afire, as Luther recommended.

Meanwhile in Spain, in April 1521, Inquisitor General Cardinal Adrian, to prevent the distribution of Lutheran works, issued a decree which, as Lea has stated, instructed the tribunals "to order, under heavy censures and civil penalties, that no one should possess or sell them whether in Latin or Romance, but should, within three days after notice, bring them to the Inquisition to be publicly burnt; the edict was to be published in a sermon of faith and, after publication, anyone possessing or selling them, or knowing that others possessed them and not denouncing the offenders, was to suffer the penalties announced by the inquisitors, while all ecclesiastical and secular authorities were ordered to render whatever aid might be necessary" (1988 III 482).

One month later, on May 12, 1521, Lutheran books and Wycliffe Scriptures were burned at St. Paul's Cathedral in London. As described by Bobrick, Henry VIII "promised the pope to burn any 'untrue translations' (having the Wycliffe Scriptures in mind) and had set his lord chancellor Cardinal Wolsey, to hunting down heretical books that were then pouring into the kingdom from overseas. On the 12th of May, 1521, Wolsey repaired in solemn procession to St. Paul's Cathedral to see his harvest burned.... Others joined the cavalcade followed by a long line of mules bearing chests full of Lutheran writings, Bishop Fisher preached a fierce sermon before the bonfires were lit" (96).

In his book burning sermon, Fisher identified Luther with past heretics—Arians, Wycliffe and others—who had caused to arise "the black cloud of heresy." Further, declared Fisher, the Arians, the Donatists, and the disciples of Wycliffe not only "infected souls," but also "murder[ed] bodies" and "slay[ed] their adversaries." This led Fisher to conclude that the heretic Luther would do the same: "And what do you suppose Martin Luther and his adherents would do if had the pope's holiness and his favorites whom he calls so often in derision *papastros* in his danger. I fear that he would use no more courtesy with them than he has with their books, that is to say with the decrials that he has burnt. And so likewise

"Bookseller Burnt at Avignon in France, for selling Bibles in the French Tongue, with some of them tied around his neck." (Courtesy Research Publications.)

I fear that he would burn them or any other Christian man that he thought might let his opinions go forward" (Mayor 344–345).

During the 1520s and after, Luther's books, along with other "heretical" writings were cast into the fires all across Europe. In his discussion of "Printing and the Reformation in the Low Countries," Andrew G. Johnston has observed that "The writings of Luther and his followers were forbidden by the central government from the very beginning. The first book burning following the pontifical bull *Exsurge Domine* (15 June 1520) took place in Louvain on 8 October 1520. Later on, book burnings took place in Antwerp, Ghent, Utrecht, Bruges, s'Hertogenbosch and Deventer. In a letter to the pontifical vice-chancellor of Rome, the legate of the Low Countries, Jerome Aleander, boasted of having burnt 400 of Luther's books, 300 of which were seized in bookshops and 100 from individuals" (178–179).

Jean-Francois Gilmont reports in his "Three Border Cities: Antwerp, Strasbourg and Basle" that "In the sixteenth century, Antwerp printers produced works in the main European languages: Dutch, English, French, Spanish, Italian and Danish, as well as Latin, Greek and Hebrew.... The Antwerp printers published Luther's works in Latin and Dutch.... Soon, however, the condemnations by the theological faculty of Louvain (7 November 1519) and by the Pope (15 June 1520) were followed by a placard by the Emperor Charles V (28 September 1520). Heretical works were publicly burnt in Louvain on 8 September 1520. In Antwerp, the first book burnings took place on 14 July 1521. In 1522, the city authorities burnt heretical books on three separate occasions" (Gilmont 191).

In 1512 in Spain, as Kinder has written, "The Headquarters (Suprema) of the Inquisition alerted provincial branches that there was a danger that books were being brought into Spain, and a letter of 27 September congratulated the Inquisition in Valencia for having detected and burnt 'Lutheran' books. In 1523, the Inquisition of Navarre was thanked for its vigilance in the ports and along the border of France. Books were seized and destroyed in Aragon too" (307). "The "infection" spreading Tyndale Bible was metaphorized into "disease," "poison," and "pestilence," all of which would "infect and contaminate the flock."

In December 1524, Edward Lee, the future Archbishop of York, wrote to the King warning him of the arrival in England of an English translation of the New Testament: "I am certainly informed, as I passed in this country [France] that an Englishman, your subject, at the solicitation and instance of Luther, with whom he is, hath translated the New Testament into English, and within a few days intended to arrive with the same imprinted in England. I need not to advertise your grace what infection and danger may ensure hereby, if it be not withstanded" (Mozley 64). As Campbell reports: "By April of that year [1525] 6000 copies had come from Worms and were being sold in England" (109). Within a year, William Tyndale's English translation of the New Testament was being burned in London.

In 1526, a public burning of the Tyndale Bible took place at Paul's Cross in London; as Worth has indicated, "The burning was accompanied by a sermon from [Bishop of London] Cuthbert Tunstall" who had "resorted to bulk purchases [of Tyndale Bibles] in Europe" (24). Bishop Tunstall denounced the Tyndale Bible as containing "heretical depravity and pernicious erroneous opinions, pestilent, scandalous, and seductive of simple minds" and containing the "pestilent pernicious poison" that would "without doubt infect and contaminate the flock, committed to us, with the pestilent poison and the deadly disease of heretical depravity, to the grievous peril of the souls committed to us and the most grievous offence of the divine majesty" (Mozley 115).

Efforts to stop the importation of the Tyndale Bibles were not successful and the book burnings continued. The buying and burning of the Bibles in 1529 has been reported in the following manner which Worth (25) describes as having "a polemical element" but which is not "inherently illogical or improbable" and Mozley describes as a "delightful tale" that "bears all the marks of embellishment" but still "likely enough that [John] Hackett [English ambassador to the Low Countries] suggested the new plan" (149–150).

The story of Bishop Tunstall's efforts to purchase Tyndale Bibles in order to set them afire reads:

> The bishop ... said: "Gentle Master Packington [London merchant], do your diligence and get them, and with all my heart I will pay for them, whatsoever they cost you; for the books are erroneous and naughty, and I intend surely to destroy them all, and to burn them at Paul's Cross.
>
> Augustine Packington came to William Tyndale and said: "William, I know thou are a poor man, and hast a heap of New Testaments and books by thee, for the which thou hast both endangered thy friends and beggared thyself; and I have now gotten thee a merchant, which with ready money shall dispatch thee of all that thou hast, if you think it so profitable for yourself."
>
> "Who is the merchant?" said Tyndale.
>
> "The bishop of London," said Packington.
>
> "Oh, that is because he will burn them," said Tyndale. "Yea, marry," quoth Packington. "I am the gladder," said Tyndale; "for these two benefits shall come thereof: I shall get money of him for these books, to bring myself out of debt, and the whole world shall cry out upon the burning of God's word. And the over plus of the money, that shall remain to me, shall make me more studious to correct the said New Testament, and so newly to imprint the same once again; and I trust the second will much better like you than ever did the first." And so forward when the bargain: the bishop had the books, Packington had the thanks, and Tyndale had the money [Worth 25].

In May 1530, Bishop Tunstall, reports Mozley, "made another of his spectacular demonstrations at Paul's Cross. He caused, says Halle, 'all his New Testaments which he had bought, with many other books, to be brought into Paul's churchyard in London, and there openly burned'" (162). In 1539, King Henry VIII in a speech before Parliament, "complained, with tears in his eyes, that the Bible was being 'disputed, rhymed, sung, and jangled in every ale-house and tavern.' Once again large quantities of the vernacular translations were pried from their owners and burned" (Bobrick 160).

Tyndale was arrested in Antwerp and August 1536, he was pronounced a heretic, degraded from the priesthood, was burned at the stake in October. According to John Foxe's description of the execution, Tyndale "was brought forth to the place of execution, was there tied to the stake, and then strangled first by the hangman, and afterwards with fire consumed, in the morning at the town of Vilvorde, A.D. 1536; crying thus at the stake with a fervent zeal and a loud voice: Lord, open the king of England's eyes" (Mozley 341).

The same year Tyndale's Bible was burned, Robert Barnes, affiliated with Tyndale, was ordered to burn some "offending books" as part of his abjuration ceremony. Barnes' attacks on various aspects of the Church led to a demand that he publicly recant, which he did on February 11, 1526. Barnes had "declaimed against the superstitious observance of holiday; the pride, pomp, and avarice of the prelates and the clergy; [their usurpation of temporal power;] the rigour and abuses of the ecclesiastical courts; the corruptions and errors of the church; and the persecution of the advocates of religious truth" (Lusardi 1372).

Barnes was confronted with various "articles ... some of them be slanderous, some be erroneous, some be contumacious, some be seditious, some be folyshe, and some be heretical" (Schuster 1381). Foxe has described the humiliating abjuration required of Barnes and the burning of the books:

> In the morning they [Barnes and four others] were all ready, by their hour appointed, in Paul's church, the church being so full that no man could get in. The cardinal had a scaffold made on the top of the stairs for himself, with six-and-thirty abbots, mitreed priors, and bishops, and he, in his whole pomp, mitered (which Barnes spoke against), sat there enthronised, his chaplains

and spiritual doctors in gowns of damask and satin, and he himself in purple; even like a bloody Antichrist. And there was a new pulpit erected on the top of the stairs also, for the bishop of Rochester to preach against Luther and Dr. Barnes; and great baskets full of books standing before them within the rails, which were commanded, after the great fire was made before the rood of Northen, there to be burned; and these heretics, after the sermon, to go thrice about the fire, and to cast in their faggots. Now, while the sermon was a doing, Dr. Barnes and the Still-yard men were commanded to kneel down, and ask forgiveness of God, of the catholic church and of the cardinal's grace [Foxe V 418–419].

While the books were reduced to ashes, Barnes was "received into the church again."

Although Barnes had abjured, he was "committed to be a free prisoner at the Austin Friars in London" and he soon learned that a writ had been issued ordering that he be burned. Barnes escaped to Antwerp, fooling the authorities into believing that he had drowned. Barnes, mistakenly, believed that he would be safe if he returned to England and in 1535 he "returned frelie into England, and lived here triumphantlye" (Lusardi 1402). That is, until 1540 when he was again imprisoned for preaching a sermon that he had been enjoined from delivering. Whereupon, Barnes was committed to the Tower and burned at the stake on July 30, 1538.

Tyndale's close associate John Frith had collaborated with Tyndale, as Bobrick has written, "on several polemical tracts, and had written a book on the doctrine of purgatory in which he claimed that neither transubstantiation nor purgatory were necessary articles of faith" (Bobrick 130). In a May 18, 1531, letter to a close friend, Oliver Cromwell refers to the King's concern about Frith: "As touching Frith ... the king hears good reports of his learning, and laments that he should misuse it in furthering the 'venomous and pestiferous works, erroneous and seditious opinions of the said Tyndale, and the other.' He hopes, however, that he is not 'so far yet uprooted' in such evil doctrines, but that he may be recalled to the right way; and he instructs you to speak with Frith if you are able, and urge him to leave his willful opinions, and like a good Christian to return to his native country" (Campbell 197).

Eventually, Henry VIII ordered Frith to be examined and "on June 20, 1533 he was tried and condemned in St. Paul's before the bishops of London, Winchester, and Lincoln, the articles with which he was charged emphasizing his denial of transubstantiation and purgatory as matters necessary to faith" (Schuster 1468). Frith was burned at the stake at Smithfield on July 4, 1533. Thirteen years later, the king issued a proclamation condemning the works of several authors whose "corrupt and pestilent teaching" had "secretly crept in by such printed books." The condemned works were to be gathered and burned: "And to the intent that no man shall mistrust any danger of such penal statutes as be passed in this behalf for keeping the said books, the King's majesty is most graciously contented by this proclamation to pardon that offense to the said time appointed by this proclamation for the delivery of said books; and commanded that no bishop, chancellor, commissary, mayor, bailiff, or constable shall be curious to mark who bringeth forth such books, but only order and burn them openly as is in this proclamation ordered" (Hughes and Larkin 375).

Just as Frith was condemned to die in the flames and reduced to ashes, so too was it ordered that his books be set afire. Others whose works were condemned in the king's Proclamation and ordered to be "openly burned" were, in addition to Tyndale, Wicklif, and Frith were "[George] Joy, [William] Roy, [Thomas] Basil, [John] Bale, [Robert] Barnes, [Miles] Coverdale, [William] Turner and [William] Tracy" (Hughes and Larkin 374).

The writings of Luther, Tyndale, Frith, Joy, and others were denounced by Thomas

More who did not hesitate invoking a variety of metaphors inviting extirpation of the works and their authors. At the outset of his *The Confutation of Tyndale's Answer,* More refers to the "pestilent" books with their "deadly poisons," "infecting" readers with "contagious pestilence." More begins: "Our Lord send us now some years plentiful good corn, as we have had some years of late plenty of evil books. For they have grown so fast and sprung up so thick full of Pestylent errours and pernyciouse heresyes, that they have enfected and killed, I fear, more simple souls than the famine of the dry years have destroyed bodies"; there are "pestilent errors" in the "abominable books of Tyndale and his fellows" (More 3). More identifies Luther's works and Frith with poison: "Then there is a book of Luther's translated into English in the name of Brightwell, but as I am informed the book was translated by Frith.... And surely Frith's prologue, if it be his as it is said ... brings to the people a draught of deadly poison" (More 9). Further, the heretical works are "books full of pestilent poisoned heresies" (More 11). The "poison" metaphors are piled one upon another; More fears that the readers of the condemned works will become "infected with some heresies" because the writings are filled with "the poison that the devil has put in them" (More 224). The "seeds of heresy," writes More, are "sown" and spring up in the books of Tyndale, Barnes, and Frith (More 11).

While Tyndale, Barnes, and Frith were all burned at the stake, More, who had refused to take the "loyalty oath" demanded by Henry VIII, was executed by decapitation. Frith had been set afire on July 4, 1533; More was beheaded two years later on July 6, 1535.

Meanwhile, across the channel in France, pro–Reformation books were being burned along with anti–Reformation books. In 1522, an anti–Luther tract written by Franciscan Thomas Murner was burned in Protestant-controlled Strassburg. As Christiane Andersson reports, Murner, who had published anti–Lutheran tracts, requested that the Strassburg authorities allow him to reply in print "to recent Lutheran attacks against him. The councilors allowed him only to post his rebuttal at twelve spots in Strassburg. Instead on December 19, 1522, Murner published his tract on the 'Great Fool' [Luther] without permission, and the council immediately confiscated and burned almost the entire edition, except for a few copies that must have escaped the censor's grasp" (50).

The title page woodcut of *The Great Luther Fool,* writes Andersson, "depicts a scene of satirical exorcism. The author [Murner], shown in his Franciscan habit and with a cat's head..., frees the 'great fool' signifying the folly of Lutheran belief: not demons but rather many small fools issue from the great fool's mouth in the process of exorcism" (50).

On May 13, 1523, a search of the home of humanist and translator Louis de Berquin led to the confiscation of his books which included, among other works, "Berquin's own translations of Luther and [German humanist and satirist] Ulrich von Hutten, and a satire aimed at the Faculty [of Theology]" (Taylor 40). The head of that Faculty, orthodox Catholic theologian Noël Beda, described by Goldstone as "one of the few among his peers to recognize the power of books—and thus the necessity of suppressing them," condemned Berquin and "was about to have him tried for heresy when Marguerite [King Francis' sister] intervened. Francis saved Berquin, but all of his books were confiscated from his library and burned just outside of Notre-Dame.... The Inquisition waited until Francis was out of Paris before hurriedly arresting Berquin, then even more hurriedly passing sentence and carrying it out. Berquin was burned at the stake in 1529" (78).

In April 1529, Berquin was sentenced to imprisonment, the sentence including the burning of his books. Further, "Parliament condemned him 'to have his tongue branded with a red-hot iron and to remain a prisoner for the rest of his life." Apr. 16 Berquin appealed to the king, and the next day Parliament, taking advantage of the king's absence at Blois, ordered Bequin to be burned at the Place de Grève" (Bonet-Maury 69).

Similarly, Taylor has written that Berquin was "condemned to die and be burned alive in the Place de Grève at Paris, and before his death, in his presence, his books were to be burned; this was done and expedited the same day so that he could not have recourse to the king or Madama the Regent, who was in Blois" (41). Bonet-Maury has taken the position that Berquin was "the first Protestant martyr of France. Theodore Beza said of him: 'If France had upheld him to the last he would have been the Luther of France'" (39).

Book printers and book sellers were also burned along with their books in France. As Febvre and Martin have reported, in 1534 "it was a printer who was burned, for having printed and bound the 'false works' of Luther" and then "it was the turn of a bookseller. On the 24th December Antoine Augereau, one of the printers of the *Miroir de l'ame pecheresse,* who had already suffered imprisonment at the time of the case involving the royal lectures, was sent to the stake. Then, on 21st January 1535, in the day-time there was a penitential procession in which the King took part through the streets of Paris, and in the evening, in the streets through which the procession passed, six heretics were burned at the stake. To complete the symbolism, three large sacks of books found in their possession were added to the pyres before the execution" (309–310).

In writing about the cathedrals and the squares as book burning locations, Mary Jane Chase has observed that they were "favorite sites for the burning of heretical books, the recantation of heretics, opinions, and the humiliation of penitent heretics. Such activities served to highlight and publicize the fate of the heretic, as well as to begin the process of the purification of the city. In 1534 the prohibited books of a condemned canon from Amiens, Jean Morand, were burned publicly in front of the cathedral. A procession to the cathedral culminated in a sermon by the noted Dominican preacher Thomas de Laurent, designed to explain and eradicate the dangerous ideas" (382). The public use of fire was seen as the most effective element to eradicate not only dangerous ideas, but also the most effective in achieving purification, especially when authors and printers were both set afire together with their books.

An edict of July 1, 1542, issued by King Francis I had as its aims, Taylor writes, "to rid the kingdom of all copies of Calvin's *Institutes,* which were to be turned in within twenty-four hours on pain of death. The edict further decreed that all clandestine printing must cease, and in all published works the printer's name and city had to be clearly displayed. Before being offered for sale, all books were to be examined by members of the Faculty. Printers were forbidden from commenting on any aspect of Christian doctrine in books covering grammar, rhetoric, logic or literature, so that such works could not be used surreptitiously to evade the censorship laws. The *parliament* also ordered Parisians to denounce preachers or cures who expounded heretical doctrines" (76). One result was that "six Parisian booksellers or publishers were put on trial between 1541 and 1544, two of whom were burnt at the stake" (Taylor 77). Then, in 1544, "a spectacular demonstration of the authorities' intentions to prosecute under the new law was given, when Parlement ordered books by both Calvin and Étienne Dolet to be burned in front of Notre-Dame while the cathedral bells were rung" (Taylor 77).

The French *parliament* ordered the burning of Étienne Dolet's books because it claimed they contained "damnable, pernicious, and heretical doctrines." Among the charges brought against Dolet at his trial were that in his writings, as Christie observes, Dolet intended "to express approval of the doctrine of predestination; that several books which had been condemned and censured as containing erroneous propositions had been printed by him with prefatory epistles of his own composition recommending perusal of them" (415–416). Further, he was charged with printing several books in the vulgar tongue; also, "that he had eaten fish in Lent and at other prohibited times; that he had walked about during the mass, and said that he preferred the sermon to the mass; and lastly, that in his writings he seemed to doubt the immortality of the soul" (Christie 416–417). The Inquisitor General Matthew Ory demanded that the books "should be burnt at the *parvis* of the church of Notre Dame at Paris, to the sound of the great bell of the church, public proclamation, accompanied by the sound of the trumpet, being at the same time made, forbidding all booksellers and printers thenceforth from possessing such books, under pain of being punished as heretics and favourers of heretics. Amongst the books ordered to be burned were *Epigrammes Dolet, Canton Chrestien, Le Nouveau Testament, imprime par icelluy Dolet en Francoys, La Bible de Genève, Calvinus intitule,* and *Les Gestes du Roy*" (Christie 443).

Two years later, as Christie records, "On the 2nd of August 1546, the First President of the *Grand Chambre,* pronounced sentence on Dolet as guilty of Blasphemy, sedition, and exposing for sale prohibited and condemned books ... and condemned him to be taken by the executioner in a cart from the prison of the Conciergerie to the Place Maubert, where a gallows was to be erected in the most convenient and suitable place, around which was to be made a great fire, into which, after having been hung on the said gallows, his body was to be thrown, with his books, and burnt to ashes, his property to be confiscated to the King" (470). On August 3, 1546, Dolet "was suspended at the gallows, and then, when he was possibly dead, but more probably still breathing, the faggots were lighted, and the author and his books were condemned to the flames" (Christie 473).

The language used in condemning heretics and their writings in 1546 continued in the tradition of relying on metaphors suggesting and inviting fiery eradication. The same year Dolet and his books were set afire, François Le Picart, the "most famous Catholic preacher in Paris from the 1530s until his death in 1556" (Taylor x), participated in the burning of fourteen condemned heretics. As Taylor has indicated, "The fourteen were bound with ropes and iron chains to a gibbet. As they were raised into the air, facing each other, those whose tongues had not been cut out sung Psalms. To drown out the voices of the heretics, the priests and the crowd sung the *Salve Regina* and *O Salutaris Hostia,* until the bodies had been burnt and fallen into the fire" (72). Le Picart declared that those who had been set afire had been "condemned to the pits of hell, and that even if an angel descended from the sky to say the contrary, it must be rejected for God would not be God if he didn't damn them eternally" (Taylor 73). Relying on the infection, cancer, and leper metaphors, Le Picart referred to "a cancer that grows silently no but continuously in the body." In his words, there is no longer "any health in the body, there is no corner on which there is not a leper; it has infected almost the entire body of the church" (Taylor 81).

On another occasion, Le Picart claimed that heresy was the cause of the problems, turmoils, and schisms of the time in France. He asserted: "The heretics are like serpents—they strike with their tails" and further, "these contemptible heretics will not last but will soon be wiped out and their heresies abolished" (Taylor 195). If heretics deserve to be in the "pits of hell" and were spreading their heretical infections, leprosy, and cancers, and were like serpents, then it would seem to follow that a heretic like Dolet and his heretical books deserved no better than to be set afire, to be "wiped out" and "abolished."

One of Dolet's editorial assistants may have been the Spanish scholar and physician Michael Servetus who, like Dolet, was burned at the stake along with his books. In his biography of Servetus, John F. Fulton has written: "Servetus had twelve happy years quietly practicing medicine near Lyons and serving as editorial assistant to local printers, including Frellon, Trechsel, and possibly also to the unfortunate Etienne Dolet who was burned at the stake by the infamous Lyons Inquisitor, Mathiew D'Ory. Dolet had met this fate in

August 1546 so Servetus must have been aware of the tremendous hazard he faced in issuing a book on which he had worked for many years in the fond hope that it would restore Christianity to the simple state in which he believed it to have been conceived" (33). In July 1553, Servetus was found guilty of heresy for, among other things, the views he expressed about the Trinity in his book *Christianismi restitutio.* The imprisoned Servetus escaped and was publicly burned in effigy, along with five thousand copies of his book (Fulton 35). His effigy was "paraded through the streets of Vienne [France] brought to the place of public execution, hanged upon a gibbet erected for the purpose, and finally set fire to, and with the five bales [of books] burned to ashes" (Willis 275).

Several months later, on October 27, 1553, Servetus was again found guilty of various heresies. This time, it was not his effigy that was set afire. In sentencing Servetus to death, the ecclesiastical court accused him of spreading "the venom of his heresy" and printing a book full of heresies "and horrible execrable blasphemies against the Holy Trinity, against the Son of God, against the baptism of infants and the foundations of the Christian religion. He confesses that in this book he called believers in the Trinity Trinitarians and atheists. He calls this Trinity a diabolical monster with three heads.... He calls infant baptism an invention of the devil and sorcery. His execrable blasphemies are scandalous against the majesty of God, the Son of God and the Holy Spirit" (Bainton 208).

In the Introduction to his *Michael Servetus: A Case Study in Total Heresy,* Jerome Friedman writes: "During his [Servetus] short lifetime he was burnt in absentia by Catholic authorities as well as in the flesh by Protestants. The Spaniard's tumultuous life led George Williams to observe that Servetus 'was indeed the veritable effigy for Catholic and Protestant alike of all that seemed execrable in the Radical Reformation.' Even in an age of widespread dissent, Servetus' writings were considered an outrage. His name was so well known all over Europe that he assumed an alias in his search for refuge" (11).

Servetus, states Friedman, "was the complete heretic. Repudiating Rome, Wittenberg, Geneva and Zurich, Servetus also rejected infant baptism, Christ's humanity, original sin, conventional concepts of prophecy and Scripture and the orthodox trinity" (133). In the conclusion of his work on Servetus, Friedman observes that Servetus "anticipated a new age where the Archangel Michael would do successful battle with the Antichrist and bring down the empire of evil," but "Servetus did not live to see the world end for after being condemned by French Catholic authorities, he was executed by Protestant authorities in Geneva. His isolation was complete for he was wanted for questioning by agencies of the Spanish Inquisition and would have fared no better had he made his way to Lutheran Germany. Perhaps in recognition of his own lonely and anomalous position against the Antichrist's forces, Servetus considered withdrawing to the newly discovered America" (136).

The sentence condemning him to be burned along with his book concluded with references to Servetus's heretical "infections" and "stinking heretical poison[s]":

And you have had neither shame nor horror of setting yourself against the divine Majesty and the Holy Trinity, and so you have obstinately tried to infect the world with your stinking heretical poison.... For these and other reasons, desiring to purge the Church of God of such infection and cut off the rotten member, having taken counsel with our citizens and having invoked the name of God to give just judgment ... having God and Holy Scriptures before our eyes, speaking in the name of the Father, Son and Holy Spirit, we now in writing give final sentence and condemn you, Michael Servetus, to be bound and taken to Champel and there attached to a stake and burned with your book to ashes. And so you shall finish your days and give an example to others who would commit the like [Bainton 208–209].

As William Hamilton Drummond has indicated in his *The Life of Micheal Servetus,* "Accounts of the last moments of Servetus vary, as might be expected" (154). While some sources refer to the burning of Servetus's "books," other sources refer only to one "book." Willis has the court declaring in its sentencing of Servetus that he is to be fastened to a stake, "to be burned alive, along with thy books, printed as well as written by thy hand, until the body is reduced to ashes" (483). Cuthbertson writes that Servetus was to be burned alive, "along with his books, printed as well as written by hand" (48). Drummond refers to "the fatal book *Christianismi Restitutio*" being strapped to the thigh of Servetus: "His body was bound to the stake by an iron chain, his neck held by a strong rope so high that his feet just touched the ground, and to his thigh was strapped a copy of the fatal book *Christianismi Restitutio.* He entreated the executioner to give him as little pain as possible; but, as the fire was tedious in performing its office, after he had suffered for some time, one or more of the spectators, moved by compassion, supplied fresh fuel and in the course of half-an-hour the holocaust was completed" (156).

To Calvin, who had denounced Servetus, the burning of Servetus and his book was not enough: "After the execution, Calvin instructed the printer Robert Estienne to hunt down any remaining copies of *Christianismi Restitutio* and see that they were burned. It was Calvin's intention to eradicate Servetus's ideas along with the man. He almost succeeded" (Goldstone 199).

The widespread book burnings in Italy matched those taking place in England, France, Spain, and other European countries. Gigliola Fragnito has written of the "traumatic" effects of the massive book burnings in sixteenth and seventeenth century Italy: "The prohibition compelled them [Italians] to deprive themselves of texts used at home (and often also at school) to follow sermons and the liturgy in Latin and which had nourished their faith for generations. This loss constituted — the sources are explicit in this regard — a veritable trauma for the common people: a trauma made more painful by the fact that, during the periodic book burnings which lit up the piazzas of Italy with their sinister glow, they were obliged to watch their Bibles, their lectionaries, and their sacred stories fed to the flames together with book by the transalpine Reformers" (34).

Putnam cites more than one source indicating the widespread book burnings in Italy in the middle of the sixteenth century. One source reported: "There was everywhere such a conflagration of books, that one was reminded of the burning of Troy. Neither private nor public libraries were spared, and many were nearly emptied.... In all the cities of Italy readers were mourning for their lost treasures." Another source declared: "In Rome, Paul IV is burning books, among others, all the writings of Erasmus. Even the works of Cyprian, Jerome, and Augustine are included because they have been rendered pernicious through the notes of Erasmus" (Putnam I 177).

Grendler reports of several book burnings in 1548 and 1549. In July 1548, "several bales of books valued at 400 scudi (possibly close to 1,400 volumes), found in the house of an unidentified clandestine bookseller who had fled were burned publicly in Piazza San Marco and at the Rialto. The father inquisitor for the period 1542–50 stated that he had burned an 'indefinite number' of books during his tenure.... [I]n July 1548, the tribunal discovered three bales of heretical books belonging to Antonio Brucioli, including titles of Luther, Bibliander, Andreas Osiander, Erasmus Sarcerius, Urbanus Rhegius, and others. The books were burned on July 12, and on November 21" (Grendler 1977 82). One year later, "the Inquisition received a denunciation involving heretical books, opinions, and associates of Francesco Stella. The investigation uncovered a library of 59 titles, including the works of Luther, Melanchthon, Bullinger, and Joachim Vadianus, among northern Protestants; and

Ochino, Curione, Vergerio, Vermigli, Giulio della Rovere, and Francesco Negri, among Italian apostates, with the majority of books having been published in Basel and Geneva in the 1540s. Ignoring the other accusations, the tribunal fined Stella *in absentia* 50 ducats and burned the books" (Grendler 1977 84).

In addition to setting fire to "heretical" books in Italy, the Church reduced thousands of copies of the "blasphemous" Talmud to ashes. On August 12, 1553, the Church ordered the burning of the Talmud and other Hebrew works: "Executed in Rome, the Congregation of the Holy Office ordered the same throughout Italy on September 12. The Venetians willingly followed suit" (Grendler 1977 106). Then, on the morning of Saturday, October 21, 1553, "'a good fire' (in the nucio's words) burned in Piazza San Marco. In the next few months the Talmud and other works were burned as far away as Crete in the Venetian Dominion, while across Italy possibly hundreds of thousands of books were burned. The Venetian government burned the Talmud before all other parts of the papal state complied with Rome's order" (Grendler 106). In the September 1553 order calling for the widespread burning of the Talmud, the Cardinals' order "exhorted" "every Christian prince, every state ruler, every Ordinary, and every Inquisitor" to seek out all copies of the Talmud "throughout the homes and synagogues of the Hebrews who dwell in their respective states and countries, and when found, to be publicly burned" (Popper). During the rest of the sixteenth century and into the seventeenth, the Church continued ordering the Talmud and other similar works be burned.

Grendler provides a listing of the titles and number of books burned in Venice in the 1560s. Two thousand four hundred volumes of various Hebrew books were burned in the Piazza San Marco. For example, one thousand copies of *Or ha-Sekhel* were burned; up to eight bales of liturgical titles published by Zorzi de' Cavalli were burned; "the Esecutori ordered 4,400 folio volumes of the *Midhrash Rabba, Be'ur al hat-Torah, Seror Ha-Mor,* or *Ha-Sekhel,* and *Moroth Elohim* burned, as well as an indefinite number of our other titles (*Eben Ha-Ezer, Abudirham, Dol-bo,* and *Mahazor*) also burned. If nearly complete runs (800–1,000) of the last four titles were destroyed, the total number consigned to the flames was between 7,600 and 8,400 volumes" (Grendler 1978 114–118).

In 1555, Jesuit Francisco de Torres declared in his *De Sola Lectione,* a work addressed to the Inquisitors, that what copies of the Talmud remained needed to be burned, especially if the salvation of the Jews was to be achieved. He wrote: "Once these books are removed ... it will soon result that the more they are without that wisdom of their princes, that is, the rabbis, so much the more will they be prepared and disposed to receiving the faith and wisdom of the word of God. For when that wisdom — or rather the insanity of their traditions, of the Jewish fables, and of the commentaries— has been blotted from memory, they will easily understand the mysteries of Christ" (Stow 441).

In his "The Talmud in History," A.S. Isaacs refers to the "continuous persecution which it [Talmud] has encountered" and to the personification of the book: "Many are the instances in history when rude hands have been laid on a book to destroy it. It might have been a version of Scripture, a scientific treatise, a whole library which must be burnt to satisfy the adversary's wrath or piety. Such examples of 'slaying an immortality rather than a life,' belong to all ages and creeds. The peculiarity of the Talmud's fate, however, is the continuous persecution which it has encountered — as if principalities and powers wished to expiate their own transgressions on this literary scapegoat, this enigmatical work.... Thou art not a book, one of its mediaeval critics all but exclaims; thou art a rabbi. Beware of the spell!" (439).

Hebrew writings were similarly being burned in Spain, along with "Lutheran books";

and within decades in the sixteenth century, the Spanish were also burning the writings of the conquered indigenous natives in the newly found colonies in the Americas.

Lea begins his "Censorship" chapter in *A History of the Inquisition of Spain* with a reference to the burning of Hebrew writings: "[A]s early as 1490, it burnt a large number of Hebrew Bibles and other Jewish books and, soon afterwards in Salamanca, it consigned to the flames in an auto some six thousand volumes of works on Judaism and sorcery" (1988 III 480). At the same time, early in the sixteenth century, the Spanish were burning "Lutheran books," as Plaidy indicates: "Adrian of Utrecht, the Inquisitor-General, sent out a command that all Lutheran books in Spain be seized. There must have been some demand for these books for in 1524 a ship, which came from Holland and was bound for Valencia, was captured and brought into San Sebastian. Lutheran books were discovered among the cargo and publicly burned. Venetian ships also brought books into Granada; these were seized and burned and the captain and crews of the ships imprisoned" (1969 105).

In Spain edicts were published everywhere in 1557, writes Lea, ordering that "bookshops were to be sedulously searched and anyone found in possession of them [corrupt Bibles] was to be punished with the greatest severity. This was followed, September 2, 1558, by an additional list of books ordered to be burnt.... [T]he excitement over the Lutherans of Valladolid and Seville suggested a comprehensive prohibition of heretic books; Valdés procured from the pope the necessary delegation of power and, in 1559, the first indigenous Index appeared. It was distributed to the tribunals with instructions that all books contained in it were to be called in; those of heretic authors were to be publicly burnt in the autos, and the rest carefully stored, making lists of them and their owners" (Lea 1988 III 486).

On September 7, 1558, a *pragmatica* was issued because church authorities had fears that, as Lea reports, "there were many heretical works in circulation, and that foreign heretics were making great efforts thus to disseminate their doctrines, while there were also many useless and immoral books"; hence, "it was ordered, under penalty of death and confiscation, that no bookseller or other person should sell or keep any book condemned by the Inquisition and all such books should be publicly burnt" (1988 III 488).

In his discussion of this same period in Spain, M'Crie has written that in 1558, Inquisitor General Fernando Valdés, "in concurrence with the council of the Supreme [the inquisitor general and three legal counselors], prepared instructions to all the tribunals of the Inquisition, directing them, among other things, to search for heretical books, and to make a public auto-de-fe of such as they should discover, including many works not mentioned in any former prohibitory index. This was also the epoch of that terrible law of Philip which ordained the punishment of death, with confiscation of goods, against all who sold, bought, read, or possessed, any book that was forbidden by the Holy Office" (254).

Not satisfied with burning the heretical books and not satisfied with punishing by death those who sold, bought, read or possessed books "forbidden by the Holy Office," Pope Paul IV issued a bull on January 6, 1559, "enjoining all confessors strictly to examine their penitents of whatever rank, from the lowest to that of cardinal or king, and to charge them to denounce all whom they knew to be guilty of this offense, under the pain of the great excommunication, from which none but the pope or the inquisitor general could release them; and subjecting such confessors as neglected this duty to the same punishment that was threatened against their penitents" (M'Crie 255).

In 1547, Fernando de Valdés had been appointed archbishop of Seville and inquisitor general and in 1559 he ordered the seizure of Archbishop of Toledo Bartolome Carranza de Miranda's "Commentaries on the Christian Catechism" which Carranza's rivals within the Church condemned as containing "many propositions which are scandalous, rash and ill-sounding, others which savour of heresy, others which are erroneous, and even some which are heretical" (Kamen 1985 51). Valdés told his inquisitors, in part: "The *Commentaries of the Catechism of Christian Doctrine* in the vernacular by the archbishop of Toledo are to be collected. And in order for it not to appear as though you are making a special effort for only this book, you should publish edicts by which it is ordered that all books that touch on Christian doctrine in the vernacular published outside these kingdoms, from the year '50 onward, are to be confiscated" (Aspe 425). As Aspe has observed, "Valdés acted with an iron hand; soon it would be a fiery one. The burning of books in Valladolid transformed itself into the burning of 'Lutheran heretics'" (425).

Valdés and other rivals of Carranza "resented the rise of men of humble birth [like Carranza] to positions of influence" and who was besides that a "liberal" (Kamen 1985 157). Lea has written of Carranza: "Moreover he was earnest as a reformer within the Church, realizing abuses and exposing them fearlessly — in fact, he declared in the Prologue that his object was to restore the purity and soundness of the primitive Church, which was precisely what the heretics professed as their aim and precisely what the ruling hierarchy most dreaded. Worst of all, he did this in the vulgar tongue" (1988 II 55). Carranza was arrested and "on the night of 28 August Carranza was shuffled into the cells of the Inquisition in Valladolid" (Kamen 1985 158). And as Lea put it, "Carranza thus disappeared from human sight as completely as though swallowed by the earth" (Lea 1988 II 66). Carranza remained imprisoned for sixteen years, his "Commentaries" were condemned and prohibited and he was required to abjure his "errors." Having become ill, Carranza died on May 2, 1576.

A few years earlier Domingo de Guzman, before being sentenced to perpetual imprisonment, was condemned to view the burning of his extensive library containing Lutheran works. Guzman, who was a son of the duke de Medina Sidonia and who entered the order of St. Dominic, had acquired "the principal Lutheran publications which he lent and recommended with uncommon industry" (M'Crie 218). On July 10, 1563, "a public auto was celebrated in Seville, at which six persons were committed to the flames as Lutherans. Domingo de Guzman appeared among the penitents of this occasion.... [T]he inquisitors were resolved to prevent the advancement of one who had embraced the reformed tenets; and after causing his books, which exceeded a thousand volumes, to be burnt before his eyes, they condemned him to perpetual imprisonment" (M'Crie 326).

The Spanish did not confine their book burnings to European Spain once they had invaded and occupied the "discovered" lands in the Americas. The Spanish conquests in the "new world" brought with them the Inquisition and the burnings of Mayan and Mexican books, idols, and shrines. As Rule has put it, the Spanish authorities seemed to agree that "while the army was destroying the natives, the Church was to annihilate the sects" (II 13). In a 1537 letter from the first Bishop of Mexico, Don Fray Juan de Zumarraga, to his Majesty, reported that the "natives continue to use Gentile rites, especially in their superstitions, and idolatries or sacrifices, although not in public as they used to do but go by night to their oratories, cues, and temples which are not yet all destroyed, and in the inmost recesses of which they have their idols" (Rule II 14). Therefore, said the Bishop, "we ... beg your Majesty to be pleased to order that those lands, and property of their temples and oratories which their *papas* and ministers possessed, be applied to our use.... We beg that we may have authority to use the stones of their temples for building churches, and that we may have power to overturn and burn and destroy the idols that are to them, for by the First Commandment, we are all bound to destroy idolatry, and the *Latria,* or Christian religion, cannot be planted there until they are rooted up and separated from their rites" (Rule II 15). In 1538, Inquisitor Juan de Zumarraga, investigating idolatry in Mexico, conducted a public burning of the prohibited Indian idols and sacrificial paraphernalia. Three Indians who had been caught in possession of the prohibited items were gagged, subjected to a sermon of their errors, and ordered to abjure their sins publicly. Zumarraga then "warned that recurrent idolatry would mean death at the stake. Their property was to be confiscated, and on November 23 [1538] they were given one hundred lashes each in the market place of Mexico City and their hair shorn. On Sunday, November 24, 1538, Zumarraga preached the sermon at Atzcapozalco and the three Indians fulfilled their penance, kneeling and abjuring their sins. The idols and sacrificial paraphernalia were then burned before the assembled populace" (Greenleaf 57).

Writing about the Inquisition in Mexico, Plaidy refers to several heretics who were imprisoned, tortured, and burned at the stake during the 1500s. On occasion, the heretics were sent to the stake with their books to be reduced to ashes. One case involved a Petro Garcia "who had written three books, uneducated though he was, which were said to contain heresy. Garcia had been whipped through the streets and was condemned to be burned at the stake. He declared that he had been misjudged but would not ask for mercy. But he changed his mind at the end when he saw the faggots about to be lighted. He was strangled before his body was burned; and the books which he had written were tied about his neck so that they might burn with his body" (Plaidy 1969 69).

Further to the south, in Peru, another heretic was burned at the stake along with books he had written while imprisoned. Francisco Maldonado de Silva was brought up a Catholic but converted to the Jewish faith. After his devout Catholic sister denounced him to the Inquisition he was imprisoned and "during the years he spent in prison he made two books out of scraps of paper, pens from egg-shells and ink from charcoal. It was thirteen years before he was finally brought out of prison and burned alive. The books he had made were hung about his neck and burned with him" (Plaidy 1969 88). This 1639 auto-da-fé, states Plaidy, "was the most important that had yet been held in Peru, because on this occasion suffered many Jews who had been rounded up in what was called the 'complicidad grande'" (88).

The same dehumanizing metaphors that had been used to define heretics in Europe became part of the language condemning heretics in the Spanish colonies. In his 1649 *Jews and the Inquisition of Mexico,* reporting on the April 11, 1649, auto-da-fé held in Mexico City, Mathias de Bocanegra, S.J. presented a summary of "the proceedings by which 109 people, of whom 108 were Jews (some of whom were dead) were found guilty of practicing Judaism, by the tribunal in the viceroyalty of New Spain" (2). Bocanegra began by highly praising the *auto* and denouncing the Jews and "the scandals of the blasphemous Jews"; in his condemnation of the Jews, Bocanegra wrote: "They conceal the hidden poison that they bring from abroad which can corrupt the Catholic blood by chicanery or stain it with dishonor. By the mercy of God, the Holy Inquisition has stopped this peril by disclosing and bringing to light the concealed and deadly poison of so many perverse Hebrews who pretended to be Catholic Christians" (Bocanegra 22). The venom-poison metaphor was combined with the wolf and weed metaphors; all, of course, inviting extermination. Two paragraphs from the report illustrate the extent to which Bocanegra relied on the metaphors leading to destruction, especially by fire:

> And you, beloved Fatherland, and Mother Mexico and New Spain, who are so occupied with so many adherents of the dead law of Moses which they have extended to the most hidden and remote corners of your empire. You must stop it with all its venom and poison as it is covertly

spreading and expanding itself throughout your provinces, cities and towns, even the smallest ones. It would succeed if it were not for the holy zeal, continued vigilance and the greatest diligence of this Holy Tribunal and of the lords who attend it, who would have liberated you from the claws of the infernal wolves. You, who are comparable to a sheep from the flock and sheepfold of Jesus Christ and whom they wish to tear to pieces.

This Holy Tribunal has discovered the cunning, the tricks, deceptions and diabolical counsels of these wicked, lost men who are molesting you. This Holy Tribunal has been the antidote, the clearer of weeds, and a source of health against the venoms and poison with which they desire to oppress you and kill the life and faith of Jesus Christ [Bocanegra 33].

Venoms, poisons, weeds (tares), infernal wolves— this centuries-old figurative language became part of the language of oppression and eradication in the New World.

In 1562, Mayan books containing "superstitions and the lies of the devil" were set afire along with Mayan idols, the books and idols being identified with the devil and defined as "pagan rites." An original source describing the 1562 burning of Mayan books is Bishop Diego de Landa's 1566 *Relación de las Cosas de Yucatán* in which he wrote: "If it was the Devil who devised this count of *Katuns,* then he did so, as he is accustomed, for his own honor; and, if it was a man, he must have been a fine idolator because with these Katuns of theirs he devised all the principal deceits, divinations, and delusions under which these people labored, together with all the other misfortunes into which they had been tricked" (123). Landa then turns to the burning of the condemned books: "These people also used certain glyphs or letters in which they wrote down their ancient history and sciences in their books; and by means of these letters and figures and by certain marks contained in them, they could read about their affairs and taught others to read about them too. We found a great number of these books in Indian characters and because they contained nothing but superstition and the Devil's falsehoods we burned them all; and this they felt most bitterly and it caused them great grief" (124).

The book burning was part of an auto-da-fé that involved the burning of Mayans and their shrines. Landa, writes Leo Deuel, "had one consuming ambition: to stamp out all vestiges of pagan rites and religion.... At last, on July 12, 1562, he staged the auto-da-fe of Mani, at which Mayans of the old faith were burnt, together with some five thousand idols and the priceless native picture books that had been sedulously rounded up by the inquisitors" (527).

Regarding another book and idol burning that possibly took place in Yucatán, Tozzer has written: "The best known and most circumstantial account of the destruction of books, idols and other antiquities is one which cannot be traced back farther than 1805. Dr. Justo Sierra, in an Appendix to the second edition of Cogolludo's *Historia de Yucatán* ... writes: 'From some notes of D. Pablo Moreno and from a letter of a Yucatecan Jesuit, D. Domingo Rodriguez to Illmo. Sr. Estevez, dated Bologna, March 20, 1805 we are able without other authority to offer to our readers the following annotation of the objects some of which were destroyed and other burned: 5000 idols of different form and dimension; 13 great stones which served as altars; 22 small stones of various forms; 27 rolls of signs and hieroglyphics on deer skin; 197 vases of all sizes and shapes'" (Tozzer 78).

As Tozzer has observed, this "famous list has been republished several times" (Tozzer 78). In distinguishing this auto-da-fé from the Mani burnings, Tozzer states: "This detailed enumeration of objects destroyed by the Spanish friars, owing to their desire to stamp out the 'lies of the devil,' has usually been taken as referring holocaust described by Landa and, inferentially, to the *auto de fe* at Mani. We have seen that in all the testimony taken at this time there are constant references to the destruction of idols but none referring to 'rolls of signs and hieroglyphics on deer skin.' It should be added that even the three extant Maya codices are not written on deer skin but upon bark of a type of fig tree" (Tozzer 78).

Whether the burned Mayan books were of deer skin or fig tree bark, there is general agreement that in destroying the idols and burning the books, the Spanish invaders and inquisitors were attempting to Christianize the native population and to eradicate their culture and history.

Half way around the world in Goa, the Portuguese were setting afire the books and idols of the native population. In 1510, the Portuguese captured Goa and the Franciscans arrived seven years later to convert the Goans to Christianity. The Jesuits followed, with St. Francis Xavier who in 1545 wrote a letter to the King of Portugal declaring that the Inquisition was needed in Goa: "The second necessity for the Christians is that your majesty establish the Holy Inquisition, because there are many who live according to the Jewish law, and according to the Mohamedan sect, without any fear of God or shame of the world. And since there are many who spread all over the fortresses, there is a need of the Holy Inquisition and of many preachers. Your Majesty should provide such necessary things for your loyal and faithful subjects in India" (D'Souza 125).

Another priest wrote in 1551 to the Father General of Rome: "This is to inform your Paternity that the Inquisition is more necessary in these parts than anywhere else, since all the Christians here live together with the Muslims, the Jews and the Hindus and, also the largeness of the country itself causes laxness of conscience in persons residing therein. With the curb of the Inquisition they will live a good life. And since the people of this country set store in their honour, if they do not mend their ways from consideration of what they owe to God, they may do so at least out of fear of the disgrace and shame of prison and other penalties." Jews who had fled Spain and Portugal to escape persecution, found in Goa Church officials bent on "persecuting insidious Judaism" because some of the population was being "infected with Judaism" (Priolkar 24–25).

The Portuguese burned the books written in the vernacular in Goa not only for religious reasons, but also as a means of destroying the native population's culture. The Portuguese historian Cunha Rivara wrote of the concerted effort to destroy Goa's language and culture: "In the first heat of conquest, temples were destroyed, all emblems of the pagan cult were shattered to pieces and the books written in the vernacular were burnt for being guilty or suspected of containing precepts and doctrines of idolatry. The wish was to exterminate also the part of the population that did not convert itself immediately, and this was not the desire only of that period, but even after two centuries there were some who with magisterial pride advised such a measure to the government" (Cundha 81). In burning the temples the Portuguese destroyed works of literature. As Borges and Feldman observe: "The Portuguese destroyed much of the ancient Goan temple art along with its literature after their arrival here in the 16th century. The same report [by a Portuguese Jesuit] mentioned above spoke of how 'some of the temples were burnt down, others were heaped as garbage and others razed to the ground, nearly two hundred and eighty of these being big and some of these very sumptuously done and of exceedingly fine workmanship.' These were repositories of literature of a mainly religious nature and were centers of learning and teaching" (58).

"All books written in Sanskrit and Marathi, whatever their subject matter," writes Priolkar, "were seized by the Inquisition and burnt on the suspicion that they might deal with idolatry. It is probable that valuable non-religious literature dealing with art, literature, sciences, etc., was destroyed indiscriminately as a consequence." Church officials ordered that books brought from "Dutch and English ships, or those of any other foreign nation" be turned over to the authorities. The forbidden books were then set afire: "Boxes containing Prohibited Books were carried in procession during Auto da Fe and burnt" (Priolkar 176–177).

While Spanish, Portuguese, French, English, Italian and other European Catholics were burning heretical, blasphemous, and impious books in Europe and in the "new world," Protestants were setting fire to Catholic writings. The dissident Protestant Anabaptists, under the leadership of Jan Matthys, established in 1533 in Munster, Germany, a regime driving out Catholics and Lutherans. The Anabaptists were condemned by the Catholics as heretics and by the Protestant establishment for, as Levy has pointed out, "Protestant establishments regarded Anabaptists with fear and loathing too, although the Anabaptists sought to emulate the primitive church of the original apostles as they imagined it to have been. They were despised for their virtues. They believed that no true Christian should serve the state, which they considered a necessary evil administered by sinful men. They would not take any oaths, not even oaths of allegiance. As pacifists they would not kill, countenance the death penalty, or serve in armies (1993 59). The Anabaptist takeover of Munster in 1533 was followed by the looting of monasteries and churches and, as Norman Cohen writes, "in a nocturnal orgy of iconoclasm the sculptures and paintings and books of the cathedral were destroyed" (245). The Munster Anabaptists established a monopoly in the interpretation of Scriptures, in part, by burning manuscripts and books in 1534: "The Anabaptists boasted of their innocence of book-learning and declared that it was the unlearned who had been chosen by God to redeem the world. When they sacked the cathedral they took particular delight in defiling, tearing up and burning the books and manuscripts of its old library. Finally, in the middle of March, Matthys banned all books save the Bible. All other works, even those in private ownership, had to be brought to the cathedral-square and thrown upon a great bonfire" (Cohen 1957 290).

Matthys was killed in March 1534 and one year later the Anabaptists were defeated by armed forces supplied by the states of the Upper and Lower Rhine: "On the night of 24th June, 1535, the besiegers launched a surprise attack and penetrated into the town. After some hours of desperate fighting the last two or three hundred surviving male Anabaptists accepted an offer of safe-conduct, laid down their arms and dispersed to their homes, only to be killed one by one and almost to the last man in a massacre which lasted several days. All the leaders of Anabaptism in Munster perished.... The clergy were restored to their offices, the city became once more officially Catholic and to forestall any further attempts at autonomy the fortifications were razed to the ground" (Cohen 1957 305–306).

The burning of both Protestant and Catholic books in Germany during the sixteenth century also took place in Poland, even though the sixteenth century in Poland was referred to as its "golden century." For example, in his history of Poland, Jerzy Topolski has written: "[T]he 16th century can rightly be called the golden age of Polish culture" and "sixteenth century Poland was marked by high political culture, in a sense exceptional in Europe. There were neither persecution of religious dissenters nor political crimes; it was 'a state without stakes'" (68–69). Similarly, *The Cambridge History of Poland* states: "In the sixteenth century Poland had been, in many respects, the most liberal and tolerant country in Europe. Not only was it open and friendly to the main Reformation currents; but it also became a refuge and a haven to all sorts of extremists" (Fox 436).

However, this "golden age" in Poland included the burning of books, paintings, and statues, both Catholic and Protestant. Janusz Tazbir reports that in 1546 "Catholic churches were turned into Protestant ones by the local squires, some Catholic religious articles such as statues and painting were burnt" (58). In 1564, "Sigismund August, at the request of the

Calvinists, ordered the burning in the Warsaw market square of Gregory Paul's treatise about the Trinity (*Tabula de Trinitate*), which advocated the Antitrinitarian principles deeply resented by the Calvinists at the time.... Twenty years later a book by Christian Francken, a man at odds with everyone else, was burnt in Cracow. Jacob Gorski, professor of the Cracow Academy, saw in the work against the dogma of the Holy Trinity such blasphemy that he advised the king to exile the author and destroy the entire printing. This was done and only two copies of Francken's book are known to have survived to this day, while the author fled to Transylvania" (Tazbir 140).

In their "The Book and the Reformation in Poland," Kawecka-Gryczowa and Tazbir refer to several other works that were set afire in Poland, with Catholics burning Protestant books and Protestants burning Catholic books. For example, they write: "Alongside supporters of Calvin, [the small city] Pinczow also housed foreign newcomers who brought ideological turmoil with them, as did Francesco Stancaro in particular. Antitrinitarian ideas grew up from debates of Stancaro's ideas on the mediation of Christ. His book *Collatio doctrinae Arii et Melanchtonis det sequacium* was burnt in 1558. This was the first occurrence of Protestant censorship" (414).

In reference to two other book burnings, Kawecka-Gryczowa and Tazbir write: "In spite of the proliferation of Protestant presses, the ecclesiastical authorities did not abandon their struggle against heretical books. They invented new procedures, such as the one known by historians as 'literary execution.' This involved burning confiscated books in public, but this practice was rarely carried out by civil powers.... In 1554, Marcin Krowlicki's *Christian Remonstrances* were burnt in front of Przenysl Cathedral. The 'literary execution' which took place in 1581 in Vilna by the order of the bishop, Jerzy Radziwill, had a particularly large impact, although the books which were burnt had been bought not confiscated" (424).

In Cracow, "in October 1574 the interior of the Protestant church ... was ransacked. The books were piled on a bonfire and burnt to the accompaniment of a choral *Te Deum Laudamus*" (Tazbir 104). Four years later, the Poznan Lutheran printer Melchior Nering began the printing of the "anti–Jesuit *Diatribe* by Jacob Niemojewski, a Calvinist." The Jesuits accused him of printing a heretical book, but the city council took no action against Nering whereupon "the servants of the bishop of Poznan, Lucas Koscielecki, then demolished Nering's shop and the episcopal court sentenced him to the stocks and whipping and the book to be burnt. The printing of *Diatribe* was interrupted and only two copies saved" (Tazbir 141). This book burning was followed with the public burning of *Equitis Poloni in Jesuitas actio primo* (Polish Nobleman's First Speech Against the Jesuits) and in 1614 with the burning of "the *Monita primata*, an anti–Jesuit book by Jerome Zahorowsky" (Tazbir 141).

Calvinists in Poland, write Kawecka-Gryczowa and Tazbir, "rather rapidly began to use the Catholic methods to fight against heretical works, although on a much more modest scale.... In 1556, Prince Mikolaj Radziwill bought up a large part of the print-run of Piotre of Goniadz's *De filio Dei homine Jesu Christo*, in order to burn it. The work is now known only through its title. However these were relatively rare events in Poland. Books were burned, rather than their authors or printers, while in western Europe people often perished with their works" (425–426).

Across Europe, during the middle and latter part of the sixteenth century, the interests of the ecclesiastical and secular authorities increasingly converged. As Lea points out: "The organization of the Inquisition was so complete, and the terror which it inspired so profound, that the State frequently used its [Inquisition's] censorship to suppress writings purely political, which one would have supposed the secular authorities amply able to deal with. The Inquisition assumed to itself this function from a passage in the instructions of Clement VIII ordering the expurgation of matters derogatory to the prince, and ecclesiastics, and contrary to good morals and Christian discipline.... In November, 1642, it prohibited and burnt a manifesto in which the Catalans accused the royal favorite Olivares of causing all the misfortune in Spain" (1967 83).

The burning of impious, heretical, blasphemous books because they not only contributed to the undermining of religion, but also because they threatened the stability of government and society had been going on for centuries. As indicated at the outset of this chapter, Stone observed that in both Greek and Roman societies "not to recognize the city's gods was to be disloyal to the city" and Levy similarly stated that "treason against the gods was close to treason against the state." By the 1600s, English jurists would be arguing that "the ecclesiastic is the prime part of the Government of England" (Nokes 43) and "to reproach the Christian religion is to speak in subversion of the law" (Nokes 48).

Before the sixteenth century was over, various royal proclamations ordered the burning of books that were not only blasphemous or heretical, but also because they were "lewd, heretical and seditious." These proclamations were issued in addition to others that simply "banned" the books or prohibited their importation and circulation or called for the "destruction" of the condemned works. However, several royal proclamations called specifically for the burning of the works containing errors condemned by both church and state.

In 1546, Henry VIII's proclamation began: "The King's most excellent majesty, understanding how under pretense of expounding and declaring the truth of God's Scripture, diverse, lewd and evil-disposed persons have taken occasion to utter and sow abroad, by books imprinted in the English tongue, sundry pernicious and detestable errors and heresies, not only contrary to the laws of this realm, but also repugnant to the true sense of God's law and his word" (Hughes and Larkin 1 373). To purge "his majesty's dominions" of the "corrupt and pestilent teaching" and "pernicious doctrines," the Proclamation ordered the burning of the works of several authors, including Tyndale, Frith, Wycliffe, Bale, Barnes, and Coverdale (Hughes and Larkin 1 374–375).

In 1555, another royal proclamation, this time issued by King Philip and Queen Mary, calling for the burning of books, linked the heresies and "false doctrines" with the preservation and safety of the "good and loving subjects": "The King and Queen our sovereign lord and lady therefore (most entirely and earnestly tendering the preservation and safety, as well of the souls as of the bodies, lands, and substance of all their good and loving subjects and others, and minding to root out and extinguish all false doctrine and heresies and other occasions of schisms, diversions, and sects that dome by the same heresies and false doctrine) straightly charge and command that no person or persons ... from henceforth presume to bring or conveyor cause to be brought or conveyed into this realm any books, writings, or works hereafter mentioned." Among the twenty-seven authors mentioned in this Proclamation were Luther, Bucer, Coverdale, Tyndale, Cranmer, Frith and Peter Martyr. The Proclamation not only called for the burning of the books and writings of these condemned authors, it also declared that the authorities were empowered to "inquire and search out the said books, writings, and works, and for this purpose enter into the house or houses, closets, and secret places of every person of whatsoever degree being negligent in this behalf and suspected to keep any such book, writing, or works contrary to this proclamation" (Hughes and Larkin ll 59).

The linkage between heretical and seditious books was most clearly expressed three years later in another Philip and Mary Proclamation:

Whereas divers books filled both with heresy, sedition, and treason have of late and be daily brought into this realm out of foreign countries and places beyond the seas, and some also printed within this realm and cast abroad in sundry parts thereof, whereby not only God is dishonored but also an encouragement given to disobey lawful princes and governors: The King and Queen's majesties, for redress hereof, doth by this their present proclamation declare and publish to all their subjects that whosoever shall, after the proclaiming hereof, be found to have any of the said wicked and seditious books, or finding them do not forthwith burn the same without showing or reading the same to any other person, shall in that case be reputed and taken for a rebel, and shall without delay be executed for that offense, according to the order of martial law [Hughes and Larkin 2 90–91].

In 1580, Queen Elizabeth devoted a Proclamation entirely to an attack on the religious community known as The Family of Love which, according to the Proclamation, was "maintained by certain lewd, heretical and seditious books" which the Queen ordered burned. The condemned books written by the founder of The Family of Love, Hendrik Niclas, included *Evangelium Regni, or a Joyful Message of the Kingdom, Documental Sentences, The Prophecy of the Spirit of Love, A Publishing of the Peace Upon the Earth.* In denouncing the "sect," the Queen's Proclamation declared, before calling for the burning of the books: "[H]er majesty, being very sorry to see so great an evil by the malice of the devil first begun and practiced in other countries to be now brought into this her realm, and that by her bishops and ordinaries she understandeth it very requisite not only to have these dangerous heretics and sectaries to be severely punished, but that also all other means be used by her majesty's royal authority, which is given her of God to defend Christ's church, to root them out from further infecting of her realm" (Hughes and Larkin 2 474).

The Queen commanded both temporal and ecclesiastical authorities that "search be made in all places suspected for the books and writings maintaining the said heresies and sects, and them destroy and burn" (Hughes and Larkin 2 475). Further, imprisonment and "bodily punishment" awaited anyone who printed or brought the condemned books into the realm.

Three years later, specifically condemning the writings of Robert Browne and Robert Harrison as "seditious, schismatical, and erroneous," Elizabeth declared in her 1583 Proclamation that the works of Browne and Harrison "do manifestly contain in them very false, seditious, and schismatical doctrine and matter, and have notwithstanding been secretly sold, published, and dispersed in sundry places within this realm, to the end to breed some schism among her majesty's subjects, being persons unlearned and unable to difference the errors therein contained." Linking "the peace of the church, the realm and the quietness of her people," the Proclamation concluded with the command "that all manner of persons whatsoever, who have any of the said books or any of like nature in his or their custody, that they and every of them do forthwith, upon the publishing hereof, bring in and deliver up the same unto the ordinary of the diocese or of the place where they inhabit, to the intent they may be burned or utterly defaced by the said ordinary" (Hughes and Larken 2 501–502).

Both Browne and Harrison, who had opposed the absolutism of the Catholic Church, became strong critics of the Church of England. As Leland Carlson has pointed out, "Harrison denounced the ministers of the Established Church as blind guides.... He accuses them of submitting without resistance to ceremonies, mumbled prayers, popish traditions, fees, and seals" (Peel and Carlson 10).

Browne had written in one of his books, *A Treatise of Reformation Without Tarying for Anie:* "We say ... and often have taught, concerning our Sovereign Queen Elizabeth, that neither the Pope, nor other Popeling, is to have any authority over her, or over the Church of God, and that the Pope of Rome is Antichrist, whose kingdom ought utterly to be taken away. Again, we say, that her authority is civil, and that power she has as highest under God within her Dominions, and that over all persons and causes" (Peel and Carlson 152). As Carlson has pointed out, "Browne's emphasis on Elizabeth's civil power, and his denunciation of the pope as antichrist, were calculated to elicit general approval, but they were irrelevant to the real question — the role of the civil power in ecclesiastical affairs. Browne's position was that neither Queen Elizabeth nor Parliament had jurisdiction over the church. The spiritual kingdom is not subservient to earthly rules.... Browne certainly wishes the magistrates to wield the civil sword, but he denounced their use of religious powers, which the clergy have surrendered so cravenly. This usurpation hinders the reformation of the church.... Therefore, the clergy should realize their obligation of reforming the church without tarrying for the commands of the magistrate" (Peel and Carlson 16). The same year the Queen's Proclamation was issued, forty copies of the works of Browne and Harrison were set afire and two printers, Coppin and Thacker, were hanged for dispersing the books (Peel and Carlson 2).

The various royal proclamations were issued; the book burnings followed. In some cases the books, but not the authors, were set afire. In other cases, books and authors were burned separately. In still other instances, authors and books were set afire together. And in some cases, the disinterred bones of the authors were burned along with the dead man's books. In the case of Martin Bucer, condemned in the royal proclamation of 1555, along with other writers, Bucer's bones were dug up and burned along with his books. In his *Acts and Monuments,* Foxe devotes several pages to Bucer and friend Paul Fagius in which he refers to the books that were ordered to be searched out and thrown into the fire with the remains of Bucer and Fagius. Of the actual burning of the disinterred bodies of Bucer and Fagius and their books, Foxe wrote:

> The vice-chancellor ... taking with him Marshal the common notary, went first to St. Michael's church, where Phagius [Fagius] was buried. There he called forth Andrew Smith, Henry Sawyer, and Henry Adams, men of the same parish, and bound them with an oath, to dig up Phagius's bones, and to bring them to the place of execution. [The same being done to Bucer.] Smith, the mayor of the town, which should be their executioner, commanded certain of his townsmen to wait upon him in harness, by whom dead bodies were guarded; and being bound with ropes, and laid upon men's shoulders (for they were enclosed in chests, Bucer in the same that he was buried, and Phagius in a new), they were borne into the midst of the market-stead, with a great train of people following them. This place was prepared before, and a great post was set fast in the ground to bind the carcasses to, and a great heap of wood was laid ready to burn them withal. When they came thither, the chests were set up on end with the dead bodies in them, and fastened on both sides with stakes, and bound to the post with a long iron chain, as if they have been alive. Fire being forthwith put to, as soon as it began to flame round about, a great sort of books that were condemned with them were cast into the same [Foxe 8 283].

Bucer, a one-time Dominican who became a Protestant reformer, had died on March 1, 1551, and as Hopf reports, years later, "A warrant 'de haeretico comburdeno' was issued against Bucer and his friend Paul Fagius. The bones were dug out, chained and burnt at the market-place in Cambridge on a day (February 6th) when all the people from outside Cambridge came to the town, as it was market day. The peasants were amazed at details of the procedure, and could not understand why the bones, which certainly could not run away, had to be chained. With the bones, heaps of books of heretical content by the two reformers and others were burnt" (30). Bucer's enemies hated him, writes Hopf, because "he had spurned the monastery himself, they hated him because he taught heresy, and they hated him because he was an outsider who threatened to steal their power away." Further, Bucer had drawn up a list of articles that his enemies saw as heretical: "These articles attacked traditional rites and practices; such as, the intercession of saints, the mass, prayers for the dead, singing in a foreign language, compulsory celibacy, and the secular power of the clergy" (15). When several witnesses spoke against Bucer and Fagius during the disinterment process and nobody spoke in their defense, "their dead bodies were dug up, and delivered to the Queen's officers.... After the pile [of chests with the dead bodies] was set on fire, they threw a great number of books of the Protestants into it, which they had gathered together, which were soon consumed by the spreading flames" (Baker 344).

Baker provides still another example, this time from Italy, of the burning of a heretic's remains, along with his books. In his 1736 work *Complete History of the Inquisition in Portugal, Spain, Italy, the East and West Indies in All Its Branches from the Origin of It in the Year 1163, to Its Present State,* Baker, after referring to the Wycliffe disinterment and the burning of his bones and after describing the Bucer and Fagius burning, Baker describes the burning of the dead body of Mark Anthony de Dominis and his books in the Campo Fiore. Early in the seventeenth century, the books of Mark Anthony were condemned as heretical in Rome. While he abjured his heresies there were suspicions that his abjuration was feigned. Whereupon he became ill and died. However, his "trial" continued and it was decided that he had died a relapsed heretic. In 1624, the sentence against Anthony was announced and the burning of his corpse, his effigy, and books followed:

> Things thus disposed, a certain parson mounted the pulpit and with a shrill voice, which rung through all parts of the spacious church, and in the vulgar language, that the common people might understand him, read over a summary of the process, and the sentence by which the Cardinals Inquisitors General, specially deputed for the affair by the Pope, pronounced Mark Anthony, as relapse into heresy.... [A]nd cast him out of the ecclesiastical court; delivered over his dead body and effigies into the power of the governor of the city, that he might inflict on it the punishment due, according to the rule and practice of the Church. And finally, they commanded his impious and heretical writings to be publicly burnt, and declared all his effects to be forfeited to the Exchequer of the holy Inquisition. After this sentence was read, the governor of the city and his officers threw the corpse, effigies, and aforesaid writings into a cart, and carried them into the Campo Fiore, a great multitude of people following after. When they came there, the dead body, which as yet in all its members was whole and entire, was raised out of the chest as far as the bottom of the breast, and shown from on high to the vast concourse of people that stood about, and was afterwards with the effigies and bundle of books, thrown into the pile prepared for the purpose, and there burnt [Baker 349].

In 1553 Servetus had been burned at the stake along with his books. In 1555 the books of Bucer and Fagius were burned along with their disinterred bones. While the bones of William Thomas, author of *A Historie of Italie* (1549) which contained passages offensive to Queen Mary, were not dug up to be burned with his book, he was hanged, beheaded, and quartered before his book was later burned. Thomas's 1549 work, the first English book dealing with Italy, was, as reported in *the Dictionary of National Biography,* "said to have been 'suppressed and publicly burnt,' probably after Thomas's execution" (*DNB* 19 674). What may have offended the Catholic Queen were Thomas's descriptions of the ceremonies and behavior of the Church and priests in Rome. For example, Thomas wrote: "Indeed the Bishop for his own ordinary keepeth a great house, but his train exceedeth all that I have seen.... And lightly there is none of them [cardinal and prelates] without three or four pages trimmed like young princes, for what purpose I would loath to tell" (Thomas 50). Further, as Thomas stated: "If I should say that under their long robes they hide the greatest pride of the world, it might happen some men would believe it, but that they are the vainest men of all other their own acts do well declare." And perhaps most objectionable to the Queen would be the following Thomas observation: "Briefly, by report Rome is not without 40,000 harlots, maintained for the most part by the clergy and their followers" (50). Eventually, Thomas was suspected of conspiring against Queen Mary, was brought to trial, and found guilty of treason. On May 18, 1554, Thomas was "drawn upon a sled to Tyburn, where he was hanged, beheaded, and quartered.... On the following day his head was set on London Bridge ... and quarters set over Crepullgate whereabouts he had perhaps previously lived" (DNB 19 676).

In the latter half of the sixteenth century, there was no let-up in the burnings of heretics and their books. In fact, increasingly, church and state authorities attempted to control the printing, distribution and possession of not only heretical-blasphemous books, but also seditious-heretical and immoral-seditious works. In the last decade of the sixteenth century, book burnings were taking place across Europe.

In 1576, the Stationers' Company adopted an order calling for the burning of books proscribed by the authorities; the order provided that "a search of all London printing houses be made once a week by the searchers.... They were required to make a weekly report showing what work each printer was then engaged in, how many impressions he made, for whom they were printed, how many apprentices were kept.... All unlawful books seized by the searchers were taken to the Stationers' Hall where they were inspected by the ecclesiastical officers. If they were merely infringement of patents or copyrights, they were turned over to the proper owner, but if they were books proscribed by the authorities they were burnt" (Siebert 84–86).

In 1586, the Archbishop of Canterbury was "wielding censorship power vested in him by the Star Chamber. No printing was allowed outside London, Oxford and Cambridge.... And in 1599 a translation of Ovid's *Elegies* by Christopher Marlowe was burning at Stationers' Hall by order of the Archbishop — and this, at last, *was* on the grounds of obscenity" (Rolph 30).

Of the repression in Spain in the sixteenth century, Lea has written: "What between its censorship and the minute supervision, which exposed to prosecution every thought or expression in which theological malevolence could detect lurking tendencies to error, the Spanish thinker found his path beset with danger. Safety lay only in the well-beaten track of accepted conventionality.... The splendid promise of the sixteenth century was blasted by the steady repression of all and progress, and, from the foremost of the nations, became the last" (Lea 1988 4 148).

In July 1560, French printer Martin Lhomme was convicted of publishing seditious pamphlets, was executed in Paris after the authorities "discovered under his bed a pamphlet entitled *Le Tigre* directed against the cardinal of Lorraine. A large crowd turned out to see Lhomme hanged and the condemned booklets burned on the place Maubert. A stranger in "the crowd, Robert Delors, was heard to make some remarks which led nearby priests to call him a "Huguenard" (Huguenot); the crowd assaulted him, and the authorities imprisoned him. Four days later ... Robert Delors was pronounced guilty of blaspheming against God and 'the Glorious Virgin Mary' and provoking public scandal and sedition. He was executed that same day on the place Maubert, on the very spot where Martin Lhomme had been hanged" (Diefendorf 56).

In 1559, Richard Breton, a Paris printer and bookseller who had participated in trading prohibited books, "fell under suspicion of the Parisian authorities" and in 1562 "a quantity of censured books was found in his house and he was ordered arrested, along with his wife and half a dozen presumed associates in the illicit trade. Since Breton had already left town on account of the religious conflicts, proceedings against him continued in absentia. The confiscated books were publicly burned in front of his house" (Diefendorf 132).

In Italy, Francesco Stella was accused of possessing a box full of heretical works, including *Martin Luther de Capivitate babilonicha, Nova methodux, Erasmi Savarii, Sermones Bernardini Ochini,* and *Le prediche del Occhino,* all of which, plus scores of others, were condemned to be burned in 1550. Stella was tried, found guilty, and part of the sentence called for burning of the books found in the box. The sentence read: "1. Books to be burned publicly in Piassa permeso la Gesia this morning [January 2, 1550]. 2. Stella within ten days of the publication of this sentence is to pay fifty ducats fine into our office. 3. If he fail to do so he is to be banished from Venice and from Portobuffole for three years. 4. Fine to be exacted from his property. 5. If he break confines, six months in the prison called Liona" (Brown 1891 120–121)

During the last decade of the sixteenth century, Hebrew works were being set afire, as they were decades earlier. In 1591, "the Nuncio in Savoy was ordered to make known to all the Inquisitors of the state the attitude of the central office, and its desire to have the Talmud and other forbidden works burned" (Popper 73). In 1592, the Talmud was reduced to ashes after a notification to the Inquisitor of Vercelli (in Piedmont), to "enforce the decree against the Talmud and similar writings, and by April 4th the Nuncio had satisfied Rome that the auto-da-fe had taken place" (Popper 73). In 1593, after the Talmud burnings in Piedmont, an edict was issued forbidding Jews "to dwell anywhere in papal territory except in Rome, Ancona, and Avignon"; it was ordered "that in Rome all books containing offensive references or heresies must be surrendered within ten days, in other places within two months; they were then to be burnt, while excommunication and confiscation of property were to be punishment for possessing them, or helping others to possess them by printing, copying, sale, or gift" (Popper 74). In 1592, Jewish homes were searched for forbidden books and works that "violated the provisions of the Index" and they were ordered "burnt, and the offenders required to pay a large fine" (Popper 92).

Jean Bodin's *Republic* (*Six Books of the Commonwealth*) was condemned and burned in Italy in the last decade of the sixteenth century. Bodin was mistrusted by the Catholic League and was subjected to two "inquisitions"; his house was searched in January 1590 and as a result "certain books from his library were publicly burned" (McRae A 11). Published in 1576, Bodin's *Republic,* as M.J. Tooley writes, marked the transition "from specifically medieval to specifically modern ways of political thinking.... He [Bodin] recognized the emergence of the state as the all-important and all-powerful instrument of men's fate" (Bodin 1955 xxxix). Of Bodin's religious inclinations, McRae observes: "True religion, he [Bodin] proclaims several times, is strictly a personal affair, the turning of an individual mind towards God. It is best practiced in solitude, requires no outward Church, and by its very nature cannot be interfered with by the state. The point is stressed more often in the later writings, but it is also stated clearly in the early years when he was closer to Protestantism. This conjoining belief in the primacy of a personal religion divorced from any church must be considered as the fundamental tenet of Bodin's religious thought" (McRae A 13). While his *Republic* was primarily a work dealing with political theory, Bodin was seen by his contemporaries as either a skeptic or an atheist.

In 1592, the Cardinal of Santa Severina wrote a letter in which he ordered the burning of Bodin's *Republic*: "I seize this opportunity to remind your reverence that from the year 1591 by order of Gregory XIII of blessed memory, the *Republic* of Jean Bodin was prohibited in whatever language it might be found or translated, since it is a work full of errors and impieties, even though it is said to have been corrected and emended. Therefore, your reverence will show diligence and give express orders that it be neither read nor possessed and that any [copies] found should be burned" (Tedeschi 279).

Meanwhile, in Holland, in 1598, Polish nobleman Andreas Wojdowski and "another anti–Trinitarian, Christopher Ostorodt, arrived in Amsterdam on their way to Leiden to bring a chest of Socinian books to the Polish students there. The Amsterdam magistrates seized the books and sent them to the Hague, from which they were sent to the Leiden theological faculty for assessment. The Calvinist professor Franciscus Gomarus and his colleagues condemned the books for 'Turkish doctrine,' the books were ordered burned and Wojdowski and Ostorodt were given ten days to leave the country" (Bangs 82). Among other reasons, the Calvinists and others found the Socinians' denial of the doctrine of the Trinity as blasphemous, hence the burning of their books.

In the last year of the last decade of the sixteenth century, the Stationers' Company in England "proscribed nine titles in addition to all of 'Nasshes bookes and Doctor Harveys books wheresoever they may be found.' On June 1, 1599 seven of the titles listed were 'burnte in the hall': John Marston's *Metamorphosis of Pigmalion's image* and *The scourge of villanie;* Edward Guilpin's *Skialetheia or a shadow of truth;* John Davies' *Epigrammes and Elegies; Microcynicon, Sixe snarlinge satyres; The booke against woemen* and Antoine de La Sale's *Fiftene joyes of maryage*" (Rostenberg 84–85).

In reference to the burning of these satires, John Peter wrote in 1956 that the satirists John Marston and Edward Guilpin "had popularized a new and thoroughly undesirable style of writing, and to the authorities it must have been only too obvious that, if nothing were done to check it, the infection was likely to spread farther and farther afield. As everyone knows, they took action in an edict issued on 1 June 1599. *Virgidemiae, Pigmalions Image, The Scourge of Villanie, Skialetheia,* and *Micro-Cynicon* were all to be brought immediately to the Bishop of London and to be burned, and so were Thomas Cuwode's *Caltha Poetarum,* Sir John Davies's *Epigrams* (with Marlowe's *Elegies,* which they accompanied), R.T.'s translation called Of *Marriage and Wiving,* and a book called *The XV joyes of marriage* that has not survived.... On the fourth of June, another entry in the Stationers' Register informs us, Marston's two books, *Skialetheia, Micro-Cynicon,* Davies's *Epigrams* and the two books on marriage were duly burned" (Peter 148). At the same time the satires were being set afire, the Archbishop and the Bishop of London ordered that no satires henceforth were to be printed unless a specific license had been issued. "This action," Kernan has written, "silenced many of the earlier satiric authors" (82).

Why these satirical works were burned was not always clear; they may have been burned because they were considered obscene or immoral or libelous or politically dangerous. As Peter has explained: "G.B. Harrison maintains that 'the burning of the satirical books was the direct sequel to the affair of Hayward's *Henry the Fourth*' (a book which Elizabeth herself took strong exception to, on the grounds that it was likely to encourage treason and insurrection), and he also says: 'Of these eleven works, four were indecent, seven satirised recognisable individuals under feigned names.' Davenport, too, in his edition of Hall's *Poems,* suggests that the censorship was designed to put down libel and 'the evident tendency ... of satirical writing to ramify from personalities into dangerous criticism of contemporary political and social affairs,' that he adds that it may also 'possibly' have been intended to discourage the publication of erotic literature" (148).

The massive book burnings of the sixteenth century were a prelude to the continued massive book burnings of the seventeenth century. Books were being set afire in the seventeenth century in such places as Holland, Spain, England, Poland, Japan, Peru, France, and Italy. The sixteenth century ended in 1599 with the trial of Giordano Bruno and the seventeenth century began with Bruno being burned at the stake along with his books.

Early in 1599, Bruno was charged with heresy and after he refused to recant he and his books were set afire on February 16, 1600. As Arthur Imerti has summarized in his Introduction to *The Expulsion of the Triumphant Beast: Giordano Bruno*: "[O]n January 14, 1599, eight heretical propositions which Vatican theologians had extracted from his [Bruno's] works, were read to the defendant. The crisis in the embattled life of Giordano Bruno of Nola had reached its climax. On January 18 he was allowed a period of six days in which to recant; but in his reply on January 25, he stubbornly insisted upon the right to defend his views. He declared on December 21, 1599, that 'he did not want to, nor did he wish to retract'; nor was there 'anything to retract'" (63).

The early charges that became the basis of the Church's case against Bruno are summarized by Imerti: "[Giovanni] Mocenigo made the following accusations: Bruno maintained that the Catholic faith is 'full of blasphemy against the majesty of God'; 'that there are infinite worlds'; that all the operations of the world are guided by fate'; and that 'souls created through the operation of nature pass from one animal to another'" (48). Bruno was further accused of having "branded all monks as 'asses,' and Catholic doctrines as 'asinine'; that he considered a blasphemy the Catholic teaching that bread is tranmuted into flesh; that he disapproved of the sacrifice of the Mass, stating that 'there is no punishment of sins'; that he denied the possibility of the Virgin Birth" (48).

Bruno, a former Dominican, was influenced by the teachings of Copernicus and as Edward Peters has observed: "When Bruno took up the ideas of Copernicus, he did so not as a mathematician or an astronomer, but as a *magus* who professed to find in Copernicus a set of physical arguments that corroborated his own larger and cosmic vision" (1998 244). The Church excommunicated Bruno and ordered "his books should be publicly burned, and their titles placed upon the *Index*" (Imerti 64). Bruno and his books were burned at the Campo di Fiori on February 16, 1600 and his "ashes were scattered to the winds" (Riehl 105).

The first decade of the seventeenth century witnessed not only the burning of Bruno's writings in Italy, but also the burning in 1600 in London of the works of preacher and exorcist John Darrell and satirist Samuel Rowlands. In 1600, Rowlands published his *The Letting of Humours Blood in the Head-Vaine* which consisted of "thirty-seven epigrams and seven satires on the abuses of contemporary society. Private persons are attacked under feigned Latin names, and types of character are depicted with incisive power. A similar effort, entitled 'A mery Meetinge, or 'tis mery when Knaves mete,' was published in the same year.... Rowland's biting tone was deemed offensive to the authorities, and both pamphlets were burnt not only in a public place, but also in the kitchen of the Stationers' Company on 26 Oct. 1600" (DNB 353). The order to burn the writings declared that these two books (*The Letting of Humours Blood* and *A Mery Meetinge*)" shalbe publiquely burnt the whole Impressions of them for that they conteyne matters unfyhtt to be published. They [are] to be burnt in the hall kytchen with other popishe bookes & things that were lately taken" (Gillett 1932 92).

While Rowland's writings were set afire because of the severity of his satire, John Darrell's *A true narration of the Strange and Grevous Vexation by the Devil of Seven Persons in Lancashire* was burned the same day. As Rostenberg has indicated, exorcist Darrell's book was "consigned to the flames at the same time. Darrell's 'pestiferous opinions,' according to a contemporary report, had been 'lately broached abroad in pamphlets and printed apologies pass[ed] underhand in the public view of rag and tag'" (85). Darrell, having taken part in an exorcism in 1596, "was suspected of complicity on the boy's false seizures" and was condemned as a fraud. In Notingham, where the exorcism had taken place, disturbances occurred between those who saw Darrell as a fraud and those who supported him, the disturbance providing the Archbishop the excuse to bring Darrell before an ecclesiastical court. Darrell appeared before a church commission in May 1593 and "was pronounced an imposter, and, along with George More, one of his confederates, degraded from the ministry and committed to the Gatehouse. He remained in prison for at least a year, but it is not known what became of him" (DNB V 517).

Three years later, Reginald Scott's *The Discovery of Witchcraft* was ordered burned by King James I: "All copies of the first edit. 1584, that could be found were burnt by the order of K. James I. an author on the other side of the question" (Wood 1 679). The full title of Scott's *Discovery* read:

> The discouerie/of witchcraft,/Wherein the lewde dealing of witches/and witchmongers is notablie detected, the/knauerie of conjurors, the impietie of inchan-/tors, the follie of south-saiers, the impudent fals-/hood of cousenors, the infidelitie of atheists,/the pestilent practises of Pythonists, the/curiositie of figure casters, the va-/nitie of dreamers, the begger-/lie art of Alcu-/mystrie,/The abhomination of idolatrie, the hor-/rible art of poisoning, the vertue and power of/naturall magike, and all conueiances/of Legierdemaine and juggling are deciphered:/and many other things opened, which/have long lien hidden, howbeit/verie necessarie to ' be knowne./Heerunto is added a treatise upon the/nature and substance of spirits and devils/&c.: all latelie written/by Reginald Scot/Esquire./I. John. 4, 1./Beeleeve not euerie spirit, but trie the spirits, whether they are/of God; for manie false prophets are gone/out into the world &c./1584 [Scott 1930 xxxiii].

As the entry in the DNB observes: "With remarkable boldness and an insight that was far in advance of his age, he [Scott] set himself to prove that the belief in witchcraft and magic was rejected alike by reason and religion, and that spiritualistic manifestations were wilful impostures or illusions due to mental disturbance in the observers. He wrote with the philanthropic aim of staying the cruel persecution which habitually pursued poor, aged, and simple persons, who were popularly credited with being witches" (DNB XVII 1002).

Right at the outset of *Discovery,* Scott declares: "The fables of Witchcraft have taken so fast hold and deepe root in the heart of man, that fewe or none can (nowadaies) with patience indure the hand and correction of God. For if any adversities, greefe, sicknesse, losse of children, corne, cattell, or libertie happen upon them; by & by they exclaime uppon witches. As though there were no God in Israel that ordereth all things according to his will; punishing both just and unjust with greefs, plagues, and afflications in manner and forme as he thinketh good: but that certeine old women heere on earth, called witches, must needs be the contrivers of all mens calamities, and as though they themselves were innocents, and had deserved no such punishments" (1964 25).

"Such faithless people," continues Scott, "are also persuaded, that neither haile nor snowe, thunder nor lightening, raine nore tempestuous winds come from the heavens at the commandment of God: but are raised by the cunning and power of witches and conjurers; insomuch as a clap of thunder, or a gale of wind is no sooner heard, but either they run to ring bels, or crie out to burne witches." Towards the end of Chapter One, Scott, writing in the same vein, asserts: "I am also well assured, that if all the old women in the world were witches and all the priests, conjurers: we should not have a drop of raine, nor a blast of wind the more or the lesse for them. For the Lord hath bound the waters in the clouds, and hath set bounds about the waters, untill the daie and night come to an end.... The wind of the Lord and not the wind of witches, shall destroie the treasures of their plesant vessels, and drie up the fountains; saith Oseas. Let us also learne and confesse with the Prophet David, that we our selves are the causes of our afflictions; and not exclaime upon witches, when we should call upon God for mercie" (1964 25–26).

King James VI of Scotland declared that Scott's opinions were "damnable" and published his attacks on Scott in a work titled *Demonologie*. Of the King's interest in and attraction to witchcraft, Williamson has written: "Ever since the matron-like witch, Agnes Sampson, had insisted on demonstrating the reality of her powers by telling the King 'the very words which passed between the King's Majesty and his Queen in Norway, the first night of their marriage,' James, who 'swore by the Living God that he believed that all the Devils in Hell could not have discovered the same,' had taken witchcraft with considerable seriousness. Among his first acts on becoming King James I of England in 1603 was the enactment of more stringent laws against witchcraft and the order that all copies of the *Discoverie* were to be burnt" (1964 23).

While heretical, blasphemous, satirical, and "damnable" books were being burned in England in the first decade of the seventeenth century, in Italy the papacy in 1605 "instructed the Venetian Inquisition to ban two works of Ferninando de las Infantes, *Tractatus de praedestinatione secundum sacram et veram evangelicam lucem, divina mediante gratia* (Paris, 1601), and *Liber divinae lucis secundum divinae et evangelicae scripturae lucem in 109, Psalmi expositionem* (Cologne, 1603). The Holy Office took the author into custody, burned the books in his presence, and extradited him to Rome in 1608" (Grendler 1977 276). In the first decade of the seventeenth century, Hebrew books continued to be set afire in Italy. In 1610, "in Rome a certain Jew named Vita was arrested and charged with holding many Hebrew books containing Talmudic errors. Sentence was passed that he be punished in accordance with the index rules of Clement VIII; his books were therefore burnt, and his property confiscated (Feb. 4, 1610)" (Popper 100).

From the outset of the seventeenth century to the beginning of the eighteenth, decade after decade, thousands upon thousands of book were burned across Europe and increasingly in the "New World." And the same dehumanizing metaphors used to define heretics and blasphemers in previous centuries continued to be invoked to "justify" the burning of their writings. In the middle of the century, heresiographer Ephraim Pagitt published his *Heresiography or, A Description of the Hereticks and Sectaries of these latter times* in which he listed over forty "sects," including Anabaptists, Antitrinitarians, Brownists, Familists, Servetians, and Socinians. The poison-plague-devil- infection-wolves-disease metaphors were invoked by Pagitt in his call for the extermination and death of those heretics and blasphemers who were threats to both church and state.

Pagitt warned on the title page of his *Heresiography*: "Beware the false prophets, which come to you in sheepes clothing, but inwardly are ravening wolves." In his "Epistle Dedicatory" to the Lord Mayor of the city of London, sheriffs, and aldermen, Pagitt asked: "What is more correspondent with the duty of Christian magistrates than to assist God's cause with your political authority? A question may be asked, whether it be lawfull for the magistrates to use the sword against heretics?" Pagitt replied: "To this I answer, such whose heresies are blasphemous in doctrine, or dangerous to the state deserve death: the reason is, because they corrupt the faith. If such as poyson waters and fountains at which men and beasts drink, deserve capital punishment, how much more they that as much as in them lyeth go about to poyson men's souls?"

As Pagitt saw it, the metaphorical heretical "plague of heresies" was greater than the literal plague: "The plague is of all diseases most infectious: I have lived among you almost a Jubile, and seen your great care and provision to keep the city from infection, in shutting up the sick, and carrying them to your pest-houses, in setting warders to keep the whole from the sick, in making fires, and perfuming streets, in resorting to your churches, in pouring out your prayers to Almighty God with fasting and almes to be propitious to you. The plague of heresy is greater, and you are now in more danger than when you buried five thousand a week."

According to Pagitt, the Familists were "unpure" and they "blasphemously pretend to be Godified like God, whereas indeed they are devillified like their Father the Devell." The Donatisticall Brownists, "who in times past hid themselves in holes; now lift up their heads, and vent openly their errors, infecting our people" (Pagitt Dedication).

In addition to relying on the dehumanizing metaphors to attack the heretics and their works, Pagitt relates heresy and blasphemy to sedition. The "Sectaries," he asserts have hurt the Church, but at the same time the Commonwealth suffers with the Church; the heresies and blasphemies are "dangerous to the State."

As Levy has observed: "In the seventeenth century, the belief that a nation's religious unity augmented its peace and strength accounted, at least in part, for the rising dominance of the state in policing serious crimes against religion. The connection of religious dissent with political subversion was old, but governments intervened more frequently to suppress nonconforming intellectuals and sectarians" (1993 73). King James believed that it was "one of the principall parts of that duties which appertaines unto a Christian King, to protect the trew church within his owne dominions, and to extirpate heresies" (Levy 1981 188). Later in the century, "soon after the Restoration the expression of unorthodox religious opinion was generally recognized as an offence at common law" (Nokes 42).

In 1647 and 1655, John Biddle's books were condemned by both secular and ecclesiastical authorities and set afire. Biddle and his Socinianism, it was claimed, spread a "poyson" which had to be extirpated. The vice-chancellor of Oxford University warned of Biddle's influence: "[T]he evill is at the doore; there is not a Citty, a Towne, scarce a village in England, wherein some of this poyson is not poured forth" (Levy 1981 214). His "damnable heresies," including the denial of the Trinity, led the Assembly of Divines to appeal to Parliament to put him to death, which Parliament did not do, but did imprison him and debarred him "from the use of pens, ink, and paper; and all his books were sentenced to be burnt (December 13th, 1654)" (Farrer 111).

Biddle's anti–Trinitarian views prompted Parliament to order the burning of his *twelve Arguments Drawn out of the Scripture, Wherein the commonly received Opinion touching the Deity of the Holy Spirit, is clearly and fully refuted*; *Gods Glory Vindicated and Blasphemy Confuted*; *The Apostolic and True Opinion*; and *Twofold Catechism* (Gillett 1932 328–333).

The voluminous book burnings in seventeenth century Great Britain have been reported to such an extent in Hart's 1872 *Index Expurgatorius Anglicanus,* Farrer's 1892 *Books Condemned to be Burnt,* and Gillett's 1932 *Burned Books* that I hesitate going over all that territory again here and hence I refer the reader to those sources for more information about seventeenth century book burning in England. In fact, Farrer states at the outset of his book that his work is "confined to books so condemned [burned] in the United Kingdom" (7). And then his book concludes basically with the end of the seventeenth century; he writes in his chapter "The Last Book Fires" in which he deals with a few early eighteenth century burnings: "The eighteenth century ... saw the hangman employed for the last time for the punishment of books" (170).

Gillett's *Burned Books* also is limited to book burnings in Great Britain and, for the most part, to the seventeenth century. At the outset of his two-volume work, Gillett writes: "The following pages present the story of the burning books, principally in Great Britain" (viii). As for the termination of the burning of heretical and blasphemous writings, Gillett declares: "Since the beginning of the eighteenth century, the condemnations have been for the most part upon political grounds" (vii).

While I see no need to redo what the above works have covered, I include here some of the book burnings in England during this period, in addition to the burnings of heretical-blasphemous book burnings that took place in other countries.

While the British in the seventeenth century were burning the books of Thomas Hobbes, John Milton, Richard Baxter, John Goodwin, John Owen, John Archer, John Fry, and scores of others, across the channel on the continent the French, Italians, Poles, and Spanish were setting their own fires, burning blasphemous-heretical works, many of them being seen as politically menacing. Across the oceans the book burning rituals were also being observed in Japan and the New England colonies.

In 1610 Italy, at a time when Christians were burning each other's books, they were also setting fire to Hebrew works. As Popper reports, in 1610 "the Inquisitor of Placentia (Piacenza) was notified that when prohibited books were presented to an Ordinary, this officer was required to deliver them to the Inquisitor for burning or correction (Jan. 24, 1610)" (100). Ten days later, in Rome, "a certain Jew named Vita was arrested and charged with holding many Hebrew books containing Talmudic errors. Sentence was passed that he be punished in accordance with the index rules of Clement VIII; his books were therefore burnt, and his property was confiscated (Feb. 4, 1610)" (Popper 100).

Some authors had the "honor" of having their books burnt in two or more countries. In 1614, Jesuit scholastic Francisco Suárez's *Defensio fidei* was burned in Paris, London, Oxford and Cambridge. Suárez wrote the book "at the instance of Pope Paul V. against James I. of England and the English oath of allegiance, in which he laid down the principle that the pope had the power to depose temporal rulers for heresy and schism, and that this must be accepted an article of faith on the ground of the power of the keys. James had the book publicly burned by the executioner in front of St. Paul's" (Zockler 124). The Spanish ambassador at London wrote to Philip III: "Two hours ago I was told that the book of Father Suarez was going to be burned with several others. I hastened to assure myself, and learned with certitude that today at noon, by order of the Archbishop of Canterbury, who has jurisdiction over London, a minister preached in the cemetery of St. Paul's Church and in the midst of his sermon produced the book of Father Suarez together with one of Becan [Jesuit Van de Beeck] and one of Scioppius. After he had informed the people of the contents, he pitched the books down from the height of his pulpit and ordered them to be burned. Immediately on the spot two sacks of books were thrown into the flames" (Fichter 299). Of the burning of Suárez's book, Farrer writes that James I "ordered it to be burnt at London, and at Oxford and Cambridge; forbade his subjects to read it, under severe penalties; and wrote to Philip III. of Spain to complain of his Jesuit subject [Suárez]. But Philip, of course, only expressed his sympathy with Suarez, and exhorted James to return to the Faith. The Parlement of Paris also consigned the book to the flames in 1614" (64).

Another author whose book was burned in both London and Paris was satirist Gaspar Scioppius who in the above Spanish ambassador's letter was identified as having his book burned along with Suárez's *Defensio fidei*. Scioppius's controversial book, *Ecclesiasticus,* which was a criticism of and attack on James I and Casaubon, was "burnt in London, and its author hanged and beaten in effigy before the king on the stage, [and] was burnt in Paris by order of the Parlement, chiefly for its calumnies on Henri IV" (Farrer 19). Theologian Isaac Casaubon wrote at the time: "Know concerning Scioppius that some of his works have been burned not only here at London by the command of our most wise King, but also at Paris by the hand of the hangsman" (Ditchfield 167).

Paris and Geneva were the sites of the burnings of two works by Agrippa d'Aubigne: *Histoire universelle* was burned in Paris in 1620 and *Aventures du Baron de Faebeste* was burned in Geneva. The latter work was condemned by the Calvinists who had the book burned in the square in Geneva. The conflict between d'Aubigne and the Calvinists was largely based on the Calvinists' attitude towards the writing of fiction. As Catharine Randall Coats explains, d'Aubigne's "work was expressed in theo-literary language, in which theological terms acquired new literary applications, while literary constructs conveyed theological convictions. This was innovative for a Calvinist, for whom literature — a focus on the self rather than on the Creator — was perceived as part of the fallen world.... The Calvinist distrust of fiction was a major stumbling block which d'Aubigne had to overcome in order to write non-exegetical works. Indeed, with the exception of d'Aubigne, we find no *literary* works by Calvinist writers" (1). Further, as Coats indicates, "much of d'Aubigne's work was not in line with scriptural motivation. It deviated because d'Aubigne licensed a discussion of the self that distracted from the focus on Scripture" (7).

D'Aubigne's *Histoire universelle* was burned because, among other reasons, it satirized Charles IX, Henry III, Henry IV, and "other French Royal personages of the time" (Farrer 19). Protestant d'Aubigne's book was condemned to be burned at the Sorbonne and the French authorities "called for the arrest of d'Aubigne and his printer, Jean Moussat" (Nichols-Pecceu 41). As Cameron has written: "When the *Histoire universelle* was condemned to be burned in 1620, the author was summoned to defend himself at the Chatlelet; he also became involved in the revolt against Luynes in the same year. In danger of his life, d'Aubigne was forced to flee the country and take refuge in Geneva" (14).

In her essay on d'Aubigne's *Histoire universelle,* Nichols-Pecceu indicates that censorship in France during this period was guided by the Edict of Chateaubriant and "what marked the conditions of writing under the Edict of Chateaubriant ... was the explicit link between religious and subversive literature and secondly, the extension of censorship from the more visible sphere of publishing and selling to the private one of owning and reading" (42–43). This link, especially the religious-subversive, made it difficult to determine whether a work was set afire because it was heretical-blasphemous or because it was subversive-seditious. Relying on religious arguments to criticize royal prerogative and actions would easily lead to a charge of being both heretical and subversive.

When in 1623, Théophile (Théophile de Viau) and his books were condemned to be set afire, he was accused of "denying the resurrection of the dead" and became "a symbol of all that was subversive of orthodoxy organized dogmatic thought and Christian religious attitudes" (Levi 885). He was condemned by the Parlement of Paris "to be burnt with his book *Le Parnasse des Poètes Satyriques,* but the author escaped with his burning in effigy, and with imprisonment in a dungeon" (Farrer 16). Théophile's play *Pyrame et Thisbe* was also burned: "on April 1623 a volume had appeared entitled *Le Parnasse satyrique,* containing audacious and partly licentious poems.... The volume was condemned on 11 July by the Paris parlement, which also ordered Théophile's arrest. He was in hiding ... when on 19 August, he was burnt in effigy with his works, including *Pyrame*" (Levi 885).

Ditchfield asserts that *Le Parnasse des Poètes Satyriques* "deserved" destruction: "His [Théophile's] poems are a mere collection of impieties and obscenities, published with the greatest of impudence, and well deserved their destruction.... His book, the cause of all his woes, was burnt with the poet's effigy in 1623" (181–182). It is surprising to find Ditchfield declaring that the poems of Théophile "deserved their destruction" because of their "impiety and obscenities" when at the outset of his 1895 *Books Fatal to Their Authors* he expresses admiration for the "constancy and courage of those who lived in less happy days. We are not concerned now in condemning or defending their opinions or their beliefs, but we may at least praise their boldness and mourn their fate" (3). Yet he condemns the "impieties and obscenities" in Théophile's poems that were published "with the greatest of impudence, and well deserved their destruction."

In Italy, at the end of the sixteenth century and well into the seventeenth, vernacular Bibles were being set afire in various Italian towns. The burning of the vernacular Bibles and other condemned religious writings, Fragnito observes, was a loss that constituted "a veritable trauma for the common people; a trauma made more painful by the fact that, during the periodic book burnings which lit up the piazzas of Italy with their sinister glare, they were obliged to watch their Bibles, their lectionaries, and their sacred stories fed to the flames together with the books from the transalpine Reformers. Prohibited and seized because the Holy Office deemed them the source of all heresy, the Holy Scriptures were thus confused in the Italian imagination with the writings of the 'heretics'; a conflation which persisted well beyond the suspension of the prohibition by Benedict XIV (1758)" (34).

The inquisitor of Genoa, Eliseo Masini, wrote in 1620 that he had "purged this city of the Aretinos, the Machiavellis, the Bodins, the Boccaccios and of innumerable other filthy authors, of vernacular Bibles, of historical compendiums, and of innumerable other totally prohibited books, having had public bonfires made, as I did with much edification of the city some years ago, when fully five or six thousand copies of books were burned" (Fragnito 35).

In 1617, Italian archbishop Marcantonio de Dominis, who had become involved in a controversy with Church officials, published his *De Republica Ecclesiastica* in which he "shows that the authority of the Bishop of Rome can easily be disproved from Holy Scripture, that it receives no support from the judgment of history and antiquity, that the early bishops of that see had no precedence over other bishops, nor were in the least able to control those of other countries. He declares that the inequality of power amongst the Apostles is a human invention, not founded on the Gospels; that in the Holy Eucharist the priest does not offer the sacrifice of Christ, but only the commemoration of that sacrifice; that the Church has no coercive power, that John Huss was wrongfully condemned" (Ditchfield 14). Such views were clearly distasteful to the pope and Dominis broke with Rome and decided in 1616 it was wise to go to England where King James rewarded him "by conferring on him the Mastership of the Savoy and the Deanery of Windsor, and he further increased his wealth by presenting himself to the rich living of West Ilsley, in Berkshire" (Ditchfield 14). However, as Akrigg points out, "by 1612 the English were tired of the archbishop and he of them" (315). Dominis returned to Rome after the accession of Gregory XV who was a relative and fellow countryman and who "ceremoniously received" Dominis back into the Church. "But then disaster struck. In July 1623 Gregory died and the new Pope handed De Dominis over to the Inquisition. Death from illness carried off the unfortunate man before e could be brought to trial, but a posthumous verdict convicted him of seventeen heresies and resulted in his body, picture and books being publicly burned in the Campo di Fiore" (Akrigg 316).

According to Ditchfield, the inquisition seized Dominis and "he was conveyed to the Castle of St. Angelo, where he soon died, as some writers assert, by poison. His body and his books were burned by the executioner, and the ashes thrown into the Tiber" (16). The *New Catholic Encyclopedia* reports in its entry for Dominis: "After Gregory XV's death Dominis was seized by the Inquisition and confined to the Castel Sant' Angelo as a relapsed heretic, where he died. His body and books were burned on Dec. 21, 1624" (Luciani 856).

In his *A State Without Stakes: Polish Religious Toleration in the Sixteenth and Seventeenth Centuries,* Janusz Tazbir refers to the sixteenth century as the "golden age" in Poland, "the well known 'refuge of heretics,' as Poland was called in sixteenth century Europe" (13). Again and again, Tazbir compares the heretic burnings in western Europe to the absence of such burnings in Poland: "In the West many writers went to the stake, in Poland only their books were burnt.... Instead of live heretics—as in some other countries—only their effigies were burned in Poland. For example in 1622, in the course of the celebration of the beatification of St. Ignatius Loyola, a puppet representing Martin Luther was paraded through the city of Lwow, mounted on a pig, and then solemnly burned. It was perhaps not the subtlest form of religious propaganda, but on the whole preferable to a Spanish auto-da-fe" (141).

If the burning of heretics at the stake were fewer in Poland, there were other forms of punishment and persecution applied: jailings, burning of churches, whippings, the stocks, forced exile. Tazbir reports: "The governor of Cracow, Gabriel Tarnowski, wanted to condemn to death the Calvinist printer Andrew Piotrowcyzk (1625) for printing the anti–Jesuit pamphlet *Gratis* by Jan Brozek.... Piotrowcyzk was sentenced instead to the stocks and a whipping and he was exiled from the city. At the same time on November 20, 1625 the public executioner burnt all the copies found at the printer's. Some more copies were also found at another printing shop, a Catholic one; the shop was ransacked and some of the staff beaten" (142).

In 1646, Jonas Schlichting published a Polish version of his *Confessio* and in 1647 he was "banished from the Commonwealth by the Diet of Warsaw and the offending document was burnt by the hangman in the capital" (Williams 113). Schlichting was one of many supporters of the anti–Trinitarian views of sixteenth century "heretic" Faustus Socinus; as described by Levy, Socinianism was "the most detested heresy in Christendom" (1993 120). Both Catholic and Protestant authorities condemned Socinianism; as Florida has observed, "the authoritarian churches of Rome and of 'genuine' Protestantism united in persecuting the Socinians and all anti–Nicene Christians. Servetus and Gribaldi both fled for their lives from Catholic lands and were executed by Protestants for their anti–Nicene beliefs. Bruno and Ochino both died in miserable exile, unwelcome in either Catholic or Protestant realms" (1974 49). The term "Socinian" eventually came to "synonymous with heretic" (Florida 1974 119).

Farrer, referring to seventeenth century writers who had survived their books that were set afire in the 1640s and were "fortunate enough not to share the burning of their books," reports: "Wolkelius [Johan Volkelius], a friend of Socinus, the edition of whose book *De Vera Religione,* published at Amsterdam in 1645, was there burnt by order of the magistrates for its Socinian doctrines, appears to have lived for many years afterwards. Schlicttingius [Schlichting], a Polish follower of the same faith, escaped with expulsion from Poland, when the Diet condemned his book *Confessio Fidei Christianae* to be burnt by the executioner" (11–12). Like the books of Volkelius and Schlichting, the manuscripts and books found in the house of Socinus had been reduced to ashes in Cracow a half century earlier. As Zockler has indicated, in 1598 Socinus was "ill-treated" when "students of Cracow, incited by Roman priests, threw him out of his sick-bed, carried him half-naked through the streets, and inflicted bloody injuries.... During the assault all the paper, manuscripts, and books found in his house were burned in the market-place" (488).

After this 1598 attack on Socinus, matters became worse for the Socinians. "In 1611, an anti–Nicene burgher of Biesk was executed for blasphemy against the holy trinity and for dishonoring a crucifix; Socinians were forbidden to meet in Lublin after 1627; and in

1638 the intellectual centre of Socinianism — the college and press at Rakow — was razed in punishment for a prank done by two Socinian schoolboys. In short, toleration in Poland while still a constitutional guarantee was hardly in practice" (Florida 34). By 1660, "there were few Socinian survivors to expel; perhaps a thousand families abjured their faith and remained in Poland while a few hundred fled" (Florida 35). As Florida has pointed out, Voltaire "took interest in the fate of an obscure Polish sect of Protestant heretics — the Socinians" and in 1773 Voltaire "wrote to Catherine II, empress of Russia, to ask her to relieve the oppression of the Socinians in Lithuania.... Catherine now had the power to make reforms in Lithuania since Poland had recently been partitioned among Russia, Prussia, and Austria. Unfortunately Voltaire's letter was at least 113 years too late to help the Socinians in Lithuania; they had been extirpated in all Polish land in 1660" (15).

About the same time Socinian books were being burned on the Continent the British were setting fire to the works of "English Socinians" Paul Best, John Biddle, and John Fry. In 1647, Best's *Mysteries Discovered* was ordered by the House of Commons to be burned "by the hangman on Monday, Friday, and Saturday following July 26, 30 and 31, between the hours of ten and twelve, in the Palace yard at Westminster, in Cheapside, and Cornhill before the Exchange" (Gillett 1932 326). For awhile, Best "had been imprisoned in the Gatehouse for certain expressions he was supposed to have used about the Trinity; and before he wrote this pamphlet [*Mysteries Discovered*] the House of Commons had actually voted that he should be hanged" (Farrer 108). While Best's "blasphemous" writings were burned and while he did spend some time imprisoned, he escaped hanging. In 1647, he was released from prison and had to "promise never again to publish his religious opinions" (Levy 1993 117).

Like Best, Socinian John Biddle was imprisoned in Gatehouse where the two became acquainted; and as with Best's writings, Biddle's *Twelve Arguments drawn out of Scripture, wherein the Commonly Received Opinion touching the Deity of the Holy Spirit is Clearly and Fully Refuted* and *Twofold Catechism* were burned. As Levy has indicated, on December 13, 1654, the House of Commons "examined Biddle, who admitted writing both books, but said that he had no congregation and refused to identify his printers. 'The Law of Christ,' he explained, enjoined him 'not to betray his Brethren.' He denied the divinity of the Holy Ghost, as earlier, and, when asked whether Jesus Christ was God 'from Everlasting to Everlasting,' he denied that the Bible said so" (127). Farrer reports that in 1654, Biddle "published his *Twofold Catechism,* for which he was again committed to the Gatehouse, and debarred from the use of pens, ink, and paper; and all his books were sentenced to be burnt (December 13th, 1654)" (111). A year later, Cromwell "banished Biddle for life, sending him under armed guard to a castle-fortress on one of the Scilly Islands, about forty miles off the southwesternmost point of England" (Levy 1993 135). Levy ends his chapter "Socinian Anti-Trinitarians" in *Blasphemy* stating: "[Biddle] was kept in prison under sickening conditions. He caught a fatal malady and died in 1662 at the age of forty-seven. His congregation did not survive him, and Socinianism, once supposedly raging in every nook and corner of the realm, almost disappeared from it" (135).

"Closely allied in the clerical mind with John Biddle and Paul Best was John Fry.... All three were dubbed 'Socinians,'" writes Gillett (1932 344). In 1648 Fry wrote *Accuser Sham'd* and in 1650 *Clergy in their True Colours,* whereupon in 1651 both books were condemned as "erroneous, profane, and highly scandalous" and were ordered by the House of Commons to be burned, "some at the New Palace in Westminster, and rest at the Old Exchange" (Gillett 1932 351). The condemned works of these three English Socinians were denounced as "poisonous, Satanic, profane, heretical, blasphemous, and pernicious" as the books were gathered to be set afire.

As indicated earlier in this chapter, the book burnings during the seventeenth century in Great Britain have been identified and discussed in Gillett's *Burned Books* (1932), Farrer's *Books Condemned to be Burnt* (1892), and Hart's *Index Expurgatorius Anglicanus* (1872); to include more pages here on seventeenth century English book burnings would be to cover material already adequately dealt with elsewhere. I have included at this juncture the burnings of the writings of Best, Biddle, and Fry because of their Socinian connections with the Continental anti–Trinitarians.

While the Europeans were burning Catholic, Protestant, and Hebrew writings, half way around the world the Church's efforts to Christianize the Japanese began early in the sixteenth century and by the end of the century the missionaries were burning Buddhist works and were ordered by the Japanese to leave. The conflict between the Japanese and the Catholic missionaries resulted in the former destroying and burning Christian churches and books and the latter burning Buddhist places of worship and idols.

In 1587, the Japanese ordered the expulsion of the missionaries, the order reading, in part: "1. Japan is the country of gods, but has been receiving false teachings from Christian countries. This cannot be tolerated any further.... 2. The [missionaries] approach people in provinces and districts to make them their followers, and let them destroy shrines and temples. This is an unheard of outrage.... 3. The padres, by their special knowledge [in the sciences and medicine] feel that they can at will entice people to become their believers. In so doing they commit the illegal act of destroying the teachings of Buddha prevailing in Japan" (Lu 197).

Several years earlier, in 1572, the missionaries in Nagasaki had "set fire to the great Buddhist temple, Jinguji, and attributed the fire to the 'wrath of God,'—after which act, by the zeal of their converts, some eighty other temples, in or about Nagasaki were burnt. Within Nagasaki territory Buddhism was totally suppressed,—its priests being persecuted and driven away" (Hearn 365–366).

As Hearn has indicated, the Church's intolerance and destruction of Buddhist temples led to local persecutions of Christians, but soon enough the central government began its policy of suppressing the "foreign creed": "The local persecution in Kyushu, for example, would seem to have been natural consequences of the intolerance of the Jesuits in the days of their power, when converted daimyo burned Buddhist temples and massacred Buddhist priests.... But from 1614—at which date there remained only eight, out of the total sixty-four provinces of Japan, in which Christianity had not been introduced—the suppression of the foreign creed became a government matter; and the persecution was conducted systematically and uninterruptedly until every outward trace of Christianity had disappeared" (338).

As seen by the Japanese authorities, the Christian missionaries were simply a prelude to their gaining economic and political control in Japan. It was not unreasonable, states Hearn, for the Japanese to suspect the motives of the missionaries:

[W]ho could reasonably have doubted that, were opportunity offered, the Roman Catholic orders would attempt to control the general government precisely as they had been able to control local government already in the lordships of converted daimyo. Besides, we may be sure that by the time at which the edict [ordering expulsion of the missionaries] was issued, Iyeyasu must have hears of many matters likely to give him a most evil opinion of Roman Catholicism: — the story of the Spanish conquests in America, and the extermination of the West Indian races; the story of the persecutions in the Netherlands, and of the work of the Inquisition elsewhere.... The edict was issued in 1614, and Iyeyasu had found opportunity to inform himself about some of these matters as early as 1600 [343–344].

Putting it a bit differently, but making the same point, Reischauer has written: "The missionaries' intolerance of other religions ... resulted in strong resistance to them by the Buddhist clergy, and Hideyoshi, after reuniting the country, began to look on Christianity as possibly subversive to unified rule. The Japanese were not unaware of the Spanish political conquest that had accompanied the introduction of Christianity to the Philippines, and some of them began to fear that Christian loyalties directed toward a distant papacy could undermine a feudal system based on purely local loyalties" (Reischauer 87).

By the end of the seventeenth century, prohibited books taken from the cargoes of ships entering Japanese ports were being set afire. In 1685, when a ship arrived in Nagasaki an examination of unloaded books took place in search of banned or suspicious books, leading to the burning of the forbidden Christian writings. As Tasaburo has described it, "When such rigorous censorship turned up books on the Christian doctrine or those that could be regarded as such, they were burnt and the ship that had carried them was forbidden to engage in any trade. The magistrate not only had the ship carry home all her cargo but prohibited the shipper and the captain from entering the port again" (Tasaburo 40).

From 1685 onward, "every book with even a single line describing *jashumon* ... (the evil (Christian) faith) had to be reported" (Tasaburo 41). From 1685 to 1720, "sixteen titles had been committed to flames or upon delectation with Indian ink ordered to ship back, because they dealt with the Christian doctrine or contained descriptions of Christian missionaries such as [Matteo Ricci] and Christian manners and customs" (Tasaburo 41–42). Most of the books were not "missionary books but dealt with astronomy, mathematics, topography, poetry, etc." One "included a description of a chapel, [which] might have been regarded as related to Christianity." Others contained European poetry and dealt with sorcery. In one instance, "the Governor of Nagasaki warned the captain of the ship as follows: 'It is the rule of our government to burn and sink both the cargo and crew of any ship that should bring in books designed to propagate the Christian faith. Next time you bring books, bear that in mind and take precautions'" (Tasaburo 42).

During the Kyoho period, 1716–1735, while there was a relaxation of censorship, several books were set afire, including one that denounced "Confucianism, Buddhism and Taoism" and glorified "Christian doctrine" and another work that asserted that "Confucianism and Christianity are based on a common creed" (Tasaburo 52).

Part of the Church's efforts to Christianize the Japanese in the sixteenth and seventeenth centuries had been to label the Japanese gods and Buddha as "devils," to the "burning of thousands of Buddhist temples, destroying countless works of art, and slaughtering Buddhist priests" (Hearn 336). These Christian practices were turned against them when in the seventeenth century the Japanese labeled the Christians "barbarians," destroyed their place of worship, killed some Jesuits and Franciscans, and set fire to Christian writings.

With the discovery of the "New World" in the Americas came the book burning practices of the Old World. As indicated earlier, the Spanish invaders burned the Mayan idols and books in 1562. In the seventeenth century, the Spaniards and the Church, in their attempts to Christianize the "natives" in Peru, took steps to stamp out idolatry and in so doing "public sessions of abjuration and absolution ensued in the traditional auto de fe: the administration of punishment, the burning of objects of worship, and the destruction of sacred sites" (Griffiths 35). At the same time European invaders were burning and destroying the Peruvian religious works, they were setting fire to Hebrew writings in Lima. In 1639, an auto-da-fé was "celebrated" in Lima at which Francisco Maldonado de Silva, an Anussim (Crypto-Jew), was burned at the stake along with the books he had written. A friar's description of the event portrays de Silva being led to the fire, "frail, gray-haired, long-bearded, and with the books he had written tied around his neck" (Lazar 179). Condemned as a relapsed-heretic, de Silva was imprisoned: "During the years he spent in prison he made two books out of scraps of paper, pens from egg-shells and ink from charcoal. It was thirteen years before he was finally brought out of prison and burned alive. The books he had made were hung about his neck and burned with him" (Plaidy 1961 88).

Lazar observes that martyrs like de Silva and others "went to the stake sanctifying their monotheistic faith ... and imitating the martyrology of the ten celebrated rabbis ... which occupies a special place in ancient Jewish lore and in the traditional prayer books. One of these sages, Hanina ben Teradyon, we are told, had been draped in a Torah scroll by his persecutors and thrown into the fire. Seeing his daughter distressed, he said to her: 'Were I to be burning alone, it would be dreadful to me; now that I am in the fire with the Torah around me, whoever will avenge the honor of the Torah will at the same time avenge mine.' His disciples asked: 'Rabbi, what do you see?' And he replied: 'Burning scrolls, I see, and letters rising in the air'" (Lazar 179). The burning of Jews along with their books had come to the "New World," along with the "letters rising in the air," as they did in Europe.

At the same time the Catholics were setting fire to condemned writings in Central and South America in the middle of the seventeenth century, the Protestant colonial invaders to the north were burning heretical works in Massachusetts. As Felice Lewis had stated: "The earliest recorded censorship actions in the colonies were directed mainly against printed matter considered blasphemous or seditious, at a time when colonial governors still had absolute control over the press.... The colonists were most edgy about blasphemy, which for a time was punishable by death in Maryland, Plymouth Colony, and Massachusetts Bay Colony. In 1638 the Deputy Governor of Massachusetts suggested to Governor John Winthrop that a book be burned because he found 'the scope thereof to be erroneous and dangerous, if not heretical.' A theological pamphlet *The Meritorious Price* of our Redemption, was ordered burned in the Boston marketplace in 1650" (1).

While the colonists fled England to escape religious censorship and persecution, they established their own censorship and oppression. As United States Supreme Court Justice Hugo Black wrote in 1962 in the Court's opinion concluding that New York's state composed prayer recited in that state's public schools was unconstitutional: "It is an unfortunate fact of history that when some of the very groups which had most strenuously opposed the established Church of England found themselves sufficiently in control of colonial governments in this country to write their own prayers into law, they passed laws making their own religion the official religion of their respective colonies" (*Engel v. Vitale* 427).

In 1650, William Pynchon's *The Meritorious Price of our Redemption* was condemned by the Massachusetts General Court which ordered the book "be burned by the common executioner in the market-place in Boston, and issued a 'Declaration' to prove its own detestation of many of these opinions and assertions, and to show that it was not privy to the publication" (Duniway 32). On October 15, 1650, The General Court ordered: "first, that a protest be drawn to notify all men that the Court, far from approving the volume, did 'utterly dislike it and detest it as erroneous and dangerous'; secondly, that the book be answered by one of the elders; thirdly, that the author be summoned to appear before the next General Court to answer for his publication; and, fourthly, that the book be burnt by the executioner, or such other person as the magistrates should appoint, in the market in Boston the next day after the lecture" (Smith 1961 26). Among Pynchon's heresies was his denial "that Christ gave himself a ransom for our sins. In his treatment of the price and merit of Christ's sufferings, he had called them 'but trials of his obedience, yet intending thereby to amplyfy and exalt the mediatorial obedyence of Christ as the only meritorious price of man's redemption,' — a dangerous divergence from the received opinion of the elders on a fundamental theological tenet" (Duniway 32). The book took the form of a discourse "between 'a Trades-man and a Divine'" and was "designed to prove that 'Christ did not suffer for us those un-utterable Torments of Gods Wrath, which commonly are called Hell-Torments, to redeem our Souls from them' and that 'Christ did not bear our Sins by Gods Imputation, and therefore he did not bear the Curse of the Law for them'" (Smith 1961 25). As Levy has pointed out, "The General Court deemed it [Pynchon's book] heretical and ordered that copies be burned. Pynchon was called to answer for his heterodoxies. Significantly, he did not deny the Trinity, and he was not accused of blasphemy. His prosecution ended when he returned to England" (Levy 1993 254).

The 1650 burning of Pynchon's heretical work was followed six years later with the burning of books and pamphlets brought to the colonies by Quakers. In 1654, the General Court in Massachusetts, fearing the appearance of Quaker books, ordered

> that all & euery the inhabitants of this jurisdiction that haue any bookes in their custody that haue lately bin brought out of England under the names of John Reeves & Lodowick Muggleton, who ptend themselves to be the two last wittnesses & prophets of Jesus Christ, which are full of blasphemies, & shall not bring or send in all such bookes now in their custody, to the next magistr, shall forfeit the sume of ten pounds for every such booke that shalbe found, or knowne to be in the hands of any inhabitant after one moneths publication hereof, the one halfe to the informer, the other halfe to the country; & as many of the sd bookes as can be or may be found by the executionor, at Boston [Duniway 36].

In 1656, two Quaker women, Mary Fischer and Ann Austin, arrived in Boston harbor from Barbados and were immediately jailed until they were shipped back five weeks later to Barbados. Their luggage had been searched by Massachusetts authorities and one hundred books and pamphlets were confiscated. Writing of this imprisonment and book burning, Winwar observes: "On the first of July the two Quaker women with their bundles of tracts landed in New England. The Puritans were ready for them. Seizing them before they had a chance to say one heretical word, they clapped them in Boston jail and made a bonfire of their literature in the market place. For five weeks the women remained in prison without anyone to plead for them, and then they were released, to disappear from the scene" (Winwar 68). Further, as Winwar reports, eight other Quakers arrived by boat, were described by the General Court as part of "the blasphemouth" sect: "They, too, came laden with books, which again were burned in the market place, notwithstanding the fact that some were volumes of the Bible. Whatever belonged to the Quakers was damned, and best put out of the way" (Winwar 68–69). As the authorities saw it, jailing the Quakers and burning their books was not enough punishment to discourage the Quakers: "It was obvious to the magistrates that half measures like cutting off the ears of the men and boring the tongues of the women with hot irons no longer sufficed to keep Hell's minions at bay. There was still the threefold corded whip, made of the dried intestines of animals and knotted with three knots, which, when applied with the full strength of the jailer's arms, laid the flesh bare to the bone" (Winwar 75).

Massachusetts law provided that Quakers who persisted in returning to Massachusetts after being banished were subject to various punishments: "[E]very such male Quaker who shall for the first offense have one of his ears cut off and be kept at work of correction till he can be sent away at his own charge, and for the second offense shall have his other ear cut off ... and every woman Quaker ... shall be severely whipt and kept at the house of correction at work till she shall be sent away ... and for every Quaker, he or she, that shall a third time herein again offend, they shall have their tongues bored through with a hot iron" (Wertenbaker 212). Quakers who returned to New Haven, Connecticut, for a second time were to be "branded on the hand with the letter H, be committed to prison and kept to work till he can be sent away at his own charge." Quakers who returned to New Haven for the fourth time, "shall have their tongues bored through with a hot iron" (Wertenbaker 213–214).

Four decades after the books of Mary Fischer and Ann Austin were burned in Boston, Massachusetts authorities ordered the burning of Quaker Thomas Maule's *Truth Held Forth & Maintained &c.* not only because it contained "wicked lies about private persons," but also because there appeared in the book "corrupt and pernicious Doctrines utterly subversive of the true Christian & professed faith" (Duniway 71). The General Council ordered in December 1695 "That the sd Bookes now under seizure both at Boston and Salem be publickly burnt here and there and that sd Thomas Maule give Bond of two hundred pounds himselfe & one hundred pounds apiece two sureties for the said Maules appearance at the next Court of Assize & General Goale Delivery, to be holden within the County of Essex to answer what shall be objected agst him on his Majtys behalfe for being the Author of said Booke" (Duniway 72–73).

In *Truth Held Forth* Maule argued "that no one could prove that Scriptures is the word of God; it was only man's interpretation of spiritual influence. He also stated that Friends believed in a Trinity (if it was understood that there was a unity of the Godhead).... Maule went beyond mere ideological quibbling and attacked the Massachusetts clergy; he also made the error of letting his name appear on the pamphlet rather than using a pseudonym" (Worrall 49). Further, the Boston clergymen "took vigorous exception to his assertion that they were as guilty of being creatures of the devil as the persons they had seen charged with witchcraft and executed for it, and to his charge that New England's recent troubles with witches and Indian invasions resulted directly from their persecution of Quakers" (Worrall 50–51). The clergy and inhabitants of New England and Massachusetts were confronted with Maule's contention that "if the Inhabitants of New England do not amend and repent, the Lord hath yet a Work to do by Pestilence and Famine, which will be more terrible than all the Lords former judgments have been, ever since they began to persecute the honest People called Quakers" (Maule 1695 207–208). When Maule was brought to trial, Justice Danforth told the jury, "you ought well to consider the horrid wickedness of Thomas Maule's setting forth the book now before you, in which there is contained a great deal of blasphemous matter against the churches and government of this province" (Chandler 146).

On December 12, 1695, a warrant for Maule's arrest was issued, stating in part: "To the Sheriffe of the County of Essex.... Whereas there is lying before the honourable Lieutenant Governour and Council a printed Pamphlet, entituled, *Truth held forth and maintained, &c* put forth in the name of Thomas Maule, said to be Thomas Maules of Salem within your County, and published without Licence of Authority, in which is contained many notorious and wicked Lyes, and Slanders, not only upon private Persons, but also upon Government, and likewise divers corrupt and pernicious Doctrines utterly subversive of the true Christian and professed Faith" (Maule 1697 53). Two days later, the sheriff's returned warrant read, in part: "According to the within Warrant, I have been at the House of Thomas Maule, and there have found thirty one of said Pamphlets, and them secured, as required and have seized the said Maule, and delivered him to the keeper of their Majesties Goal in Salem" (Maule 1697 54).

Before he came to trial, writes Philathes (Maule), "they imprisoned him and sacrificed sixteen pounds worth of his Books, a burnt Offering to their Anger and Revenge, though upon his Tryal the Jury could not find him in the least guilty of any evil fact, relating to their Charge about his book" (Maule 1697 55). At his trial Maule had declared that "he had suffered ten times in their Jurisdiction, five times by imprisonment, three times by the loss of Goods taken from him, and twice by cruel Whipping, and now before this Tryal they had both imprisoned him, and burnt sixteen Pounds worth of his books" (Maule 1697 57).

On a much larger scale the burning of impious, blasphemous, and heretical books in Europe continued in the latter half of the seventeenth century, especially in France, England, Spain, Denmark and Austria. The works of some noted writers, such as Blaise Pascal, John Milton, and Thomas Hobbes were set afire when their books were condemned as "repugnant to the holy Scriptures, Decrees of Councils, Writings of the Fathers, and Faith and Profession of the Primitive Church: and also destructive of the Kingly Government, the safety of his Majestie's person, the Publick Peace, and Laws of Nature, and bonds of human Society" (Gillett 1932 516). The books were burned because they were an affront and threat to both ecclesiastic and secular authorities.

In 1657, Blaise Pascal's *Lettres à un Provincial* was burned in France and again in 1660, because, as Farrer has put it, Pascal "made too free with the dignity of authorities, secular and religious" (12). As Wight has stated in his Introduction to *The Provincial Letters*, "They were not suffered to pass without censure of the high places of the Church. The first effect of their publication indeed, was to raise a storm against the casuists, whom Pascal had so effectually exposed" (117). Referring to the burning of Pascal's work, Wight continues: "Unable to answer the Letters, they [Jesuits] succeeded in obtaining, in February, 1657, their condemnation by the Parliament of Provence, by whose orders they were burnt on the pillory by the hands of the common executioner" (118).

In his reference to the burnings of Pascal's *Lettres à un Provincial*, Cole has pointed out that "by challenging the commonsense reading of a Papal Bull and ridiculing the verdict against Arnauld [condemned by Jesuits] in the Sorbonne, he [Pascal] opened himself to censure by the Church as well as the state. The Parlement of Aix condemned the *Provinciales* for troubling public order and defaming the Sorbonne, the Dominicans, and the Jesuits; on 9 February 1657, the judges sentenced Letters 1–16 to be burned by the Hangman (reportedly keeping their own copies of the offending pamphlets and putting the torch to an unwanted almanac).... Finally, on 23 September 1660, the conscil d'Etat in Paris formally sentenced Wendrock's Latin version to be lacerated and burned, forbidding all subjects to print, sell, purchase, or even retain the book in any form" (181).

Writing in 1872, O.W. Wight observed that "few books have passed through more editions than the Provincials.... The Letters were translated into Latin during the lifetime of Pascal, by his intimate friend, the learned and indefatigable Nicole, under the assumed name of 'William Wendrock, a Salzburg divine.'" Further, "the Provincials have been translated into nearly all the languages of Europe," with the Spanish translation being suppressed by order of the Inquisition (121–122). In the entry for Pascal in *The New Schaff-Herzog Encyclopedia of Religious Knowledge,* Lachenmann writes that the *Lettres* are a "literary masterpiece possessing a high dramatic unity. In place of dry scholastic discussions on technicalities, Pascal has given vivacious dialogue, sparkling with humor. The figure of the genial Jesuit, expounding the secrets of his casuistical library with smug complacency to the curious Louis de Montalte, is worthy of Moliere at his best; and the strong, clear, sober style makes the book one of the finest monuments of French prose" (363). A year before he died, Pascal had been asked if he "repented of having written the Provincial Letters." His reply was: "[F]ar from repenting, if I had it to do again, I would write them yet more strongly" (Wight 125).

While Pascal, before he died in 1662, saw the burning of his books in 1657 and 1660, the French heretic Simon Morin was set afire together with his books in Paris in 1663. While Pascal's *Lettres* was praised as a masterpiece, Morin's *Pensees de Simon Morin* was berated at the time of its burning and subsequently two centuries later. Writing in 1892, Farrer saw little value in Morin's book: "Simon Morin was burnt with all the copies of his *Pensées* that could be found, on the Place de Greve, at Paris, March 14th, 1663. Morin called himself the Son of Man, and such thought of his as survived the fire do not lead us in his case to grudge the flames their literary fuel" (10). Similarly, Ditchfield wrote in 1895: "The seventeenth century was fruitful in fanatics, and not the least was Simon Morin, who was burnt in Paris in 1663. His fatal book was his Pensees de Simon Morin ... which contains a curious mixture of visions and nonsense, including the principal errors of the Quietists and adding many of how own" (51).

At the time of the of Morin with his *Pensées,* the attacks on the book and Morin relied on the centuries-old dehumanizing metaphors suggesting a need for extirpation: pestilence, plague, infection, vermin, wolves, weeds. Such was the language in a 1663 work titled: *An Exact and True Relation on the Birth, and Life of Simon Morin Who Professed Himself to be Jesus Christ: For Which, and other Detestable Heresies, Together with His Book Entituled Pensées du Morin, He was Condemned and Burnt at Paris in the End of February Last, 1662/3.* In this work by W. Griffith, Morin and his *Pensées* were portrayed as dangers to both church and state; his followers were, according to Griffith, "a considerable number, and too great to be trusted by the Magistrate, was infected with his Errors: which (as we are informed from France) were found in his Conviction to be many more, and his Practices very dangerous, both to the Church and to the State" (4). When the heretics' aim "is Innovation both of Church and State" it is "the best Prudence and Policy of a Prince, or State, to eradicate and root-up those Weeds out of the Gardens of their Government, while young and tender; or, as we deal with Wolves, when got at liberty, unkennel all the Mastiffs in a Country to worry them, e're they come to litter, and fill the soil with so pestilent a Vermine" (Griffith 2).

Turning to the public burning of Morin and his book, Griffith refers to Morin's trial and refusal to repent: "[H]e was after Tryal condemned and publickly burnt; his Errors at the same time suffering the same Condemnation, and forbidden to be propagated, or published; a Book, wrote by him, entituled *Pensees du Morin,* (or *The Opinions of Morin*) containing, as it should seem, the substance of his Erroneous Doctrine being burnt together with him; for which reason it is impossibel to give you an exact Catalogue of his other Errors; but it may be sufficient to know, that they were so monstrous, that the Civil Magistrate thought them not fit to come to the knowledge of any elite, lest they might be liable to the same Infection" (5).

While Morin's *Pensées* was criticized by Ditchfield for its "curious mixture of visions and nonsense, including the principal errors of the Quietists," he had some good words for the Quietism of Michael Molinos, the founder of Quietism and whose *Guia Espirituale* was ordered burned by the Inquisition in 1687: "Molinos has been considered the leader and founder of the Quietism of the seventeenth century. The monks of Mount Athos in the fourteenth, the Molinosists, Madame Guyon, Fenelon and others in the seventeenth century, all belonged to that contemplative company of Christians who thought that the highest state of perfection consisted in the respose and complete inaction of the soul, that life ought to be one of entire passive contemplation, and that good works and active industry were only fitting for those who were toiling in a lower sphere and had not attained to the higher regions of spiritual mysticism" (Ditchfield 6). Referring to the eleven-year imprisonment of Molinos, Ditchfield wrote in 1895: "The pious, devout and learned Spanish divine was worthy of a better fate, and perhaps a little more quietism and a little less restlessness would not be amiss in our busy nineteenth century" (6).

Amongst the blasphemous, heretical, and seditious ideas Molinos was accused of holding were, as summarized by Lea: "Of the articles the most important were his justifying the sacrilege of breaking images and crucifixes; depreciating religious vows and dissuading persons from entering religious Orders; saying that vows destroyed perfection; that, by the prayer of Quiet, the soul is rendered not only sinless but impeccable, for it is deprived of freedom and God operates it, wishing us sometimes to sin and offend him, and the demon moves the members to indecent acts" (1988 IV 56). Or, as explained in the "Quietism" entry in the *Oxford Dictionary of the Christian Church,* in the view of Quietists "man, in order to be perfect, must attain complete passivity and annihilation of will, abandoning himself to God to such an extent that he cares neither for Heaven nor Hell, nor for his own salvation.... Quietism was condemned in the person of M. De Molinos by Innocent XI in his bull 'Coelestis Pastor' of 19 Nov. 1687" (Cross 1357).

The strangulation and burning of Molinist Maria de los Dolores Lopez presents an example of the fate of some Molinists. Plaidy refers to Molinos in her discussion of the heresy and burning of Dolores who at the age of twelve lived with her confessor and became his mistress and then again later had a sexual relationship with another confessor, the latter eventually confessing to church authorities of this relationship. Dolores "assured the Inquisition that, since she was four years old, she had been in communication with the Virgin Mary and had been married to Christ in heaven" (1969 168). Dolores "insisted on defending her sensuality with the doctrine called Molinist after Miguel de Molinos. The theme of this was that what appeared to be evil to ordinary mortals was not so if condoned by God. She maintained that the relationship which she had enjoyed with her men friends had in no way offended Christ and the Virgin and therefore was not evil. This was, of course, in direct contrast to the teaching of the Church and could only come under the heading of heresy." Dolores was declared a heretic and was set afire: "[S]he was conducted to the *auto de fe*; and it was necessary to put a gag in her mouth, for she insisted on shouting her dangerous views to the crowd. But the sight of the faggots ready to be kindled broke her spirit as no amount of talking could do. Dolores broke down, confessed, and was strangled before the wood at her feet was set alight" (Plaidy 1969 168–169).

While in the second half of the seventeenth century the Spanish were burning Molinos' books and the Japanese were burning Christian writings and the French were burning the books by Morin and the Italians were burning Hebrew writings and the British were burning books by John Owen, Charles, Blount, Daniel Defoe, John Fry, John Milton, Thomas Hobbes and others (see Gillett 1932), and Quaker books were being set afire in New England, polygamists were witnessing their books being burned in Denmark and Poland.

In 1676, Johann Lyser published his work on polygamy *Theophili Alethaei discursus politicus de Polygamia,* the second edition titled *Polygamia triumphatrix,* and "on account of the strange views expressed in this work he was deprived of his office of Inspector, and was obliged to seek protection from a powerful Count, by whose advice it is said that Lyser first understood the advocacy of polygamy.... He was imprisoned by the Count of Hanover, and then expelled. In Denmark his book was burned by the public executioner" (Ditchfield 56–57). Lyser argued that "not only was polygamy lawful, but that it was a blessed estate commanded by God" (Ditchfield 56). Lyser was "threatened with capital punishment if he appeared in Denmark, and his *Discursus Politicus de Polygamia* was sentenced to public burning (1677)" (Farrer 17). At the beginning of the next century, another book dealing with polygamy was set afire, this time in Poland. Samuel Friedrich Willenburg, a doctor of law at the University of Cracow wrote *De finibus polygamiae lictae* which in 1715 was commanded by the High Court of the King of Poland to be burned. (Ditchfield 59).

As I indicated earlier, I have not dealt here with the widespread burning of heretical-blasphemous books in seventeenth century England because Gillett has already provided us with a complete treatment of those burnings. However, not to totally ignore the English book burnings of that specific period it is appropriate here to conclude the seventeenth century with reference to several book burnings in England in the last two decades of that century.

On July 21, 1683, the Oxford University *Judgment and Decree* ordered the public burning of the books identified in the *Decree*. The title page read: "The Judgment and Decree of the University of Oxford Past in their Convocation July 21, 1683, Against certain Pernicious Books and Damnable Doctrines Destructive to the Sacred Persons of Princes, their State and Government and of all Humane Society. Rendered into English, and Published by Command. Printed at the Theatre, 1683." This pro-royalist document calling for the banning and burning of the condemned works listed twenty-seven "Propositions" that were not to be tolerated: "We decree, judge and declare all and every of these Propositions to be false, seditious and impious; and most of them to be also Heretical and Blasphemous, infamous to Christian Religion, and destructive of all Government in Church and State" (*Judgment and Decree* 7).

The condemned books and propositions were seen as threats to both secular and ecclesiastical authorities, the *Decree* referring to "the honor of the holy and undivided Trinity, the preservation of Catholic truth in the Church: and that the King's Majestie may be secur'd from attempts to open and bloudy enimies, and the machinations of Traiterous Heretics and Schismatics" (2). What followed was the listing of the condemned "Propositons," books, and authors such as John Goodwin, Samuel Rutherford, George Buchanan, John Milton, John Owen, Richard Baxter, and Thomas Hobbes. The "Propositons" began with: "1. All Civil Authority is derived originally from the People. 2. There is a mutual compact tacit or express, between a Prince and his Subjects; and that if he perform not his duty, they are discharg'd from theirs. 3. That if lawful Governors become Tyrants, or govern otherwise then by the laws of God and man they ought to do, they forfeit the right they had unto their Government." The list concludes with: "26. King Charles the first was lawfully put to death, and his murtherers were the blessed instruments of Gods glory in their Generation. *Milton. Goodwin. Owen.* 27. King Charles the first made war upon his Parliament; and in such case the King may not only be resisted, but he ceaseth to be King. *Baxter.*" These unacceptable "propositions" were followed with a final paragraph that made it clear that the people were to submit to the "King and all that are in Authority, that we may lead a quiet and peaceable life in all godliness and honesty; for this is good and acceptable in the sight of God our Savior" (8).

The *Decree* ordering the burning of the books containing the impious-heretical-seditious ideas was defended by royalists as a means of protecting the population from "poisonous" books, just as the populace is protected from poisonous drugs: "'Tis the same thing in Books, and Principles; Only a Poysonous Position does more hurt than a Poysonous Drug. The one kills it's Hundreds, and other it's Thousands" (Gillett 1932 511).

In an ironic turn of events, the 1683 *Decree* ordering the burning of the condemned books was itself condemned in 1710 by Parliament which ordered it to be burned. On March 23, 1710, it was "Resolved, by the Lords Spiritual and Temporal in Parliament assembled,

That the said Judgment and Decree contains in it several Positions, contrary to the Constitution of this Kingdom, and destructive of the Protestant Succession, as by Law established" and hence it was ordered that the *Judgment and Decree* "shall be burnt by the Hands
of the Common Hangman, in the Presence of the Sheriffs of London and Midd[lese]x, at
the same Time and Place when and where the Sermons of Doctor Henry Sacheverell are
ordered to be burne" (Gillett 1932 513). In a 1709 sermon Sacheverell had "inveighed against
the popish party, denounced toleration, advocated nonresistance..., and attacked the Whig
government," declaring that "the Great Security of our Government and the very Pillar upon
which it stands, is founded upon the steady Belief of the Subject's Obligation to as Absolute,
and Unconditioned Obedience to the Supreme Power, in All Things Lawful, and the utter
Illegality of Resistance upon any Pretence whatsoever." As Gillett points out, "This was a
distinct return to the positions assumed by the Oxford Convocation of a quarter of a century before" (606), hence, the fiery destruction of Sacheverell's sermons along with the
Judgment and Decree.

In August 1690, Arthur Bury, rector of Exeter College at Oxford, saw his *Naked Gospell*
set afire. As reported by Anthony Wood: "Aug. 19, Tuesday, Convocation in the morning,
where a decree pas'd the house that Dr. Arthur Bury's book *Naked Gospell* containing a great
deal of Socinianisme should be burnt" (1898 III 338). Bury's book was denounced as containing heresies and blasphemies; as Levy has observed, "Bury argued that Christians had
perplexed and persecuted one another too long because of bitter differences about the doctrine of the Trinity. When Bury's identity as author of the book was uncovered, a convocation of the entire university consigned *The Naked Gospel* to the flames as heretical and
blasphemous, deposed from office and fined him (1993 229).

Three years later, on December 15, 1693, William Freke's *A Dialogue by way of question and answer concerning the deity* and *A brief and clear confutation of the doctrine of the
trinity* were set afire in the Palaceyard at Westminster. Wood has written of this book burning: "These two things were printed together about the beginning of Dec. 1693, and sent
inclosed, by way of peny-post letters, to several parliament men, who thereupon supposed
that they had been written by a quaker. But the books being communicated, and laid open
before the house of commons, they, upon perusal of, finding much blasphemy in them, voted
them to be burnt; accordingly, 13 Dec. 1693, they were burnt in the Palaceyard at Westminster." Freke was "tryed at the King's-bench bar for writing the said Socinian pamphlets
against the trinity; and, being found guilty, was fined" (1820 IV 741).

The following excerpt from *A brief and clear confutation of the doctrine of the trinity*
indicates what the authorities would find so objectionable; early in the book Freke states
that he hopes to

> show beyond all doubt, both that the Doctrine of the Trinity is unscriptural, nay, and Idola-
> trous too, and contrary to all known reasonings of mankind. And thus, First, this doctrine
> destroys the very unity of God. Our Trinitarians talk indeed of a Trinity of unity, and that Nat-
> ural religion teaches us, that there is but one God, a white, black, or an one set of Gods they
> mean, or how else they can say that many personal Gods can make one God, God only knows,
> for I don't; this I am sure, had the heathen of old us'd this argument, even an angel must have
> despaired of ever convincing them of politheism, though they had 100000 Gods. So also our
> Trinitarians, would tell us, that God is the most pure and simple being; and yet again they can
> say that he is 3 persons, has 3 wills and 3 understandings, etc. Good God! that men can pretend
> to any conception of such a mock simplicity and unity [Freke 10].

On December 13, 1693, and January 3, 1694, the House of Commons and House of Lords
condemned Freke's anti-trinitarian work and ordered it burned by the common hangman.

While the English House of Commons ordered the burning of Freke's "blasphemous" books, the Irish House of Commons ordered the burning of a "heretical" work by John Toland. In 1697, Toland had the "honor" of having his *Christianity Not Mysterious* burned at two different sites in Dublin. The title page of his work read: "Christianity not Mysterious or, a Treatise shewing, That there is nothing in the Gospel Contrary to Reason, nor Above it: And that no Christian Doctrine can be properly call'd A Mystery." Gillett says of Toland's book: "The book at once occasioned controversy and was one of the initial publications in the deistic movement. His purpose was not destructive, but rather the contrary.... Toland's desire was to remove stumbling blocks, by showing that the gospel was not burdened with tenets which had to be accepted whether they appealed to the common sense of men or not" (1932 538). Farrer similarly wrote in 1892 that the condemnation of Toland's work was a "case of a book whose title far more suggested heresy than its contents substantiated it.... It is difficult now to understand the extreme excitement caused by Toland's book, seeing that it was evidently written in the interests of Christianity, and would now be read without emotion by the most orthodox. It was only the superstructure, not the foundation, that Toland attacked; his whole contention being that Christianity, rightly understood, contained nothing mysterious or inconsistent with reason, but that all ideas of this sort, and most of its rites, had been aftergrowths, borrowed from Paganism, in that compromise betweens the new and old religion which constituted the world's Christianization" (149).

Toland's book was burned "by the hangman before the Parliament House Gate at Dublin, and in the open street before the Town-House, by order of the Committee of Religion of the Irish House of Commons, one member even going go far as to advocate the burning of Toland himself" (Farrer 149).

The Eighteenth Through Twentieth Centuries — Burning Fewer Heretical Works

In terms of book burnings, the eighteenth century began much like the seventeenth ended. In 1700, Robert Calef's *More Wonders of the Invisible World* was burned at Harvard College in Boston. In 1702, Daniel Defoe's *The Shortest Way With Dissenters* was burned by the common hangman in the public square of New Palace, London. In 1703 and 1707, John Asgill's *An Argument Proving that According to the Covenant of Eternal Life, revealed in the Scriptures, Man may be Translated from Hence into that Eternal Life without Passing Through Death, although the Human Nature of Christ Himself could not be Thus Translated till He had Passed Through Death* was ordered burned by the English and Irish parliaments. In 1708, Jonathan Swift's *The Predictions for the Ensuing Years* was burned in Ireland and Portugal. In 1710, Matthew Tindal's *The Rights of the Christian Church asserted against the Romish, and all other priests who claim an independent power over it* was set afire in England. In 1711, the "blasphemies" of the Talmud led to the continued burning of this work and other Hebrew books in Germany. In 1713, Hebrew books were publicly burned in Amsterdam and Breslaw by rabbis who found in the books ideas contradictory to Judaism.

So began the eighteenth century which later witnessed the burnings of Voltaire's *Dictionnaire philosophique* and *Lettres philosophiques sur Anglais* and Rousseau's *Social Contract* and *Emile*. At the end of the century, the books on magic, occultism and blasphemy by Count Cagliostro and others of his "sect" were burned by the Christians in Rome, just as Christian images and books were, as "inauspicious, filthy things," burned in China to "weed out the tares."

As the eighteenth century came to an end, burning heretical-blasphemous authors and their books, compared to previous centuries, declined, the book burners becoming more interested in setting fire to subversive-seditious works (see Chapter 3). By the end of the eighteenth century, it became less clear whether the anathema to certain works was based on perceived attacks on religious doctrine or on criticism, in religious language and allusions, of secular authorities. Increasingly, it became less clear whether a sermon was a religious statement or a secular attack. Religious language and concepts were drawn in on more secular concerns. While the book burners in the eighteenth century were still concerned with blasphemy against God, there was a significant decrease in books being burned because of apostasy and church related heresies. Where in earlier centuries there were burnings of condemned authors and books expressing heretical views on the Trinity, baptism, reincarnation, predestination and transubstantiation, the eighteenth century witnessed an increased interest in protecting the populace from immoral, libelous, and seditious speech. Church doctrine — whether baptism was necessary for salvation or whether bread and wine were the body and blood of Christ or whether there was one God or a Trinity — slowly was overshadowed by whether the writings were immoral, attacks on secular authorities, undermining the state, insults to the royalty, or libelous of individuals and the state.

Writing in 1892, Farrer concluded his *Books Condemned to Be Burnt* with a chapter titled "Our Last Book Fires" in which he stated: "The eighteenth century, which saw the abolition, or the beginning of the abolition, of so many bad customs of the most respectable lineage and antiquity, saw also the hangman employed for the last time for the punishment of books. The custom of book-burning, never formally abolished, died out at last from a gradual decline of public belief in its efficacy" (170). Book burning, of course did not "die out at last."

There were, however, signs that changes were taking place in the eighteenth century affecting the burning of books and their authors. As Levy has observed, "Book burnings ... were as typical of the eighteenth century in character as of the seventeenth. But a proceeding against an author's writings instead of against the author represents a leap in toleration" (1993 276). Also, while the demise of the Inquisition was still decades in the future, there were indications that the inquisitors were losing their influence and power at the end of the eighteenth century. In his *The Spanish Inquisition* Tuberville refers to the 1797 suggestion that "the Holy Office should be abolished": "The spirit of the age, reflected in the attitude of the Court and the ministers, was too strong for the Inquisition; it no longer possessed the authority and respect that it had hitherto enjoyed, and many of its scantily-paid officials grew slack and indifferent. When it acted with its old assurance it met with no support from educated classes and even sometimes with popular hostility. Some high-handed proceedings on the part of the tribunal at Alicante led to the suggestion, brought forward in 1797 and the two succeeding years, that the Holy Office should be abolished" (210). In his two volume work focusing on book burnings in England, Charles Gillett concludes: "After the Restoration, measures of repression were adopted, but usually fire was allowed to do its work. Some books were suppressed, but their number was not large, and even burning gradually went out of fashion and occurred only sporadically" (12). "Sporadically" or not, the books continued to be set afire in England, New England, France, Italy, Poland, Spain, China, and other countries.

In 1700, New Englander Robert Calef's *More Wonders of the Invisible World,* published in England because Calef could find no printer for the book in the colonies, was devoted to an attack on witchcraft as practiced in New England and on criticism of Cotton Mather who claimed Calef had libeled him. While many sources assert that Calef's book was burned at Harvard College in 1700 by Cotton's father, Increase Mather, a few sources question whether such a burning ever took place. In its entry for Calef, *The National Cyclopedia of American Biography* reports that "The title [of Calef's book] was suggested by that of Mather's celebrated work, 'The Wonder of the Invisible World' (1692), and the book, which was largely a compilation was aimed at the ministers of Boston — the Mathers especially. Increase Mather, then president of Harvard, ordered copies publicly burned in the college yard" (8 165). Similarly, *Who Was Who in America*'s entry for Calef reads: "Started dispute with Mather family by accusing Cotton Mather of attempt to start 'witch hunt' similar to one at Salem Mass., 1693; believed that witches existed, but denied possibility of proving anyone to be a witch; expressed his view in More Wonders of the Invisible World, 1697, copy of book publicly burned in Harvard Square by Increase Mather" (91).

Still other sources report that *More Wonders of the Invisible World* was publicly burned in the Harvard College Yard by order of President Increase Mather. In his *Narratives of the Witchcraft Cases: 1648–1706* Burr states in his Introduction to Calef's book: "Why it found no printer in New England can be guessed; the storm it raised when it appeared in print is well known. President Increase Mather 'ordered the wicked book to be burnt in the college yard,' and his son's diary is eloquent with vexation" (1914 293). Finally, the *American National Biography*, in its Calef entry, reports that a copy of Calef's book "was burned in Harvard Yard at the order of Increase Mather, president of Harvard College" (Garraty and Carnes 4 210)

However, a few sources, while not overtly denying the book burning took place, have hedged a bit. The authors of a biography of Cotton Mather put it this way: "Tradition based solely on the testimony of one man has it that Increase Mather, still president of Harvard, ordered the book burned in Harvard Square" (Boas 1928 147). Similarly, another source stated: "According to a rather slim tradition, Increase Mather, then president of Harvard, ordered the book to be burned in Harvard Yard" (Kunitz and Haycraft 126).

In 1693, Cotton Mather had published *The Wonders of the Invisible World* in which he defended and advocated the hunting of witches, declaring: "I have indeed set my self to Countermine the whole Plot of the Devil against New England, in every Branch of it, as far as one of my Darkness can comprehend such a Work of Darkness" (Burr 1914 211). Calef, however, saw the witch hunters as a "dreadful enemy": early in his book, after referring to "comman calamities" in New England and the "devastations and cruelties of the barbarous Indians," he wrote: "But this is not all, they [New Englanders] have been harrast (on many accounts) by a more dreadful Enemy, as will herein appear to considerate. Were it as we are told in *Wonders of the Invisible World,* that the Devils were walking our Streets with lengthned Chains making a dreadful noise in our Ears, and Brimstone, even with a Metaphor, was making a horrid and a hellish stench in our Nostrils...." After listing the witch hunting tragedies—"to let loose the Devils of Envy, Hatred, Pride, Cruelty, and Malice against each other; yet still disguised under the Mask of Zeal for God, and left them to the branding one another with the odious Name of Witch; and upon the Accusation of those above mentioned, Brother to Accuse and Prosecute Brother, Children their Parents, Pastors and Teachers their immediate Flock unto death ...; Estates seized, Families of Children and others left to the Mercy of the Wilderness (not to mention here the Numbers prescribed [condemned to death] in Prisons, or Executed, etc.)— ." Calif observes: "All which Tragedies, tho begun in one Town, or rather by one Parish, has Plague-like spread more than through that Country. And by its Eccho giving a brand of Infamy to this whole Country, throughout the World" (Burr 1914 299). Mather contended that he had been libelled and filed a lawsuit against Calef which was subsequently dropped.

Other colonial writings condemned as, among other things, profane, were set afire in New England early in the eighteenth century. On December 5, 1705, the General Court in Massachusetts ordered that "two Irreligious prophane & scandalous printed Pamphlets sent to this Court, with a Letter Subscribed John Rogers & John Rogers, jun. be burn'd in the great Street in Boston neer the whipping Post, by the Common Executioner, on the morrow at one oclock afternoon" (Duniway 79). Seven years later, in April 1712, "John Green, of Boston, mariner or schoolmaster, was fined five pounds and put under bonds for publishing 'a most prophane, filthy & obscene discourse or sermon, tending to vilify the word & ordinances of God, & to debauch & corrupt the morals of the youth of this place.' Furthermore, 'the original book and copies thereof' were ordered to be publicly burned by the common hangman" (Duniway 79).

In the eighteenth century, the book burning rituals continued in Europe, but the fires reducing the blasphemous-heretical books to ashes decreased towards the end of the century. Increasingly, burnings of blasphemous-heretical works gave way to burnings of seditious and obscene publications. However, well into the eighteenth century, the "poisonous," blasphemous works of such writers as Voltaire, Rousseau, Diderot, and others were being burned in such countries as England, Ireland, France, Holland, Switzerland, and Italy.

At the outset of the century, John Asgill had the "honor" of being elected to both the Irish and English parliaments *and* being expelled from both *and* having his books ordered to be burned by both, in 1703 and 1707. Asgill had published in 1700 a work titled *An Argument Proving that According to the Covenant of Eternal Life revealed in the Scriptures, Man may be Translated from Hence into that Eternal Life without Passing Through Death, although the Humane Nature of Christ Himself could not be Thus Translated till He had Passed Through Death.* The book was condemned as being blasphemous and "the [Irish] house ordered his pamphlet on death to be burnt by the hangman, and fortnight afterwards (11 Oct. 1703) expelled him and declared him incapable of sitting again" and on December 18, 1707, the book was ordered by the English parliament "to be burnt, and Asgill, having appeared in his place and made his defense (published in 1712), was expelled" (*DNB* 1908 1 632).

As Farrer has indicated, "In this book of 106 pages Asgill argued that death, which had come by Adam, had been removed by the death of Christ, and had lost its legal power. He claimed the right, and asserted his expectation, of actual translation; and so went by the nickname of 'Translated Asgill'" (Farrer 145). At the outset of his condemned book, Asgill wrote: " *Ante obitum felix nemo, supremaque fata* is a fiction of Poets. And that old Motto (worn upon tombstones) *Death is the Gate of Life,* is a lie. Whereas it is just so far out of the way" (Asgill).

There is some question as to whether Asgill really was sincere in expressing these beliefs about achieving eternal life without passing through death. Farrer writes that "Asgill clearly wrote in all honesty and sincerity, though the contrary has been suggested" (147), and the *Dictionary of National Biography* reports: "Asgill's seriousness in the pamphlet on death was doubted at the time. A German traveller in 1710 ... gives a report that it was written in answer to a lady's challenge to show his skill in maintaining paradoxes. The book itself indicates no want of sincerity, though some ludicrous phrases were very unfairly wrested by the committee of the English House of Commons to colour the charge of blasphemy" (*DNB* 1908 1 632). Whether sincere or not, Asgill's work was considered serious enough by the Irish and English parliaments to warrant setting it afire.

While Asgill and his opponents were arguing about death, resurrection, and eternal life, William Coward was in dispute with his adversaries over the issues of immortality and the soul. Coward had published two books in 1702 that were condemned by Parliament

and publicly burned in 1704. In ordering the burning of the books by the common hangman in the Palace Yard at Westminster Parliament asserted that the books contained
"offensive doctrines." The House of Commons resolved, "That the said books do contain
therein divers Doctrines and Positions, contrary to the Doctrine of the Church of England,
and tending to the Subversion of the Christian Religion" (Gillett 1932 588).

The title page of one of the condemned books read: *Second Thoughts concerning human
soul, demonstrating the notion of Human soul, as believ'd to be a spiritual immortal substance,
united to human body, to be a plain heathenish invention, and not consonant to the principles of philosophy, reason, or religion; but the ground only of many absurd, and superstitious
opinions, abominable to the reformed churches, and derogatory in general to true Christianity.* The title of the other work that also was set afire read: *Grand Essay; or a Vindication of
Reason and Religion against Impostures of Philosophy.*

At the outset of Coward's *Second Thoughts concerning human soul,* an "Epistle Dedicatory" is presented in which he attacks the superficiality and absurdity of churchmen and
philosophers: "For as to the authority of the Fathers, whose pious ignorance in former
times may be a just excuse for their errors rendering it invincible, I cannot nor indeed
ought in reason to be obliged by, or subservient to, because their scrutinies into the mysteries of religion, seem in many cases, as appears, by their writings, to be very superficial,
and slight, resolving them into an implicit faith, where the difficulty seemed too knotting
for their apprehensions."

"As to the philosopher's notion of the soul of man," wrote Coward, "I think, I have
abundantly proved in the following papers, to the satisfaction of any reasonable judge,
upon what ridiculous and absurd foundation their opinion of the nature and essence of
human soul, called the substantial form of men, is built; how incoherent and inconsistent
with it self, and the common principles of reason it appears to be; therefore I will not trouble you to recite here, by way of anticipation, what I have more fully explained elsewhere,
and you may read, if you please."

In Chapter Five, Coward argues: "That it is a doctrine or belief most consonant to the
principles of philosophy, that human soul will cease to be when the body dies, and consequently the philosophical notion of it, commonly received, is erroneous" (125). In Chapter Six he argues: "That it is a doctrine of belief most consonant to the dictates of right
reason, that human soul will cease to be, when the body dies, and consequently it cannot
be a substantial immortal spirit united to the body" (145). Chapter Seven: "That it is a doctrine or belief most consonant to the whole tenor of the Holy Scriptures, that human soul
and life are the same thing, and consequently the notion of a spiritual immortal substance
in man is erroneous; and according to the common course of providence man's immortality begins not until the resurrection" (177). Coward's willingness to recant "anything contrary to religion or morality" did not save his books from being set afire by the common
hangman (*DNB* 4 1298).

In March 1710, the writings of Henry Sacheverell and Matthew Tindal were set afire,
along with the 1683 *Judgment and Decree* of the Oxford Convocation, and several other
condemned works. The attacks on these books included both religious and political elements. While the Sacheverell and Tindal publications were denounced as seditious, they
were also condemned as blasphemous libels. Extracts from Tindal's books were denounced
as "scandalous, seditious, and blasphemous libels, highly reflecting upon the Christian Religion, and the Church of England, and tend to promote Immorality and Atheism, and to
create Divisions, Schisms, and Factions, among her Majesty's Subjects" (Gillett 1932 613).

In the *Articles of Impeachment* of Sacheverell, Article IV read: "He, the said Henry

Sacheverell, in his Sermons and Books, doth falsely and maliciously suggest, That her Majesty's Administration, both in Ecclesiastical and Civil Affairs, tend to the Destruction of the Constitution, and that there are Men of Characters and Stations in Church and State, who are False Brethren.... [A]nd that his said malicious and seditious suggestions may make the stronger Impressions upon the Minds of her Majesty's Subjects: He, the said Henry Sacheverell doth wickedly wrest and pervert divers Texts and Passages of Holy Scripture" (*Articles of Impeachment* 4). As indicated in the *Dictionary of National Biography,* in the St. Paul's sermons of November 1709, "Sacheverell spoke strongly in favour of the doctrine of non-resistance, declared that the church was in danger from toleration, occasional conformity, and schism, openly attacked the bishop of Salisbury ... and pointed at the Whig ministers as the false friends and real enemies of the church" (*DNB* 1909 7 570).

While Sacheverell was declared guilty, the sentence was "merely that he should be suspended from preaching for three years; he was left at liberty to perform other clerical functions, and to accept preferment during that period. His two sermons were ordered to be burnt by the common hangman. Such a sentence was felt to be a triumph for him and the high-church and Tory party" (*DNB* 1909 7 571). *Cobbett's Parliamentary History* reported that "the Sermon was ordered to be burnt, in the presence of the Lord Mayor and sheriffs of London; and this was done.... The Lords also voted, that the Decrees of the university of Oxford, passed in 1683, in which the absolute authority of princes, and the unalterableness of the hereditary right of succeeding to the crown, were asserted in a very high strain, should be burnt with Sacheverell's Sermon" (7 885).

There were, however, other books condemned to be burned at the same time: "The Commons also, upon a Complaint made: to them of a book entitled, 'Collections of Passages referred to by Dr. Sacheverell, in his Answer to the Articles of his Impeachment,' ordered the same to be burnt. On the other hand, the Doctor's friends complained to the House, of a Book entitled, 'The Rights of the Christian Church, &c.' and a defence of it, in two parts, with a Letter from a Country-Attorney to a Country Parson, concerning the Rights of the Church; and Le Clerc's judgment of that book in the Bibliotheque Choisie. All of which were condemned to the flames; as was also a Treatise of the word Person, by John Clendon of the Inner-Temple" (*Cobbett's Parliamentary History of England* VII 887).

This exchange of book burnings has been referred to by Farrer: "At all events, Sacheverell won for himself a place in English history. That he would have brought the House of Lords into conflict with the Church, causing it to condemn to the flames, together with his own sermons, the famous Oxford decree of 1683, which asserted the most absolute claims of monarch, condemned twenty-seven propositions as impious and seditious, and most of them as heretical and blasphemous, and condemned the works of nineteen writers to the flames, would alone entitle his name to remembrance. So incensed indeed were the Commons, that they also condemned to be burnt the very *Collections of Passages referred to by Dr. Sacheverell in the Answer to the Articles of Impeachment*" (160).

As indicated above, when Parliament ordered the burning of Sacheverell's writings, an order also went out to burn the works of Matthew Tindal, Jean Le Clerc, and John Clendon. The burning of the works of these three authors took place two days before Sacheverell's sermons were reduced to ashes.

In 1706, Tindal had published his *The Rights of the Christian Church asserted Against the Romish, and all other Priests who claim an Independent Power over it, with a Preface concerning the Government of the Church of England, as by Law Establish'd* which as the DNB reports, "was ordered by the House of Commons to be burnt by the common hangman along with Sacheverells sermons (25 March 1710) by way of proving, apparently, that the whigs did not approve deists" (DNB XIX 884). Tindal has been referred to by Farrer as a "brilliant writer" and Levy calls him "one of the foremost deists of the early eighteenth century" (1993 292). In praising Tindal's *Rights of the Christian Church,* Farrer says of this "immortal work": "In those days, when the question that most agitated men's minds was whether the English Church was of Divine Right, and so independent of the civil power, or whether it was the creature of, and therefore subject to, the law, no work more convincingly proved the latter than this work of Tindal; a work which, even now, ought to be far more generally known than it is, no less for its great historical learning than for its scathing denunciations of priestcraft" (160).

Tindal's 416 page work begins with an eighty page Preface that declares at the outset: "Nothing is more disputed at present, than who is the best Churchman, both High and Low Church laying claim to it; and therefore it can't be doubted but both will approve my Design in setting this Dispute in a fair Light, and showing what is meant by the Church of England as by law established: wherein I shall make it appear that they who raise the greatest Noise about the Danger of the Church, are the greatest Enemies to it, by asserting such Notions as undermine both Church and State, and are in direct opposition to the Principles of the Reformation; and that they mean some other Church besides the Church of England, which being established by Acts of Parliament, is a perfect Creature of the Civil Power" (Tindal iii–iv).

The Table of Contents of the ten chapter work provides an introduction to Tindal's claims:

Chap. 1. That there cannot be two Independent Powers in the same Society.
Chap. 2. That the Spirituality's which Clergymen claim, are either such as are peculiar to the Divine Nature, or else were only bestow'd on the Apostles: And that both these serve 'em as a Pretence for invading the Rights of the People, and of their Representatives.
* * * *
Chap. 5. The Clergy's indeavouring at an Independent Power, not only prevents the further spreading of the Gospel, but is the cause of its having already lost so much ground.
Chap. 6. That the Clergy's claiming an Independent Power, is of all things the most destructive to the Interest of Religion, and is the Cause of those Corruptions under which Christianity Labours [Tindal xc–xci].

Levy, referring to the burning of Tindal's books, observes that "his works were burned as blasphemous, his printers suffered prosecution for publishing against the government, honing Tindal's appreciation of the freedom of religion and of the press" (1993 292).

Dutchman Jean Le Clerc's *Bibliothéque Choisie* was set afire because in his review of Tindal's work, Le Clerc "argued on behalf of basic ideas in harmony with his own beliefs which were not yet fully acceptable to the traditionally-minded in Holland and England" (Golden 79). In his review, Le Clerc "said he was embarrassed for lack of space not to have done more for the rest of the book and simply listed the ten chapter headings which elaborated on the points which had been mentioned in the introduction" (Golden 81). Le Clerc's review included long extracts from *The Rights of the Christian Church*; and to the thinking of those burning Tindal's writings it made little sense to burn Tindal's book and not to burn a review containing long extracts from it.

During the same week that Sacheverell's sermons were set afire, a thirty-two page tract titled *Collections of Passages referred to by Dr. Sacheverell* was also burned. Just as both Tindal's books and Le Clerc's book containing passages from Tindal's work were set afire, so too was it that Sacheverell's sermons were burned along with *Collections of Passages* containing "material that his lawyers had read aloud to the Lords and the audience" (Levy 1993

286). In both cases the original works were burned and in both cases books containing passages from their works were also burned. In one week in March 1710, the words of Sacheverell, Tindal, Le Clerc, and Clendon went up in smoke. Deist, Trinitarian, and anti–Trinitarian books were reduced to ashes. As explained by Farrer, "Parliament was in a burning mood; for Sacheverell's friends, wishing to justify his cry of the Church in danger, easily succeeded in procuring the burning of Tindal's and Clendon's books" (160).

Thirteen years later, in 1723, a book that had been burned two centuries earlier, *Christianismi Restitutio* by Michael Servetus, was again set afire in London. During the preparation for the 1723 publication of the Servetus book in England, an employee working for the printer notified the bishop of London that "heresy was being promulgated in his city." The bishop, Dr. Edmund Gibson, "one of a number of conservative clergymen who had managed to preach and prosper ... immediately sought and received an injunction under the Blasphemy Laws from the Censor of the Press. On May 27, 1723, Drummer [a Unitarian who had brought a transcription of *Christianismi Restitutio* to England] opened his door and found himself face to face with the police. The proof sets that were in his home were confiscated and subsequently burned, and Drummer himself was fined. He was lucky to escape prison" (Goldstone 250).

The same year the heretical-blasphemous book by Servetus was set fire in London, Pietro Giannone's *Civil History of the Kingdom of Naples* was immediately condemned by the Church in Rome. As the translator of Giannone's work reports in his Preface, "the Work no sooner appear'd in Publick, A.D. 1723, than the Court of Rome was alarm'd: It was Censur'd, Condemn'd, and the Sale and Reading of it prohibited, under severe Penalties" (Ogilvie Preface).

In writing of the censorship of the seventeenth century and its effects, M'Crie refers to the burning of Giannone's works in Italy in the eighteenth century. After writing that "not satisfied with exerting a rigid censorship over the press, the [Spanish] Inquisitors intruded into private houses, ransacked the libraries of the learned and curious, and carried off and retained at their pleasure such books as they, in their ignorance, suspected to be of a dangerous character" (M'Crie 383). Then, turning to Italy, M'Crie states: "In Italy the same causes produced the same effects. Genius, taste, and learning were crushed under the iron hand of inquisitorial despotism. The imprisonment of Galileo in the seventeenth and the burning of the works of Giannone in the eighteenth century, are sufficient indications of the deplorable state of the Italians, during a period in which knowledge was advancing with such rapidity in countries long regarded by them as barbarous" (386). What was being set on fire was Giannone's 1723 *Istoria civile del regno di Napoli*.

As soon as the work was published, it was denounced by the Holy Office as "scandalous and seditious, on no account to be read or translated by the faithful, and a copy of it would be ceremonially burnt. In Naples the cardinal-archbishop excommunicated the author; the newly appointed Viceroy, himself a cardinal, advised Giannone to flee for his life" (Trevor-Roper 659). In his essay "Pietro Giannone and Great Britain," Trevor-Roper expresses high praise for Giannone and his "great work": "That great work, though essentially a work of scholarship, was both historically and politically revolutionary: historically, because it ignored the traditional and privilege separation of ecclesiastical from political history; politically, because it justified the programme of those reformers who sought, throughout catholic Europe, to remove ancient 'feudal' obstructions to modern progress and 'enlightenment'" (659).

Ogilvie, the translator of Giannone's work, in expressing praise for it provides more than a hint why the Church condemned the work and set it on fire; Oglivie writes: "The Author [Giannone] tho' in Communion with the Church of Rome, has not been afraid to tell a great many bold Truths, nowise consistent with the Credit and Honour of that Court. To give one Instance among many; throughout the Course of the History, he clearly shews us, how that Monster of a Spiritual Monarchy, an *Imperium in Imperio,* was conceiv'd, brought forth, and nourish'd till it came to full Maturity. The Reader will likewise see what Opinion he had of Relicks, Pilgrimages, Image-worship, the great Number of Holy-days, and other Practices introduc'd during the Ages of Ignorance and Darkness" (Preface).

Ditchfield, also praising Giannone's book, states: "This remarkable work occupied the writer twenty years, and contains the result of much study and research, exposing with great boldness the usurpations of the Pope and his cardinals, and other ecclesiastical enormities, and revealing many obscure points with regard to the constitution, laws, and customs of the kingdom of Naples" (104).

While M'Crie, Trevor-Roper, Ditchfield and others have acclaimed *The Civil History of Naples,* the 1913 edition of the *Catholic Encyclopedia* (with the Church's imprimatur) asserts that Giannone's work is "a compilation of biased attacks and mistatements" with a "bitter anti-ecclesiastical bias" (VI 548). Referring to the burning of Giannone's work, Farrer writes that the five volume book was "burnt by the Inquisition, which, for his escape, would have suppressed the author as well as his book, for his free criticisms of Popes and ecclesiastics. His escape saved the eighteenth century from the reproach of burning a writer" (21). While Giannone was not burned at the stake, he was captured and imprisoned for the last twelve years of his life, dying on March 7, 1748.

Two years earlier, Denis Diderot's *Pensées philosophiques* had met the same fiery fate as Giannone's *Civil History of the Kingdom of Naples,* being accused of "presenting to restless and reckless spirits the venom of the most criminal opinions that the depravity of human reason is capable of" (Furbank 30–31). Referring to the burning of Diderot's work, Crocker writes: "On the seventh of July [1746], the Parlement of Paris condemned the work and ordered it be burned in effigy, an honor it shared with many other famous books of the century. They accused it of 'presenting to restless and bold minds the most absurd and most criminal thoughts of which the depravation of human nature is capable, and of placing all religions, by an affected uncertainty, nearly on the same level, in order to end up by not recognizing any'" (68).

In summarizing the main points of Diderot's *Pensées philosophiques,* Fellows wrote in 1989: "Three main points can be extracted from the work. [T]he first of these is a defense of the passions or, more exactly, an attempt to view biological and psychological man with greater understanding. The second is ostensibly a relentless attack against fanaticism, and religious dogma, but in reality, against any highly organized, stultifying force or forces. The third point, itself very much with us today, is that adherence to any faith, whether it is a personal or group conviction, should pass through the necessary process of critical reasoning" (32).

In his defense of the passions Diderot wrote: "I. People are for ever declaiming against the passions; they attribute to them all the pains that man endures, and forget that they are also the source of all his pleasures.... Without them, there is no sublime, either in morality or in achievement; the fine arts return to puerility, and virtue becomes a pettifogging thing. II. Sober passions make men commonplace.... III. Deadened passions degrade men of extraordinary quality. Constraint annihilates the grandeur and energy of nature" (Jourdain 27–28).

As to skepticism and beliefs, Diderot maintained: "XXXIII. It is as hazardous to believe too much as too little. The danger of being a polytheist is neither greater nor less than the danger of being an atheist; now skepticism is the only defence, in any period and any place, against these two opposite extremes. XXX. What is a sceptic? A philosopher who has questioned all he believes, and who believes what a legitimate use of his reason and his senses has proved to him to be true."

Turning to the subject of impiety, he asserted: "XXXV. I hear cries against impiety on every side. The Christian is impious in Asia, the Mussulman in Europe, the papist in London, the Calvinist in Paris, the Jansenist at the top of the rue St. Jacques, the Molinist at the bottom of the faubourg St. Medard. What is an impious person, then? Either everybody, or nobody. XXXVI. When the pious declaim against scepticism, it seems to me that they either do not understand their own interest, or are inconsistent. If it is certain that a true faith, to be embraced, and a false faith, to be abandoned, need only be fully known, surely it must be highly desirable that universal doubt should spread over the surface of the earth, and that every race should consent to the examination of the truth of its religion. Our missionaries would find a good half of their work already accomplished" (Jourdain 45–47)

Such views were, of course, anathema to both the ecclesiastic and Catholic secular authorities. Diderot's local parish priest, complaining to the police in 1747, denounced Diderot in the following terms: "He utters blasphemies against Jesus Christ and the Holy Virgin that I would not venture to put into writing.... In one of his conversations he admitted to being the author of one of the two works condemned by the *Parlement* and burned about two years ago. I have been informed that for more than a year he has been working on another work still more dangerous to religion" (Furbank 47).

Diderot died on July 31, 1784, and according to his daughter, his last words were: "The first step toward philosophy is disbelief" (Mason 1982 29). The skeptic Diderot, or the "atheist" as some called him, was given a somewhat extravagant funeral after "a priest watched over the bier, while the house was sumptuously draped in black.... The body was carried to the parish church of Saint-Roch, and, the words of absolution pronounced, was lowered beneath the slabs in the Chapel of the Virgin" (Crocker 436). According to Furbank, "The funeral took place at the church of Saint-Roch, and Vandeul [son-in-law] arranged things in great style. It was the custom to hire priests (at 1 *livre* apiece) as attendants at funerals, and Diderot had no less than fifty to see him into his grave. He was buried in the Chapelle de la Vierge, and his bones have long since disappeared" (430). Or as Crocker has put it, "And, strangely enough, it is not known, nor in all probability will it ever be known, where the remains of Diderot have found their last resting place" (436).

Diderot's fellow skeptic and "atheist," Claude Helvetius was to see his *De l'esprit* burned in 1759, just as Diderot had witnessed the burning of his *Pensées philosophiques* thirteen years earlier. Published in 1758, *De l'esprit* was immediately and forcefully attacked by ecclesiastic and secular authorities. The extent of the denunciations of Helvetius' work is described by Smith who writes: "No book during the eighteenth century, except perhaps Rousseau's *Emile* [see Chapter 3] evoked such an outcry from religious and civil authorities or such universal public interest. Condemned as atheistic, materialistic, sacrilegious, immoral, and subversive, it enjoyed a remarkable *succes de scandale.*... It was attacked in Church periodicals and in polemical pamphlets, in the literary *salons* and in popular songs, from bishops' pulpits and from the stage of the *Théâtre français.* Though Helvetius retracted his book three times, he was condemned by the Archbishop of Paris (Nov. 1758), the Pope (Jan. 1759), the Parlement of Paris (Feb. 1759), the Sorbonne (Apr. 1759), and by various bishops" (1964 332).

A similar account of the fierce condemnations directed against Helvetius and his book has been provided by Grossman: "The general aims of the book — to present man realistically without the adornment vested on it by religion and idealistic philosophy, to found a system of morality, based on what he thought to be the true nature of man—conflicted with the arbitrary authority imposed by Church and State.... The book was attacked as being subversive of all morality and religion.... The sale of the book was forbidden by order of Council. It was burned, together with the *Encyclopedia*" (16–17).

Condemning *De l'esprit* immediately after it was published in 1758, the authorities swiftly acted to destroy it by fire at the outset of 1759: "The book was referred to the <u>parlement</u> of Paris on 23 January 1759, and after the judicial address of the attorney-general commissioners were appointed to examine it.... On 31 January Pope Clement XIII declared it scandalous, licentious and dangerous. A few days later, on 6 February 1759, the parlement duly condemned it and the gloomy issue reached its climax when, on the 10th, *De l'esprit*, in the company of Voltaire's poem *Sur la loi naturelle,* was torn and publicly burned at the foot of the great staircase of the Palais" (Cumming 84).

In condemning the persecution of Helvetius, Voltaire wrote: "It is a little extraordinary ... that they should have persecuted, disgraced, and harassed, a much respected philosopher in our days, the innocent, the good Helvetius, for having said that, if men had been without hands they could not have built houses, or worked in tapestry. Apparently, those who have condemned this proposition, have a secret for cutting stones and wood, and for sewing with the feet" (Helvetius ix). In *De l'esprit* Helvetius had asserted: "If Nature, instead of hands and flexible fingers, had terminated our wrist with the foot of a horse, mankind would doubtless have been totally destitute of art, habitation, and defence, against other animals. Wholly employed in the care of procuring food, and avoiding the beasts of prey, they would have still continued wandering in the forests, like fugitive flocks" (12).

Through his satire Voltaire ridiculed the "injudicious persecution" of Helvetius: "Who would believe, that, in the eighteenth century, a philosopher would have been dragged before the secular tribunals, and treated as impious by others, for having said that men could not have exercised the arts if they had not had hands. I have no doubt that they will soon condemn to the galleys the first who shall have the insolence to say, that a man cannot think without his head; for, some bachelor will tell him, the soul is a pure spirit, the head is nothing but matter; God can place the soul in the nails, as well as in the scull, therefore I prescribe you as impious" (Helvetius x).

In one form or another, attacks on religion, Christians, and Catholics appear throughout *De l'esprit.* At one point, Helvetius discusses the intolerance, cruelties, and crimes perpetrated in the name of religion and Christianity:

> At length fanaticism arms afresh the hand of Christian princes, and orders the Catholics to massacre the heretics: then again appears on the earth the tortures invented by the Phalarises, the Busirises, and the Neros; it prepares, it kindles, in Spain the flaming pile of the inquisition; while the pious Spaniards leave their ports, and traverse the seas, to plant the cross and desolation in America. If we cast our eyes to the north, the south, the east, and the west, we everywhere see the sacred knife of religion held up to the breasts of women, children, and old men; the earth smoking with the blood of victims sacrificed to the false Gods or to the Supreme Being; every place offers nothing to the sight but the vast, the horrible, carnage caused by a want of toleration [182–183].

Such criticisms of religion and the Church could not be tolerated, especially by ecclesiastical authorities who identified *De l'esprit* with "poison": "On 9 April [1759] the Faculté de Théologie de Paris announced its anticipated conclusions. The servile Sorbonne attacked the literary value of *De l'esprit* and decided that of all modern literature it contained 'the essence of poisons'" (Cumming 85). The book was burned in 1759; Helvetius died in 1771, a year after the burning of his friend Paul-Henri Holbach's *Le Système de la nature*.

The views of Holback and Helvetius had enough similarities that at the time *The System of Nature* was published in 1770, the anonymously published work "was first attributed to Helvetius, and then to Miarabeau" (Holbach iv). By order of the Parlement of Paris, Holbach's *The System of Nature* was burned in August 1770 for Holbach "had lurched out into as severe a criticism of the State as of the Church" (Wickwar 208). In his discussion of government and rights, Holbach declared: "A society of which the chiefs, aided by the laws, do not procure any good for its members, evidently loses its right over them: those chiefs who injure society, lose the right of commanding. It is not our country without it secures the welfare of its inhabitants; a society without equity contains only enemies; a society oppressed is composed only of tyrants and slaves; slaves are incapable of being citizen; it is liberty — property — security, that render our country dear to us; and its' the true love of his country that forms the citizen" (70).

As for religious issues, there was no shortage of assertions that would be condemned by the ecclesiastics who argued for the burning of *The System of Nature*. Holbach concluded that "the most simple reflection upon the nature of the soul, ought to convince man that the idea of its immortality is only an illusion of the brain" (118). Towards the end of *The System of Nature,* Holbach devotes several pages defending atheists and atheism in which he states: "Atheism is only so rare because every thing conspires to intoxicate man, from his most tender age, with a dazzling enthusiasm, or to puff him up with a systematic and organized ignorance, which is [of] all ignorance the most difficult to vanquish and to root out. Theology is nothing more than a science of words, which, by dint of repetition, we accustom ourselves to substitute for things; as soon as we feel disposed to analyze them, we find that they do not present us with any actual sense" (328).

Holbach's attack on religion and the ecclesiastics was too radical for Voltaire who, himself a deist, had criticized the Church and its priests. Upon publication of Holbach's work, Voltaire responded with a refutation, *Dieu et les hommes,* that was also burned along with *De l'esprit.* As Besterman has observed: "[W]hen Voltaire published a refutation of Holbach, that also was condemned, as when the public prosecutor Antoine Louis Seguier delivered a *Requisitoire* which led to the public burning of works by Holbach and Voltaire's *Dieu et les hommes,* which was directed against them" (1976 523). Setting fire to Holbach's work did not seriously detract from its influence; as Richardson writes in his Preface to *The System of Nature:* "Holbach was one of William Godwin's major sources for his ideas about political justice, and Shelley, who discussed Holbach with Godwin, quotes extensively from *The System of Nature* in *Queen Mab.* Furthermore, Volney's *Ruins,* another important book for Shelley, is directly descended from *The System of Nature.* On the other side, Holbach was a standing challenge to such writers as Coleridge and Goethe and was reprinted and translated extensively in America, where his work was well known to the rationalist circle around Jefferson and Barlow" (vi).

Church authorities were interested in condemning not only books questioning the existence of the soul or immortality or God, but also books dealing with alchemy, magic, and the occult. On March 21, 1791, the Inquisition in Rome denounced alchemist, magician, charlatan, and Freemason Alessandro Cagliostro and ordered the burning of his book titled *Egyptian Masonry.* Taking on the title of Count, he conducted séances, practiced clairvoyance, and portrayed himself as a healer of the sick. Grete de Francesco devotes a chapter in his *The Power of the Charlatan* to Cagliostro which begins: "Cagliostro was the most renowned of all the charlatans in the eighteenth century. No other stimulated so strongly the minds of representative literary men to criticism, admiration, or poetic expression. Goethe, Schiller, Tiek, and Dumas made him a leading character in various literary productions; he was a genuinely popular figure, occupying the imagination of the best men of his time" (209).

When the Inquisition ordered the burning of *Egyptian Masonry*, the sentence imposed on Cagliostro identified him with not only "heretics, dogmatics, heresiarchs, and propagators of magic and superstition," but also with Freemasonry: "Giuseppe Balsamo [Cagliostro] ... has been found guilty and condemned to the said censures and penalties as decreed by the Apostolic laws of Clement XII and Benedict XIV, against all persons who in any manner favour or form societies and conventicles of Freemasonry, as well as by the edict of the Council of State against all persons convicted of this crime in Rome or in any other place in the dominions of the Pope" (Trowbridge 300). The order to burn the book followed: "[T]he manuscript book which has for its title *Egyptian Masonry* is solemnly condemned as containing rites, propositions, doctrines, and a system which being superstitious, impious, heretical, and altogether blasphemous, open a road to sedition and the destruction of the Christian religion. This book, therefore, shall be burnt by the executioner, together with all the other documents relating to this sect" (Trowbridge 301).

Schnur reports that Cagliostro "had been imprudent enough not to destroy his papers. His correspondence, the manuscript of the Egyptian ritual and a quantity of Masonic regalia were found and impounded" (299). After having been found guilty by the Inquisition, "the manuscript on Egyptian Masonry and the Masonic regalia found in his possession were to be publicly burned by the hangman" (Schnur 303). After the burning of the book and regalia, Cagliostro was imprisoned in a dungeon in an almost inaccessible fortress near Montefeltro where he died in 1795.

Just as it was not always clear whether heretical-blasphemous books were being burned in Europe because they were threats to orthodox religious beliefs or because they were perceived as seditious and undermining secular authorities, so too was it not always clear in China where the "tares" and "poisonous" books were also being reduced to ashes. Various scholars have commented on the Asians' fear that the proselytizing of the Catholic and Protestant missionaries had as its goal the subversion of political institutions and of destroying national security and unity. As Sansom has explained: "What the Jesuits were doing in Japan as well as in India and China, was to challenge a national tradition and through it the existing political structure" (129). One of the strongest objections appearing in anti–Christian treatises in Japan "was that to deny the national deities was to imperil the state" (Sansom 175). While the first Christians in Japan in the middle of the sixteenth century were received with a positive response, "the missionaries' intolerance of other religions, however, resulted in strong resistance to them by the Buddhist clergy, and [Japanese ruler] Hideyoshi, after reuniting the country, began to look on Christianity as possibly subversive to unified rule" (Reischauer 87).

Similarly in China, the Christian missionaries were seen as "barbarians" who constituted a threat to Chinese culture, politics, and civilization. Huang Zhen strongly warned: "You may be sure that the Barbarians will not immediately seek to destroy Confucianism. Their plan is to operate initially by means of seduction and to proceed in a furtive manner. Through seduction they can win a joyful welcome in the sight and knowledge of all. By proceeding in a furtive manner, they can win a secret welcome without any anxiety. In the first case they immediately proceed to denigrate Confucianism. In the second, they undermine it" (Gernet 126).

As some Chinese saw it, the missionaries were encouraging revolution when they demanded that converts to Christianity destroy Buddhist writings, statues, and temples. In his condemnation of the missionaries urging these burnings and destructions, Huang Zhen, as a strong critic of the Jesuits, wrote of their ordering supporters to bring them the statues of "sovereign lords": "And they cut the heads off all of them and put them down the latrines or throw them into the fire.... These are things that I myself have seen with my own eyes. So in this way, they incite people to revolt against the Saints [of China]. There is no greater cruelty. These are great crimes and sacrileges" (Gernet 180). As Young has observed, "In essence, Huang was charging the Jesuits with engaging in some form of ideological invasion. The cultural and ideological challenge of the Jesuits could therefore become a political threat" (75). Similarly, Stainton concludes that "by the nineteenth century, Christianity had come to be seen as a heretical teaching with implicit danger to society" (136).

Since, as Huang Zhen claimed, some "gentry and important literati" were "poisoned" by the false teachings and printed books by the Jesuits, one method to help eliminate the poison was to burn the Christian writings. On more than one occasion, Huang Zhen relied on the "poison" metaphor in condemning the "barbarian" Jesuits; he declared: "[Jesuit] Aleni says that more than 7,000 books [of their doctrine] have entered China. There are more than one hundred to be found today in Zhangzhou.... If they continue to upset everything and spread everywhere, these books will end up by destroying the tradition of the Saints. These people will never be satisfied until they have caught everybody in their nets and have spread their poison everywhere" (Gernet 128). And then on another occasion he wrote: "Alas! Our glorious China is disturbed by the pernicious ideas of the Barbarians. Their poison is spreading everywhere and threatens to contaminate millions of generations" (Gernet 128).

In 1800, the Emperor concluded that "the sectarian chieftain Liu Chi-hich" had founded "heretical societies which had spread like poison through five provinces" (Groot 374). Five years later, an Emperor's Decree ordering the burning of some Christian works invoked the "contagion" metaphor: "Since even Buddhism and Taoism are untrustworthy, how much more so is that religion of Europe. It is now of the greatest moment to cleanse one's self of the old contagion, and not again to listen to heretical talk, or believe in it" (Groot 394). The same "poison," "contagion," and "purify" metaphors used by the Church in condemning heretics and their works to be burned were now being used by Asians in setting fire to Christian writings.

An 1811 decree calling for the return of Europeans "back to their own land" further provided: "And the Europeans who remain in Peking in Government employ, shall be kept under control with increased strictness, in order that their intercourse with Bannermen may be effectively stopped, and the poison emanating from them be kept away from the provincial districts. Since Europeans are no more wanted in Government employ, why should they be allowed to go there by stealth and spread their heretical religion? Every Viceroy or Governor shall strictly examine with all his energy whether any such be roaming about in his jurisdiction, in which case he shall immediately track them, arrest them, and prosecute them one by one, in order to purify both root and stem" (Groot 401).

The "tares" metaphor was invoked in condemning other "sects" as heretical. An 1812 Decree warning against "heretical religions and seditious societies" declared that "happiness proceeds from complying with orthodoxy (ching), and misfortune from following heresy (sie). If then some few people belonging to the tares of society contrive means to fan the fire of seduction, but find no one ready to join them, their baseness must gradually die out, and the good manners and customs (fung-suh) together with the hearts daily gain more purity" (Groot 417). Those who possessed unorthodox religious books and images were given the opportunity to escape punishment if they turned over to the authorities the books and images to be burned and destroyed. Once this occurred, "the eyes of the people, all in possession of heavenly (natural?) loyalty, shall be opened to the seductions (to which they were prey); with heartfelt respect they shall keep and observe the Imperial institutions and energetically co-operate to the realization of Our dearest wish affectionately to nurture Our babes (the people), to convert the people to what is right and ameliorate their customs, and weed out the tares for the insurance of rest and peace to the loyalists" (Groot 443).

Punishments inflicted on the propagators of the European religion included arrest, exile, and enslavement. A 1785 Decree was issued calling for the burning of Christian writings and the exile and enslavement of proselytizing Christians: "Europeans propagating their religion here, and thereby leading the people into error, are extremely fatal to the manners and customs and to the human heart" and native Christian pastors "must be banished to Ili, and there be given as slaves to the Oelot" (Groot 332). As stated in the Decree: "[T]hose whom they [Christians] have drawn over to act as propagandists, shall be sent into slavery to the Oelot in Ili, in order that it be publicly shown that there exist punishments to deter from such things. And as for natives who keep the Christian commandments and profess that religion because it was handed down to them by their grandparents and parents, they shall, of course, be forced to conversion; and so their books, writings, and other things brought to light must be melted and burned" (Groot 333).

The 1805 Emperor's Decree ordered several Chinese Christian proselytizers to be sent into enslavement for propagating "their misleading doctrines": "They shall, pursuant to the verdict of the Board of Punishments, be sent to Ili, and there given as slaves to the Oelot; and without using heavy cangues, they shall be exhibited therein for three months, to show that there are punishments to deter people from such crimes. The woman of the Yang tribe, married in that of Chien, who has done duty as leader of the female community, is still more strictly to be reckoned amongst those who did not quietly do their duties. She must therefore be sent up to Ili, and there be given as slave-woman to the soldiery; and she shall not be exempt from wearing the cangue, nor be allowed to redeem her punishment" (Groot 388). The same Decree ordered that two other proselytizers "be placed in the cangue for three months, and when this term expired, be sent up to Ili and there given as slaves to the Oelot" (Groot 389).

While some of the proselytizing Chinese Christians were being yoked and sent off to the remote Ili region in Mongolia to become slaves to the Oelot tribes, the Christian missionaries were burning and destroying Chinese and Japanese religious idols and books. The missionaries demanded that "anyone wishing to be receive baptism had ... first to get rid of everything in his home which might remind him of superstition; Taoist and Buddhist books, works on divination, statuettes and images of deities" (Gernet 178). In one of his letters, Jesuit missionary Matteo Ricci wrote: "Another repentant man who, in penitence, had a long time eaten no meat or fish or eggs or milk, having seen and read the Catechism, brought his idol and his books to us to be burnt and falling on his knees and repeatedly striking his head upon the ground, he begged us to make him a Christian" (Gernet 178). On another occasion, Ricci wrote of a Chinese specialist in the areas of geomancy and horoscopes who set fire to his books: "He had an excellent library and it took him three whole days to inspect it and destroy by fire the works which were forbidden by our Law and of which he possessed a large number, especially those that related to this art of divination — mostly manuscripts — which he collected with great zeal and at much cost" (Gernet 178).

While the Christian missionaries were setting fire to Asian religious idols, sutras, and books, the Chinese themselves were burning the books and woodblocks of their own authors. Goodrich has provided a good sampling of the eighteenth century Chinese edicts ordering the censorship that took place during the "literary inquisition of Ch'ien-lung." The edicts indicate the orders to burn the books were primarily concerned with secular, not religious, matters. Books were condemned to be burned because they were "scornful of the Manchus," because they insulted previous dynasties, and contained "false and rebellious statements." In his *The Literary Inquisition of Ch'ien-lung*, Goodrich provides eight tests that were used by Chinese officials to "determine a book's fitness to exist":

A. Was it anti-dynastic or rebellious?

B. Did it insult previous dynasties which were, in a sense, ancestral to the Ch'ing?

C. Did it concern the northern and northwestern frontiers and military or naval defense?

D. Was it by, or did it contain the writings of certain authors: Ch'ien Ch'ien-i, Ch'u Ta-chun, Chin Pao, Lu Liu-liang, Hsu Shu-k'uei...?

E. Did it contain heterodox opinion on the Confucian canon?

F. Was the Style un-literary?

G. Did it give a biased, or, in Manchu eyes, unfavorable account of any incident or series of events in the Chinese-Manchu period of conflict of the seventeenth century?

H. Did it concern such political parties as the Tung-lin and Fu-she, which flourished at the end of the Ming? [44–54].

As Goodrich concludes, Ch'ien-lung "seems to have been primarily anxious to suppress anything of rebellious tendence; secondly, he was conscious of his duty to act as the preserver of what was orthodox in thought, morals, and taste" (53). Of the eight "tests," only one deals exclusively with religion: "Did it [the book] contain heterodox opinion on the Confucian canon?" All the other tests sought to restrict writings dealing with rebellion, military defense, insults to previous dynasties, and political parties; hence, the burning of these subversive-seditious books will be dealt with in the next chapter.

While Asians were setting fire to Christian works and Christians were burning Asian religious writings and idols, the Church continued in Europe to reduce to ashes various Hebrew works. The Talmud and other Hebrew writings were condemned and then "the censors decided to carry out their sentence against the majority of works by burning them" (Popper 113). In 1757, in Poland "the order was given that copies of the Talmud should be confiscated wherever found and consigned to the flames.... So a search was instituted by the officers of the church, the police, and the Frankists, without opposition, and all books except the Bible and Zohar were confiscated; in all, 1000 copies were thrown into a ditch and burnt. Daily visits were then regularly made to the houses of Jews in search for additional books" (Popper 127).

At the same time Christians were burning Jewish writings, Jews themselves were setting fire to Hebrew works denounced as heretical and abominable. When in the seventeenth century Shabbetai Tzvi proclaimed himself the Messiah destined to redeem the Jewish people, he and his "prophet" Nathan of Gaza "effected a veritable revolution in the Jewish communities" (Carmilly-Weinberger 60). Various Jewish leaders condemned the Sabbatean (also Shabbatean) movement and imposed bans on the movement's publications. One of the more militant defenders of Sabbateanism, Nehemiah Hiyya Hayon, published *Meheimanuta de Khola,* the printed text "surrounded by two original commentaries: Oz L'Elohim (Power of God) and Beit Kodesh HaKodashim (The House of the Holy Holies)" (Carmilly-Weinberger 62). Various rabbis called for the burning of the book and in 1714 Rabbi David Nieto published a work in which he argued that Hayon's ideas were heretical.

As Carmilly-Weinberger has observed, "Nieto's principal argument for the burning of *Oz L'Elohim* naturally centered around the heresies it contained. Hayon, he said, had 'lifted up his hand against the King of the Universe ... and had attributed to Him traits that were totally false and contrary to our faith, which we received by tradition from our forefathers, our prophets and our sages as a heritage transmitted [in an unbroken chain] ever since Adam, the first man, and down to this very day'" (65).

One rabbi, invoking the "poison" metaphor, "appealed to all the Jewish communities, near and far, to react as one and to defend themselves, lest they perish from the evil poison"; another rabbi denounced Hayon's works as "abominable and filthy books" written by "the accursed excommunicated writer Nehemiah Hiyya Hayon, and entitled by him *Beit Kodesh HaKodashim* and *Oz L'Elohim*" (Carmilly-Weinberger 67).

While Hayon's adversaries were demanding that his books be burned, the Hayon supporters in Amsterdam declared "a ban on anyone possessing literature ... attacking Hayon's Beit Kodesh HaKodashim or Oz L'Elohim" and in a "herem declared in the summer of 1715, Rabbi Solomon ben Jacob Aryylon and the officers of Amsterdam's Portuguese community announced that anyone having in his possession copies of the book *Shever Poshim* by R. Moses Hagiz, in which the author attacked Hayon, was under orders to deliver the book to them within two days so that all copies might be incinerated forthwith" (Carmilly-Weinberger 68). Hayon's books were banned and burned in cities such as Breslau, Frankfurt, and Nikolsburg, Moravia, and in 1713, one of Hayon's strongest critics, Rabbi Moses Hagiz, wrote that "all the books that Hayon had already managed to sell were to be collected, piled up in the middle of the street and publicly burned" (Carmilly-Weinberger 68). As his books were being set afire, the excommunicated "snake" Hayon was forced to flee from city to city and finally moved to Africa where he died.

Two decades later, another Jewish writer, Rabbi Moses Hayyim Luzzatto, a Cabbalist and Sabbatean, published several books, including *Zohar Tinyana,* and *Tikkunim LeYad HaHazakah,* and *The Book of 150 Psalms.* The books were "labeled heretical literature forbidden to Jews, and fit only to be destroyed"; hence, they were banned by the rabbis all across Europe, including the cities of Prague, Hamburg, Amsterdam, Berlin, and Breslau. In a proclamation distributed to all the synagogues of Venice, the rabbis condemned his ideas that "pollute the air and fill it with stench and threaten to destroy the world": "All must keep a distance of at least one arrow's shot away from them [Luzzatto's books] so that they will be set apart from Jewish congregations and from every sacred thing, for they and we cannot be partners in building up the House of the Lord. Moreover, let all his books, letters, poems, psalms and all his writings of any sort whatsoever be henceforth considered heretical and there be burned along with the Divine Names spelled out in them" (Carmilly-Weinberger 82).

In an effort to establish a compromise between Luzzatto and his adversaries, Rabbi Samon Morpurgo in 1735 suggested that Luzzatto's works be buried, not burned. As explained by Carlebach, anti–Sabbatean Moses Hagiz and his supporters "had condemned Luzzatto's writings to the pyre. Morpurgo urged that the writings be gathered and buried, rather than burned. This would still achieve the desired effect of removing them from circulation, but it would leave Luzzatto's supporters with their dignity intact. Burial was appropriate for writings which were liable to be misunderstood by the masses, but it did not carry the shameful stigma of burning which was reserved for works of outright heresy.... Morpurgo's efforts were not completely in vain"; Luzzatto's writings were sent to Rabbi Jacob Popers who "convened an ad hoc court to decide the fate of the writings. He informed Hagiz that he had burned a portion of the manuscripts, but the majority had been consigned to burial. 'And even this was done in a manner that they will soon molder and crumble away'" (Carlebach 246).

Another rabbi accused of being a Sabbatean, Rabbi Jonathan Eybeschuetz, came under strong attacks by Rabbi Jacob ben Tzvi Emden who wrote several books denouncing Eybeschuetz. In 1753, "at its session in Jaroslaw [Poland] the Council of the Four Lands banned [Emden's] *Torat HaKenaot* and *S'fat Emet V'Lashon Zehorit*" and its ruling declared: "We are [therefore] burning these papers atop the thornes, the briars and the thistles so that his [i.e., Emden's] pamphlets may never again be mentioned by any Jew nor be remembered by anyone in the world.... They shall be bidden: Go hence! and all of them shall be subject to destruction, and the best form of destruction is incineration. They were [already] burned here, in the streets of this city, in front of the entire holy congregation" (Carmilly-Weinberger 88).

While the anti–Sabbateans were burning Sabbatean books and Sabbateans were setting fire to anti–Sabbatean works, "both the protagonists and the antagonists of the Sabbatean movement joined in burning and banning the works of Abraham Michael Cardozo" who initially was a follower of Shabbetai Tzvi, but when the latter converted to Islam, Cardozo broke with him. Cardozo wrote two books, *Boker D'Avraham* and *D'rush Tov Adonai LaKol,* that were attacks on Sabbatean Rabbi Samuel Primo who "fought back vigorously and ... had both books burned. Other books by Cardozo were also burned and in the end Cardozo himself was excommunicated" (Carmilly-Weinberger 93–94). In *Abraham Miguel Cardozo: Selected Writings,* David Halperin referred to the burning of Cardozo's books: "The war between the two men [Cardozo and Primo] had been declared even before their public confrontation. Primo had taken copies of *Abraham's Morn* and had them burned. Another of Cardozo's treatises, *The Lord Is Good to All,* would later go up in flames. No doubt Primo would have been pleased to burn the writer along with his books. But this was impossible. He had to content himself with discrediting and humiliating Cardozo in full public view, and then driving him from the city [Edirne, Turkey]" (Halperin 92). Cardozo himself wrote of the book burning in his "Autobiographical Letter": "When it came to my attention that a certain rabbi [Samuel Primo] had burned my treatise *Abraham's Morn,* I waged a terrific struggle against him. I told him, in the presence of the entire Jewish community [of Edirne], that he was a deceiver and seducer of the Jewish people. That very night, by consent of the rabbis and officials of thirteen congregations, he ordered it proclaimed throughout the town that no one might come to my house to learn Torah from me" (Halperin 281). Cardozo who had already been expelled from various cities, from Leghorn to Ismir to Constantinople to Rodosto to Edirne to Candia [Crete], was again sent into exile in 1697, ending up in Egypt; in 1706 "Cardozo was stabbed to death by his nephew" (Halperin xxxi).

While Jews were setting fire to "heretical" Jewish writings, Muslims were burning Islamic books condemned as betraying and corrupting Islam. In the eighteenth and nineteenth centuries the rise of Wahhabism in the Near East was accompanied with the censorship and elimination of condemned Islamic works. In 1744, theologian Muhammad ibn 'Abd al-Wahhab "launched a campaign of purification and renewal. His declared aim was to return to the pure and authentic Islam of the Founder, removing and where necessary destroying all the later accretions and distortions" (Lewis 2003 120). Wahhabism denied "all esoterism or mysticism, and rejects the idea of Saints, including the visiting of Saints tombs or any tomb or grave, exception being made only to the pressure of universal custom as regards visiting the tomb of the Prophet.... They also reject all notions of the holiness or sacredness of objects or places as detracting from the exclusive holiness of God and as infringing Divine Unity" (Glasse 471).

Referring to the Wahhabis' book burnings, Bernard Lewis has written: "Wherever they could, they enforced their beliefs with the utmost severity and ferocity, demolishing tombs, desecrating what they called false and idolatrous holy places, and slaughtering large numbers of men, women, and children who failed to meet their standards of Islamic purity and authenticity. Another practice introduced by Ibn 'Abd al-Wahhab was the condemnation and burning of books. These consisted mainly of Islamic works on theology and law deemed contrary to Wahhabi doctrine. The burning of books was often accompanied by the summary execution of those who wrote, copied, or taught them" (122–123).

Just as the Jews burned their "heretical" Jewish books and Muslims burned the Islamic books containing impure doctrines, Christians were burning the Bible in Ireland during the 1850s, and Catholics were burning the King James version of the Bible. In 1852, a Franciscan friar, John Bridgman, concerned about Protestant attempts to convert Catholics, "retaliated by denouncing them and their missionary efforts. Assaulting their religious beliefs and their Bible, he climaxed his bad judgment by publicly burning the King James Version of the New Testament as he loudly proclaimed it to be not the word of God but the word of the devil 'and the Devil's Book — Luther's Bible, or your Heretic Bible'" (Levy 1993 462). He was brought to trial for blasphemy and "a mixed jury of Protestants and Roman Catholics convicted. The sentence was light: "Brother John was bound over to keep the peace and be of good behavior for seven years" (Levy 1993 464).

Levy refers to another Bible burning that took place two years later, the Bible burner who vilified it as he set it afire also being convicted. The following year, 1855, a Roman Catholic priest, Vladimir Petcherine, instructed his followers in Ireland to burn "immoral and infidel publications" in the chapel yard; a bonfire was lit and some Protestants "claimed to have seen their Bible thrown into the flames." Petcherine was brought to trial and as Levy has summarized, the presiding judge "instructed the jury that, even if they believed that a Bible had been burned, they must hold the defendant not guilty unless they were convinced that he was responsible for its burning and that he had the blasphemous intent ascribed to him by the indictment. He must, that is, have burned it to show his hatred and contempt of it. The jury, consisting of both Protestants and Catholics, deliberated for about three-quarters of an hour. Its verdict of not guilty provoked 'rapturous cheers' from the people in and outside the courtroom" (1993 466).

Just as Catholic priest Petcherine in Ireland instructed his followers in Ireland to burn "immoral and infidel publications," the *Catholic Review* in Chile condemned Francisco Bilbao's "Chilean Sociability" as "blasphemous, seditious, and immoral," leading to the burning of all copies of the newspaper in which the article appeared in June 1844. As Arciniegas has observed, immediately after Bilbao's article was published, "The *Catholic Review* entered a fiery protest, and Bilbao was tried for abuse of the press.... His book was officially burned by the hangman in a public bonfire" (386).

Bilbao had written in his "The Nature of Chilean Society": "Our past is Spain.... Spain is the Middle Ages. The soul and body of the Middle Ages were Catholicism and feudalism" (Crawford 69). Further, Bilbao wrote of the effects of Catholicism on women, children, the individual, and thought: "The wife is subjected to the husband. Slavery of the wife.... The child irremediably subjected to the father. Slavery of the child.... The individual subjected to authority. Slavery of the citizen.... Thought chained to the text, intelligence bound to dogma. Slavery of thought" (Crawford 70). As Crawford has explained, for Bilbao "it was Catholicism that carried out to its logical conclusion the medievalism of Spain; it was Catholicism that put the same stamp on the colonial regime in America" (70).

When Bilbao was brought to trial for blasphemy, sedition, and immorality he declared:

"I, a blasphemer? I who have dedicated myself to seeking God everywhere, I who have devoted myself to seeking truth? ... because God resides in the absolute truth.... My conscience is clean, gentlemen.... I am not a blasphemer, because I love God; I am not immoral, because I love and look for the duty which perfects itself; I am not seditious, because I wish to avoid the exasperation of my oppressed fellow-men" (Lipp 19). Bilbao was found guilty, paid a fine, and was "ousted from his chair at the university and his doctrines were condemned from the pulpit" (Arciniegas 386).

By the end of the nineteenth century and into the twentieth, fewer and fewer "blasphemous, heretical, and sacrilegious" books were being set afire. While some religious groups took it upon themselves to burn "Satanic," "dirty," and "blasphemous" works, the courts in the United States increasingly declared that the state authorities were not empowered to suppress heretical blasphemous expression. In 1872, the U.S. Supreme Court asserted that "the law knows no heresy, and is committed to the support of no dogma, the establishment of no sect" (*Watson v. Jones* 728). This personification of the law "knowing" no heresy subsequently appeared in other court decisions involving religious issues. In 1944, in a case that dealt with the sending of "fraudulent" and "untrue" religious claims through the U.S. mails to solicit funds and members, Justice Douglas, writing for the Court and drawing on the personification, stated: "The law knows no heresy.... It [the First Amendment] embraces the right to maintain theories of life and of death and of the hereafter which are rank heresy to followers of the orthodox faiths. Heresy trials are foreign to our Constitution. Men may believe what they cannot prove" (*United States v. Ballard* 86).

Again, in 1968, when the U.S. Supreme Court declared unconstitutional an Arkansas "anti-evolution" statute that prohibited "the teaching in its public schools and universities of the theory that man evolved from other species of life," Justice Fortas, delivering the opinion of the Court, declared: "The law knows no heresy.... This has been the interpretation of the great First Amendment which this court has applied in many and subtle problems which the ferment of our national life presented for decision within the Amendment's broad command" (*Epperson v. Arkansas* 104).

The U.S. Supreme Court, in 1952, was faced with the constitutionality of a New York statute which permitted the banning of films on the ground that they were "sacrilegious." The film involved was the Italian movie *The Miracle* which the New York State Board of Regents had determined was "sacrilegious" and ordered that a license to exhibit the film be rescinded. The Court stated that the state could not "ban a film on the basis of a censor's conclusion that it is 'sacrilegious.'" Justice Clark, delivering the opinion of the Court, wrote: "Since the term 'sacrilegious' is the sole standard under attack here, it is not necessary for us to decide, for example, whether a state may censor motion pictures under a clearly drawn statute designed and applied to prevent the showing of obscene films. That is a very different question from the one now before us. We hold only that under the First and Fourteenth Amendments a state may not ban a film on the basis of a censor's conclusion that it is 'sacrilegious'" (*Burstyn v. Wilson* 506).

While the U.S. Supreme Court and the lower courts asserted again and again that "the law knows no heresy" and that states could not ban "sacrilegious" films, Christian and conservative groups took it upon themselves to clean the land of "anti–Christian" writings, whether through banning or burning. When in 1975 the Board of Education, Island Trees Union Free School District, removed from the school libraries several books, including *Go Ask Alice, The Fixer, The Naked Ape,* and *Slaughterhouse-Five,* the works were characterized as "anti–American, anti–Christian, anti–Semitic and just plain filthy" (*Board of Education v. Pico* 857). The book banning was challenged in the courts and when the case reached the U.S. Supreme Court, the Court decided against the school board and in so doing cited the now famous metaphor from *West Virginia v. Barnette* in which the Court decided for students of the Jehovah's Witness faith who had refused to salute the flag: "If there is any fixed star in our constitutional constellation, it is that no official, high or petty, can prescribe what shall be orthodox in politics, nationalism, religion or other matters of opinion.... If there are any circumstances which permit an exception, they do not now occur to us" (*West Virginia State Bd. of Ed. v. Barnette* 642).

While the U.S. Supreme Court decided in 1982 against the banning of *Slaughterhouse-Five,* ten years earlier the book had been burned in Drake, North Dakota. In November 1973, as the American Library Association's *Newsletter on Intellectual Freedom* put it: "The mid–November chills that come to Drake, North Dakota, foreshadow the winter gales that sweep across the northern plains. But the fire the school officials of the hamlet started was not to drive off the cold. It was to burn copies of Kurt Vonnegut's *Slaughterhouse-Five*" (January 1974 4).

Expressing strong objections to the burning of his book, Vonnegut wrote at the outset of his November 16, 1973, letter to the chair of the Drake School Board: "I am writing to you in your capacity as chairman of the Drake School Board. I am among those American writers whose books have been destroyed in the now famous furnace of your school." Vonnegut's letter of condemnation concluded: "If you and your board are now determined to show that you in fact have wisdom and maturity when you exercise your powers over the education of your young, then you should acknowledge that it was a rotten lesson you taught young people in a free society when you denounced and then burned books—books you hadn't even read" (Vonnegut E19).

Four years after the Drake, North Dakota, book burning, Warsaw, Indiana, was the scene of the burning of copies of a controversial high school textbook, *Values Clarification.* Tracy Metz reported in his "The New Crusaders of the USA": "A group of senior citizens in the town of Warsaw, Indiana, requested the school board to hand over a number of forbidden textbooks to them so that they could burn them in a parking lot in the middle of town. Their request was granted and the books were destroyed" (20).

Los Angeles Times staff writer Larry Green described the Warsaw, Indiana, book burning ritual: "In a parking lot next to the senior citizen's center, someone moved a wire trash basket into place. The day was cold, a good day for a fire. There was snow on the ground. The basket was partially filled and a flammable liquid was poured over the contents. A match was lit. Some of the elderly participants smiled. Some did not. In a few seconds of flames and smoke it was over. The books were burned. The ceremony destroyed 27 copies of a textbook that had been banned at the high school by the local school board" (Green 1). On December 15, 1977, the Warsaw *Times-Union* "published a photograph of a group of senior citizens burning forty copies of *Values Clarification*" (Jenkinson 63). The book burners setting fire to the condemned textbook saw the work as indoctrinating students with "anti–Christian" secular humanism and moral relativity.

The school board's removal of several books from the high school classroom and library was challenged in court by a student who sought to reverse the board's removal order. When the case reached the U.S. Court of Appeals, Seventh Circuit, the court, while concluding that the burning of the books by senior citizens in the parking lot was not directly relevant to the case, took the opportunity to condemn the fiery destruction of the books: "This contemptible ceremony, which has greatly animated the discussion of this case by the *amici curiae,* took place in December, 1977. No self-respecting citizen with a knowledge of history can look upon this incident with equanimity" (*Zykan v. Warsaw Community School Corp.* 1302).

The public burning of "satanic" and "anti–Christian," and "anti–God" books continued as the twenty-first century began with the bannings and ceremonial fiery destruction
of the Harry Potter books (*Harry Potter and the Sorcerer's Stone, Harry Potter and the Chamber of Secrets,* and *Harry Potter and the Prisoner of Azkaban*), the novels of J.R.R. Tolkien,
the *Complete Works of Shakespeare,* and various CDs and videos. ABC News reported on
March 26, 2000, that "the congregation of a church in suburban Pittsburgh gathered around
a bonfire Sunday night to burn *Harry Potter* books, Disney videos, rock CDs and literature
from other religions, purging their lives of things they felt stood between them and their
faith" (DailyNews/book-burning010326.html). In addition to videos such as *Pinnochio* and
Hercules and CDs by Pearl Jam and Black Sabbath, the bonfire reduced to ashes pamphlets
of the Jehovah's Witnesses. The news item reported that Reverend George Bender of the
Harvest Assembly of God Church in Butler County declared: "We believe that Harry Potter promotes sorcery, witchcraft-type things, the paranormal, things that are against God."

Again reminiscent of Savonarola's 1496 bonfire of vanities, on December 30, 2001, a
book burning "of works written by J.K. Rowling and others ... took place outside" Alamogordo, New Mexico's Christ Community Church. As reported in *American Libraries,* "The
book burning was held on church property after a half-hour prayer service, and drew several hundred congregants. Across the street were as many as 800 counter protesters.... After
Pastor Jack Brock sermonized about fire as a cleansing instrument, some worshippers placed
into the bonfire personal copies of the Potter series as well as such items as J.R.R. Tolkien
novels, issues of *Cosmopolitan* and *Young Miss* magazines, AC/DC recordings, the *Complete
Works of William Shakespeare,* and Ouija boards. Brock, who organized the demonstration,
characterized the Potter series as 'a masterpiece of satanic deception'" (*American Libraries*
19).

Christians condemned the Potter series and demanded the banning of the "satanic"
works, because "the books are based on sorcery, which is an abomination to the Lord"
(*Newsletter on Intellectual Freedom* 49 March 2000 50). A parent in Arab, Alabama, calling
for the banning of the Potter books, declared: "It was a mistake years ago to take prayer
out of the school because it left Satan in" and "we need to put God back in the schools and
throw the Harry Potter books out" (*Newsletter on Intellectual Freedom* 50 January 2001 11).
At the Alamogordo, New Mexico, bonfire, one seventeen-year-old participant "discarded
a Backstreet Boys music tape, among other items. It [burning them] will strengthen my life
in Jesus Christ and my relationship with him" (*School Library Journal* 27).

While at the end of the twentieth century and beginning of the twenty-first some
Christians in the United States were setting fire to books promoting "Satanism," "sorcery,"
and "witchcraft," Muslims and Hindus in Asia were burning books condemned as "filthy"
and "blasphemous." Earlier in the twentieth century, *Aangarey,* a collection of one play and
nine short stories by several authors, was denounced by Muslims in India as "blasphemous," "dirty," and "filthy" and was banned and burned in 1933. The publisher of the book
"confessed to his mistake in bringing out the book and apologized in a written statement
of February 27, 1933. He apologized for infuriating the feelings of the Muslim community.
He readily agreed to surrender unsold copies of the book to the Government. Now the
book-burning spree had begun in the right earnest. Not only the copies in the custody of
local administration had been disposed of in similar fashion, but festive burning also took
place of copies of the book found on the shelves of local bookstores" (Kumar 122).

The stories were "humorous, satirical, blasphemous and unconventional," Kumar has
stated, and "there were mentions of religious angels and earthly religious preachers in it.
They were all tarred with the same brush" (116–117). "Serious objection," says Kumar, "was

taken to the stories by Sajjad Zaheer and S. Ahmed Ali in particular, because of critical references to God, Prophet Mohammed, Archangel Gabriel and the place of women in Islam" (119). For example, Zaaheer "bemoans the fate of women in Islam by putting words in their mouth: 'What a life! Manipulated off and on at will, we are always at the receiving end. What else are we fated for, except to suffer? Our birth in Muslim households is a curse. May God put such a faith to sword.'" Also, two stories by S. Ahmed Ali were condemned as being irreligious: "Ahmed Ali must have bordered on being blasphemous, when one of his characters cries out in desperation, 'Why doesn't he listen? Does he exist at all? Who would he be? He must be totally unjust and cruel.... Religion is wholly and solely responsible [for this state of affairs]. He is the main hurdle to progress. Poor are lectured to remain poor. Was it the only way to reach God?'" (Kumar 120).

The most famous case of the twentieth century involving the Muslims' banning and burning of a Muslim work by a Muslim author was that of Salman Rushdie's *The Satanic Verses*. In January 1989, a group of Muslims in Manchester and Bradford, England, burned *The Satanic Verses* after it was denounced by Iran's Ayatollah Khomeini who called for a fatwa for the assassination of Rushdie. The Bradford book burning was attended by 1,500 people and Rushdie responded: "I think they went too far.... It [the book burning] got people concerned about me, sympathetic toward me, who had been content to sit on the sidelines. There were Labor Party M.P.s—Asians representing Bradford—who attended that book burning; that's a horrible thought for many people. They get to thinking, 'If it's him today, it's me tomorrow'" (*Newsletter on Intellectual Freedom* May 1989 107).

After the public burning of his book, Rushdie wrote in *The New York Review of Books*:

> Nowadays ... a powerful tribe of clerics has taken over Islam. These are the contemporary Thought Police. They have turned Muhammad into a perfect being, his life into a perfect life, his revelation into the unambiguous, clear event it originally was not. Powerful taboos have been erected. One may not discuss Muhammad as if he were human, with human virtues and weaknesses. One may not discuss the growth of Islam as an ideology born out of its time. These are the taboos against which *The Satanic Verses* has transgressed (these and one other; I also tried to write about the place of women in Islamic society, and in the Koran). It is for this breach of taboo that the novel is being anathematized, fulminated against, and set alight [26].

Towards the end of his one-page essay, Rushdie observed: "How fragile civilization is; how easily, how merrily a book burns" (26).

Four years later, a fatwa was issued in September 1993, calling for the death of Bangladeshi writer Taslima Nasrin whose *Lajja* especially had offended Muslims and was set afire. Describing Taslima's works, Weaver has written: "Strong, often startling challenges to Islamic taboos on the role of women, and on female sexuality, are an essential ingredient of her work. 'Religion is the great oppressor, and should be abolished,' she has frequently said. Even by Western standards, her views are radical and her poems daring, ripe with sexual imagery" (Weaver 49).

In 1992, Taslima received "the Indian state of West Bengal's most distinguished literary award and began work on a novella, 'Lajja' ('Shame'), which is a fictionalized account of the brutalization of a Hindu family by Islamic fundamentalists in Bangladesh after Hindu fanatics in India razed a sixteenth-century mosque.... The book, published in February of 1993 — only three months after the razing of the mosque — resulted in the first fatwa against her, issued by an obscure mullah in a northern provincial town, in the name of an obscure organization the Soldiers of Islam" (Weaver 55).

While Hindu fundamentalists distributed copies of *Lajja*, Muslims burned hundreds of copies: "Hindu fundamentalists from India's Bharatiya Janata Party circulated thousands of pirated copies and lionized Taslima in the streets— anyone who exposed Muslim excesses was their natural ally. Muslim fundamentalists in Bangladesh, on the other hand, burned hundreds of copies and called for her death" (Weaver 55).

Ten years later, it was reported in March 2001, that "about 200 right-wing Hindus burned copies of the Muslim Korans and tore up posters of Islamic shrines in New Delhi. The burning of the Muslim holy book is a form of protest and retaliation against the destruction of ancient Buddhist statues in Afghanistan by the Taliban, which includes two centuries-old massive Buddhas in Bamiyan province" ("Kashmir Leader Held on Holy Book Burning Protest" (1).

In the 1990s, during Taliban's control of Afghanistan, the Taliban's penal code provided that "a person who engages in sorcery, his or her books will be burned and the sorcerer will be jailed for so long that he or she seeks forgiveness from God" (*New York Times* December 2, 2001 WK7). Also, during the Taliban efforts to rule the nation, "the Taliban burned more than 1,000 reels of stock [film] when they took Kabul. 'They started doing it here in the office,' said Timur Hakimian, head of the company [Afghan Films], waving a hand in front of his face. 'You can't imagine the smell. Since it was asphyxiating them as well as the rest of us, they went to the stadium and made a public spectacle of their bonfire. Fortunately, Taliban censors didn't know the difference between prints and negatives; what they burned was mostly replaceable, and the negatives, hidden elsewhere, survived'" (*New York Times* March 10, 2002 AR20).

During the first decade of the new millennium, Christians set fire to the Koran, Muslims burned newspapers carrying satiric articles, and anti–Semites firebombed a Jewish school's library and books. Norimitsu Onishi, writing from the Ivory Coast in 2000, stated in his *New York Times* report "2 Religions Clashing in Ivory Coast" that when Christians in Abidjan, Ivory Coast, attacked the Aisha Niangon Mosque in Abidjan, the building was gutted and "scorched copies of the Koran lay scattered on the staircase in the muezzin's tower" (A12). Two years later, Marc Lacy reported of newspapers being burned in Kaduna, Nigeria, when a Miss World contest being held in Nigeria was criticized by Muslims and this criticism then satirized by the newspaper: "Making light of Muslim protests of the [Miss World] event, an article published on Nov. 16 in the Lagos-based newspaper *This Day* said Muhammad himself might have taken one of the young women as a wife" (A3). The burning of the newspapers was followed by rioting and Christians retaliating: "A crowd of mostly young people took to the streets to seize and burn copies of the offending publication. The newspaper's Kaduna offices were burned, and rioting broke out throughout the town on Nov. 20. Muslim youths gathered at churches, where they pounded through the walls, rushed inside and destroyed everything they could. By Friday, Christians were retaliating, giving Kuduna's mosques similar treatment" (Lacy A3).

As in earlier centuries, motivations for burning books at the outset of the twenty-first century were not always entirely clear. At times books were being set afire for political and religious reasons. In April 2004, a Canadian Jewish school library and 10,000 books were burned while the students and teachers were away on Passover holiday. In its July,\ 2004 coverage of this firebombing, the *Newsletter on Intellectual Freedom* reported: "Calling it a 'cowardly and racist act,' Canadian Prime Minister Paul Martin condemned as a hate crime the March 5 firebombing that incinerated the library of the United Talmud Torahs elementary school in the Montreal, Quebec, suburb of Saint-Laurent. A message taped to the front of the building claimed the bombing was linked to the March killing of radical Islamist Sheik Ahmed Yassin by the Israeli military in Gaza and promised more attacks. Only one box of 25 books was salvaged from the 10,000-volume library that served some 230 students" (137).

Through the centuries, into the twenty-first, religious hatreds, combined with political fears and hostilities, transformed the burning books into disease, vermin, pestilence, plague, tares, filth, contagion; the titles of the books may change, but the language of the book burners remains much the same: from the Theodosian Code's "polluted contagions of the heretics" in 391, to the "pestilence and contagion" of heretical and Hebrew writings condemned by fifth century Christians, to the Inquisition's "poisons of disbelief and detestable plague of heresy" of the sixteenth century, to the "filthy blasphemies" of Muslim books in India in the twentieth century, to the "Satanism and dirt" of the Harry Potter books burned by Christians in the twenty-first century. The persistent use of this metaphoric, bibliophobic language has been an integral part of reducing to ashes the vermin infested, disease carrying, cancerous, pestilent, satanic inspired books.

In the twentieth and twenty-first centuries, as in earlier times, the condemnation of writings because they were anti–Christian, satanic, and blasphemous was often a pretext for destroying by fire books suspected of being a threat to the unity and stability of the political institutions. For example, the books of Monteiro Lobato and Jorge Amado were burned in the 1930s in Brazil not only because they were "anti–Catholic," but also because they were "anti–Brazilism, anarchistic, and communistic." Kurt Vonnegut's *Slaughterhouse-Five* was condemned and burned in the United States in 1973 not only because it was "anti–Christian," but also because it was "anti–American, anti–Semitic, and just plain filthy." The burning of the Muslim holy book in India in 2001 was not only a religious act, but also part of the political conflict over Kashmir. The firebombing in 2004 of the Jewish school library and 10,000 books was an anti–Semitic religious "hate crime" as well as a fiery destructive act related to the political Israel-Palestinian conflict.

The twentieth and twenty-first century book burnings and the book burners' persistent reliance on condemnatory, menacing, dehumanizing language are a reminder that there continues to exist a mindset not much different from that which existed a long time ago when the heretical-blasphemous-subversive works of Bruno, Servetus, Wiclif, Milton, Hobbes, Voltaire, Pascal, Diderot, Halbach, and scores of others were burned along with the Talmud, Koran, and Bible.

3

BURNING SEDITIOUS-
SUBVERSIVE BOOKS

Antiquity Through the Eighteenth Century

Just as over twenty centuries witnessed the burning of heretical-blasphemous religious books, so too did those same centuries experience the burning of politically subversive-seditious writings. While in the earlier centuries ecclesiastical and secular authorities were burning books ostensibly because of heretical-blasphemous content, they saw the same books as undermining civil authority, but they publicly condemned the works for their religious impiety and heresy and not their direct threats to secular institutions. In the later centuries, proclamations were issued explicitly calling for the burning of "heretical and seditious" works. Eventually, heresy was of little concern and seldom mentioned in the edicts and proclamations ordering the burning of books. While this transition took place over the centuries, early authorities set fire to books for primarily secular reasons, just as they had burned books primarily for ecclesiastical reasons.

The metaphoric language used to condemn to the fires "heretical-blasphemous" books was equally applied to works burned because they were "seditious-subversive." The seditious-subversive writings and their authors were identified with and linked to pestilence, cancer, excrement, filth, arsenic, and disease. In the Theodosian Code defamatory writings became "poisonous weapons." When Voltaire's *Philosophical Dictionary* was burned in the eighteenth century, one of his adversaries, Charles Bonnet, "rejoiced at the fate of 'the most detestable book of this pestilential author.'" During the Nazi book burnings in 1933, Propaganda Minister Joseph Goebbels told the book burners that "never before have the young men had so good a right to clean up the debris of the past.... The old goes up in flames, the new shall be fashioned from the flame in our hearts." While Goebbels spoke of clearing up the "debris of the past," the Franco regime in Spain set fire to Catalan books and "public libraries were closed for 'purification.'"

When in 1945 the Nazis deliberately were destroying libraries in Poland, Greece, Czechoslovakia, and elsewhere, "between 500 and 600 libraries and institutions in Yugoslavia were pillaged. By official decree, Germans demanded all Slovene books; library buildings in larger centers were torn down and books, if they were not pulped or sent away for other purposes were ceremoniously burned." In the Netherlands the Germans ordered all libraries to lock up "politically undesirable" books in "poison rooms" (*New York Times* April 4, 1945 12).

The centuries-old metaphoric "parasites" invoked when blasphemous-heretical books were being set afire became part of the Chinese *People's Daily* editorial in 1966 praising the Red Guards; the article pointed out that "'none of the old parasites hidden in dark corners can escape the sharp eyes of the Red Guards' who 'are pulling out the bloodsuckers, these enemies of the people one by one'" (Barnouin and Changgen 99).

In 1973, the Pinochet junta in Chile embarked on a campaign to "extirpate the Marxist cancer"; and "although the new authorities have disavowed acts of book burning," the *New York Times* reported, "Leftist literature remains highly suspect and has been removed from the shelves of most bookstores and libraries" (September 28, 1973 2).

While the Nazis referred to "poison rooms," the Chinese to "parasites," the Pinochet regime to "the Marxist cancer," the Vietnamese in 2002 were destroying "poisonous cultural products," including "44,000 CDs, videodiscs and CD roms, 2,833 books and 570 advertising banners" (*New York Times* July 12, 2002 A6).

Over the centuries, the book burnings of seditious-subversive writings "purified" the land, ridding society of the parasites, disease, and vermin, just as fires were ignited to cleanse the land of heretical blasphemous works, and just as fire had been used by farmers to rid their lands of the literal pests, tares, and vermin.

In 213 B.C.E., the first Ch'in emperor, Shih-huang-ti, held a banquet attended by seventy scholars who praised the emperor of his achievements; one of the speakers, Li Ssu, one of the most important advisers to the emperor, suggested the burning of books as a means of controlling "evil speaking" and maintaining power. Grand Councilor Li Ssu warned: "To cast disrepute on their rule they [critics] regard as a thing worthy of fame; to accept different views they regard as high (conduct); and they lead the people to create slander. If such conditions are not prohibited, the imperial power will decline above, and partisanships will form below. It is expedient that these be prohibited." This warning was followed with a call for burning books:

> Your servant suggests that all books in the bureau of history, save the records of Ch'in, be burned; that all persons in the empire, save those who hold a function under the control of the bureau of the scholars of wide learning, daring to store the *Shih,* the *Shu,* and the discussions of the various philosophers, should go to the administrative and military governors so that these books may be indiscriminately burned. Those who dare to discuss the *Shih* and the *Shu* among themselves should be executed and their bodies exposed on the market-place. Those who use the past to criticize the present, should be put to death together with their relatives....
>
> Those who have not burned them (i.e., the books) within thirty days after the issuing of the order, are to be branded and sent to do forced labor. Books not to be destroyed will be those on medicine and pharmacy, divination by the tortoise and milfoil, and agriculture and arboriculture. As for persons who wish to study the laws and ordinance, [let them take the officials as their teachers] [Bodde 82–83].

A year later, "it being discovered that upwards of 460 scholars had violated the prohibitions, they were all buried alive in pits, for a warning to the empire, while degradation and banishment were employed more strictly than before against all who fell under suspicion" (Legge 9).

As Bodde has pointed out, "There were three classes of literature against which the Burning of the Books was particularly directed: first, the collection of poetry and of historical speeches, etc., known respectively as the *Shih* and *Shu;* secondly, histories of other states besides Ch'in; and thirdly, the 'discussions of the various philosophers.' The *Shih* and *Shu,* which during the Han dynasty became known as the *Shih Ching* (Book of Odes) and the *Shu Ching* (Book of History), and which have since formed the cornerstone of the Chinese classics, were considered especially objectionable" (164).

Li Ssu's advocacy of book burning was nothing new. A century earlier, the Legalist statesman Shang Yang (390–338 B.C.E.) had advised Duke Hsiao "to burn the Book of Odes and Book of Documents and elucidate the laws and regulations, to reject the private requests of powerful families and concentrate upon furthering the interests of the royal family; to forbid people to wander about in search of political office, and to glorify the lot of those who devote themselves to agriculture and warfare" (Watson 82). Duke Hsiao put Shang's "suggestions into practice, and as a result the position of the ruler became secure and respected, and the state grew rich and powerful. But eight years later Duke Hsiao passed away, and Lord Shang was tied to two chariots and torn apart by the men of Ch'in" (Watson 82).

As a Legalist, Shang had "resolutely opposed returning to the past, retrogression, and conservatism" and "he openly stood for 'rule by law.' This, in essence, was to advocate reform — to replace the dictatorship of the slave-owning class by the dictatorship of the landlord class" (Liang Hsiao 182–184). He "encouraged farming and war, abolished the hereditary system of slave-owning aristocrats, established the prefecture system, strengthened central authority, and ordered 'burning the *Book of Poetry* and the *Book of History* in order to manifest the laws and regulations'" (Liang Hsiao 192).

Referring to the Burning of the Odes and History, Duyvendak writes: "[W]e must assume as certain that a strong opposition to the study of these two books existed in the circles influenced by the Law School. Han Fei-tzu ["the greatest of all the Legalist philosophers"] is very explicit on this point. In one of his most important chapters he says: 'Therefore in a state of an intelligent ruler, there is no literature of books and bamboo tablets, but the law is the only doctrine; there are no sayings of former Kings, but the officials are the only models'" (125). "It was this anti-cultural teaching of the School of Law," continues Duyvendak, "which had prepared the mind of Ch'in Shih-huang-ti for the deed by which he incurred the hatred of all later generations: the Burning of the Books in 213. Li Ssu in advising him to this action, merely put into practice what the Law School had been teaching for decades, and he found a ear in his master" (126).

Relying on the "parasite" metaphor, Shang wrote: "Farming, trade, and office are the three permanent functions of a state. Farmers open up the soil, merchants import products, officials rule the people. These three functions give rise to parasites, six in number, which are called: care for old age, living on others, beauty, love, ambition, and virtuous conduct. If these six parasites find an attachment, there will be dismemberment. If farmers live in affluence, they seek leisure in their old age; if merchants have illicit profits, there will be beauty and love, and these will harm the means for enforcing the law; if officials are set up, but are not utilized, ambition and virtuous conduct will be the end. If the six parasites become a pervading custom, the army will certainly suffer great defeats" (Duyvendak 306–307).

Where Shang spoke of "parasites," a century later Han Fei Tzu relied on the "vermin" metaphor calling for rulers to "wipe out such vermin." Scholars "cast doubt upon the laws of the time"; "speechmakers propound false schemes ... forgetting the welfare of the state's altars of the soil and grain"; people worried about military service turn to bribing influential men, "in this way escaping the hardship of battle"; "merchants and artisans spend their time making articles of no practical use, and gathering stores of luxury goods, accumulating riches, waiting for the best time to sell, and exploiting the farmers." Han Fei Tzu concludes: "These five groups are the vermin of the state. If the rulers do not wipe out such vermin, and in their place encourage men of integrity and public spirit, then they should not be surprised, when they look about the area within the four seas, to see states perish and ruling houses wane and die" (Watson 117).

In 233 B.C.E., fellow Legalist Han Fei-tzu was imprisoned and committed suicide by taking a poison supplied to him by Li Ssu. Li Ssu, however, met the same fate as Shang Yang who had in 339 B.C.E. been executed by being cut in two at the waist. In 208 B.C.E., Li Ssu was "condemned to be cut in two at the waist upon the market-place of Hsien-yang," being executed along with his son, followed by the "extermination of their kindred to the third degree" (Bodde 52).

The 213 B.C.E. book burning has been referred to by Wylie as the "first bibliothecal catastrophe" (xiii). Other bibliothecal catastrophes subsequently occurred during various Chinese insurrections and wars. In the first century B.C.E., a collection was made of several thousand classical, philosophical, poetical, medical, mathematical, and military works: "This collection, which had been amassed with so much care, was not allowed to remain long undisturbed, for during the insurrection of Wangmang at the close of the dynasty, the imperial edifice was reduced to ashes, and scarcely a vestige remained of the well-assorted library. This is considered the second great 'Bibliothecal catastrophe'" (Wylie xiv). In the second century C.E., during internal disorders, "the palace at Loyang was burnt and the greater part of the books again lost"; similarly, near the end of the fifth century, a library of 18,010 books "was burnt by troops at the overthrow of the dynasty, and the greater part of the contents was lost" (Wylie xv–xvii).

While the Chinese were setting fire to works that were condemned as undermining dynastic authority and detrimental to establishing unity, the Romans in 12 B.C.E. began burning secular books considered seditious, having political ramifications. In his essay "Bookburning and Censorship in Ancient Rome," Cramer has observed that in 12 B.C.E. "oracular books and other writings of this sort" were burned ostensibly for religious reasons, but essentially were set afire for political reasons: "It was a great *auto da fe* of scrolls and books that Augustus held at that time, but it was possible to camouflage the political character of such an unprecedented act. For he ordered the bookburning not in his capacity as secular ruler of the Roman realm, but in that of high-priest (pontifex maximus), making it thus appear as an ecclesiastical action, not as one of political importance" (167). More than two thousand scrolls, pamphlets, and books "were condemned to a fiery death, and the first mass *auto da fe* of this kind was solemnly held in Rome" (Cramer 167).

The oracular writings, with their predictions of societal, political, and personal changes to occur in the future, prophesied "drastic changes affecting Augustus and his regime. As a source of perpetuating the hopes of the political opposition, these writings were therefore a legitimate object for governmental suppression, that is, if governmental suppression of the written word can ever be called legitimate. In any case, the *auto da fe* of 12 B.C. preceded by only two decades the introduction of the burning of secular writings by the secular government, i.e., Augustus" (Cramer 168).

Various authors have identified Labienus as the first writer to have his works burned in C.E. 12 for political criticism of the authorities. Rhetorician Seneca the Elder had written in the first century of the "new punishment" imposed on "eloquent genius" Labienus: "His freedom of speech was so great that it passed the bounds of freedom: and because he savaged all ranks and men alike, he was known as Rabienus [a play on *rabies,* "madness"]. And amid all his faults, he had a great spirit — one that was, like his genius, violent.... It was for him that there was first devised a new punishment: his enemies saw to it that all his books were burnt. It was an unheard of novelty that punishment should be exacted from literature" (357).

Seneca the Elder then went on to condemn those who "put a match to literature": "What appalling mania harries these madmen? I suppose familiar cruelties are insufficient punishment. Go ahead, look for fresh ways to perish — yourselves: and as for anything that nature has removed from all suffering—genius, and the memory of a name—find a way of subjecting it too to the ills that afflict the body. How great is the savagery that puts a match to literature, and wreaks its vengeance on monuments of learning; how unsatisfied with its other victims! Thank god that these punishments for genius began in an age when genius had come to an end! The man who had pronounced this judgment on Labienus' writings lived to see his own writings burnt: no longer an evil penalty, once it became *his*" (357–359).

In one of his essays, Montaigne wrote of Labienus and the burning of his books: "There were several people who were jealous of the Labienus I am referring to; he also probably had enemies among the courtiers and favourites of the contemporary Emperors for his frankness and for inheriting his father's innate hostility towards tyranny which we may believe coloured his books and writing. His enemies prosecuted him before the Roman magistrates and obtained a conviction, requiring several of the books he had published to be burnt. This was the very first case of the death-penalty being inflicted on books and erudition; it was subsequently applied in Rome in several other cases" (449).

More recent scholars also have identified Labienus as the first Roman to suffer the burning of his books. In his *Tacitus: The Man and His Work,* Mendell has written that in the first century, "Vituperation and eulogy would tend to bulk large; historians and biographers hostile to the emperors or too enthusiastic for liberty might be eliminated and their books burned" (44). Mendell goes on to identify the burning in C.E. 12 of Labienus's books as "the first instance of this penalty applied to an historian" (45).

When Seneca the Elder referred to "the man who had pronounced this judgment [to burn Labienus's books] lived to see his own writings burnt," he was alluding to Cassius Severus whose own works were burned by the imperial government and who was condemned in C.E. 24 to exile on "the barren little island of Seriphos, a penniless beggar" (Cramer 173). In his reference to the book burnings of this period in Roman history, Syme writes: "The last years of Augustus witnessed stern measures of repression against noxious literature. Public bonfires were instituted—but not for such trifles as the *Ars amatoria* of Ovid. Contemporary political literature provided the cause—and the fuel" (486). Severus, who was "hated and feared for his bitter tongue and incorrigible love of independence," had "prosecuted Augustus' friend Nonius Asprenas on a charge of poisoning. His activities were not confined to the courts—he composed libellous pamphlets, assailing illustrious persons of both sexes, without restraint or distinction, among them P. Vitellius the procurator, whose grandfather, he said, was a cobbler, his mother a baker's daughter turned prostitute" (Syme 486–487).

As the entry for Severus in *The Dictionary of Greek and Roman Biography and Mythology* reports: "Severus was banished by Augustus to the island of Crete on account of his libellous verses against the distinguished men and women at Rome; but as he still continued to write libels, he was deprived of his property in the reign of Tiberious, A.D. 24, and removed to the desert island of Seriphos, where he died in great poverty in the twenty-fifth year of his exile" (Smith 1902 504). While both Labienus and Severus suffered the burning of their books, the former died by suicide and the latter died in forced exile.

A year after Severus was "deprived of his property" and removed "to the desert island of Seriphos," another Roman, historian Cremutius Cordus, also was condemned for his political writings that were set afire. As recorded by Dio, Cordus "was accused of having praised Cassius and Brutus, and of having assailed the people and the senate; as regarded Caesar and Augustus, while he had spoken no ill of them, he had not, on the other hand, shown any unusual respect for them. This was the complaint made against him, and this it was that caused his death as well as the burning of his writings; those found in the city at the time were destroyed by the aediles" (Dio 181).

Like Dio, Tacitus provides a description of events that led to Cordus's death and the burning of his books: "The year [C.E. 25] began with the prosecution of Aulus Cremutius Cordus on a new and previously unheard-of charge: praise of Brutus in his *History,* and the description of Cassius as 'the last Roman.'" Cordus began his defense by declaring: "Senators, my words are blamed. My actions are not blameworthy. Nor were these words of mine aimed against the emperor or his parent, whom the law of treason protects. I am charged with praising Brutus and Cassius. Yet many have written of their deeds—always with respect" (Tacitus 174). Following his speech in defense of himself, "Cremutius walked out of the senate, and starved himself to death. The senate ordered his books to be burnt by the aediles." Tacitus comments: "But they [books] survived, first hidden and later republished. This makes one deride the stupidity of people who believe that today's authority can destroy tomorrow's memories. On the contrary, repressions of genius increase its prestige. All that tyrannical conquerors, and imitators of their brutalities, achieve is their own disrepute and their victims' renown" (Tacitus 174–175).

Centuries later, Montaigne, after pointing out that Cordus had been accused of having praised Brutus and Cassius, stated: "That slavish base and corrupt Senate ... condemned his writings to the pyre: it pleased him to keep his books company as they perished in the flames by starving himself to death" (450).

Ten years after Cordus's works were set afire, the speeches of Aemilius Scaurus were burned along with his play titled *Atreus.* The Elder Seneca, after expressing strong criticism of Scaurus's oratory, stated that Scaurus "published seven speeches, later burnt at the senate's decree"; and then Seneca sarcastically declared: "The fire served him [Scaurus] well" (Seneca 353).

Cramer refers to the "trumped-up charge of literary treason" brought against Scaurus: "In the end ... Scaurus met his fate. His final downfall occurred in 34 A.D. The charges were numerous, but the only reason for his trial was the mortal enmity of the then omnipotent *praefectus praetorio* Macro. A trumped-up charge of literary treason was based upon a line in one of Scaurus' plays.... Nevertheless to seal Scaurus' doom, magic practices were preferred as the official reason for the charges, in almost ludicrous contrast, one of Rome's gayest blades was furthermore accused of adultery" (190). As to the burning of Scaurus's writings, Cramer states that seven of Scaurus's speeches were burned and "there are some grounds for the assumption that his *Atreus* along with the rest of his works was also sentenced to death, the fiery one of the stake" (191).

The Theodosian Code of the fourth and fifth centuries ordered not only the burning of heretical-blasphemous writings, but also the fiery destruction of defamatory and seditious works. The Code's Title 34 decreed the burning of defamatory writings: "Our glorious father provided that writings which are called defamatory shall be destroyed, if possible. He ordered also that such writings shall not be admitted to his own cognizance or to public cognizance. Therefore, neither the life nor the rank of any person shall be shattered and shaken by such devices, for We decree that all such defamatory writings shall be burned" (Pharr 250).

In the previous chapter dealing with the burning of heretical-blasphemous books, I wrote that the voluminous book burnings in seventeenth and eighteenth century Great Britain have been reported to such an extent in Farrer's 1892 *Books Condemned to Be Burnt* and Gillett's 1932 *Burned Books* that I hesitate going over all that territory again here. Similarly, the reader is referred to those two works for a coverage of the burning of seditious-subversive English books up to the eighteenth century, involving such authors and works as: John Wolfe's *Henry IV,* burned in 1600; John Cowell's *The Interpreter,* burned in 1610; William Prynne's *Histrio-Mastix,* burned in 1633; George Wither's *Justiciarius justificatus,* burned in 1646; John Milton's *A Defence of the People of England,* burned in 1660; and Thomas Delaune's *Plea for the Nonconformists,* burned in 1683.

On August 13, 1660, King Charles II issued a Proclamation ordering the burning of John Milton's *Eikonoklastes* and *Defensio* and John Goodwin's *The Obstructors of Justice.* The Proclamation asserted at the outset that in both of Milton's books "are contained sundry treasonable passages against us and our Government, and most impious endeavours to justify the horrid and unnatural murder of our late dear Father of Glorious Memory." The Proclamation concluded with the order "to cause the same [books] to be publicly burnt by the hand of the common hangman" and commanded that "no man hereafter presume to print, sell, or disperse any of the aforesaid books" (Milton 1848 xxxviii).

Milton's *Defensio* was published in Latin, in 1651, as a response to Salmasius' *Defensio Regia,* a work defending Charles I against the charges that he was a tyrant and traitor. In his defense of the absolute powers of a king, Salmasius asserted, among other things, that "a king is one who has supreme authority in the kingdom, who is answerable only to God; who unfettered by laws, gives laws; who judges all and is judged by none.... Charles is compared to the ancient Jewish kings. Kings can do what they please, without fear of laws and judgments. God alone is the avenger of the unjust King" (Milton 1966 340).

Milton, in his attack on Salmasius' position, wrote in *Defensio:* "While he [Salmasius] defines a king ... as one whose power is supreme in the kingdom and responsible to none but God, one who may do as he will and is not subject to the laws, I shall be able to prove the opposite, not merely by my own theories and evidence but by his as well; that is, no nation or people of any size ... has ever granted such rights or power to its king that he should be subject to the laws, that he might do as he will, that he should judge all and be judged by none" (Milton 1966 340).

Goodwin's condemned book was titled *The Obstructours of Justice or A Defence of the Honourable Sentence passed upon the late King, by the High Court of Justice* in which he defended the execution of Charles I and condemned the absolute power of kings. Goodwin arguing that kings were not "above the law," asserted: "It is a frivolous pretence to say, that King's are accountable unto God, when they transgresse his law, though not unto men." [Further] "The people are not of, sprang from Kings, but Kings of, and from the people" [and] "A people or State formerly Governed by Kings, may very lawfully turn these servants of theirs out of their doors" (Gillett 1932 429).

After the burning of scores of seditious books in the seventeenth century, the English began the eighteenth century by burning a work by the author of *Robinson Crusoe, Moll Flanders* and *A Journal of the Plague Year;* in 1702, Daniel Defoe's satirical *The Shortest Way With Dissenters* was declared a "seditious libel" and was ordered by the House of Commons to be burned by the common hangman in the public square of New Palace. At the time, as Fitzgerald has indicated, the Dissenters "were tolerated — but no more than tolerated. They could worship as they pleased; but no Dissenter could hold State or municipal office unless he had first taken the communion in an Established church. In law, at any rate, Dissenters were still regarded as public enemies, as potential levelling revolutionaries" (119).

In *The Shortest Way with Dissenters* Defoe incorporated many of the ideas and language used by the Tory anti–Dissenters and on the surface the work appeared to be an attack on the Dissenters, but was instead Defoe's satirical attack on the High Churchmen and Tories. As Fitzgerald has observed, "Defoe's caricature of the ferocious High Churchmen came off so brilliantly — it was so true to life — that his irony was taken in earnest.... When the truth leaked out, the dreadful truth that Defoe had written the pamphlet and that it was a hoax — a satire — the anger of the High Church and the Tory party was intense" (121). The denigrating metaphors used by the anti–Dissenters were included in Defoe's satire when he wrote, for example,

> This is the time to pull up this heretical Weed of Sedition, that has so long disturb'd the Peace of our Church, and poisoned the good Corn. 'Tis Cruelty to kill a Snake or a Toad in cold Blood, but the Poyson of their Nature makes it a Charity to our Neighbours, to destroy those Creatures, not for any personal Injury receiv'd, but for prevention; not for the Evil they have done, but the Evil they may do.
> Serpents, Toads, Vipers, etc. are noxious to the Body, and poison the sensative Life; these poyson the Soul, corrupt our Posterity, ensnare our Children, destroy the Vitals of our Happyness, our future Felicity, and contaminate the whole Mass [Boulton 94–95].

So brilliant was Defoe's irony that at the outset some Dissenters were alarmed at the attack on them and some High Churchmen expressed appreciation of the hard line taken against Dissenters. As Boulton has stated, "Defoe's irony misfired. It was hailed by the Tories as a pungent expression of their case; it was denounced by the Dissenters whose cause it aimed to serve; though Defoe felt that 'if any man take the pains seriously to reflect upon the Contents, the Nature of the Thing and the Manner of the Stile, it seem Impossible to imagine it should pass for anything but an Irony.' When true intention of the pamphlet was recognized, the Government acted quickly" (87).

On February 25, 1703, the House of Commons "found the pamphlet a reflection on Parliament 'tending to promote Sedition' and ordered it to be burned by the common hangman in the New Palace Yard, Westminster, and that 'the Sheriffs of *London* and *Middlesex* do assist the Serjeant at Arms, attending this House, to see the same done.' The *English Post* for 1 March reported that it was, in fact, burned on 26 February as a 'seditious libel'" (Backscheider 103). Defoe was imprisoned for several months and was required to stand three times in the pillory.

Just as Defoe had used satire in *The Shortest Way With the Dissenters* to rebuke the Tories and anti–Dissenters, with the book being reduced to ashes, six years later Jonathan Swift's satirical *Predictions for the Year 1708* was burned in Ireland and Portugal. Swift's book was ordered burned by the Portuguese Inquisition "no doubt because of the serious matters foretold of continental affairs and personages" (Scott 1907 298). The Irish burned the book because as "such uncanny prescience could not otherwise than signify collusion with the evil one himself" (Haight 30). Writing under the name Isaac Bickerstaff, Swift satirized the Almanackmakers and their predictions; the beginning paragraph of the work leads the gullible reader to believe that the astrologers are his target: "I have considered the gross abuse of astrology in this kingdom, and upon debating the matter with myself, I could not possibly lay the fault upon the art, but upon those gross imposters, who set up to be the artists. I know several learned men have contended, that the whole is a cheat; that it is absurd and ridiculous to imagine the stars can have any influence at all upon human actions, thoughts, or inclinations; and whoever has not bent his studies that way may be excused for thinking so, when he sees in how wretched a manner that noble art is treated, by a few mean, illiterate traders between us and the stars." The unsuspecting reader is further hoodwinked in the second paragraph when Swift writes: "I intend, in a short time, to publish a large and rational defence of this art, and therefore shall say no more in its justification at present, than that it hath been in all ages defended by many learned men, and among the rest by Socrates himself, whom I look upon as undoubtedly the wisest of uninspired mortals" (Scott 1907 301).

Swift's first prediction is related to John Partridge, an astrologer and Almanack-maker, who predicted the death of King James II and was widely thought to be "instrumental in toppling James II by predicting the King's death" (Lowe 75). According to Lowe, "Swift's main reason for attacking Partridge ... was not to expose a quack but to attack a politically dangerous adversary whose influence over the vulgar masses had in the past proved crucial" (78). At the outset of his predictions, Swift wrote: "My first prediction is but a trifle, yet I will mention it, to shew how ignorant those Scottish pretenders to astrology are in their own concerns: it relates to Partridge the Almanack-maker; I have consulted the star of his nativity by my own rules, and find he will infallibly die upon the 29th of March next, about eleven at night, of a raging fever; therefore I advise him to consider of it, and settle his affairs on time" (Scott 1907 305).

The month of April, writes Swift, "will be observable for the death of many great persons. On the 4th will die the Cardinal de Noailles, Archbishop of Paris: on the 11th, a great peer of this realm will die at his country-house." Other predictions included: On July 14th, "a shameful discovery will be made of a French Jesuit, giving poison to a great foreign general: and when is put to the torture, he will make wonderful discoveries" and in September "the Pope having long languished last month, the swellings in his legs breaking, and the flesh mortifying, will die on the 11th instant; and in three weeks' time, after a mighty contest, be succeeded by a Cardinal of the imperial faction, but a native of Tuscany, who is now about sixty-one years old" (Scott 1907 305–308). Swift's hoax, his April Fools' joke, with its predictions of things to come in European religious and political matters, was not appreciated in Ireland and Portugal where the satire was condemned, burned and forbidden upon pain of excommunication if read (Mayhew 280).

In France, the "false, scandalous and seditious" *Antonii Santarellis* by Jesuit Sanctarel was condemned by the Sorbonne in Paris and ordered by the French Parlament to be burned. The 1626 order commanding the book be burned had a title page which read: "A COPIE OF THE FIRST ARREST OR DECREE OF THE Parlament of Paris, against the Books of Santarellus the Jesuit; Commanding it to be burned, and the Provincial of the Jesuits with others, to come to the Court the next morning to be heard. With, the Parlaments demands, the Jesuits answers, their Declaration of their destestation of the said Book, with the Censure of the Sorbon Doctors against the same." The document condemning the book and ordering it be set afire stated at the outset: "The court has declared, and does declare the propositions, and Maxims of the said book, to be false, scandalous, and seditious, tending to the subversion of Sovereign powers ordained, and established by God, to the insurrection of subjects against their prince, withdrawing them from their obedience, inducing to attempt against their persons, and states, to disturb the public peace, and tranquility; and the said book, as such, to be torn and burned in the Court of the Palace by the Executioner of high justice" (*A Copie of the First Arrest or Decree of the Parlament of Paris*, etc. Title page).

On April 4, 1626, the Sacred Theological Faculty of Paris focused on the two chapters in *Antonii Santarellis* that contained the following condemned propositions: "That the Pope can punish Kings, and Princes with temporal punishments, depose, and deprive them of their kingdoms for the crime of heresy, and free their subjects from their obedience, and that this has ever been the custom of the Church. And not only for heresy, but also other causes; to wit, for their sins. If also it be expedient: if princes be negligent: if they be unable and unprofitable. Moreover, that the Pope had power over spiritual things, and also over all temporal. And that by the law of God there is in him both spiritual and temporal power" (*A Copie of the First Arrest or Decree of the Parlament of Paris*, 11).

The Faculty of Paris, in April 1626, "disproved, and condemned the doctrine contained in these propositions ... as new, false, erroneous, contrary to the word of God; making the Pontifical dignity to be odious; opening the way to schism; derogating from the supreme authority of kings, which depend only upon God, hindering the conversion of infidel, and heretical princes, disturbing the public peace, and overthrowing kingdoms, states, and commonwealths, and in brief, with drawing subjects from the obedience, which they owe to their sovereigns, and inducing them to factions, rebellions, and seditions, and to attempt against the lives of their princes" (*A Copie of the First Arrest or Decree of the Parlament of Paris,* 12).

The Parlement document forbade, "under pain of Treason all booksellers, and printers to print, sell, utter, and all persons of what state, and condition soever they be, to have, keep, retain, and communicate, to print, or cause to be printed, or to publish the said book" (4). Further, it was ordered that "the Provincial, three Rectors, and three Ancients of the Jesuits" appear before the Parlement "to be heard." The Jesuits appeared on March 24, 1626, and "the Parlement asked them, Do you approve the wicked book of Santarellus?" The Parlement continued its questioning: "Answer these two things, do you believe that the King is all Powerful within his Estates, and do you think, that any foreign Power can, or ought enter in, or any than in the person of the King can disturb the peace of the Gallican Church?" The Jesuits answered: "No, Messieurs, we believe him all powerful, as for temporal." Parlement: "As for temporal, speak plainly, and tell us, if you believe, that the Pope can excommunicate the King, free his subjects from their oath of allegiance, and expose his kingdom to spoil?"

At the end of the questioning, the Jesuits requested a bit more time to confer together. A few days later, the Jesuits signed a document which said in part: "We underwritten do declare, that we disallow, and detest the wicked Doctrine contained in the book of Santarellus, in that which concerns the person of kings, their authority, and their states, and that we acknowledge their majesties to depend immediately upon God, that we are ready to shed our blood, and expose our lives in all occasion for the confirmation of this truth" (5–7).

According to Peignot, it had been decided that "if these priests did not disapprove of the doctrine of Sanctarel they would be treated as criminals.... Fear forced the bishops to condemn their colleague's doctrine by the official signing on the 16th of March 1762. That same year the Sorbonne censured the work and on the 13th of March the Parlement of Paris condemned it to be shredded and burnt by the hand of the executioner. Several other faculties of the kingdom followed the Sorbonne's example" (II 114).

To Voltaire went the honor of the French author who had more different titles set afire than any other writer. Farrer observed in 1892 that "no one writer ... of the eighteenth century contributed so many books to the flames as Voltaire" (Farrer 15). However, to paraphrase Farrer in the twenty-first century, no one writer in all history has provided so many different books to the flames as Voltaire. Many authors have had one or two of their titles set afire, but only Voltaire has had at least ten different titles reduced to ashes in such cities as Paris, Geneva, and Berlin. Between 1734 and 1771, the following works by Voltaire were burned: *Candide; Diatribe du docteur Akakia; Dictionnaire philosophique; Dieu et les Hommes; Le Diner due Comte de Boulainvilliers; L'Homme aux quarante ecus; Lettres philosophiques; Poème sur le désastre de Lisbonne; Poème sur la loi naturelle; La Pucelle; Temple du goût. Lettres philosophiques* was first published in English in 1733 under the title *Letters Concerning the English Nation.* As one of Voltaire's biographers has indicated: "When the letters were published in France the following year, the clergy demanded their suppression. The doom of the book was sealed. It was condemned by the Parliament as a menace to the religious and civil order of society, and was publicly burned by the executioner"

(Brandes 1 200). Further, "The authorities were outraged at the book, and when sentence was imposed, it prescribed that the work 'being scandalous, and offensive to religion, good morals and the respect owed the State, should be burned by the executioner, at the foot of the great stairway.' This was done" (Brandes 1 266).

Another biographer has summarized what it was that so offended the French that led to the Parliament's order to burn the book:

> England came off far the better in Voltaire's comparison between the two countries. But over and above that, there was something wounding about the tone in which the book was written, whether the opinions it offered were just, as they sometimes were, or unjust.... The book also troubled people's consciences. It cast poisoned darts at religion and French institutions. To old Cardinal Fleury, it seemed to make fun of hallowed institutions, feudal privilege, and royal absolutism. Instead of being heavily castigated by a long-winded and virtuous reformer fulminating against injustice, France's political apparatus was compared, in the simplest, most straightforward manner, to the wise customs of England. Voltaire made use of an irony by which the odiousness of French customs often seemed to be surpassed only by their ridiculousness, and their cruelty only by their absurdity [Orieux 107].

It is not as though there had not been previous critics of French institutions; but as Orieux has explained, earlier attacks on French institutions "were intended to stimulate and strengthen Church and throne, whereas Voltaire's lightning darts were meant to kill the institutions they were aimed at. That was what was new about the *Lettres,* as those in power fully realized" (107).

The same year *Lettres philosophiques* was burned, Voltaire's *Temple du goût* was also set afire. Haight reports: "*Temple du Goût,* a satire on contemporary French literature, was condemned. Copies were seized and burned, and a warrant was issued against the author, who was not to be found" (33). As Noyes has observed, *Temple du goût* "created immense excitement in Paris; but it delivered so many shrewd thrusts that it inevitably made trouble for its author.... The victims of his satire in this delicious piece of poetical persiflage seized every opportunity to revenge themselves by twitching the sleeve of authority and pointing out the destructive nature of his thought" (176).

In 1752, Voltaire became involved in a dispute with a scientific academician Pierre-Louis Moreau de Maupertuis, favored and praised by Frederick II, King of Prussia, who attacked Voltaire in print. Voltaire "was not disposed to accept Frederick's polemic as the final word in the affair. He responded with a satire, *Diatribe du docteur Akakia,* ridiculing Maupertuis savagely. Frederick, incensed by this direct challenge to his own authority, ordered the work to be lacerated and burned on all the public squares of Berlin on 24 December. So the wheel had turned full circle. Voltaire, who had gone to Prussia to escape persecution, had now suffered exactly the same condign punishment to his work in Berlin as his *Lettres philosophiques* had undergone in Paris in 1734" (Mason 1981 63).

In his biography of Voltaire, Thaddeus provides the following information related to the 1752 burnings of *Diatribe du docteur Akakia:* "Voltaire, looking out of his window, sees a sight he has often seen in France but never before in Prussia. A great fire in the street, a man (who looks very like the public executioner) tearing a book to pieces, and throwing it leaf by leaf to the flames. 'I think,' he says softly, with a little smile, 'It is my Doctor they are burning!' ... The official paper of Berlin carries the following item about the deceased Doctor — 'Sunday, at noon, a horrible pamphlet, entitled The Diatribe, etc., was burned publicly in different places by the hand of the executioner. M. De Voltaire is said to be the author of its'" (184–185).

"Frederick may have consoled himself and Maupertuis by his *auto-da-fe,* but Europe howled with laughter, both at the *Diatribe* and at the old goings-on of the philosopher-king" (Besterman 1976 338). Voltaire was imprisoned for almost a month in Frankfort and after being released, not allowed to re-enter France, he settled in Geneva.

Three years later, Voltaire's mock-epic poem of Joan of Arc, *La Pucelle,* was burned in Paris and Geneva. In his biography of Voltaire, Besterman devotes a chapter to *La Pucelle,* beginning the chapter with: "Very many unkind things have been said about the *Pucelle,* which became widely known at this time. The most recent history of French literature, by a French university professor, refers to the 'continuous obscenity' and the 'crushing pornography' of this poem. This was by no means the view ... Certainly, Voltaire's treatment of St. Joan was often condemned, but it was usually for religious and patriotic reasons, as in the Inquisition decree of 1757" (1976 389). Besterman concludes that Voltaire was not "in the least inclined to write with conventional respect even about a national heroine. Those who find these things shocking will be duly shocked. But all this is incidental. The main theme is a huge joke: the mystical importance attached to Joan's virginity. Voltaire found irresistibly funny the notion that the fate of France could depend on the preservation of this peasant-girl's maidenhead.... Voltaire developed this theme in fugue and counterpoint, in some of his most successful verse, pausing only here and there to sink his blade into some of man's inhumanities and stupidities" (1976 396). Joan of Arc was burned at the stake in 1431 and as Knapp has written: "Ironically, *The Maid,* Joan of Arc, was again burned — this time not in the flesh, but in paper replica, on August 5, 1755" (61).

In 1756, Voltaire published *Poème sur le désastre de Lisbonne (Poem on the Lisbon Earthquake)* and *Poème sur la loi naturelle (Poem on Natural Law).* In his *Poem on the Lisbon Earthquake,* Voltaire "attacks optimism, and deals harshly with Providence and the Catholic Church. He said the poem was not anti–Christian, but unfortunately the printer, to fill out the poem, had bound the poem up together with Voltaire's *Poème sur la loi naturelle.* The volume was sentenced to be burned in 1759, despite Voltaire's preface proclaiming his Catholic zeal" (Orieux 294). In his *Poem on Natural Law* Voltaire "forwarded the notion of a universal morality independent not only of organized religions but of all concepts and systems relating to the Supreme Being. Again he decried the evils of fanaticism, as witnessed in the Spanish and Portuguese inquisitions organized by the Catholic Church, where Moors and Jews were burned at the stake in an *auto-da-fé,* or 'act of faith'" (Knapp 15).

In his reference to the burning of *Poem on Natural Law,* Brandes writes: "The *Lettres philosophiques* were burned by the hangman. The *Poème sur la loi Naturelle* was likewise burned by order of Parliament" (Brandes 2 107). According to Crowley, the *Poéme sur la loi Naturelle* "was, in the company with other liberal works, torn to bits and burned on the tenth of February, 1759" (Crowley 232).

Also in 1759, immediately after Voltaire had published *Candide* the book was condemned and a few months after publication the now classic work was ordered burned. In March 1759, the Geneva Council "ordered that it should be burned by the hangman at once. This was done, to Voltaire's anger. He took revenge shortly by flooding Geneva with brief anti–Church and anti–Christian pamphlets. The authorities of Paris as well as of Geneva were furious. The encyclopedists had almost got the best of them. The clergy urged that some decisive action should be taken. Helvetius's book *De l'Esprit,* which had caused a considerable sensation, was condemned by the Parliament and burned by the hangman on February 10, 1759" (Brandes 2 146).

In 1764, Voltaire published his *Dictionnaire philosophique* and it was ordered by the Parliament of Paris that the work be burned by the hangman (Brandes 2 220). As Brandes has indicated: "More dangerous than his repudiation of the concept of 'Revelation' in the

Dictionnaire proved his allusions to the Parliament; for instance, in the article titled 'Tyrant' he said "it is better to have to do with a single tyrant than with a whole flock of little tyrants—the Parliament took this as applying to itself" (221). *Dictionnaire philosophique* was, as Besterman points out, "repeatedly condemned by the civil and religious authorities in several countries, but nowhere with more congenial venom than in Geneva" where the public prosecutor denounced Voltaire's works as "errors, malignity and indecency," "contageious poison," "temerarious, impious, scandalous, destructive of revelation" (1976 477).

One of Voltaire's adversaries, Charles Bonnet, described *Dictionnaire philosophique* as a "detestable book" by a "pestilential author" which "is to the conscience what arsenic is to the intestines" (Orieux 409). "When Voltaire simply smiled to see his *Dictionary* burned, the pastor [Bonnet] was furious: 'This man no longer produces anything but excrement, and countless people are ready to swallow it,' he wrote, dipping his own pen in the chamber pot" (Orieux 409).

In 1765, a nineteen-year-old Chevalier de la Barre was brought to trial on the charge of blasphemy for not genuflecting, using "godless language," spitting at pictures of the Saints, and speaking ill of the Virgin Mary. He was found guilty and decapitated. At his trial in 1766, La Barre's possession of several books was used against him: "[H]is library proved to be his undoing, for in France at that time, people were punished for the books they possessed, on unfair assumption that a man's books betrayed the exact way of thinking of their owner. Now it was revealed that La Barre had possessed books which either ignore or attacked the Church: Voltaire's *Dictionnaire philosophique,* Helvetius' *De l'Esprit* and several others" (Brandes 2 228). After the decapitation, La Barre's body, "together with Voltaire's *Dictionnaire Philosophique Portatif,* was burned to ashes and strewn to the winds" (Brandes 2 228). The book was burned in Paris, Geneva, the Netherlands and Rome.

The news of La Barre's execution caused Voltaire "deep distress and shame ... at the legal injustices of which France was capable. Alarming too had been the report that he might be implicated in the La Barre affair, seeing that a copy of his *Dictionnaire philosophique* was publicly burnt in the flames that consumed La Barre's corpse" (Mason 1981 109).

The burning of *Dictionnaire philosophique* was followed in 1771 with the burning of *L'Homme aux quarante ecus:* "After La Barre had been executed as a victim of the brutality and stupidity of the Parliament of Paris, Voltaire's hatred of the various Parliaments of France had increased daily. His ingenious tale *L'Homme aux quarante ecus* (of February, 1768), which tried to teach the government and the people some common sense notions of economics, and strove especially for a reformation of the unfair French tax system, was sentenced by the order of the Parliament to be burned on the pyre — which glorious sentence was repeated in Rome and carried out on November 29, 1771" (Brandes 2 268). Referring to the rejection of Voltaire's work, Orieux has written that in 1768, Voltaire published "the delightful tale, *L'Homme aux quarante ecus* (The Man with Forty Crowns), in which his allusions to the cruel rapacity of financiers made him enemies among the royal fiscal authorities" (423).

Two other works by Voltaire that were reduced to ashes were *Dieu et les Hommes* and *Le Diner du comte de Boulainvilliers* (Farrer 15; Peignot 189). The latter, as summarized by Besterman, "is a series of dialogues about religion. The first is a conversation before dinner between an abbe and a count, who maintains that free thought is superior to the Roman Catholic religion.... Dinner is served, and the conversation broadens into light-hearted but extremely outspoken fun about the grosser absurdities of the *Bible* and religion. After dinner the conversation takes a practical turn. Is religion necessary to enforce morality? The general conclusion, in which even the abbe eventually joins, is that human nature requires religion, but only when purified from superstition and the priesthood" (518).

Voltaire died in 1778 and the contentiousness of his life followed him to his grave — graves. Amidst some controversy he was given a Catholic burial. Thirteen years later, Voltaire's body was exhumed and ceremoniously transferred to the Pantheon in Paris. In 1814, royalists who believed that it was an outrage to have Voltaire buried in a site that had once been a church, decided to secretly remove his remains: "One night in May 1814 Voltaire's coffin, together with that of Rousseau, nearby, was opened, emptied of its contents, and carefully closed again. Nobody breathed a word about it. The remains were taken to a piece of wasteland at Bercy used as a dump for refuse and scrap, buried in quicklime, and covered with rubbish. The conspirators stamped down the ground to hide their traces" (Orieux 500).

At the same time the French and others were setting fire to Voltaire's books, they were also burning the books of Jean-Jacques Rousseau. While the two authors shared little in matters related to religion, politics, and art, they did share, in addition to a common grave, seeing their books burned in Paris, Geneva, and the Hague; in 1764, "Jean-Jacques' *Lettres de la Montagne* and Voltaire's *Dictionnaire philosophique portatif* were to be reconciled by being burned on the same fire, in the courtyard of the Palais in Paris" (Guehenno 133). In 1762, Rousseau published both his *Social Contract* and *Emile,* the former in April and the latter in May. Both were immediately condemned and set afire in June. In his biography of Rousseau, Miller, referring to the burning of Rousseau's works, writes that the government of Geneva banned "*Emile* and the *Social Contract* declaring both books subversive and the author *persona non grata*" (xii). As Miller indicates, Rousseau's books were burned because they were condemned as being both impious and subversive: "On June 7, [1762,] the faculty of the Sorbonne called Rousseau 'a great master of corruption and error,' condemned *Emile,* primarily on religious grounds — the idea of natural goodness contradicted the Church's doctrine of original sin. Two days later, the Parliament of Paris followed suit, making clear that the bravado involved in signing such an impious book ought not to go unpunished. But political issues were at stake as well. According to the attorney for Parliament, Rousseau's work contained not only impieties but also 'propositions that tend to give a false and odious character to sovereign authority, to destroy the principle of obedience that is his due, and to weaken respect and love of peoples for their Kings'" (Miller 78). In condemning *Emile,* the Judgment of the Parlement described the book as "impugning the veracity of the Holy Scriptures, disputing the divinity of Jesus Christ and the existence of the Christian religion, asserting blasphemous, ungodly, and detestable principles, containing indecent material offensive to propriety and modesty, together with propositions subversive to sovereign authority, setting forth maxims of education which could only produce men devoted to scepticism and toleration, abandoned to their passions, men given over to the pleasures of the senses, dominated by pride and listening to no other voice than that of nature" (Cranston 5).

In Geneva, the authorities "condemned *Emile* and the *Contract social* ... to be burned, as 'rash, scandalous, impious, tending to destroy the Christian religion and all governments...,' and added a warning that Rousseau would be arrested if he set foot on Genevan soil. Other condemnations followed, in Berne, and of course in Rome" (Rousseau xx). The hostility towards Rousseau was reflected in a letter from Genevese scientist Charles Bonnet to Bernese biologist Albrecht von Haller: "Two hundred years ago, we would have roasted Rousseau: this time we have only roasted his books" (Cranston 9).

The burnings of *Emile* and the *Social Contract* were followed with the fiery destruction of Rousseau's *Letters from the Mountain* in 1764 and *Lettres écrites de la montagne* in 1765. In *Letters from the Mountain* Rousseau satirized the government and religion of Geneva and denounced Voltaire. Miller says of the book burnings: "A trail of smoke seemed to follow it [*Letters from the Mountain*] wherever Rey [Rousseau's publisher] marketed the book. Burned in Berne and at the Hague, it was forbidden in Neuchatel, censured in Geneva, condemned by the Court of Holland, committed to the flames in Paris" (126). Cranston states that while the Genevese authorities condemned the book they "stopped short of actually burning the book" (108).

In response to attacks from the Genevan public prosecutor, Rousseau published *Lettres écrites de la montagne* in which he defends *Emile* and the *Social Contract*. Rousseau "made it his task to establish by irrefutable proofs that the [Geneva] Council had not only shown exceptional severity, but had violated the laws of the Constitution, in its treatment of him — so that even had he been guilty of the offences with which he was charged, his condemnation would have been unjustly pronounced. In the second and third letters, he appeals to the principles and history of the Reformation to support his declaration that he had not in *Emile* attacked or opposed any of the doctrines of the reformed faith" (MacDonald 116–117). Immediately after its publication, *Lettres écrites de la montagne* "was condemned to be burnt at Geneva, at Paris, and this time, also at the Hague" (MacDonald 117). Green also writes that the book was "publicly burnt at The Hague in January 1765" (1955 324)

Rousseau died on July 2, 1778, one month after Voltaire's death; like Voltaire, he was buried in the Pantheon. However, there is disagreement amongst biographers as to what happened to the remains of the two men after they were placed in coffins in the Pantheon. For example, one source states: "In 1814, on the collapse of the Empire, the Pantheon was invaded and Voltaire's remains — like those of Rousseau — scattered no one knows where" (Andrews 149). Similarly, another source declares: "One night, in the month of May, 1814, the bones of Voltaire and of Rousseau were taken out of their coffins of lead, tumbled into a common sack," carried to "a piece of waste ground" where "the sack of bones was emptied into the pit; a sack of lime was poured upon them. The hole was filled up with earth, all traces of the burial were obliterated as far as possible, and the party then separated in silence" (Parton 2 628).

However, Rousseau biographer Cranston argues that the bones of Rousseau and Voltaire remain in their coffins in the Pantheon: "A rumour arose and came to be widely credited that the coffins were then desecrated and the bones within them removed and scattered. To scotch the rumour once and for all, a commission of distinguished citizens was appointed in 1897 by the Minister of Instruction and Fine Arts and charged with determining the truth. The commission found that both coffins were still in an underground vault of the Pantheon, now again a secular building, and that their contents had been undisturbed. Rousseau's skeleton, the commission reported, 'was perfectly preserved, the arms crossed on the chest, the head slightly bent to the left, like a man asleep'" (188–189).

While Rousseau and Voltaire "conceived a strong aversion from each other" (Besterman 1976 206) and while Voltaire saw Rousseau as a "scoundrel" and a "hypocrite" (Cranston 102) and Rousseau "convinced himself that there was not room in Geneva for both Voltaire and himself"(Guehenno 7) — the two adversaries shared the honor of seeing their books burned and after their deaths sharing some time together in coffins in the Pantheon and in the end perhaps sharing a common unknown grave in a "piece of waste land at Bercy used as a dump for refuse and scrap" (Orieux 500).

Four years before Voltaire died, he had expressed high praise for dramatist Pierre Beaumarchais whose *Memoirs* were burned in 1774. Voltaire wrote of Beaumarchais: "What a man! He embraces in himself: intellect, earnestness, reason, humor, energy. He knows how to appeal to the feelings. In short, he is successful in every kind of eloquence" (Brandes 2 286). After Voltaire's death, it was Beaumarchais who took on the responsibility of publishing Voltaire's *Secret Memoirs for Use in Writing the Life of Voltaire* and, at great expense, the seventy-two octavo volumes were published between 1784 and 1789, ending up a financial disaster for Beaumarchais (Orieux 506). However, when two centuries later Theodore Besterman published his definitive *The Complete Works of Voltaire,* he paid tribute to Beaumarchais: "A respectful salute is addressed to the memory of those who laid the foundations of this edition by assembling and preserving numerous manuscripts of Voltaire's correspondence: above all to Beaumarchais [and others]" (Besterman 1968 85 xxxi)

In 1773, Beaumarchais had become involved in a dispute involving payment of attorney fees to Louis-Valentin Goezman who subsequently wrote pamphlets against him. Beaumarchais responded by publishing five memoirs against Goezman who was charged with government corruption; the *Memoires* were immediately "hailed as a masterpiece of polemics in France and all over Europe. The Parlement had no other choice but to dismiss Goezman from office while imposing the infamous sentence of blame on Madame Goezman as well as on Beaumarchais and condemning his *Memoires* to be burned" (Sungolowsky 20). The entry for Beaumarchais in the *Guide to French Literature: Beginnings to 1789* reads, in part: "The *Memoires* were a huge success. Thousands of copies of each had been sold, culminating in the sale of 10,000 copies of the fourth in three days. On 5 March [1774] they were publicly burnt" (Levi 42).

Beaumarchais, who wrote *Le Barbier de Seville* and *Le Mariage de Figaro,* received high praise for *Memoires* from Voltaire who stated: "Beaumarchais' *Memoires* are the strongest, boldest, most comic and interesting thing I have ever seen, and the most humiliating for the author's enemies" (Orieux 442). Brandes has summarized why the authorities condemned the work and had it burned:

> The importance of the four *Memoirs,* which Beaumarchais published (1774–1778) in connection with his trial, is the fact that in them the future author of *Figaro* raised the question: was the private citizen who had no powerful protector without defense against the arbitrariness and partiality of the courts? ... Beaumarchais revealed, as Voltaire had done before him, the tricks and subterfuges which the administration of justice employed, and like Voltaire he struck at the roots of the tyranny under which the population was suffering. In its haughtiness the Parliament had been so careless as to overlook the possibility that among those it injured there might be a genius capable of taking revenge [Brandes 2 286].

As Farrer has put it, *Memoires* "has condemned to the flames for its imputations on the powers that were" (22).

A contemporary of Beaumarchais, Rousseau, and Voltaire was one-time Jesuit Guillaume Raynal whose *History of the Two Indies* was ordered burned by the Parlement of Paris which condemned the work as impious, blasphemous, seditious, tending to provoke the people against sovereign authority and to overthrow the fundamental principles of the civil order (Peignot 2 71). Raynal's three thousand page work was smuggled into France and "was read and discussed all over Europe; smuggled copies soon found their way into France; and eventually, by May 1781, *Parlement* condemned it to be burned and Raynal was threatened with arrest and had to take refuge abroad" (Furbank 418).

The full title of the work was *The Philosophical and Political History of Settlements and Commerce of the Europeans in the Two Indies,* the two Indies being the West Indies and India. Raynal and his collaborator Diderot advocated social and political liberty, condemned slavery and fanaticism; as Salmon has observed, "Together they [Raynal and Diderot] condemned superstition, privilege and despotism; and they extolled liberty, toleration, the spirit of humanity, and progress through enlightenment. Both regarded the clergy as the instrument of oppression, and religion as at best the servant of morality" (114).

When his work was attacked by the Faculty of Theology at the Sorbonne, Raynal responded with his *Reply to the Censure* in which he "called upon 'the kings of the earth' to 'draw the people from the lethargic slumber in which the priests would have them repose,' to employ 'reason to unmask the hypocrisy of the audacious sect,' and to show 'courage to enlighten humanity.' He ranked himself beside Voltaire and Rousseau, and denounced the concept of sin as the malicious invention of St. Augustine" (Salmon 116).

Eventually, ten years after his work had been burned for being seditious and impious, Raynal disavowed most of what he had written in *History of the Two Indies:* "He had come to regret the extremism of the *Philosophical History,* and occupied himself preparing a new edition which would omit some of the offending passages" (Salmon 117). When Raynal died in 1796, it was not as a revolutionary, but as someone sympathetic to the royalists and monarchy.

One year before Raynal died, radical socialist and journalist François Babeuf was arrested and his newspaper *Tribun du peuple* was "solemnly burnt in the Théâtre des Bergères by the *jeunesse dorée,* the young men whose mission it was to bludgeon Jacobinism out of the streets and cafes" (*Encyclopædia Britannica* 3 93). Babeuf, known as "Gracchus" Babeuf, argued that the French Revolution had not gone far enough in bringing about equality and justice. As John Scott has stated: "The first years of the Revolution saw the unfolding of a tremendous struggle in the countryside for the abolition of feudal dues, services and taxation. Babeuf strove to widen and deepen this movement, to give it direction. He appeared in the first instance as a leader of the peasantry in the struggle against these exactions, but this was for him only a beginning.... No revolution, in Babeuf's view, could be considered complete that did not result in the abolition of private property and of the division of society into exploited and exploiting classes.... Land division ... would, he thought, be for French people an important first step toward a society without class differences and without exploitation" (5–6).

In 1797, Babeuf was brought to trial and his indictment read that he was involved in a conspiracy "to destroy the government, to overthrow the established authorities, to massacre a huge number of ordinary people, and to organize the looting of private property" (Babeuf 31). In his defense speech, Babeuf referred to the emphasis placed by the prosecution on his *Tribune of the People:* "The prosecution has traced the origins of the alleged conspiracy to my newspaper *Tribune of the People,* which has been in circulation since 13 vendémiaire. The prosecution, indeed, has built a major part of its case around the publication of this journal" (40).

In his courtroom speech, Babeuf quoted extensively from the condemned *Tribune of the People* in which had had written: "Man's condition ought not to have deteriorated in passing from a state of nature to a state of social organization. In the beginning the soil belonged to none, its fruits to all. The introduction of private property was a piece of trickery put over on the simple and unsuspecting masses. The laws that buttressed property operated inevitably to create social classes— privileged and oppressed, masters and slaves.... [The] three roots of our public woes— heredity, alienability, and the differing values which arbitrary opinion assigns to different types of social product — proceed from the institution of private property" (Babeuf 52–53). "It did not take me long to draw the following conclusions," continued Babeuf. "If the earth belongs to none and its fruits to all; if private ownership of public wealth is only the result of certain institutions that violate fundamental human rights; then it follows that this private ownership is a usurpation; and it further follows that all that a man takes of the land and its fruits beyond what is necessary for sustenance is theft from society" (54) .

Babeuf was convicted under a law that "decreed the death penalty for advocacy by word or in writing of the overthrow of established authority, of the re-establishment of the Constitution of 1793, or of the division of the lands" (Scott 1967 11). Babeuf and a colleague, A.A. Darthe, were executed on May 27, 1797. Historically, Babeuf's "importance lies in the fact that he was the first to propound socialism as a practical policy, and the father of the movements which play so conspicuous a part in the revolutions of 1848 and 1871" (*Encyclopædia Britannica* 3 94).

Across the Atlantic, the House of Representatives in the Massachusetts colony, in October 1754, "had occasion to assert the privilege of its members to be free from annoying public criticism. Some one had published an anonymous pamphlet entitled 'The Monster of Monsters,' containing a satirical account of the debate of the House upon an unpopular excise bill. The pamphlet was really nothing more than a harmless piece of humor; but the affronted representatives resolved that it was a false, scandalous libel, reflecting upon the proceedings of the House in general and on the members in particular. The hangman was ordered to burn it in King Street below the courthouse, and the messenger was required to see the order carried out" (Duniway 115).

Kidder places the burning of *The Monster of Monsters* in the following context: "Regardless of its authorship, the origin of the pamphlet can be traced to the action of the Massachusetts legislators, who, considering the importance of the traffic in rum, imposed an excise upon wines and other spirituous liquors. The regulation excited great opposition and in every town the law was more or less denounced; the press teemed with pamphlets in which the members of the House were attacked with great violence; and prosecutions were instituted against some persons who were most bitter in their opposition" (47–48). The suspected printer of *The Monster of Monsters*. Daniel Fowle, was arrested, imprisoned for a brief period, and fined; he took his case through the court system and eventually, on December 8, 1766, the House ordered that "Fowle be granted twenty pounds 'on Account of ye Sufferings mentioned in this Petition,' which action was approved by the Council the following day. Thus, with the receipt of the additional twenty pounds, Daniel Fowle ceased his claim for compensation for the injury to his person and character resulting from his illegal arrest and imprisonment for the supposed printing of *The Monster of Monsters* over twelve years before" (Kidder 54). The satirical account of the House debates that led to the order to burn *The Monster of Monsters* began: "There lately appeared, in this Metropolis, a MONSTER of the most hideous Form, and terrible Aspect; such an one as was never before seen in America by any Man's Eyes; and, I believe, no where else; to be sure not in the British dominions. There was indeed one formerly a little like him in Turkey; another in Italy; and, as some say, there is one in France at this Day. He had more Heads and Horns than the He-Goat in Daniel. His Teeth resembled those of an overgrown Lion ... his Claws, like those of a Bear, only much bigger; and for a Tail, Gulliver's Monkey was a Fool to him" (3–4). The satire has a woman's club suggesting the Monster be taken to be viewed by the public: "For the Entertainment and Delight of the Publick ... we have resolv'd to hire a great Number of Persons to carry him thro' the Country for a Sight. So good a show will certainly give infinite Pleasure to People of every Rank; at the same Time that it will bring in Cash enough to find us all, in Tea, and Coffee, in Equipages and Fine Clothes, in Citron Water and gaming Money, as long as we live" (6). The imposition of new taxes is alluded to when we read: "For although I sometimes speak of this Creature, as being of the Male

Gender, I would now acquaint the Reader, that it is really an Hermaphrodite; and has a Multitude of large Teats; at which many hope to hang in Rows, like so many sucking Pigs, or rather like Imps at the teats of Witches. Nor need I observe here, what every one knows already. That though Monsters are said not to breed; yet they frequently give Milk in prodigious Quantities. But then it takes the Produce of a whole Country to feed one. And indeed, is this should live, I fear we shall find the old Proverb concerning the Sterility of Monsters, erroneous" (11).

During the eighteenth century, especially during the latter half of the 1700s, the Chinese were setting fire to subversive-seditious books and woodblocks. In 1769, the Emperor Chi'en-lung issued an edict ordering the burning of works by Ch'ien Ch'ien-i, a seventeenth century poet and scholar. The edict declared: "Now Ch'ien Ch'ien-i is already dead, and his bones have long since rotted away. We will let him be. But his books remain, an insult to right doctrine, and a violation of [the principles of] loyalty.... They must early be done away with. Now therefore let every governor-general and governor see to it that all the bookshops and private libraries in his jurisdiction produce and send [to the yamen] his *Ch'u Hsueh Chi* and *Yu Hsueh Chi*. In addition, let orders be dispatched to small villages, country hamlets, and out of the way regions in mountain fastnesses for the same purpose. The time limit for this operation is two years. Not a volume must escape burning" (Goodrich 26). Goodrich comments: "Such was to be the formula for every author similarly accused used time and again with ever great success during the next twenty years" (26). Often the order to burn the subversive books included the demand that the woodblocks also be set afire.

The edict ordering the burning of the "seditious poetry and prose" of Ch'u Ta-chun asserted: "The poems and essays of Ch'u Ta-chun are seditious; long ago and many times since have I ordered them proscribed, and forbade people privily to keep them. But as I have often proclaimed, all these rebellious words were the bigoted views of former writers and have no relation to our times. In case the books contain language that is anti-dynastic, then the woodblocks and printed sheets must both be put to the flames"(Goodrich 125).

Four years later, in June 1778, "the Grand Council reported to the emperor that so many condemned books and the woodblocks used for printing them had piled up in the Military Archives Commission that the councillors were afraid some volumes would be lost or misplaced. The imperial rescript, dated 11 June, ordered the councillors to 'cast the books to the flames.' That imperial orders were carried out is indicated by a report of 12 November 1781, that 52,480 woodblocks for printing seditious books, weighing 36,530 catties, had been broken up for firewood" (Guy 171).

Year after year edicts were issued ordering the burning of "rebellious," "seditious" and "treasonable" works; "memorials" followed indicating that the orders had been carried out. 1777: "In regard to carrying out of the edict for the suppression of books, I humbly report that on ten distinct occasions I have handed over a total of 1,863 *pu* [volumes], to be delivered to the Supreme Council for burning." 1779: "Since my arrival at this post in the 6th moon, I have found and forwarded books to the number of over 880, directed to the Grand Council to be burned." 1787: "Edict on the Writings of Li Ch'ing": "Let all the copies of the *Ssu-k'u* that have been stored in the four halls, together with the three additional copies, be purged of his work, and let it be destroyed by fire. Further, let all references to it in the annotated catalogue be completely cut away." These and other edicts and memorials are presented by Goodrich in his valuable *The Literary Inquisition of Ch'ien-lung*.

In the Introduction to her translation of the Chinese novel *Shui Hu Chuan (All Men Are Brothers),* "one of China's most famous novels," Pearl Buck refers to the 1799 burning of this work. *Shui Hu Chuan* is set in the thirteenth century, a story of 108 men who in opposition to oppressive government "flee from society to take refuge on a great mountain set in a lake and surrounded by a reedy marsh.... Here these fugitives gather and organize themselves into a complex group having their own rigid laws not only for warfare but of conduct and of courtesy. There is good authority for believing that the tale is based on history.... Their reputation was very high among common people ... and this fame spread far and wide and was told from generation to generation" (Buck vi). The author of the "tale" remains unknown. As Buck observed in 1933, "Naturally such a novel has been extremely popular among the people of China, although equally naturally it has often been forbidden"; an Imperial mandate of 1799 ordered the burning of the book: "All bookstores which print the licentious story 'Shui Hu Chuan' must be rigorously sought out, and the work prohibited. Both the wood blocks and the printed matter should be burned" (vi). Buck concludes in the Introduction to her 1933 translation: "Today the newest and most extreme party in China, the Communist, has taken the 'Shui Hu Chuan' and issued an edition with a preface by a leading Communist, who calls it the first Communist literature of China, as suitable to this day as to the day it was written" (ix).

Subversion, "breaking down respect for authority and for authorities," was also the rationale behind the burning of Aleksandr Radishchev's *A Journey from St. Petersburg to Moscow* during the reign of Catherine II; that the book be burned by the public executioner (Haight 42). As Thaler states in the Preface of the English translation of Radishchev's work, "*Journey from St. Petersburg to Moscow* made educated Russians think about the problem of serfdom.... [The] book presented a serious criticism of serfdom and of the entire Russian social order.... Radishchev ... had condemned equally the sovereign's despotism, the gentry's tyranny, and the peasants' violence. He wanted to make revolution unnecessary. He wanted reforms, and wanted them in time" (Radishchev vii).

In condemning the book, Catherine declared that the purpose of the work "is clear on every page: its author, infected and full of the French madness, is trying in every possible way to break down respect for authority and for the authorities, to stir up in the people indignation against their superiors and against the government.... The Empress was furious at Radishchev's 'praise of Mirabeau, who deserves not once but many times over to be hanged'" (Radishchev 10).

Radishchev, who had received part of his education at the University of Leipzig, had studied the works of Raynal, Voltaire, Rousseau, Helvetius, and Milton, all of whom, according to Catherine had "infected" Radishchev. Milton's influence is reflected in the book's longest chapter which is devoted to an historical account and condemnation of censorship. Milton had written in *Areopagitica* in 1644: "For who knows not that Truth is strong next to the Almighty? She needs no policies, nor stratagems, nor licensing to make her victorious; those are the shifts and the defences that error uses against her power." A century and a half later, Radishchev wrote in his *A Journey from St. Petersburg to Moscow,* "But if in these days of enlightenment one were to undertake to forbid or burn books that deal with divination or preach superstition, would it not be ridiculous for truth to lift the cudgel of persecution against superstition? Need truth seek the support of tyrannic might and the sword to overcome error, when the very sight of it is the most cruel scourge of error?" (173).

In Radishchev we have a confluence of matters related to censorship and book burning: first, his university education included studying authors whose books had been burned; second, he devoted a significant part of his own condemned book to a denunciation of censorship; and third, his own work is then set afire. Early in July 1790, Radishchev was arrested, imprisoned, and a few days later was condemned to death; in September, the Empress "commuted Radishchev's sentence to banishment for ten years to Ilimsk in eastern Siberia" (Radishchev 11). In 1802, he committed suicide.

The Nineteenth Through Twenty-first Centuries — Burning More Seditious-Subversive Books

An 1817 book burning that took place in Wartburg, Germany, has been referred to by Leo Lowenthal in his discussion of the now-famous Nazi book burnings in 1933. Lowenthal explains:

> [I]t is worth consideration that both the Wartburg Festival and the book burnings of May 10, 1933, hark back to Luther's burning of the bull of excommunication, as if it were a matter of a legitimate continuity of consciousness with a quasi-religious coloring. If one looks more closely at the Wartburg Festival, one finds that despite the quite different ideological rationalizations, extraordinary similarities mark the self-styled liberal and anti-absolutist *Burschenschaftsbewegung* (student association movement) and the National Socialist Fuehrer-ideology. The rituals of book-burning accompanied by anti–Semitic outbreaks, the screaming student choirs, the infamous participation of university professors who aided this ill deed at the Wartburg Festival as well as in German university towns in 1933, are expressive of the similarities between 1817 and 1933 [Lowenthal 16–17].

At the 1817 Wartburg Festival, students and professors took part in a book burning ritual, celebrating (1) the three hundredth anniversary of the Reformation and Luther's burning of the Papal Bull of excommunication, and (2) the 1813 German victory over the French at the Battle of Leipzig. Twenty-five to thirty books and papers were set afire, "including *Haller's Restauration der Staatswerk* of 1816 (which gave its name to the whole period) and the *Code Napoleon*" (Ritchie 628). As Snyder describes the event, "on October 17 to 19, 1817, at Wartburg Castle in Saxe-Weimar, hundreds of students from some thirteen universities gathered at a great festival to celebrate jointly the three hundredth anniversary of Luther's promulgation of the Ninety-Five Theses and the fourth anniversary of the Leipzig Battle of the Nations, Napoleon's last fight on German soil. The celebration began in a solemn and dignified manner, but, on the evening of the 19th, the students worked themselves into a political orgy. After a torchlight procession, a great bonfire was kindled, and books of 'anti-student' and 'reactionary' tendency were cast into the flames, along with a bagwig, a pair of guardman's stays, and a corporal's cane — symbols of the military authoritarian state" (154). According to Friedenthal, the bonfire consumed the writings by "well-known reactionaries" such as "Haller's *Restoration of Political Science,* pamphlets by the hated Sohmalz in Berlin, who denounced all students' associations, and books by the German playwright and Russian Councillor of State Kotzebue, who sends secret reports to Russia" (454).

The slavery issue in the United States provoked both sides to setting fire to a variety of publications. On July 30, 1835, "Charleston citizens, having learned that the mail steamer had brought to town packages of these [anti-slavery] propaganda writings, broke into the post office, and took them into the street and burned them" (Filler 97). The following year, the Virginia legislature "passed a law requiring postmasters to notify justices of the peace whenever they received incendiary publications or publications 'denying the right of masters to property in their slaves and inculcating the duty of resistence to such right.'" If the justice of peace found such publications they were to be "burned in his presence" (Eaton 268).

In 1838, "the Reverend R.J. Breckenridge, of Baltimore, editor of a religious magazine, had one number of his magazine burned because it contained an article on Biblical slavery. He was an anti-abolitionist, so that the action was not directed against abolitionists but against his right to discuss slavery Biblically or otherwise without consent. This occurred in Petersburg May 8, 1838, in the presence of the mayor and the recorder" (Savage 100).

Copies of Rowan Helper's *The Impending Crisis of the South* were burned in the South after its publication in 1857. As Blumenthal reports: "Hinton Rowan Helper's *Impending Crisis*..., a work of racial bigotry, advocated the sending of Negroes back to Africa. It aroused the fury of Southern slave-holders. At High Point, North Carolina, ten copies were publicly burned in the civic center. Some fifty volumes of the British anti-slavery author, Charles Haddon Spurgeon, were burned in 1860 behind a bookstore in Montgomery, Alabama" (18). Helper's book presented his "scheme for the abolition of slavery in the Southern States." He listed several "mottoes which, in substance, embody the principles, as we conceive, that should govern us in our patriotic warfare against the most subtle and insidious foe that ever menaced the inalienable rights and liberties and dearest interests of America" (Helper 155). Included in his "mottoes" were: "3rd. No Co-operation with Slave-holders in Politics— No Fellowship with them in Religion — No Affiliation with them in Society.... 5th. No recognition of pro-slavery men, except as Ruffians, Outlaws, and Criminals.... 10th. A Tax of Sixty Dollars on every Slaveholder for each and every Negro in his Possession at the present time, or any intermediate time between now and the 4th of July, 1863 — said Money to be Applied to the transportation of the Blacks to Liberia, to their Colonization in Central or South America or to their Comfortable Settlement within the Boundaries of the United States" (Helper 156).

Writing of the influence of Helper's *Crisis,* Holbrook stated: "No one, so far as records show, was ever hanged for owning a copy of Mrs. Stowe's *Uncle Tom's Cabin,* or even arrested. Such was not the case with *The Impending Crisis,* the 413 pages of carefully prepared and concentrated dynamite that Helper wrote and published in 1857. Men *were* hanged for possessing this book. Many more men were mobbed, and the legislatures of the South passed laws specifically forbidding its sale, purchase and even its possession" (108). Gilbert also reports that "three residents of Arkansas were reputedly hanged for owning copies" and that "many Southerns viewed the book as a serious threat to their property and social structure" (64). While Helper argued for the demise of slavery in the South, his goal was to improve the lot of white southerners, he said, by ridding the land of degrading and uneconomical slavery. Helper had little sympathy for the slaves and was critical of attempts to bring about equal treatment of the races. Even though he shared the racism of the slave owners, his advocacy of ridding the South of slavery was not to be tolerated and hence the burning of his book.

In 1909, Helper committed suicide in Washington, D.C., and *The Literary Digest,* in reporting his death referred to the significance of *The Impending Crisis in the South:* "Recently an old, destitute, and friendless man died by his own hand in a Washington garret. Some fifty years ago he wrote a book which eventually had almost as much influence on the slavery agitation of the day as did 'Uncle Tom's Cabin' or John Brown's Raid. His book also became a real factor in promoting the election of Lincoln" (A Forgotten Hero of Slavery Days, 569).

While Southerners were burning anti-slavery publications, abolitionist William Lloyd Garrison set fire to a copy of the Fugitive Slave Law, the Constitution, and the Declaration of Independence. In May 1854, Anthony Burns, a slave from Virginia escaped by boat to

Boston where he was arrested and ordered by a judge Loring that he be taken back to Virginia. Anti-slavery activists conducted a July 4 rally to protest the return of Burns to slavery in Virginia and it was on this Independence Day celebration that William Lloyd Garrison burned not only the Fugitive Slave Law, the Constitution, and the Declaration of Independence, but also judge Loring's decision ordering the return of Burns to Virginia: "Producing a copy of the *Fugitive Slave Law*, he set fire to it, and it burnt to ashes. Using an old and well-known phrase, he said, 'And let all the people say, Amen'; and a unanimous cheer and shout of 'Amen' burst from the vast audience. In like manner, Mr. Garrison burned the decision of Edward C. Loring in the case of Anthony Burns, and the late charge of Judge Benjamin R. Curtis to the United States Grand Jury in reference to the 'treasonable' assault upon the Court House for the rescue of the fugitive — the multitude ratifying the fiery immolation with shouts of applause. Then, holding up the U.S. Constitution, he branded it as the source and parent of all the other atrocities—'a covenant with death and an agreement with hell'— and consumed it to ashes on the spot, exclaiming, 'So perish all compromises with tyranny! And let all the people say, Amen!'" (Garrison 412).

Responding to critics, especially the *Commonwealth* periodical, who asserted that Garrison more appropriately might have burned the Constitution in his own private bonfire, "without outraging the feelings" of his audience, he declared: "Let me tell the *Commonwealth* that slavery is a public, not a private concern — a national, not a local system; that it is silly and impertinent to suggest privacy of action against it; that, in this struggle for its overthrow, I neither seek nor take advantage of any man unfairly; that my testimonies, in whatever form given, are for the nation, not for the chimney corner.... I burnt a PRO-SLAVERY Constitution, in my judgment, in the judgment of the nation ever since its adoption, and therefore was faithful to the slave in so doing" (Garrison 413).

With the advent of the twentieth century, there was a significant increase in the number of countries where book burnings were conducted: Argentina, Brazil, Cambodia, Canada, Chile, China, El Salvador, Guatemala, Germany, Iran, Italy, Indonesia, Korea, Malawi, Spain, Turkey, the Soviet Union, the United States, among others. Various labels were applied to the books as they were set afire, labels such as "rebellious," "subversive," "seditious," "reactionary," "leftist," "poisonous," "cancerous," "decadent," "debauched," "profane," "pernicious," "un–German," "un–American." Decade after decade, all through the twentieth century, the fires consuming the condemned books continued to burn, and in many cases the authors murdered, imprisoned, or exiled. The book burners of seditious-subversive books were increasingly active in the first half of the twentieth century and even more so in the second half. In every decade, books were being set afire somewhere in the world.

The century began with Chinese authorities ordering in 1900 the burning of the "rebellious books" published by the "rebellious wolves" K'ang Yuwei and Liang Ch'ich'ao. The two authors called for "national political reform, including the exposure of official corruption and the introduction of the western ideas of 'liberty,' 'democracy' and 'constitutional reform'" (Yutang 94). Their writings were banned by imperial decree; as Lin Yutang has observed, "The imperial edict of January 15th, 1900, banning the publications of K'ang and Liang, shows their influence over the Chinese public and the great feeling of annoyance of the Manchu Court" (97).

An edict order the burning of the works of these two writers, K'ang and Liang, read, in part: "These rebellious wolves ... still persist in their agitations along the coastal provinces, publishing newspapers and inciting the Chinese people with their eloquence. Such rebellious activities make one's hair stand on end.... *If nobody will buy their papers, then the rebels can do no harm.* The provincial governors shall, therefore, strictly enforce the punishment of anyone who buys or reads their papers. In addition, the rebellious books published by these criminals shall be also burned when found in people's possession, in order to carry out the law of the land and keep the human heart at peace" (Yutang 98).

Writing in 1935, Edgar Snow reported that "suppression of civil liberties in China, growing ever harsher since 1928 until it has reached an all-time severity, is Generalissimo Chiang Kai-sheck's answer not only to Communist propaganda but to all forms of liberal and progressive thought" (381). Referring to the book burnings under Chiang Kai-Shek's regime, Snow writes: "Suppression of the press has its natural corollary in the burning of books. At literary bonfires in important cities during 1934 thousands of volumes were destroyed. These included, of course, translations of all Marxist, Communist and Socialist books that had survived earlier purgings, but also many books of history and economics distasteful to Blue Jacket [a secret fascist organization created to combat communism and to promote Chaing Kai-Shek] leaders, who directed the campaign" (383). The burning of the books was accompanied with the banning of "149 books, including many of the best works of contemporary Chinese writers.... Among the Western writers whose works are forbidden in translation are John Dos Passos, Theodore Dreiser, Strindberg, Bertrand Russell, Maxim Gorky, Upton Sinclair and even Maeterlinck and Romain Rolland" (Snow 383).

Similarly, Lee-hsia Hsu Ting has written that under the Chiang Kai-Shek regime the writings of "leftist writers" were banned and burned; for example, in 1934, "149 books in the humanities were outlawed for 'advocating class struggle' ... Some [condemned works] were reference books: a dictionary of literature for students. Foreign writers who made the list included Maxim Gorky, A.V. Lunacharsky, K.A. Fedin, A. Serafimovich, Upton Sinclair, Theodore Dreiser, Maurice Maeterlinck, Romain Rolland, and Bertrand Russell.... A list of leftist writers was thus compiled and all their writings outlawed. Instructed by KMT [Chiang's Kuomintang Party] Central Headquarters, the Party official in Shanghai visited booksellers and publishers on February 19 [, 1934,] and ordered them to submit all copies and stereotypes of such books to the Party headquarters to be burned" (92).

When at the beginning of the twentieth century the Japanese annexed Korea, as Chung has reported, "one of the first things the Terauchi administration did after the annexation was to collect all books of Korean history and biographies of illustrious Koreans from schools, libraries and private homes and to burn them. Priceless treasures of historical value records were thus destroyed by this needless vandalism of the Japanese" (125). Reducing the biographies and history books to ashes was one more way to eradicate history and identity.

In the first half of the twentieth century, the fear of Marxist, "leftist," "communist" books led governmental authorities and private citizens in various countries, democratic and dictatorial, to cleanse the land of these pernicious, "rebellious," and "subversive" writings. In 1928, Lenin's *Proletarian Revolution in Russia* was burned by Canadian officials. In his Introduction to the 453-page work, Louis Fraina, states that "the material comprised in this volume, consists largely of a mass of articles written by Lenin and Trotzky during the actual course of the Revolution; the material accordingly is not alone a record of history, *but a maker of history*— original sources" (xix). Writing in his Introduction to the book published in 1918, Fraina declares at the outset: "History is the history of class struggles. Revolution is the culmination of the class struggle; and history, accordingly, is equally a history of revolutions, of cataclysmic epochs when the antagonisms of the class struggle flare up into revolutionary and decisive action. In these great crises of universal history, the ordinary aspects of the class struggle assume a violence, catastrophic expression, developing into war, civil war, and into the searing, magnificent upheavals of the Revolution" (iii).

In the book section titled "International Socialism," Lenin declared: "The international duty of the Russian working class has become very evident these days" and he called for "active internationalism." In his call for action, Lenin wrote: "Good people often forget the cruel, savage paraphernalia of a world-wide imperialistic war. Phrases and naive sentimental desires are impotent. There is only one way of being a genuine internationalist: to strain all our energies in an endeavor to develop the revolutionary movement and speed the revolutionary struggle in our own land, to support that struggle in every way, by propaganda, sympathy, material aid, and support *only that* struggle, in every country without exception. Everything else is a snare and a delusion" (144–145). Ten years after the publication of this work, it was reduced to ashes in Canada.

In the 1930s, the Brazilian authorities ordered the burning of books by Monteiro Lobato, Jorge Amado, and Gilberto Freyre because the works were politically unacceptable. As Hallewell has indicated, the criteria applied in seizing and burning the books "could of course be outspokenness of language or eroticism of theme or treatment, just as well as political unacceptability.... Books by Monteiro Lobato were publicly burnt in Bahia while works of Jorge Amado were burnt both there and in the state of Sao Paulo" (272). Further, "even holders of such moderate views as Gilberto Freyre had their books burned and were publicly attacked as subversives. *Casa Grande e senzala* [by Freyre] was berated as pernicious, anti–Brazilian, anti–Catholic, anarchistic, communistic, with an author deserving to be burnt at the stake to save his soul" (Hallewell 273).

The nationalistic, dictatorial president of Brazil, Getulio Vargas, imprisoned Jorge Amado and ordered that his books be burned. In 1936, Amado was briefly imprisoned "on the pretext that he had somehow supported an abortive military revolt against the Vargas regime the year before" (Chamberlain 5). After his release, he traveled to several Latin American countries and the United States, meeting with such notables as Diego Rivera, Jose Orozco, David Alfaro Siqueiros, Michael Gold, and Paul Robeson. When he returned to Brazil in October 1937, "he was arrested in Nanaus and his books were banned nationwide. Thousands of copies were publicly burned in Salvador and Sao Paulo, along with the works of other authors, in early November. Within a week, Getulio Vargas proclaimed the Estado Novo (New State) dictatorship" (Chamberlain 5).

In 1937, Amado published *Capitaes de areia* (Captains of the Sand) which is a work of social criticism, dealing with "the life of a group of abandoned adolescents who live in a warehouse on the waterfront of Bahia. The narrative gives us a realistic picture of this gang and their fight for survival in search for food and money" (Oliveira 168). According to Oliveira, "The intention of *Capitaes de areia* was to draw attention to the neglected adolescents and not necessarily to call for a proletarian revolution. Nevertheless this novel was censored by the government in 1937, and hundreds of copies were burned in public by the Bahian militia. The main character, a youth named Pedro Bala, has a counterpart in a novel by Mario Vargas Llosa, *La ciudad y los perros* [The Time of the Hero]. Here the society in a military academy is also pictured as violent, and the hardships endured by the young cadets are quite similar to what the Capitaes de Areia gang goes through. It is also interesting to know that Vargas Llosa in his turn had his novel burned by the militia in Lima" (168).

The most widespread burning of thousands of books in the 1930s occurred in Nazi Germany in May 1933. With the rise of Nazism in the 1920s and 1930s came the massive book burnings in Berlin, Munich, Breslau, Kiel, Heidelberg, Frankfurt-am-Main and other

German towns. Into the bonfires went the "un–German" books by such authors as Sigmund Freud, Karl Marx, Friedrich Engels, Upton Sinclair, Jack London, Heinrich Mann, Emil Ludwig, Arnold and Stephan Sweig, Erich Maria Remarque, Helen Keller, Albert Einstein, John Dos Passos, Thomas Mann, Leon Feuchtwanger, and Arthur Schnitzler.

On May 11, 1933, Fredrick T. Birchall reported in *The New York Times* on the previous night's book burnings:

> To work up enthusiasm when fresh consignments [of books] reached the fire a student barker began to name the authors:
> "Sigmund Freud—for falsifying our history and degrading its great figures!"
> The crowd cheered.
> "Emil Ludwig—burned for literary rascality and high treason against Germany!"
> Loud cheers.
> Then Erich Maria Remarque—"for degrading the German language and the highest patriotic ideal"; Alfred Kerr, late dramatic critic of the Tageblatt, denounced as "a dishonest literary adventurer." ...
> So it went until there appeared, amid Nazi salutes and protected by uniformed satellites, the attraction of the evening, Dr. Paul Joseph Goebbels, the Minister of Propaganda. Mounted on a tiny swastika-draped rostrum, he spoke.
> "Jewish intellectualism is dead," he declared. "National socialism has hewn the way. The German folk soul can again express itself.
> "These flames do not only illuminate the final end of the old era, they also light up the new. Never before have the young men had so good a right to clean up the debris of the past" [12].

In Munich, "A hundred massively bound volumes—the works of 'un–German' writers—were publicly burned in the Koenigsplatz ... after a picturesque torchlight parade of students. All the books destroyed came from the university library, but they were consigned

The 1933 Nazi book burning bonfire. National Archives (W&C_986)

to the flames lit by the students' inquisitorial tribunal because of their 'disintegrating influence.'" In Frankfurt-am-Main, "Marxist literature and other 'un–German' books went into the flames on the Romerberg ... to the strains of Chopin's Funeral March as thousands of students of the University of Frankfurt in full regalia stood at attention." In Breslau, "Five thousand pounds of 'heretical' literature, among it books by Emil Ludwig, Erich Maria Remarque, and Thomas Mann, went into the students' bonfire in the Schlossplatz." In Kiel, "The crusade against the 'un–German spirit' culminated ... with the public burning of about 2,000 examples of pacifist literature and erotic publications gathered by the students of Kiel University" (*The New York Times* May 11, 1933 12).

Five years later, after the German troops marched into Austria in March 1938, a public book burning took place in Salzburg on April 30. As reported in *The New York Times* on May 1, 1938, "The ceremony began at 8 o'clock [in the evening] when a schoolboy threw Dr. Schuschnigg's [ousted Austrian Chancellor] book, 'Three Times Austria,' on a gasoline-soaked pyre at gaily illuminated Residenz Square. Next came books on Chancellor Engelbert Dolfuss and his regime, then propaganda books and works by Jewish authors.... The burning was largely symbolic, however, for only one copy each of 2,000 different books was consigned to the flames. The rest, said to consist of more than 30,000 volumes collected from the university and other libraries, are to be burned later" (35).

While this work does not deal with the massive book burnings that occurred as a result of "collateral damage" during times of war, we must be reminded that during wartime books and libraries have been intentionally targeted for fiery destruction; they have not been reduced to ashes as "collateral damage." For example, after the German invasion of Poland in 1939, books and libraries were deliberately set afire in such cities as Warsaw, Lublin, Poznan, Bedzin, and Vilna. In Bedzin and Poznan, as Philip Friedman has observed, "special German 'Brenn-Kommandos' (arson squads) were assigned to burn synagogues and Jewish books. Jews attempting to save Torah Scrolls or books from the burning buildings were shot or thrown into the flames" (1997 85). In Kovno, "soon after the German invasion, the books in the famous Mapu Library were publicly burned. The ceremony was witnessed by high German officials, while a military band played and Storm Troopers danced around the fire.... The most valuable books were transported to Germany, and the remainder was turned over for pulp to a paper mill" (Friedman 1997 90).

The German newspaper *Frankfurter Zeitung* reported in 1941 the Nazis' pleasure and delight in burning the books and library of the Lublin Yeshiva: "For us it was a matter of special pride to destroy the Talmudic Academy, which was known as the greatest in Poland.... We threw the huge Talmudic library out of the building and carried the books to the market place, where we set fire to them. The fire lasted twenty hours. The Lublin Jews assembled around and wept bitterly, almost silencing us with their cries. We summoned the military band, and with joyful shouts the soldiers drowned out the sound of the Jewish cries" (Shavit 48–49).

Until the Nazis were driven out of Poland in early 1945, the book burnings continued. As Borin reports: "The National Library in Warsaw was burned in September 1939, along with many of its notable collections, including 500 manuscripts from the Rapperswill collection, while the main stacks of the Warsaw Public Library were burned on the eve of evacuation, 15 January 1945" (446). In his essay titled "The Tragic Fate of Polish Libraries After 1939," Dunin writes: "During the last stage of war operations on the territory of Poland, especially at the time of the Warsaw Uprising, many buildings were destroyed by fire and many of the books in them perished. Some buildings were set on fire on purpose by the German fire-squads, the *Brandkommando*. The Zaluski Library, the library of the Krasinski estate, the Central Military Library, the bookstacks of the Warsaw Public Library and hundreds of other libraries, big and small, private and public, were destroyed in the fires" (8). Further, as Sroka has observed, "During the Warsaw Uprising of 1944, Ludwig Fischer, governor of Warsaw, gave personal orders to set the Raczynskich Library on fire. The building as well as 300,000 volumes of precious books were burned to the ground.... The libraries in Elblag, Gdansk, and Poznan were almost completely wiped out. The Nazis also destroyed 70 percent of all Jewish books in Poland during the war years" (12).

Like their Nazi allies, the Italian Fascists were setting fire to Jewish books: "In Turin, a city with 4,060 Jews in 1938, the Holocaust did not begin with a huge October roundup. Italian Fascists in effect served notice of pending trouble early that month when they broke into the Jewish Community Library, seized most of the books, and burned them in a great bonfire in the Piazza Carlina" (Zuccotti 156).

Just as the Germans and Italians were purposely setting fire to books and libraries, their Axis power Japan, "burned, with systematic efficiency, nearly every collection of books in the Philippine Islands, with exception of valuable scientific and other works which they carried off to the homeland" (Shaffer 82).

Devastating as the book burnings were, the Nazis' burning of paintings and other artistic works was even more catastrophic inasmuch as many of them were irreplaceable. As Grunberger has indicated, in 1939 the Nazis gathered up sixteen thousand paintings, drawings, etchings and sculptures denounced as "degenerate," including: "1,000 pieces by Nolde, 700 by Haeckel, 600 each by Schmidt-Rottluff and Kirchner, 500 by Beckmann, 400 by Kokoschka, 300–400 each by Hofer, Pechstein, Barlach, Feininger and Otto Muller, 200–300 each by Dix, Grosz and Corinth, 100 by Lehmbruck, as well as much smaller numbers of Cezannes, Picassos, Matisses, Gauguins, Van Goghs, Braques, Pisarros, Dufys, Chiricos and Max Ernsts. Of that total, 4,000 were actually burned in the courtyard of the headquarters of the Berlin fire-brigade in 1939" (425)

While the Nazi book burnings were denounced in the United States as contemptible, uncivilized, and dangerous, copies of John Steinbeck's *Grapes of Wrath* were being set afire in 1939 in California, Illinois, and Oklahoma because the book, according to the book burners, was "filthy," "vile propaganda," and "false sensationalism" (*Look* 15). *The Publishers Weekly* reported on November 25, 1939: "Most spectacular so far as the local attempts to suppress John Steinbeck's 'The Grapes of Wrath' is the order by the Library Board of East St. Louis, Illinois, that three copies of the novel be burned" (1994). Steinbeck's novel was condemned especially by large agricultural anti-labor interests in California who objected to both the "obscenity" and the portrayal of the migrant workers as being brutally mistreated and living in misery and poverty. The president of the Associated Farmers of Kern County, California, declared: "We are angry ... because we were attacked by a book obscene in the extreme sense of the word.... It is too filthy for you to point out its vile propaganda ... false sensationalism.... Americans have the right to say what they please, but they do not have the right to attack a community in such words that any red-blooded American would refuse to allow his daughter to read them" (*Look* 15) A photograph of *The Grapes of Wrath* being set ablaze in a metal container appeared in *Look* magazine with the caption: "*The Grapes of Wrath* is burned and banned in Bakersfield, Cal. with the approval of W.B. Camp, president of the Associated Farmers of Kern County" (*Look* 15).

During the fascist takeover of Spain in the 1930s and during the next decades of Franco's dictatorial rule, massive censorship and book burnings became commonplace in the effort to "purify" and "cleanse" the land of the "infectious virus " of liberalism and communism. The disease-cancer-virus metaphors were continually applied in condemnations of leftist writers and their books. In his efforts to achieve complete power, Franco decreed that "all books of Leftist tendencies should 'be destroyed as a matter of public health'" (Lloyd 141). As Lloyd has indicated, "even Hollywood, it seemed, could affect the national hygiene. Turning a censorial eye on the movies, he [Franco] banned from his territories all films to which the following 'radicals' had contributed: writers Upton Sinclair, Clifford Odets, Liam O'Flaherty, Dudley Nichols, and Humphrey Cobb; film stars Paul Muni and Luise Rainer; directors Lewis Milestone and Frank Tuttle, and producer Kenneth MacGowan" (142).

In 1973, two years before Franco died, Diego Dieguez wrote that "censorship has been in force since the Civil War and its shape today is scarcely different from the war years [1936–1939] when it was imposed by an openly fascist and totalitarian movement.... When the war ended in 1939, virtually everything was forbidden. Many private libraries had been burnt and went on being burnt until long after, liberal education establishments like the Free Institute of Education were shut down, and other democratic cultural centres like the Atheneum were taken over" (92). The "foreign virus" of liberalism, as Michael Richards has observed, "which bred communism, was infection which had to be expunged," according to the fascists (47).

One of Franco's chief press officers, Don Gonzalo Aguilers, carried the disease metaphor even further when he spoke of "infection, plague, and virus": "In healthier times— I mean healthier times spiritually, you understand — plague and pestilence could be counted on to thin down the Spanish masses. Held them down to manageable proportions, you understand. Now with modern sewage disposal and the like they multiply too fast. The masses are no better than animals, you understand, and you can't expect them not to become infected with the virus of bolshevism. After all, rats and lice carry the plague. Do you understand now what we mean by the regeneration of Spain?" (Whitaker 108).

Once Franco and his Nationalists won the war in 1939, "a flood of atrocity stories filled the newspapers and bookshops, while liberal or 'Marxist' books were ordered to be taken from even the private shelf. Symbolic book-burnings of Marxist books were carried out in large cities" (Thomas 1977 923). After the murder of Federico Garcia Lorca in 1936, "his books were publicly burned and his plays banned until the 1970s" (Wilkinson A24).

While the Spanish fascists were setting fire to socialist works, the Italian fascists were burning Jewish library books in Turin in 1938. After reporting of the increased roundup of Jews in October 1938, a month during which "the Holocaust in Italy was in full swing," Zuccotti writes: "In Turin, a city with 4,060 Jews in 1938, the Holocaust did not begin with a huge October roundup. Italian Fascists in effect served notice of impending trouble early that month when they broke into the Jewish Community library, seized most of the books, and burned them in a great bonfire in the Piazza Carlina. Most Turinese Jews seem to have gone into hiding soon after that incident, much sooner than Jews elsewhere" (155–156).

When Sergei Eisenstein's film *Battleship Potemkin* was released, it was banned in several European countries, including Poland, Czechoslovakia, Germany, Great Britain, and France. The film depicting a successful rebellion against political authority, was viewed as a threat to discipline and encouraging rebellion. A 1926 order of the German War Ministry declared that the film was to be "shunned" by soldiers of the armed forces "for the show presents a threat to discipline" (Marshall 122). In 1928, "the Censorship Committee of the London County Council ... categorically prohibited the showing of the Soviet moving picture *The Battleship Potemkin*" (Marshall 151). In France, the film was not only banned, but also "the French police burned every copy that they could find" (Baets 481).

At the same time the French were burning copies of Eisenstein's classic film, they were also burning the writings of militant Bretons who saw the French authorities as bent on destroying the Breton language and culture. The long-time French efforts to stamp out the use of the Breton language led to government efforts to establish French as "the only acceptable language of education" and resulted in burnings of some writings supporting the Bretons: "In the second half of the 1930s certain of the Breton separatist groupings were seen as siding opportunistically with the fascists. The French authorities, intent on counteracting any threat to the unity of the French nation, were suspicious of the Breton Movement. In 1939, the [Breton] journal *Breiz Atao* was suspended. The place in Rennes (the Breton capital) where *Breiz Atao* was raided, the books in Breton found there were seized and burnt" (Barbour 297).

In the 1930s, seeking an independent Breton state, militant Bretons took the position that "the enemy of our enemy is our friend," and began siding with the Germans who the militants expected to establish a separate Breton homeland (Reece 149–150). For example, "in March 1938 *Breiz Atao* editorially praised the Nazi takeover in Austria and sarcastically noted Paris's 'indignation at the destruction of the rights of a small nation'" and in May the anti–French Bretons "argued that Germany had a clear right to Czechoslovakia's Sudetenland on the basis of 'the fundamental principle of the rights of nationalities'"(Reece 143). Referring to the suppression of *Breiz Atao,* Reece has written: "The end came for *Breiz Atao* in August 1939.... In what turned out to be their last issue of *Breiz Atao* they demanded in a banner headline on 27 August that Daladier resign as prime minister and called on Bretons not to die for Danzig.... A few days later Paris suppressed *Breiz Atao* by administrative decree.... Breton nationalists had apparently become in the eyes of French justice what *Breiz Atao* charged in September 1932 they always had been: outlaws" (148). The rationale for burning the Breton books was no longer to control simply the Breton language and culture, but also to control anti–French, pro-German propaganda just as France was becoming involved in World War II.

This effort by governments to control the language and culture of segments of society is exemplified also by the Soviet Union's attempt in the 1930s to suppress, partly by book burnings, the Arabic language and the Muslim influence. As Frantz has reported, "By 1929, the Soviets had banned Arabic in an attempt to eradicate Muslim influence in Azerbaijan and the republics of Central Asia. Azeri remained, with a Latin script. A decade later, Stalin abolished the Latin alphabet and insisted on only Cyrillic script in a deliberate attempt to isolate Azerbaijan from its Muslim past and the influence of its larger neighbor, Turkey, which had switched from an Arabic to a Latin alphabet" (8). According to Frantz, "The Soviets went on book-burning rampages throughout Azerbaijan to eradicate the Arabic language" (8).

Then, after the collapse of the Soviet Union, the president of Azerbaijan ordered in 2001 that "official documents, magazines, newspaper and signs be written in the Latin script used in the West instead of the Cyrillic used for Russian"; in his decree, the president declared: "In order to strengthen Azerbaijan's independence, to respect its history and cultural development, it is necessary to observe the norms of the Azeri language and namely the Latin script" (Frantz 8). These language and script changes, among others in Azerbaijan's history, states Betty Blair, "has caused amnesia of the nation.... Things that should be common knowledge have disappeared" (Frantz 8).

The 1940s and 1950s witnessed an increase in the number of book burnings around the world. "Book burning in 1940?" asked Professor of Education Harold Rugg in Chapter One of his 1941 work *That Men May Understand.* "Yes," he answered, "and not merely in little towns like Bradner, Ohio." It was in Bradner that Rugg's social science books were burned in April 1940. The *Cleveland Press* reported on April 9, 1940: "Books on civics and social science ... have split this little western Ohio town wide open in a row over the 'teaching of Communism.' The rural Red hunt ... has resulted in: explosion of a dynamite charge and the burning of a fiery cross in front of the home of school board president.... Dramatic burning of a dozen library schoolbooks in the school furnace.... The books ... seized at a board meeting the other night and shoved in the furnace were mostly those in the social-science series by Harold Rugg" (Rugg 3). The social science texts were condemned by the self-proclaimed patriots as being "un–American," anti–free enterprise, and giving the child "an unbiased viewpoint instead of teaching him real Americanism." A suggestion to burn Rugg's books was made the same month in Binghamton, New York, where "a member of the Board of Education's teacher committee proposed that a 'bonfire be made' of the 180 Rugg social-science textbooks, formerly used in local schools, and said she would recommend such a motion at the board's next meeting" (Rugg 4).

The burning of "un–American" books continued well into the 1940s. In his *A History of Book Publishing in the United States,* John Trebbel identified a book burning that took place in Oklahoma City as the "most celebrated censorship case of the forties"; the case involved "the Progressive Bookstore in Oklahoma City, and its owner, Robert Wood. A Father Webber, head of the local vigilante organization, advised his radio audience in the summer of 1940 that certain books bought in the bookstore would be publicly burned in the Oklahoma City stadium, and so they were" (Trebbel 85).

Publishers Weekly, tracing the history of this case, reported on July 5, 1941: "The history of the case goes back to about a year ago, when an unofficial raid, previously announced over the radio by one Father Webber, was made on the store by a vigilante organization. The shop is at 129½ West Grand Avenue. Father Webber also announced that the books seized would be burned in the Oklahoma City stadium. This later took place, and among the publications destroyed were many copies of the Declaration of Independence and the Constitution" (140 21).

In the midst of the McCarthyism of the 1950s there was an increase in the United States of book bannings, book burnings, and blacklisting of writers who were labeled "un–Americans" by Senator Joseph McCarthy, the U.S. House Un-American Activities Committee, and the various state investigating committees. As a result, books by such "un–American" authors as Howard Fast, Philip S. Foner, Dashiell Hammett, Langston Hughes, Lillian Hellman, Theodore White, and Herbert Aptheker were removed from U.S. Information Service Libraries located in countries around the world. James C. Conant, former president of Harvard University and in 1953 U.S. High Commissioner for Germany, was interrogated by McCarthy and was asked what he would do about removing the "un–American" books from the U.S. overseas libraries:

McCarthy: What do you propose to do with these [30,000] books when they have been removed?
Conant: I would not have an answer to that. It would seem to me a relatively minor problem whether they were stored somewhere or what was done.
McCarthy: What would you store them for? What are you going to save them for?
Conant: They might be sold as excess property here in the U.S.
McCarthy: Would you burn them?
Conant: I certainly would not burn them.
McCarthy: What would you do, pay for storing them?
Conant: I think I would be able to make a deal by which I could get rid of them as secondhand books for one purpose or another.
McCarthy: By secondhand books, do you mean for someone to read?
Conant: Yes, in the United States.
McCarthy: In other words, you are trying to sell those 30,000 books so that the people in the United States could read them?

Of course, McCarthy was not interested in having "people in the United States" read these works by "un–American" authors and his question about burning the books was not far-fetched, especially as a "suggestion" coming from the senator so ready to stigmatize, discredit, and blacklist those whom he labeled "communist sympathizers" and "traitors." The actual number of "un–American" books banned or burned at the overseas libraries because they contained "subversive" messages remains indefinite. Then Secretary of State John Foster Dulles stated that it was possible that in one or two places a total of eleven books may have been actually burned (*U.S. News and World Reports* 40).

Writing in the summer 1953 issue of *American Book Collector,* Blumenthal reported: "In June, 1953, some 300 books by eighteen authors were 'purged' from U.S. Information Service Libraries abroad on order of the State Department, because they were alleged to be Communist propaganda or by suspect authors. A few were said to have been burned, but most were sold for pulping or otherwise destroyed" (18).

It was during this period of McCarthyism in American history that President Dwight Eisenhower declared in a speech delivered at Dartmouth College on June 14, 1953: "Don't join the book burners" (*The New York Times* June 15, 1953 10). In effect, Eisenhower was telling the American people not only don't become, literally, book burners, but also don't become book banners. There was good reason for the President's warning: "At Sapulpa, Oklahoma, February 11, 1952, a handful of books in the High School Library was burned at the request of a women's civil group" (Blumenthal 18). The condemned books were set afire not only because they "approved" of socialism, but also because they "dealt too frankly with sex." The vice-president of the Sapulpa Board of Education said that "some books in the Sapulpa High School Library had been burned by the school after being criticized by a women's civic group for the way they dealt with socialism and sex" (*York Times* February 12, 1952 29).

Further, in Cleveland, Ohio, on August 27, 1952, "the U.S. Attorney, John J. Kane sought a Federal court order to burn thousands of copies of two 'obscene' French novels, shipped there and seized by the Collector of Customs. The titles were *The Black Mistress* and *Where They Breed,* both written by Louis-Charles Royer.... In Chicago on April 12, 1953, a mob broke up a meeting of the Council of American-Soviet Friendship. More than one hundred books, including nineteen copies of Dr. Corliss Lamont's *Soviet Civilization* were burned or otherwise destroyed in the street" (Blumenthal 18).

While Eisenhower was warning Americans not to join the book burners, the United States government was supporting the Guatemalan military dictatorship which was burning "subversive books" such as *Les Misérables* and Miguel Ángel Asturias's novels *El Señor Presidente* and *The Green Pope* (Karolides 308). In 1954, the democratically elected president of Guatemala, Jacobo Arbenz, was overthrown by the right-wing National Liberation led by Castillo Armas who was supported by the United States, especially by the CIA and State Department. Once Armas took power, a series of repressive measures were instituted: "At the CIA's behest, Castillo Armas announced on July 19 [1954] the creation of a 'National Committee of Defense Against Communism.' A few weeks later, he followed that action by decreeing the Preventive Penal Law Against Communism. The Penal Law established the death penalty for a series of 'crimes' that could be construed as 'sabotage,' including many labor union activities. Meanwhile, the National Committee was given the power to meet in secret and declare anyone a Communist with no right of defense or appeal" (Schlesinger and Kinzer 221). This was followed by book burnings and the cancellation of reforms established by Arbenz; as Schlesinger and Kinzer reported: "On August 10, he [Armas] outlawed all political parties, labor confederations and peasant organizations. A week later, he restored Ubico's secret police chief, José Bernabe Linares, to his former post. Soon Castillo Armas subordinates began burning 'subversive' books, including Victor Hugo's *Les Misérables,* Dostoyevsky novels, the writings of Arevalo [former reformer President Juan Arevalo], and other revolutionaries and novels by Guatemala's Nobel Prize–winning writer, Miguel Ángel Asturias, a biting critic of United Fruit" (221–222). Secretary of State John Foster Dulles "expressed no displeasure at these actions" and Arbenz went into exile in Mexico (222–223).

During the next two decades, 1960–1980, there was a significant increase in reports in books burnings in several South American countries ruled by right-wing military governments. In the 1960s, the Argentine government led by Juan Carlos Ongania, in addition to ordering widespread censorship, "seized magazine editions, closed theatres on morality grounds, ordered imported textbooks such as Marx and Engels to be burned by the Post Office" (Graham-Yooll 43).

The books burnings in Argentina continued into the 1970s. Nick Caistor reported in his article "Cleansing the Teaching Area": "In Cordoba on April 1976 the local commander carried out a great book-burning that was shown on television, and claimed that he was destroying the pernicious texts of Marx, Che Guevara, Castro, etc.: 'To avoid Argentinean youth being led into error over what our true patrimony is, namely our national symbols, our family, our church, and our cultural heritage founded on God, the homeland, and the hearth'" (20).

The Argentine government's seizure and burning of "subversive" writings instilled in the populace a fear of being found with suspicious literature and as a result citizens began burning their own books, as reported by Andrew Graham-Yooll, when "the Cordoba paratroop regiment set a new example on 29 April by burning seized subversive literature, some of it genuinely guerrilla copyright, but also much that had been taken from the political shelves of established book stores. This 'auto-da-fe' led to pyromaniac behaviour in a large part of the population: not a day goes by without a woman, a man, a couple, a youth, alone with their fears, admitting that they have burned every book, paper or pamphlet which might be even remotely related to Marxism in fear of an imagined imminent raid on their homes"(Graham-Yooll 28).

In his report on the censorship practices and arrests in the 1970s in Argentina, Caistor quotes from Army Commander General Vilas who declared: "Until we can cleanse the teaching area, and the professors are all of Christian thought and ideology, we will not achieve the triumph we seek in our struggle against the revolutionary left." Caistor then reports on the seizure and burning of books: "In Mendoza, the military rector of the University of the Cuyo, Air Force colonel Hector Ruiz, had the homes of lecturers and students searched for subversive material. As a result, some 10,000 books were seized, which the colonel displayed at a press conference, and dozens of arrests were made. In Cordoba on 3 April 1976 the local commander carried out a great book-burning that was shown on television, and claimed that he was destroying the pernicious texts of Marx, Che Guevara, Castro, etc." (20).

In his *The Press in Argentina, 1973–1978* Andrew Graham-Yooll refers to several other book burnings in Argentina. He reports on the July 1973 burning of "25,000 copies of Henri Lefebvre's *Marxism,* in its Spanish-language version ... destroyed by fire caused by a bomb at a store-house owned by the Buenos Aires University publishing company" (1979 1). A December 1973 report states: "Officials of the Buenos Aires Municipality, in a ceremony with almost ritual connotation, burn one million magazines seized from news stands on the grounds that they are 'pornographic, obscene, and immoral.' The parents' Association

(Liga de Padres de Familia) praises the burning.... Incendiary bombs are thrown against the *Gran Rex* cinema, where the film 'Hitler's Last Ten Days' is being shown — after the attack, exhibition is cancelled" (Graham-Yooll 1979 38).

When in March 1964 a military coup in Brazil established a right-wing dictatorship, "those who had usurped power did their utmost to combat all intellectual endeavour. To be a writer or artist in Brazil became dangerous" (Moura 8). Writing in 1979 in his essay "Climate of Terror," Moura referred to the book burnings and bannings imposed by the 1964 dictatorship in Brazil: "Fourteen years of censorship in Brazil: a culture demeaned, crushed, humiliated. Books, radio, television, theatre, cinema, and universities clothed in the straitjacket of a new Inquisition. Hundreds of books seized, burnt, destroyed, or withdrawn from circulation" (8). Elaborating on the objectives of the military in institutionalizing censorship and burning condemned books, Moura has observed: "To switch off the national memory: this was one of the immediate objectives of the military. They objected to *A New History of Brazil,* a first attempt at a modern view of our history" (8). The military officials "saw Marxist tendencies in this work. Its authors were prosecuted, the book seized and burnt (8).

Meanwhile in Peru the highly acclaimed novel *La Ciudad y los perros* by Vargas Llosa was set afire not long after it was published in 1963. "That *La ciudad y los perros* touched political nerves in Peru," writes Sommers, "was evident in the public reception it received. In response to the fact that the novel had been awarded a major literary prize in Spain, the military leaders commanding the Colegio Leoncio Prado in Lima (the military school which Vargas Llosa had attended and which is the novel's setting) held a special convocation. At this function, to which school alumni were invited, copies of the novel were ceremonially burned" (4).

As the *Handbook of Latin American Literature* has indicated, "*La ciudad y los perros* was acclaimed as one of the best novels written in Spanish during the previous thirty years.... The novel probes the effects of authoritarianism and blind discipline on morals and ethics in a dog-eat-dog world of exploiters and exploited.... In Peru, the reaction to the novel by the military was not surprising: one thousand copies were publicly burned at the military school" (Foster 232–233).

Next door in Chile, after the overthrow of the government of President Salvador Allende in 1973, the Pinochet authorities not only imposed widespread censorship and detained thousands of "foreign extremists" and "subversives," but also set ablaze "huge quantities of books" in the streets. Sanders reported in his "Book Burning and Brutality" that "a few days after the coup d'état, a major search raid was carried out in the residential district of Santiago known as the Torres San Borja.... Searching soldiers flung piles of books and magazines considered subversive out of the windows. These were collected below and piled onto bonfires. My own books and magazines, including poetry by Neruda and novels by Gabriel García Márquez and others, were burned before my eyes in the courtyard of the 6th Comisaria of Carabineros in Santiago, on 21 September, 1973, subsequent to my detention in my house" (11).

Pinochet's right wing junta, reported Chavkin, "broke into bookstores and libraries, seized thousands of books which they decided were Leftist in character and fed them to the flames. Up in smoke went copies of the works of Neruda, as well as those of such giants as Garcia Lorca, Pio Baroja, Unamuno, Walt Whitman, and John Steinbeck, to mention just a few" (218).

In his *The Murder of Allende,* Robinson Rojas Sandford described the events surrounding the death of Nobel Prize winner Pablo Neruda. The military denied Neruda medical attention as he lay dying from prostate cancer and at the same time "the troops sacked his house, smashing the poet's belongings, burning his books, stealing his money. Neruda's house in Santiago, at the foot of San Cristobal Hill, was also sacked, or rather, 'searched,' which is the same thing in the mouths of generals who do not lie. Neruda's books were burned, and his possessions stolen" (219).

In September 1973, Marvin Howe, writing for *The New York Times,* reported from Santiago that a U.S. professor, James G. Ritter, was one of dozens of arrests made in Santiago on September 24 of "extremist leaders" who were suspected of being "sympathetic of President Allende's Marxist regime. Four other Americans are unaccounted for in the widespread arrests that began two weeks ago with the overthrow of President Allende" (4). In addition to the "7,000 Chileans and foreigners held prisoner in the National Stadium," the military authorities turned to book burnings to silence opposition: "Widespread book-burning during the raids was reported. The military was said to have seized not only Marxist literature, but sociological literature in general and newspapers and magazines" (Howe 4).

The massive book burnings in Chile prompted the American Library Association to issue the following condemnation: "*Whereas,* There has been repeated evidence of the widescale burning of books by the military government of Chile; and *Whereas,* the burning of forbidden books is a despicable form of suppression ... *Therefore, Be It Further Resolved,* That the American Library Association vigorously condemns this violation of the fundamental rights of the people of Chile" (*Newsletter on Intellectual Freedom* March 1974 42).

The Chilean government continued burning "subversive" books up to the end of the Pinochet regime in 1988; *Article 19 Report, Information Freedom and Censorship* reported that in 1986, "the public burning of books has occurred in Chile ... with the destruction of 14,000 copies of the Gabriel García Márquez novel, *Clandestine in Chile: The Adventures of Miguel Littin*" (422).

After a 1973 military coup in Uruguay, there occurred massive dismissals of university professors and a "purifying" of the libraries. Delgado reported that "apart from material of Marxist content or supposed sympathies, other works which have ended up on bonfires or in paper processing plants are complete editions of *Cuadernos Americanos,* a Mexican publication which for over 30 years has published the best of Latin American thought, and all copies of the English publication *Past and Present* (because of its Marxist 'connections')" (50). Some of the more "foolish" examples of censorship and book burning in Uruguay, writes Delgado, are the suppression of Freud's theories because they are "repugnant and pornographic"; the prohibition of modern art and Cubism because "representational art is generally suspect and because that particular term can lead to mental associations with Cuba. This sort of foolishness on the part of the military was confirmed by their destruction of the private library of the eminent psychoanalyst, Dr. Galeano, when eight volumes on the Cubist school were carefully weeded out and burned" (51).

In the 1970s and 1980s, the military governments in El Salvador, supported by the United States, were responsible for various assassinations of opponents, including Archbishop Oscar Romero in March 1980, and the arrests and deaths of students and professors, plus the burning of "subversive" books. Poet and novelist Claribel Alegría, reporting on the Salvadoran authorities' arrests, killings, and book burnings, has written: "On 26 June 1980, the nation's most visible manifestation of culture — the University of San Salvador — was occupied by army troops who sacked the campus buildings and laboratories and killed and captured an undetermined number of students. In my personal experience, when

Arturo Molina's dictatorship closed it [university] down, in 1972, government troops made a bonfire in which thousands of supposedly subversive books were burnt, including almost the entire edition of one of my books of poetry as well as an economic study by the then-rector, Rafael Menjivar. Both books had just been published by the University press" (30).

Half way around the world some of the same books being set afire in the Americas were being condemned as "leftist" and reduced to ashes. In the Mideast, Iranian authorities of the Shah's regime, and later the Ayatollah Khomeini's, imposed not only widespread censorship, but also ordered extensive books burnings. Writing in 1978, Reza Baraheni began his essay "The Perils of Publishing" with: "Censorship in Iran has always been brutal"; Baraheni then identifies some of the journalists, novelists, and intellectuals in Iran who had suffered imprisonment and torture or had been "liquidated." "A recent development," he wrote in 1978, "in bookshops shows the intensity of government interest. Salespeople must record the names and addresses of everyone who buys books, so that, if a book is blacklisted after distribution, the government has access to the names and addresses of those who have bought copies. These can then be collected from their owners, burned or turned into pulp" (16). Blacklisted writers were both Iranian and foreign and "not only avowedly Marxist books are illegal. The works of John Steinbeck, Arthur Miller, Jack London, Jean-Paul Sartre, Aimé Césaire, Franz Fanon, Maxim Gorky, Sholokhov, Chernishevsky, Shchedrin, and any book on any revolutionary movement, from the time of Spartacus to the French workers' and students' strike in 1968, is considered to be illegal" (Baraheni 16).

Iranian author Gholam Hoseyn Sa'edi, who had been imprisoned during the Shah's reign and who left Iran after becoming disillusioned by the Khomeini revolution, wrote in 1984: "The publication of books was a fundamental subject, and it was one of the crowning achievements of the Islamic Republic to burn books, bookstores, and libraries. Nor was it only Marxist literature and the books of the leftists they destroyed, but even ancient and respected texts.... Printing houses were searched without warning, supposedly to find clandestine newspapers or circulars, or newspapers which were 'counter-revolutionary'" (20).

Iran's neighbor, Turkey, also imposed extensive censorship and turned to book burning in 1971 when a military coup implemented "measures that were directed at anyone suspected of left-wing tendencies (although many of the thousands of people subsequently arrested declared that they were not only liberals but also opposed to communism) and at curtailing many aspects of intellectual life. In the months that followed the coup, scores of newspapers and long lists of banned titles were circulated" (*Index on Censorship* Spring 1973 3). Dogan Ozguden reported that "on 28 July 1972, some 3,000 policemen headed by civil authorities empowered by a decision of the Istanbul Martial Law Headquarters raided 30 publishing houses in Istanbul. They confiscated between 250,000 and 500,000 books (650 titles, including some by Agatha Christie) and detained over 50 publishers, distributors and booksellers" (8). Among the books seized by the Turkish authorities were *Black Power* by civil rights activist Stokely Carmichael, *Selected Works* of Mao Tse Tung, *The Theory of Relativity* by Albert Einstein, *Arts and Literature* by Lenin, and *Peasants' Struggles* by Engels (Ozguden 8).

On January 29, 1973, the London *Daily Telegraph* reported under the heading "Books to Be Burnt": "Some 137 leftist publications are to be burnt in Turkey by order of a martial law prosecutor. They include the works of Nazim Hikmet, a communist who is considered to be the finest poet Turkey has produced" (*Index on Censorship* Spring 1973 19).

In 1990, the *Index on Censorship* provided the following statistics on political repression and book burnings in Turkey: "According to a 'balance sheet of repression' published by the daily *Cumhuriyet* in its 12 December 1989 edition, in the period since the September

1982 military coup 210,000 people have been indicted by military justice, 171 people have been killed under torture, 30,000 people have fled the country for political reasons, eight daily newspapers have been banned for a total of 198 days, 133,000 books have been burnt and 118,000 destroyed by other means, 937 films have been banned from public projection, 2,792 writers, journalists and translators have been tried by tribunals; and 23,667 associations have been closed down or had their activities suspended" (June/July 1990 42).

During the second half of the twentieth century, the Chinese were burning books condemned as "reactionary," "decadent," and "poisonous weeds." In 1950, an editorial in *The New York Times* criticizing the Chinese book burnings began: "The Western World has just learned that on May 25, Mao Tze-tung, the Communist leader of the Chinese People's Government, ordered the burning of books which his regime considered 'reactionary and anti-people.' On his list could be found the works of Confucius, the Chinese Book of Poetry, and The Book of History, along with the more contemporary writings of Sun Yat-sen and 'China's Destiny,' by Chiang Kai-Shek." The editorial concluded: "The destruction of books is always a symptom of weakness, for the act is an admission that the controlling power has no respect for the intelligence and dignity of its citizens. The power that orders the burning of books admits that it governs not by reason and logic but by violence and mood" (August 24, 1950 26).

During the Cultural Revolution of the 1960s, the Chinese Red Guards set fire to condemned books metamorphosed into "poisonous weeds." Describing the Red Guard's book burnings, Jung Chang has written: "The saddest thing of all for me was the ransacking of the library: the golden tiled roof, the delicately sculpted windows, the blue painted chairs.... Bookshelves were turned upside down, and some pupils tore books to pieces just for the hell of it.... Books were major targets of Mao's order to destroy. Because they had not been written within the last few months, and therefore did not quote Mao on every page, some Red Guards declared that they were all 'poisonous weeds.' With the exception of Marxist classics and the works of Stalin, Mao, and the late Lu Xun, whose name Mme. Mao was using for her personal vendettas, books were burning all across China" (292).

When Chang's father was accused of having "reactionary books" on his bookshelves "he made a faint attempt to protect his books by pointing at the sets of Marxist hardbacks. 'Don't try to fool us Red Guards!' yelled Mrs. Shau. 'You have plenty of "poisonous weeds"'! She picked up some Chinese classics printed on flimsy rice paper"; the books were thrown into "huge Jute sacks they had brought with them. When all the bags were full, they carried them downstairs, telling my father they were going to burn them on the grounds of the department the next day after a denunciation meeting against him. They ordered him to watch the bonfire 'to be taught a lesson.' In the meantime, they said, he must burn the rest of his collection" (Chang 330).

Again and again, the books set afire during the Cultural Revolution were transformed into "weeds," "pests," and "viruses." In his "Why a Cultural Revolution?" Chinese communist leader Lin Biao, speaking in 1966 of the need for a cultural revolution and how it was to be carried out, stated: "What is the essence of old culture and old ideology? We can use a great many words to express it and call it old culture, old ideology, poisonous weeds, ox-monsters and snake-demons, reactionary authorities, old academic, old morals, old art, old laws, old educational systems, old world outlook, etc." (Schoenhals 17).

An article praising the Red Guards and their efforts to destroy the traditions of landlords and the bourgeoisie declared: "The revolutionary young fighters want precisely to make a clean sweep of the remaining viruses of feudalism, eliminate the germs of capitalism" (Schoenhals 47). In a list of "One Hundred Items for Destroying the Old and Establishing the New," item number 34 directed: "Bookstores for classical books must this minute stop doing business. Children's bookstores must immediately destroy all pornographic children's books, and all bookstores and libraries must be internally purified and must clear away all poisonous weeds" (Schoenhals 216).

In his description of Red Guard book burnings, Liu Yan has written of the "Beijing No. 11 Middle School Red Guard" bonfire: "Except for those books whose covers featured Chairman Mao's portrait, almost all of the books in the library were removed and carried out to the center of the sports ground by the 'Black Gang' [reactionary-bourgeois elements]." Forcing them to do this were my classmates— Red Guards brandishing leather belts with brass buckles. The Red Guards insisted that these books had spread feudalist, capitalist, and revisionist ideas and that therefore they had to burned.... Finally the books— by now a small mountain — were set on fire by the Red Guards" (Schoenhals 337–328).

In August 1966, the Red Guards began their efforts in Tibet to get rid of the "Four Olds"— old ways of thinking, old culture, old habits and old customs— which were to be replaced with the "Four News." As Craig has reported, on August 23, 1966, "Urged on by the Chinese and intoxicated with excitement, bands of China-educated Tibetan youths invaded Tibet's holiest place, the Jokhang Cathedral, and indulged in an orgy of destruction, destroying and mutilating treasures stored there.... For days, the young fanatics rampaged round the courtyards, burning scriptures, beheading the Buddhas, smashing and defiling centuries-old images" (168). Donnet has written of the sacking of the venerated Jokhang Temple: "For five days, the crowd of Red Guards kept a bonfire burning, in which they threw all the relics they found.... Unique pieces of Tibet's cultural heritage were burnt to ashes" (78). Similarly, Avedon has reported that the Central Cathedral (Jokhang) was "invaded by Red Guards. Hundreds of priceless frescoes and images ... were defaced or destroyed" and for five days "mobs burn[ed] scriptures" (281).

The burning and destruction of the Tibetan Buddhist past have been observed in Dhondub Choedon's short autobiography when she writes that Tibetan songs and dances were prohibited and the Red Guards "showed contempt for the Tibetan script and banned Tibetan songs and dances. Further, religious objects and articles were confiscated and the Red Guards "burnt all the ancient holy scriptures. They cut off the long hair of all the men and women and killed all the dogs" (64–65).

The bonfires, into which were thrown the condemned Tibetan Buddhist scriptures, continued to burn in 1967 when countless ritual objects and sacred scriptures "were thrown into huge bonfires in the grounds of the monasteries. The Red Guards would invite the Tibetan masses to attend these 'celebrations'" (Donnet 82). The destruction of monasteries and the burning of scriptures occurred "under red flags— with drums, trumpets and cymbals providing fanfare — [and] local Tibetans were forced to demolish each monastery. Giant bonfires were lit to burn thousands of scriptures" (Avedon 291).

As the twentieth century came to an end, the Chinese authorities turned to burning the books of the Falun Gong "meditation-exercise" sect. In August 1999, Seth Faison reported in *The New York Times* in a news report headed "China's Crackdown on Sect More Talk Than Action" that followers of the Falun Gong sect were being detained, but "China's fierce-looking crackdown on Falun Gong, the spiritual movement that claims tens of millions of followers, is turning out to be far less severe than it first looked, with more propaganda than action.... Most of those detained are being released within a few days and sent home, apparently because officials at many levels of government fear the enormous disruption that would be caused by mass arrests for the innocuous crime of practicing a variant of an ancient form of meditation and exercise" (August 6, 1999 AS). The news report was accompanied with a photograph indicating "books and other materials relating to the Falun Gong sect were set afire in the Chinese city of Shouguang on Wednesday [August 4, 1999]."

Two years later, Chinese author Wei Hui was denounced as "decadent, debauched and a slave to Western culture" as her novel *Shanghai Baby* was banned and burned by Chinese officials. In August 2001, the *London Times* reported: "Forty thousand copies of this novel [*Shanghai Baby*] were publicly burnt last year" and the author was "officially condemned by China as 'decadent, debauched and a slave to Western culture'" (August 4, 2001 20c). Charles Wilson wrote in his *New York Times* review of *Shanghai Baby*: "Banned and burned in the author's native China, Wei Hui's book tells of Coco's [heroine] relationship with two men — Tian Tian, who is tenderhearted, impotent and drug-addicted, and Mark, a married German businessman.... As she vacillates between her two lovers, we tour with her the city's nightspots and attend theme parties with her friends, hard-core pleasure-lovers and romantics with names like Madonna and Flying Appel. There is a destructive streak in Coco, who reads Freud, listens to Marilyn Manson and is passionate about the novels of Henry Miller.... She is a searcher, a female Kerouac on a road of her own devising" (24).

In an explanation of what might have led the Chinese banning and burning of *Shanghai Baby*, Vanora Bennett has written: "Even more than the author's playful references to discontents, intellectual internationalism and consumerism of her designer-obsessed Generation X contemporaries, even more than her explicit sex scenes, it may be her half-nostalgic games with the symbolism of Shanghai colonialism that infuriated the authorities" (20c).

While the Communist Chinese were burning "reactionary" books, Falun Gong writings, and thousands of copies of a novel in which the heroine reads the works of Freud and Henry Miller, across the Taiwan Strait in anti–Communist Taiwan the manuscript of the memoirs of dissident Lei Chen was, as reported in the *Index on Censorship*, "burned at a military prison in April [1988]. Lei Chen had been a member of the ruling Kuomintang (KMT or National Party) hierarchy until the late 1950s when he became disenchanted with the one-party dictatorship of the KMT.... He was arrested in 1960 and sentenced to 10 years imprisonment. He was released in 1969 and died in 1979" (October 1988 40). After his death, continues the report, his widow asked for an investigation of the arrest and imprisonment of her husband; she was promised that "her husband's memoirs would be returned to her. It was later revealed, however, that the national Security Bureau had ordered the destruction of the manuscript" (40).

In the latter half of the twentieth century, books were being set afire in other Asian countries, including Indonesia, Cambodia, and Vietnam. On May 3, 1964, *The New York Times* published a short news item with the heading "Jakarta Burns Books for Its Education Day": "Indonesia celebrated National Education Day today [May 2] by burning about 500 books. A spokesman said the burning symbolized Indonesia's opposition to 'cultural subversion through ideas and theories contrary to Indonesian ideas and theories.' The ceremony was held in the courtyard of the Government education building beneath an Indonesian flag. The spokesman refused to name the authors and titles of the burning books but said they were written in English, French, German and Dutch and consisted mainly of textbooks in history and languages" (2).

In 1981, two novels by Indonesian journalist and writer Pramoedya Ananta Toer, *This Earth of Mankind* and *A Child of All Nations*, were banned and burned in Jakarta. Both novels were "stories about the early Indonesian nationalist movement in 1896–1916, told by Pramoedya to his fellow prisoners on Buru Island in 1973 and written down in 1975 during his confinement without trial there.... The first printings of the novels (tens of thousands of copies) were sold out immediately, but further printings were banned, confiscated, or burned in Jakarta.... The attorney general claimed that the books represented a threat to security and order and that Pramoedya 'had been able by means of historical data smuggle in Marxist-Leninist teachings'" (Baets 283). In the Foreword to his memoir *The Mute's Soliloquy,* Pramoedya wrote that the notes he had kept while imprisoned in Buru "were burnt by the authorities following a search for papers in my unit" (Toer x).

With the beginning of the twenty-first century, more book burnings were taking place in Indonesia. In August 2001, *World Press Review* reported, under the heading "Who Is Behind the Book Burning?": "Anti-Communist Alliance (AAK) has raided bookstores in several cities and burned books that, in its view, promote communism. The works of Indonesia's prominent man of letters Pramoedya Ananta Toer, which have enjoyed a surge of popularity and a flurry of reprints since the fall of the New Order regime [of former President Suharto], are among their targets (Pramoedya was a supporter of Lekra, a literary organization subordinate to the Indonesian Communist Party in the 1960s)" (38).

The Economist also reported on the book burnings conducted by the "anticommunist alliance," composed of more than thirty right-wing and Muslim groups in Indonesia in May 2001. The activities of the alliance (AAK) "in recent weeks in Jakarta and other cities have included purges of bookshops' shelves, burning of suspect books and attacks on left-wing politicians and their offices. On May 20th alliance supporters marked one of the anniversaries of Indonesia's nationalist movement with a menacing 'sweep' of Jakarta's bookshops" (May 26, 2001 40). *The Economist* report further indicated that the "alliance suffers from a lack of obvious books to burn. So it has tried to suppress a critical book on Karl Marx by a Roman Catholic priest; the works of Pramoedya Ananta Toer, Indonesia's most famous novelist; 'The Prophet' and other books by Kahlil Gibran, a Lebanese poet; and 'Chicken Soup for the Soul,' a self-help best-seller. Bookshop owners have been alarmingly quick to purge their shelves, showing that the self-preservation instincts bred under President Suharto still linger" (41).

While the right-wing and Muslim groups in Indonesia set fire to Karl Marx and Pramoedya Ananta Toer, the communist authorities in Vietnam burned books in 1975 to "root out all remnants of what they term the 'decadent culture of the south.' One of their chief targets has been literature. Between July and September, all published materials available in the south were collected and subjected to a process of evaluation which culminated in September 1975 with the posting in all public places of lists of banned works.... People fearful of being denounced for harbouring prohibited literature disposed of their books, and piles of books were burnt in several places. Afraid that an infamous parallel with the massive book burning drive of emperor Chin Tse Huang ti (3rd century B.C.) would be drawn, the Vietnamese authorities hasten to point out that the book burning incidents had taken place spontaneously. This indeed may well have been the case. At any rate, the offending works have disappeared from circulation" (Ho 18). Nguyen Ho titled this report of his "Erasing Vietnam's Past."

Similarly in Cambodia, when the Khmer Rouge came to power, "the publishing and teaching of history came to a halt. A spokesman proclaimed that '2000 years of history has ended.' Dissident historical views were suppressed. Many historic temples at Angkor and other religious shrines and monasteries were used as storehouses. Most of the books, bibliographical records, and newspaper collections in the National Library were burned, but the archives suffered less damage, although they clearly contained information contradicting the Khmer Rouge view of history" (Baets 88).

In a 1989 report about a Cornell University effort to help rebuild the collection of the

National Library in Phnom Penh, the *New York Times* referred to the book burnings in Cambodia during the late 1970s: "In their drive to purge Cambodia of the perceived taint of religious and imperialistic influences, the brutal Khmer Rouge tried to wipe out any record of these influences. Nearly all of Cambodia's 60 librarians were killed under the Khmer Rouge reign from 1975 to 1979. At the National Library in the capital, Phnom Penh, all but a few hundred of the tens of thousands of Khmer language titles were burned. The library was used to house pigs" (*New York Times,* July 26, 1989 B9).

In south central Africa, the Malawi government of President Hastings Banda who in 1966 had declared himself life-president and eliminated political opposition, issued a "death warrant" on a work titled *Chief the Honourable Minister.* In an interview published in 1979, London *Daily Times* reporter and BBC correspondent Victor Ndovi, writing of his imprisonment in Malawi and the censorship practices in Malawi, referred to the burning of the book; he was asked by interviewer George Theiner: "Can we now take a look at the way censorship operates in Malawi. Your experience certainly shows that, as in many other countries, the work of a journalist in Blantyre is fraught with danger, but I imagine the press is not the only sufferer." Ndovi replied: "In Malawi, the hypersensitive and extremely nervous political leaders employed literally scores of men and women, many with dubious academic credentials, to scrutinize every written word.... Less than two years ago, a non-fiction book called *Chief the Honourable Minister* and written by the Nigerian novelist T.M. Aluko, was banned for unexplained reasons.... The book was being used as an English textbook in secondary schools. Teams of plain-clothed policemen from the Special Branch descended on the school to issue 'death warrants' on the book. All the copies were taken to a central place to be burnt. After this 'funeral service' the police had to present written testimony of the books' destruction" (Ndovi 24).

All through the history of burning seditious-subversive books, the "funeral service" followed the "death warrants." Such personifications were no different from earlier ones involving books being "hanged" and "killed." The hangings, killings, deaths, and funerals of books would, the book burners hoped, "erase history," "switch off national memory," or bring about "amnesia of the nation." Since literally burning the author is no longer viewed as acceptable, the book burner, using the metonymy, can exclaim in Chile, "Burn Neruda" or in Peru, "Vargas Llosa deserves to be thrown into the flames" or in Malawi, "Into the fire with Aluko" or in China, "Wei Hui is condemned to the flames" or in Indonesia, "Pramoedya Toer must be burned" or in the United States, "Set Steinbeck afire" or in Germany, "We burn Freud for falsifying our history" and "Burn Remarque for degrading the German language."

All through history, with a "light of the match" the seditious-subversive books have been literally destroyed by the flames, figuratively killed, the author metonymically set afire, and the land metaphorically cleansed of "poisonous weeds, germs, viruses, and pests," and some history erased and eliminated.

4

BURNING OBSCENE-IMMORAL BOOKS

Antiquity Through the Seventeenth Century

While for centuries church and state authorities set fire to blasphemous-heretical works that were metamorphosed into "tares," "pestilence," "plague," and "disease," the fiery destruction of obscene writings came years later as they were metamorphosed into "filth," "dirt," "smut," and "deadly poison." For centuries, the church and state officials gave higher priority to punishing blasphemous-heretical works than to obscene expression. The reasons for this late church-state involvement are varied; there are several explanations why the banning and burning of obscene-erotic books began relatively late, as compared to the burning of heretical-blasphemous and subversive writings. First, the obscene-erotic works were less available to the masses of people; such works were primarily in the hands of the wealthy. Further, there were fewer writers publishing obscene books, as compared to the number of authors writing controversial religious and political books. Also, secular and ecclesiastical authorities were more interested in controlling the dissemination of heretical and subversive writings than in getting involved in the examination and banning of obscene works; the stability and power of the church and state were seen as threatened more by heretical and seditious works than by obscene writings.

As Lea has indicated in his *A History of the Inquisition in Spain*, "The dissociation of religion from morals—the incongruous connection of ardent zeal for dogma with laxity of life—was stimulated by the Inquisition. As we have seen, it paid no attention to morals and thus taught the lesson that they were unimportant in comparison with accuracy of belief" (4 509). Or as Morris Ernst has put it, "for the Church the index of the good life was freedom from heresy and not from obscenity" (142).

In his discussion of the different types of libels—blasphemous, defamatory, and obscene—Alec Craig observes: "Obscene libel was a last and late comer to the category of libels" (23) Similarly, Robertson points out that in the sixteenth century, "the Elizabethan censorship was concerned with book which challenged faith or government. Many dissidents were hanged, drawn, and quartered for publishing Catholic propaganda, but there is scant evidence that the licensing system was operated to suppress either popular or bawdy literature" (17).

In the United States obscenity was not a major concern of the founders of the nation: "For eighty years, that is up to 1870, there was practically no legislation banning that indefinable subject known as obscenity" (Haight 133). Felice Lewis has similarly observed: "The initial years of the Republic seem to have been singularly free from worry over obscenity.... The earliest recorded censorship actions in the colonies were directed mainly against printed matter considered blasphemous or seditious.... The colonists were most edgy about blasphemy, which for a time was punishable by death in Maryland, Plymouth Colony, and Massachusetts Bay Colony" (1978 1).

Emphasizing that in the nineteenth century obscene writings were not so readily accessible to most people in England, Sigel has explained: "Pornography belonged primarily to the upper 4 percent. Pornography was not created equal and it held no pretensions to egalitarianism. Instead, it stood as an artifact for a specific part of society — those with wealth, education, social advantages, and even some form of political power. The people who bought pornography needed to be literate, sometimes not only in English but also in Greek, Latin, or French. They needed to be wealthy" (90).

In the United States there was another factor to be considered in explaining so little concern about obscene writings being available to the general population: in the United States there was no indigenous erotic fiction being published. As Lewis has observed: "Before 1890 only a very limited amount of erotic literature seems to have circulated in this country, chiefly continental European and English classics which often reached America in expurgated form, and some underground pulp novels that were outside the mainstream of literature.... In fact, unlike other countries, we had almost no tradition of indigenous erotic fiction, perhaps because our literature was born in the early nineteenth century, with Washington Irving and William Cullen Bryant, at a time when its English model had become extremely sedate. Also, of course, it was born into a largely puritanical society that had long assumed the sexual impulse to be a dangerous passion that should be ignored as far as was possible" (1978 13).

As long as obscene books were available only to the rich and educated, censorship of such works was minimal; it was only when the secular authorities felt it necessary to protect the morality of an increasingly literate citizenry that anti-obscenity laws and decisions appear in significantly greater number. As Charles Rembar has indicated, "Censorship is ancient, but censorship of obscenity is not"; the law of obscenity, he points out, began relatively late "because there were not many books until late in history. Literary censorship is an elitist notion: obscenity is something from which the masses should be shielded. We never hear a prosecutor, or a condemning judge ... declare his moral fibre has been injured by the book in question" (30).

In his dissenting opinion in *U.S. v. 12 200-Ft. Reels of Film,* Supreme Court Justice William O. Douglas, arguing that the material involved in this case deserved constitutional protection, wrote: "The advent of the printing press spurred censorship in England, but the ribald and the obscene were not, at first, within the scope of that which was officially banned. The censorship of the Star Chamber and the licensing of books under the Tudors and Stuarts was aimed at the blasphemous or heretical, the seditious or treasonable. At that date, the government made no effort to prohibit the dissemination of obscenity. Rather, obscene literature was considered to raise a moral question properly cognizable only of ecclesiastical, and not the common-law courts" (134). In another obscenity case, *Paris Adult Theatre I v. Slaton,* Justice Douglas declared in another dissenting opinion that "prior to the adoption of our Constitution and Bill of Rights the Colonies had no law excluding 'obscenity' from the regime of freedom of expression and press that then existed" (70).

When by the end of the nineteenth century obscenity became a target of the censors and book burners, some of the metaphoric language used to condemn blasphemous, heretical, and seditious works was applied in denunciations of obscene books: poison, vermin, plague, Satanic. However, the condemnatory metaphors used in denouncing heretics and their writings — tares, pestilence, ravening wolves, foxes destroying the vineyards — were of less interest to the book burners setting fire to obscene books. Instead, the censors and book burners metamorphosed the condemned obscene works into "filth," "dirt," "rubbish," "smut," "germs," and "trash." However, these "filthy, smutty, dirty" metaphors are seldom consistently applied to heretical and seditious works, although at times the book burners have referred to heretical works as "unclean" and "filth," especially when the "leprosy" and "disease" metaphors are invoked.

The obscene book being set afire is identified as "dirt," "filth," and "slime" and becomes "dirty" and "filthy" since obscenity is associated with the body, nudity, sex, and excretion. The graphic description of nudity or sexual intercourse becomes "dirt" and "smut." The U.S. courts have on more than one occasion denied First Amendment protection to obscene writings and pictures because they appeal to "prurient interest." As the U.S. Supreme Court declared in its 1957 landmark decision *Roth v. United States,* "obscene material is material which deals with sex in a manner appealing to prurient interest" (487). Then in a footnote to this assertion the Court included a definition of "prurient": "A thing is obscene if, considered as a whole, its predominant appeal is to prurient interest, e.g., a shameful or morbid interest in nudity, sex, or excretion, if it goes substantially beyond customary limits of candor in description or representation of such matters" (487). The Court pointed out at the outset of its Roth decision that the federal obscenity statute prohibited the distribution of "every obscene, lewd, lascivious, or filthy book, pamphlet, picture, paper, letter, writing, print, or other publication of an indecent character" (479).

In their *Prophets of Deceit,* Lowenthal and Guterman, while focusing on political speech and writings of the agitator, provide some insights that apply to the metaphoric condemnations and burnings of obscene works. In their discussion of the agitator's reliance on such imagery as "rodents, reptiles, insects, and germs," Lowenthal and Guterman refer to the agitator's talk of "cleaning the house," of "disease germs," and ridding the land of "dirt and filth": "Like the Low Animal metaphor [insects, rats, vipers, etc.] this hygienic metaphor [dirt, germs, filth, etc.] occurs too consistently and too profusely to be dismissed as accidental.... Stereotypes utilizing the symbols of dirt, filth, and odor are used to impress the audience with the fact that all speeches and literature put out by the enemy should be discarded at once" (102–103). Further, "The prevalence of moral and material rubbish demands the most thorough sanitary measures" (105).

Fire, of course, is a "most thorough sanitary measure" to eradicate the "dirty, foul, filthy" obscene books. The burning of the "smut" and "garbage," the book burner promises, will bring with it cleanliness and purification since the condemned book is reduced to unthreatening, harmless ashes. The burning of the "filth and smut" provides a hygienic, sanitary cleansing of something associated with "dirty" sex, lust, and excretion. The application of these metaphors to condemn obscene books has been less an accurate description of the books than an invitation to ban and burn them. As Theodore Schroeder has warned:

> Much of the justification for intolerance derives its authority from false analogies, wrongfully carried over from physical relations into the realm of the psychic.
>
> Thus some argue that because, by laws, we protect the incompetent against being (unconsciously) infected with contagious disease, therefore the state should also protect them (even though mature and able to protect themselves by mere inattention) against the literature of infectious moral poison. Here a figure of speech is mistaken for an analogy. "Moral poison" exists only figuratively and not literally in any such sense as strychnine is a poison.
>
> Ethics is not one of the exact sciences. Probably it never will be. Until we are at least appropriately as certain of the existence and tests of "moral poison," as we are of the physical characteristics and consequences of carbolic acid, it is folly to talk of "moral poison" except as a matter of poetic license [56].

Schroeder's warning has hardly been heeded. In the middle of the nineteenth century, "the House of Lords was passing a bill to regulate the traffic in [literally] poisons, and few days after he sentenced the pornographer, Lord Campbell [Chief Justice in England] introduced a companion measure in a speech which is reported in *Hansard,* the official record of Parliamentary proceedings: 'He was happy to say that he believed the administration of poison by design had received a check. But from the trial which had taken place before him on Saturday he had learned with horror and alarm that a sale of poison more deadly than prussic acid, strychnine or arsenic — the sale of obscene publications and indecent books was openly going on'" (Loth 132).

In 1880, the New York Society for the Suppression of Vice stated in its Report: "The result of this literary poison, cast into the very foundations of social life, is found everywhere. It is infecting the pure life and heart of our youth" (Beisel 70). The 1875 Report of the NYSSV had warned of the "shrewd and wily" dealers of obscene materials who had "succeeded in inject[ing] a virus more destructive to the innocence and purity of youth, if not counteracted, than can be the most deadly disease in the body. If we had the ear of all the teachers, parents, and guardians, in our land we would plead with them, 'Guard with ceaseless vigilance your libraries, your closets, your children's and wards' correspondence and companionships, lest the contagion reach and blight the sweetness and purity of your homes'" (Beisel 57–58).

It has not been unusual to find lower court judges in the United States, in deciding to deny constitutional protection to "obscene" materials, inserting the condemnatory metaphors into their judicial opinions. In 1884, in deciding against August Muller who had been charged with selling "indecent and obscene photographs, representing nude females in lewd, obscene, indecent, scandalous and lascivious attitudes and postures," a New York court metamorphosed obscenity into "contamination and pollution": "The statute makes the selling of any obscene and indecent picture a misdemeanor. There is no exception by reason of any special intent in making the sale. The object of the statute was to suppress the traffic in obscene publications, and to protect the community against the contamination and pollution arising from their exhibition and distribution" (*People v. Muller* 408).

When in 1963 the Court of Appeals of New York concluded that Henry Miller's *Tropic of Cancer* was an obscene book, Chief Judge Desmond wrote a two and a half page concurring opinion in which he referred to "filth" and "filthy" six times. For example, he wrote: "From first to last page it is a filthy, cynical, disgusting narrative of sordid amours." Three sentences later, Judge Desmond reiterated: "The whole book is 'sick sexuality,' a deliberate, studied exercise in the depiction of sex relations as debasing, filthy and revolting." *Tropic of Cancer,* the judge asserted, is "crowded with filth" (*People v. Fritch* 718).

Ten years earlier, Judge Stephens, writing for the United States Court of Appeals concluded that both *Tropic of Cancer* and *Tropic of Capricorn* by Henry Miller were obscene, and in so doing the judge metamorphosed the words in the books into "smut," "dirt," and "slime": "Practically everything that the world loosely regards as sin is detailed in the vivid, lurid, salacious language of smut, prostitution, and dirt.... These words of the language of smut, and the disgraceful scenes, are so heavily larded throughout the book that those portions of which are deemed to be of literary merit do not lift the reader's mind clear of their sticky slime" (*Besig v. United States* 145).

In 1964, when the Superior Court of New Jersey concluded that John Cleland's *Memoirs of a Woman of Pleasure (Fanny Hill)* was "sufficiently obscene to forfeit the protection of the First Amendment," Judge Pashman referred to the New Jersey statute that prohibited the sale and distribution of any book "of an indecent character, which is obscene, lewd, lascivious, filthy or indecent." With the "filthy" incorporated into the state statute, Judge Pashman decided to include the metaphor in his opinion, with "filth" and "trashy" appearing several times in the opinion of the court; at one point he cites another obscenity case in which a New York court had said, "filth, even if wrapped in the finest packaging, is still filth" (*G.P. Putnam's Sons v. Calissi* 922).

How to rid the land of the "filthy, poisonous virus"? In some states the answer was public burning. For example, the public burning of obscene materials was provided for in Missouri's Revised Statutes, §542.420: "If the judge or magistrate hearing such cause shall determine that the property or articles are of the kind mentioned in section 542.380 [dealing with obscenity], he shall cause the same to be publicly destroyed, by burning or otherwise." On December 12, 1957, a circuit judge in Missouri "filed an unreported opinion in which he overruled the several motions [to quash the search warrants, etc.] and found that 100 of the 280 seized items were obscene. A judgment thereupon issued directing that the 100 items, and all copies thereof, 'shall be retained by the Sheriff of Jackson County ... as necessary evidence for the purpose of possible criminal prosecution or prosecutions, and when such necessity no longer exists, said Sheriff ... shall publicly destroy the same by burning within thirty days thereafter'" (*Marcus v. Search Warrant* 724). When the case reached the United States Supreme Court, Justice William Brennan, delivering the opinion of the Court, concluded: "Mass seizure in the fashion of this case was thus effected without any safeguards to protect legitimate expression. The judgment of the Missouri Supreme Court sustaining the condemnation of the 100 publications therefore cannot be sustained" (*Marcus v. Search Warrant* 738).

Historically, just as heretical-blasphemous writings were condemned to the fires because they were seen as subverting government and society, so too have obscene books been denounced as "corrupting" society, as contributing to "social disobedience," and "weakening the bonds of civil society." When in 1599, Christopher Marlowe's translation of Ovid's *Elegies* was burned in England, the Archbishop of Canterbury, as Moulton has written, saw linkage "of wantonness, corrupt doctrine, and social disobedience"; and "works thought of as ribald or licentious were not differentiated from political subversive or heretical works, but were included in a broad range of material which could seduce the innocent" (77–78).

In 1727, a British court concluding that obscenity was punishable by a temporal court, sentenced Edmund Curll to the pillory for publishing *Venus in the Cloister or the Nun in her Smock,* and as Loth points out, Curll "paid the first fine ever levied against obscenity in England" (107). One of the judges argued that the printing of Curll's book "to be punishable by common law, as an offence against peace, in tending to weaken the bonds of civil society, virtue and morality" (Grazia 1969 4).

In the United States, a Pennsylvania court decided in 1815 against Jesse Sharpless and others who had been charged with exhibiting at a house "a certain lewd, wicked, scandalous, infamous, and obscene painting, representing a man in an obscene, impudent, and indecent posture with a woman, to the manifest corruption and subversion of youth, and other citizens of this commonwealth, to the evil example of all others in like case offending, and against the peace and dignity of the commonwealth of Pennsylvania." In deciding against Sharpless, Judge Tilgman declared: "The law was in *Curll's* case established upon true principles. What tended to corrupt society, was held to be a breach of the peace and punishable by indictment. The Courts are guardians of the public morals, and therefore have justification in such cases. Hence it follows, that an offence may be punishable, if in its nature and by its example, it tends to the corruption of morals; although it be not committed in public" (*Commonwealth of Penn. v. Sharpless* 38).

In a concurring opinion, Judge Yeates asserted that "the destruction of morality renders the power of the government invalid, for government is no more than public order. It weakens the bands by which society is kept together. The corruption of the public mind in general, and debauching the manners of youth in particular by lewd and obscene pictures exhibited to view, must necessarily be attended with the most injurious consequences, and in such instances the Courts of Justice are, or ought to be, the schools of morals." Judge Yeates invoked the "poison" metaphor when he asserted that it was clear that the exhibition of the lustful painting was punishable: "The question then in this part of the case is narrowed to a single point; — Whether the exhibition of a lewd, wicked, scandalous, infamous, and obscene painting, representing, &c. to certain individuals in a private house for money, is dispunishable by the sound principles of common law? On this question I cannot hesitate. It is settled, that the publication of libel to anyone person renders the act complete.... No man is permitted to corrupt the morals of the people. Secret poison cannot be thus disseminated" (39).

These arguments asserting that the publication and distribution of obscene materials contribute to the corruption of society, to breach of the peace, to the weakening of the "bonds by which society is kept together," contributed significantly to the establishment of the relationship between obscenity and the subversion of society and government. Further, establishing, through persistent use, a relationship between obscene works and "poison," "filth," and "disease" contributed to the call for the undesirable and dangerous elements in society.

The arguments for censorship seemed logical as one reduced them into syllogisms: First premise: All writings that corrupt society and subvert government must be eliminated. Second premise: Obscene writings corrupt and subvert. Therefore, obscene writings must be eliminated. The conclusion follows from the two premises.

Another syllogism: First premise: All filth, poisons, and disease must be eliminated. Second premise: Obscene works are filth, poisons and disease. Therefore, obscene works must be eliminated. The conclusion follows from the two premises. In both cases, of course, what must be questioned are the premises. In the first case, the two premises are susceptible to criticism and attack. In the second case, of course, the meanings of the words have been changed and hence the fallacy of equivocation renders the argument invalid. This type of reasoning, as we noted in an earlier chapter, played a crucial role in the burning of heretical-blasphemous writings. The religious inquisitors had argued (1) All tares, vermin, and pestilence must be eliminated, especially by fire. (2) Heretical-blasphemous books are tares, vermin, and pestilence. (3) Therefore, heretical-blasphemous books must be eliminated, by fire.

Some of the earliest burnings of obscene books occurred in Italy. After Antonio Beccadelli's [Panormita's] *Hermaphroditus* was published in 1425, it was set afire in various Italian cities. Referring to these burnings, O'Connor has written: "When initially circulated in the fall of 1425, the *Hermaphroditus* was praised by fellow poets and humanists, but soon after it became a cause of public censure; only a few years after its initial publication, the book was condemned by the pope and copies of it were burned in Bologna, Ferra, Milan, and other Italian cities. Subsequent moralists have condemned it for its obscenity and its unabashed treatment of sexuality" (1).

In describing the sexual nature of Panormita's work, O'Connor states: "The *Hermaphroditus,* befitting its name, is a book filled with transgressions of boundaries, sexual and otherwise"; further, Panormita makes "arguably cruel jokes about physical infirmities ... sexual odors ... and urine and excrement, usually in connection with some sexual practice" and "the common targets of this 'joke' literature were priests, cuckolded husbands, and lustful women; the language used was sexual and scatological" (16–18).

The Church's concern about obscene literature was expressed in 1564 when it issued "The Ten Rules of the Tridentine Index" as a "guide and instruction for all ecclesiastics or other authorities who might thereafter be charged with the duty of literary censorship" (Putnam 1906 1 182). While the Church was primarily concerned with such matters as heresy, Bible translations, and impiety, it did devote one short section, "Rule VII," to "lascivious or obscene" works: "Books professedly treating of lascivious or obscene subjects, or narrating or teaching these, are utterly prohibited, since not only faith but morals, which are readily corrupted by the perusal of them, are to be considered. and those who possess them shall be severely punished by the bishop. But the works of antiquity, written by the heathen, are permitted to be read, because of the elegance and propriety of the language; though on no account shall they be suffered to be read by young persons" (Putnam 1906 1 185). Hence, while with one hand the Church was prohibiting "books professedly treating of lascivious or obscene subjects," it was with the other hand permitting access to the works of Ovid and Catullus who would be, of course, available only to the wealthy and literate in the sixteenth and seventeenth centuries.

Sixteen years later, in July 1580, schoolmaster Angelo Mazza was put on trial by the Church officials who charged him "first, of having dictated obscene and lascivious Latin passages to his students; second, of having possessed pedagogical and lexical works by such forbidden authors as Erasmus, Melanchthon ... third, of having prepared a sacrilegious and superstitious composition in the company of a converted Jew" (Tedeschi 322–333). Mazza was found guilty and the sentence included the fiery destruction of his "dirty Latin verses": "[I]n regard to the charge of dirty Latin verses, they are to be burned in the sight of all those assembled in front of the Cathedral church in the presence of all the people and in sight of Angelo Mazza, hatless, humbly silent and penitent. And the above named Angelo must oblige himself publicly and openly, even in a document subscribed to in his own hand and in the possession of the court, never to fall into similar errors, but to refrain in *perpetuo*" (Tedeschi 325).

In his essay titled "Italian Literature on the Index," Ugo Rozzo, writing of censorship in Italy during the fifteenth and sixteenth centuries, refers to the occasional book burnings of literary works of that period: "Literary works were first subjected to large-scale prohibition by the first universal index of the Roman Church promulgated by Pope Paul IV in 1559. Hitherto the inquisitors, much preoccupied with the circulation of texts of Protestant inspiration, had largely neglected literature, whether licentious or otherwise. In truth, there had been some occasional condemnations of ancient authors or contemporary humanists in the quattrocento, a case in point being the prohibition for obscenity that Pope Eugene IV pronounced in 1431 against Hermaphroditus by Antonio Beccadelli (il Panormita), which led to its public burning in several of Italy's town squares" (194).

Into Savonarola's 1497–1498 bonfires of vanities went, in addition to the works of Plato, Petrarch, and Dante, "licentious" writings: Luigi Pulci's *Morgante maggiore*, Boccaccio's *Decameron* (Rozzo 194) and "the works of licentious writers, and especially of poets like Morganti" (Madden 1 366). In the following century, "in 1545, a work entitled *II dio Priapo* and other (similar?) texts printed without a license were burnt, while in the following year it was forbidden to sell works by Franceso Berni" (Rozzo 198).

In comparing the writing of Pulci and Rabelais, Bart refers to the obscenity appearing in their works: "Obscenity, which bulks so large in Rabelais, is relatively absent from Pulci" (161). Pulci "attracted the notice of key critics and poets. Coleridge lectured on his works, and Leigh Hunt summarized parts of his poetry in *Stories from the Italian Poets*. Sir Walter Scott also read Pulci.... Lord Byron translated the first part of Pulci's *Morgante* ...

and the Italian poet's style is evident in the mock-heroic tone of his Don Juan" (Tommaso 425).

As the sixteenth century came to a close, several obscene-erotic writings were set afire in England by order of the Archbishop of Canterbury and the Bishop of London. The works that were reduced to ashes in that order of 1599 included: John Marston's *Pigmalion with certaine other Satyres* and *The Scourge of villanye;* John Davies' *Epigrammes and Elegies;* Christopher Marlowe's translation of Ovid's *Elegies;* Edward Guilpin's *Skialetheia, or a Shadow of Truth in Certain Epigrams and Satires;* and Antoine de La Sale's *Fyftene Joyes of Maryage* (Rostenberg 84).

Hugh Walker describes Marston's *Pygmalion* as "simply one of the most licentious poems of a period in which licentiousness was among the prevailing vices of verse" (80). As to Marston's *The Scourge of Villany,* Walker writes: "The eleven pieces of *The Scourge of Villany* considerably extend Marston's range. Like Juvenal, he thinks it difficult to refrain from satire. He declares that vice is the way to success, while honesty leads to ruin, and that procrastination has taken away the hope of reform, for each man is resolved to abandon his vice — to-morrow. All this is expressed with the utmost violence of vituperation, in verse harsher than the harshest written by other satirists" (80).

In his observations about Marston's satirical writing, Alden writes that Marston "shows an unpleasant satisfaction in dwelling on unclean details; and, as Warton observes, 'the satirist who too freely indulges himself in the display of that licentiousness which he means to proscribe, absolutely defeats his own design.' The most curious illustration of Marston's method of doing just this, is the *Pigmalion's Image* — the starting point of his satire. It is one of the most frankly indelicate poems of the period" (135).

John Davies's condemned *Epigrams* had been printed together with Christopher Marlowe's translation of Ovid's *Elegies* and their works, bound together, "perished" in the fire ordered by the church authorities: "Marlowe's translation of the *Amores* in all the editions is accompanied by Sir John Davies's *Epigrams.* The only mention of the work in the Stationers' Register is its inclusion among books to be publicly burnt by order of the Archbishop of Canterbury and the Bishop of London on 1 June 1599. The book was unlicensed and the imprint of Middleburgh (in Holland) on the title-page as the place of publication was in all probability spurious" (Boas 1940 29).

Legman, referring to the fiery destruction of *Epigrams* and *Elegies,* has stated: "Harking back to the oldest love poet of them all ... the playwright Marlowe's translation into English of *All Ovid's Elegies* was published secretly abroad, in Middleburg, Holland, in 1598, but was seized on being smuggled into England. It was condemned by the Archbishop of Canterbury and Bishop of London (probably on account of Davies' satirical poems, published with it), almost all known copies being burnt. This is one of the earliest examples outside Italy on the publication of 'erotica' in the clandestine fashion reserved otherwise almost exclusively at that time, to works of religious controversy" (82). Bakeless also has indicated that the Bishops' "wrath was probably directed mainly at the Davies Epigrams, which could not be disguised as anything but simple pornography, whereas Marlowe's Ovid had the respectability of the classics" (171).

One year after the burning of these licentious, bawdy, satirical works by Marston, Marlowe, Davies, Guilpin and La Sale, two books by Samuel Rowland, "one of the most prolific of popular writers in London during the first decade of the seventeenth century" (Alden 165), were set afire. The two satirical works were titled *A Mery Metinge, or 'Tis Mery when Knaves Mete* and *The Letting of Humours Blood in the Head-Vaine* and were burned because the *A Mery Metinge* epigrams "seem to have given offence through personal allusions"

(Alden 166) and *'Tis Mery when Knaves Mete* contained "matter unfit to be published" (Greg 20). Referring to the burning of *Letting of Humours Blood* Alden wrote: "The epigrams in the *Letting of Humours Blood* seem to have given offence through personal allusions, and there is a record in the Stationers' Register of the fining of twenty-nine stationers ... for 'their Disorders in buying of the bookes of *humours letting blood in the vayne* being new printed after it was first forbidden and burnt'" (166). Greg reports that "Samuel Rowland's *Letting of Humour's Blood* was licensed by Zachariah Pasfield in 1600, in spite of the pelates' prohibition of satires the year before, but it was condemned to be burned in the kitchen at Stationer's Hall, only to be surreptitiously reprinted" (61). As for Rowland's *A Mery Metinge, or 'Tis Mery when Knaves Mete,* Greg indicates that the Stationers' Company officials "publicly burned the whole impression of a book of sonnets called *'Tis Merry When Knaves Meet'* as containing 'matter unfit to be published,' although it had the approval of the rector of a London parish" (20).

In seventeenth century England, books referred to as "Merry books," considered coarse and offensive were condemned and burned as containing material that led to the corruption of manners. In 1656, John Phillips' published a work carrying a title page which read: *Sportive Wit: The Muses Merriment, A New Spring of Lusty Drollery, Joviall Fancies, and A la Mode Lamponnes, On some heroick persons of these late Times, Never before exposed to the publick view* which was burned because it contained "much scandalous, lascivious, scurrilous, and profane matter." Clyde, referring to the burning of Phillips' work, writes: "*Sportive Wit,* first of these merry books, although it passed the licenser and was duly entered at Stationers' Hall, was, however, too coarse to be palatable even to a Government which permitted ballads: parts of it were frankly obscene. A committee of the Council reported that it contained 'much Scandalous, Lascivious, Scurrilous, and Profane matter,' and copies of the book were ordered to be seized and to be 'forthwith publicly burnt.' The same fate was reserved for *Choice Drollery, Songs and Sonnets,* entered in the Stationers' Register on 9 February. It was suppressed for being 'stuffed with profane and obscene matter tending to the corruption of manners'" (274–275).

"Intolerable foulness," "a pariah amongst books," "diabolic humor," "indecent burlesque"— such was the language used in the seventeenth century to describe John Wilmot's [Earl of Rochester's] *Sodom.* The DNB entry for Wilmot includes a paragraph devoted to his *Sodom*: "A second play (in heroic couplets) of intolerable foulness has been put to Rochester's credit. It is entitled 'Sodom,' and was published at Antwerp in 1684 as 'by the E. of R.;' no copy of this edition is known; one is said to have been burnt by Richard Heber. Two manuscripts are extant.... The piece is improbably said to have been acted at court; it was doubtless designed as a scurrilous attack on Charles II.... Internal evidence unhappily suggests that Rochester had the chief hand in the production. French adaptations are dated, 1744, 1752, and 1767" (XXI 538).

In his discussion of whether there existed a 1684 printed edition of *Sodom,* Prinz has written: "As Pisanus Fraxi [erotica collector] believes, a copy of this edition [of *Sodom*] was in Richard Heber's collection and was destroyed by his executors together with one or two other obscene books.... The fact that not a single copy of the book has come down to us is certainly apt to render its existence doubtful, although it must be acknowledged that a pariah amongst books such as *Sodom* is exposed to greater perils than respectable works, and is much more liable to suffer the fate of complete extermination" (391). In his description of *Sodom,* Prinz observes: "It need not be emphasized that *Sodom* is most painful reading, and that one hardly feels tempted to enquire whether, apart from its value as a historical document, the piece has any further merits. This much is certain, however, that never has a satire come forward in which the vice of pederasty is scourged in such a horrifying manner and, at the same time, with so much literary skill, energy, concentration, and graphic power" (169).

Rochester himself ordered late in his life that his writings be burned. Love reports that "Rochester's own manuscripts of his writings were burned by his command, shortly before his death in July 1680, as a testimony to his conversion" (xxx). Prinz also refers to Rochester's order to burn his writings: "There is also a report, shortly before his death, Rochester gave strict orders to burn 'all his profane and lewd Writings, as being only fit to promote Vice and Immorality, by which he had so highly offended God, and shamed and blasphemed that Holy Religion into which he had been Baptiz'd and all his obscene and filthy Pictures, which were so notoriously scandalous'" (235).

Rochester's "conversion" is reflected in a letter he wrote one month before his death; he wrote to Gilbert Burnet: "If God be yet pleased to spare me longer in this World, I hope in You Conversation to be exalted to that degree in Piety, that the World may see how much I abhor what I so long loved, and how much I glory in Repentance and in God's Service. Bestow you Prayers upon me, That God would spare me (if it be his good will) to shew a true Repentance, and amendment of Life for the time to come; or else, if the Lord pleaseth to put an end to my Worldly Being now, That he would mercifully accept my Death-Bed Repentance" (Prinz 295).

During the seventeenth and eighteenth centuries, the French were setting fire to obscene books, along with effigies of the authors. As Farrer has reported, "In 1623, The Parlement of Paris condemned Théophile [Théophile de Viau] to be burnt with his book, *Le Parnasse des Poètes Satyriques,* but the author escaped with his burning in effigy and with imprisonment in the dungeon" (16). *Le Parnasse satryrique* was published in April 1623, "containing audacious and partly licentious poems included in a section signed by Théophile. The volume was condemned on 11 July by the Paris parlement, which also ordered Théophile's arrest. He was in hiding with Montmorency at Chantilly when, on 19 August, he was burnt in effigy with his works, including *Pyrame*" (Levi 885). In her examination of Théophile's "cabaret poetry," Gaudiani has written: "What traits distinguish Théophile's tavern verse from the plethora of obscene, satiric, Bacchic, and libertine poetry of his time? First, Théophile perceives, describes, and accepts two opposing aspects of sexuality: its constructive and destructive qualities. While his contemporaries generally espoused either a cynical, negative perspective or, less often, a joyful, positive view of love and women, Théophile writes easily in both modes. To the extent that sexuality brings physical pleasure, affection and love, it is a positive force. To the extent that it recalls human temporality, loneliness, and physical decomposition, it is a negative force" (46). In one of his 1611 poems, Théophile "combines the delicate natural setting of the country with the obscene language of the drinking song of the watering Latin scholars. There is no sense of degradation of the woman as the sex partner. The couple participates together in a joyful pursuit of sexual gratification" (Gaudiani 47). Ditchfield, asserting that Théophile's poems "deserved destruction," wrote: "Théophile was condemned to be burned at Paris on account of his book *Le Parnasse des Poètes Satyriques, ou Recueil de vers piquans et gaillards de notre temps...,* but he contrived to effect his escape. He was ultimately captured in Picardy, and put in a dungeon. He was banished from the kingdom by order of the Parliament.... His poems are a mere collection of impieties and obscenities, published with the greatest of impudence, and well deserved their destruction" (181). Whether Théophile's writings "deserved destruction," has been disputed by those who see his poems as part of "a literary tradition that dates back to Roman times" (Gaudiani 23).

Just as an effigy of Théophile was set afire along with his writings, so too was the effigy of Michel Millot burned along with his "bawdy, lewd" book titled *L'Ecole des filles*. In her essay "The Politics of Pornography: L'Ecole des Filles," Joan Dejean writes: "The volume [*L'Ecole des filles*] had just been printed, since only a few copies had been bound, when, on June 12, 1655, officers of justice seized all the copies they could find and began questioning suspects. After numerous interrogations, sentences were handed down on August 7. The symbolic hanging of Millot took place on August 9, and all known copies of the book were burned" (112). As to the importance of *L'Ecole des filles,* Dejean states: "In France, at least, pornography appears to enjoy a privileged relation to beginnings. Those who have worked in this field will tell you without hesitation that *L'Ecole des filles* is the original work of pornography published in French" (110). Similarly, Legman identifies Millot's work as "the first erotic work in French, for which the author was burnt in effigy on the Isle du Palais in Pris, along with all copies of his book that could be found, most of them having been seized in the form of unbound sheets at the printer's" (91).

Some writers have referred to "Helot" as the author of *L'Ecole des filles* and the person who was burned in effigy. Peignot reported that *L'Ecole des filles* was "a very scandalous work, written by a man called Helot" who was "hung in effigy and all copies of his book were burnt at the foot of the gallows.... Few people have proof of who was burnt in Paris with the book" (I 175). Farrer states: "Helot ... escaped with a burning in effigy when his *L'Ecole des filles* was burnt at the foot of the gallows" (17). Ditchfield observes that Helot was "hung in effigy, and his books were burnt.... Some think that Helot was burnt at Paris with his books" (182).

While there have been differences as to whether the author of *L'Ecole des filles* was "Helot" or "Millot" and whether he was hung in effigy or burned in effigy, and whether he was burnt along with his books, there is no disagreement that *L'Ecole des filles* was condemned and set afire.

As to the lewdness of the book and its burning, we read in the January 13, 1668, entry in Samuel Pepys' diary that he saw at his bookseller's "the French book which I did think to have had for my wife to translate, called 'L'escholle de Filles,' but when I came to look into it, it is the most bawdy, lewd book that ever I saw" (21). Then on February 9, Pepys again refers to the "lewd" book and his setting fire to the work: "Lords day. Up, and at my chamber all the morning and the office, doing business and also reading a little of 'L'escolle des Filles,' which is a mighty lewd book, but yet not amiss for a sober man once to read over to inform himself in the villainy of the world"; then in the evening, "I to my chamber, where I did read through "L'escholle des filles," a lewd book, but what do no wrong once to read for information sake and after I had done it, I burned it, that it might not be among my books to my shame; and so at night to supper and then to bed" (59).

The Eighteenth Through Twentieth Centuries — Burning More Classic "Obscene" Books

While Pepys burned his copy of the "lewd" *L'escholle des Filles* in 1668, the court of the King's Bench at the outset of the 1700s first argued in *Queen v. Read* that "writing an obscene book, as that entitled, 'The Fifteen Plagues of a Maidenhead,' is not indictable, but punishable only in the spiritual court" (Grazia 1969 3). Whether obscenity was to be "punished" was for the ecclesiastical court to decide, not the temporal or secular courts. However, twenty years later, the same court concluded in *Dominus Rex v. Curl* that the publication of *Venus in the Cloister* was punishable because, as one judge was inclined to believe, "this is to be punishable at common law, as an offense against the peace, in tending to weaken the bonds of civil society, virtue, and morality" (Grazia 1969 3). In deciding against Curl, the court imposed a small fine and sentenced him to be pilloried at Charing-Cross; a sympathetic "mob" gathered and "when he was taken down out of the pillory, the mob carried him off, as it were in triumph, to a neighbouring tavern" (Thomas 1969 83). It is significant that Charles Gillett devotes only one short chapter, four pages, in his two-volume work on book burnings in England up to the end of the eighteenth century, to books set afire because they "offended against morality" (90–93).

In France, "lewd" and "immoral" works continued to be burned. Among the few books listed by Farrer as being burned for their "immoral tendency" is *Princesses malabares, ou le célibat philosophique* which he attributed to "Dufresnoy" (17). However, in her work devoted to Nicholas Lenglet Dufresnoy, Sheridan has raised questions about the authorship of this work: "Not surprisingly, considering the reputation which Lenglet [Dufresnoy] had acquired ... through his editions and original works in the *libertin* tradition, he became one of those figures whose name was automatically raised in connection with other anonymous publications of a suspect nature.... [One] such work was the novel entitled *Les Princesses malabares ou le célibat philosophique,* an allegorical satire on the history of the Catholic church, and particularly on the divisions within France itself, which obviously aimed at undermining the whole basis of the religious tradition. The work was condemned to the fire by the order of the Parlement of 31 December 1734" (160–161). Sheridan then asserts that "on the word of the abbe Goujet the work has been more generally attributed to a certain Louis-Pierre de Longue, who was a member of the Conti household at the time he wrote it" (161). While there may be disagreement as to whether Dufresnoy was the author of *Les Princesses malabares,* there is agreement that it was burned by order of the French Parlement in 1734.

Seven years later, Andre-François Baureau Deslandres' *Pigmalion or the Animated Statue* was burned in France as one of several burned in the eighteenth century because, as Farrer has put it, of their "real or supposed immoral tendency" (17). Peignot also identifies Deslandres' work as one that was "condemned to be burnt by the Parlement of Dijon" (I 101).

In 1748, François-Vincent Toussaint published his *Les Moeurs* which, according to Niklaus, was "one of the earliest expositions of a *morale naturelle* independent of any religious belief or cult. The Parlement of Paris condemned it to be burnt" (263). Farrer lists Toussaint's book as another one of the works burned in the eighteenth century because of their "real or supposed immoral tendency" (16–17). *The New Oxford Companion to Literature in French* entry for Toussaint consists of a short paragraph stating: "French *philosophe* now remembered only for *Les Moeurs* (1748), a work of social and moral criticism at first attributed to Diderot and condemned to be burnt. He took refuge in the Low Countries and then Berlin, working as a journalist and publishing novels" (807).

While these lesser known "lewd, immoral, lascivious" works were being set afire during the middle of the eighteenth century, the writings of a more well-known author, the Marquis de Sade, were burned as the century ended and the nineteenth began. At the outset of her *Must We Burn de Sade?* Simone de Beauvoir points out that Sade's "private journals have been lost, his manuscripts burned — the ten volumes of *The Days of Florbelle,* at the instigation of his own son — his books banned" (9). In 1789, when the Bastille, where de Sade was jailed, was stormed his cell was sacked, "his furniture, his suits and linen, his library and, most important, his manuscripts, [were] burned, pillaged, torn up and carried off'" (Sade 1965 101).

Then in 1807, other Sade manuscripts were burned by the authorities. Now imprisoned at Charenton, Sade's rooms at the asylum were searched for licentious writings which were seized and eventually burned. As Donald Thomas has indicated: "In June 1807, soon after the work [*Days of Florbelle*] was finished, Sade's room at Charenton was raided by the police. They took away a number of manuscripts, including that of *Days at Florbelle*, alleging that they were obscene and blasphemous. The notebooks were added to the official collection of Sade's manuscripts in police custody, some of which dated from the raid on [publisher] Masse's premises in 1801. Sade never saw his work again" (1976 146). Referring to *Days of Florbelle*, Lever states that "This literary monument was taken to the prefecture along with an armful of other notebooks in the same hand. Sade would never see them again: *Les Journées de Florbelle*, as the play later came to be entitled, would be consigned to the flames after his death on orders of prefect Delvau and at the request of his son Claude-Armand, who personally witnessed the auto-da-fe" (525).

As Donald Thomas has put it, Sade's son "endeavoured to restore the family's good name. He went to the Ministry of Justice and requested that such material as *Days of Florbelle* should be burnt. The police agreed, and the notebooks were consigned to the flames in the presence of the anxious nobleman. The same fate overtook other manuscripts of Sade's which Donatier-Claude-Armand [Sade's younger son] discovered in the possession of the Bibliotheque Royale (later the Bibliothèque Nationale)" (146). Frenchmen were warned: "We must lock away the poison, contain the epidemic, and build a pyre of those inflammatory books which destroy the heart's purity" (Harrison 1995 132). One Sade critic Charles Villiers called for the burning of Sade's *Justine:* "Let all decent and respectable people conspire together to destroy as many copies of *Justine* as they can lay their hands upon. For myself, I am going to purchase the three copies which are still at my booksellers and consign them to the fire" (Sade 1965 xviii). Sade had the honor of being perhaps the only author who had his writings taken from him while he was jailed and burned by the authorities and had seen private citizens burning their copies of his works and had a son who requested the police to reduce to ashes his father's notebooks and manuscripts.

At the same time Sade's writings were being burned, one member of the Directory, Louis-Sebastien Mercier, denounced the distribution of obscene works, incorporating into his condemnation the "poison," "garbage," and "foul" metaphors: "Some people display nothing but obscene books whose titles and engravings are equally offensive to decency and good taste. They sell these monstrosities everywhere, along the bridges, at the door of theaters, on the boulevards. The poison is not costly; ten sous the volume.... One could say that these purveyors of brochures are privileged merchants of garbage: they seem to exclude any title that is not foul from their display" (Hunt 312).

Soon after the French burnings of Sade's works, the "crusade" against obscene materials began in the United States, the "crusaders" using the same "poison," "dirty," "disease" metaphors to condemn lascivious, erotic writings. Compared to Europe, the burning of works because of their obscene content came late in the United States. A relevant point is made by Michael Perkins when he writes: "Unlike French erotic writers, American writers had almost no indigenous tradition to draw upon. Until the sixties (1960s) American censors had been so effective that it is only possible to name a few books and note a few trends before exhausting the subject of an American tradition in the genre.... Fearful of censorship, American writers did not write specifically erotic novels. Instead, they attempted to insert bedroom scenes in mainstream novels. Thus the erotic element in twentieth-century American literature is contained in a few passages in a few novels by almost every notable American writer, from Erskine Caldwell through Norman Mailer" (90–91).

The United States had no Christopher Marlowes, John Marstons, Théophiles, or de Sades writing erotic epigrams and books. The best the Americans could do in this regard, in the middle of the nineteenth century, was Walt Whitman's *Leaves of Grass.* In 1856, a year after *Leaves of Grass* was published, the English publication *Saturday Review* suggested that the "obscene" work should be burned: "After every five or six pages ... Mr. Whitman suddenly becomes very intelligible, but exceedingly obscene. If the *Leaves of Grass* should come into anybody's possession, our advice is to throw them immediately behind the fire" (Karolides et al. 387). And that is exactly what John Greenleaf Whittier did. As Haight reports: "Whittier, in a rage of indignation, threw his first edition [of *Leaves of Grass*] into the fire, although he himself had suffered persecution for his abolitionist poems" (52). While *Leaves of Grass* did receive high praise in some quarters, there were strong denunciations labeling the work with the condemnatory metaphors: muck, filth, garbage. In 1856, a review of the book appearing in Boston's *Christian Examiner* asserted that "we are bound in conscience to call it [*Leaves of Grass*] impious and obscene" (Hindus 62). Others saw the book as a "gathering of muck," a "mass of stupid filth"; another asked, "Who is this arrogant man who proclaims himself Poet of Time, and who roots like a pig among the rotten garbage of licentious thought?" (Sweig 266).

When the burning and banning of obscene materials did begin in the United States, the authorities, critics, and private citizen groups devoted most of their time denouncing "smutty," "filthy," and "dirty" periodicals, "girly" magazines and "nudist-nature" publications. Foreign erotic classics were also condemned by anti-vice societies, but often whether such publications should be suppressed was decided in the courts. For example, in 1894, a New York court had to decide whether certain classic works—*Arabian Nights, Tom Jones,* Ovid's *Art of Love,* and Boccaccio's *Decameron*—could be sold for the benefit of the creditors of a receivership. The Society for the Suppression of Vice, established in 1873, sought to prohibit the sale of the "immoral" books, but the court concluded that the works could be sold, the court declaring: "It is very difficult to see upon what theory these world-renowned classics can be regarded as specimens of that pornographic literature which it is the office of the Society for the Suppression of Vice to suppress, or how they can come under any stronger condemnation than that high standard literature which consists of the works of Shakespeare, of Chaucer, of Laurence Sterne, and other great English writers, without making reference to many parts of the Old Testament Scriptures, which are to be found in almost every household in the land.... The works under consideration are the product of the greatest literary genius.... They are not corrupting in their influence upon the young for they are not likely to reach them. I am satisfied that it would be a wanton destruction of property to prohibit the sale by the receiver of these works, —for if their sale ought to be prohibited the books should be burned — but I find no reason in law, morals, or expediency why they should not be sold for the benefit of the creditors of the receivership. The receiver is therefore allowed to sell these volumes" (*In re Worthington* 362–363).

Several years later, the Society for the Suppression of Vice argued in a New York court that the sale of Théophile Gautier's *Mademoiselle de Maupin* constituted a violation of New York's Penal Law which provided that "a person who sells any obscene, lewd, lascivious, indecent, or disgusting book is guilty of a misdemeanor." After citing various sources arguing that the book is "an exquisite work of art," and is not vulgar, the court concluded that it was "for the jury, not for us, to draw the conclusion that must be drawn. Was the book as a whole of a character to justify the reasonable belief that its sale was a violation of the Penal Law? The jury has said that it was not. We cannot say as a matter of law that they might not reach this decision" (*Halsey v. New York Society for Suppression of Vice* 219).

During the late nineteenth century and early twentieth, Anthony Comstock, along with the New York Society for the Suppression of Vice, persistently attempted to suppress obscene materials by metamorphosing them into that which is dreadful, insidious, and dangerous: leprosy, disease, devil. Comstock relied on the fear of leprosy when he wrote: "There seem to be a criminal indifference and recklessness on the part of many writers and publishers as to what results flow from the dissemination of their leprous products"; the distribution of "unclean stories" is a kind of "devil seed-sowing"; dealers selling such "dirty books" are venders of "filth"; then piling one condemnatory metaphor on another, Comstock attacked the obscene "classics": "Garbage smells none the less rank and offensive because deposited in a marble fount or a gold or silver urn. So these foul stories and unclean tales of ancient writers find no justification on the moral world simply because clothed in smooth verse or choice rhetoric. Decaying matter breeds a disease, whether confined in costly receptacles or ash-barrels. So this wretched tainted matter, stolen from ancient writers, which is made to appear to the depraved taste, is equally deadly in it polluting effects" (Comstock 1891 161–167). Comstock titled the 1891 article in which this language appeared "Vampire Literature." Leprous, devil, filth, vampire, pollution — such condemnatory metaphors are less a precise definition of the literature than an invitation to cleanse the land of the publications.

In the 1920s, a "Clean Books" crusade was organized to rid the country of unclean, filthy, poisonous obscene writings, with churches joining in the "crusade." As Boyer has indicated, the Methodists' *Zion's Herald* was one of the church periodicals to strongly advocate censorship; in 1922, it published "an impassioned editorial excoriating postwar fiction as a 'sea of filth' and many recent books as 'literary garbage wagons' fit for 'the jungle and the sty'" (100). Sympathetic letter writers supported the demand for censorship and denounced the obscene writings in the following language: "Go to it. Hit the thing hard. Scorch it with flame — vitriolic acid may reach it"; "We muzzle mad dogs. Why should we give literary charlatans unbridled license to prey upon our people?"; "Books that leave a 'bad taste' for adults should be burned"; "Authors of literary filth ought to have treatment similar to the purveyors of deadly disease germs" (Boyer 101). Ministers supporting the censorship "spoke of 'poison gas' and 'the bubonic plague' in discussing current fiction"; another minister metaphorized the producers of obscene works into "human rats" who had to be dealt with "peremptorily"; finally, like others, a minister suggested the use of fire, expressing "the hope that the *Zion's Herald* editorial would be 'the torch to start a great conflagration'" (Boyer 101).

These calls to rid the land of the "filth, germs, poison, and plague" appeared just as the writings of James Joyce were being burned by the United States Post Office. In 1922, five hundred copies of Joyce's *Ulysses* were set afire by the Post Office; three years earlier, the "filthy" *Ulysses* episodes were reduced to ashes when in 1919 the literary magazine *The Little Review* published installments of *Ulysses* and as a result the magazine was burned by the United States Post Office: "*The Little Review* had serialized about half of Joyce's novel by the time that [John] Sumner, Comstock's successor, struck, but even before that happened, the United States Post Office had seized from the mails and burned three issues of the magazine because of Joyce's 'obscene' prose. The first seizure was in January 1919 (the 'Lestroygonians' episode), the second in May ('Scylla and Charybdis'), and the third in January 1920 ('Cyclops')" (De Grazia 13–14). The publisher of *The Little Review*, Margaret Anderson, said of the burnings of her literary journal: "It was like a burning at the stake as far as I was concerned. The care we had taken to preserve Joyce's text intact; the tears, prayers, hysterics and rages we used on printer, binder, paper houses; the addressing, wrapping,

stamping, mailing; the excitement of anticipating the world's response to the literary masterpiece of our generation.... And then a notice from the Post Office: BURNED" (De Grazia
1992 14).

After the burnings of *The Little Review,* copies of *Ulysses* mailed from France were
burned by the United States Post Office: "A good number of copies sent by ordinary book
post to the U.S.A. got through to their various destinations, but some time between October 1922 ... and December 1922 the U.S.A. censorship authorities evidently became suspicious; copies were held up and accumulated at the U.S.A. post offices until finally 400–500
copies were confiscated and burnt" (Ellman 1959 521). *Ulysses* was set afire also in England,
Ireland, and Canada (Loth 175). In 1923, four hundred ninety nine copies of *Ulysses* were
"seized at Folkestone harbour under the Customs Act of 1867 and burned in 'the King's
Chimney' before Miss Weaver [publisher], who hurried to their rescue, could take any legal
action" (Craig 1962 79). Vanderham also reports that the burnings of *Ulysses* took place in
Canada, England, and Ireland and thus by 1923 *Ulysses* was largely banned in the English-
speaking world" (82–83).

By 1933, however, United States District Court Judge John Woolsey decided in *U.S. v.
One Book Called "Ulysses"* that the book was not obscene and could be admitted into the
country; Woolsey concluded in his now famous opinion: "I am quite aware that owing to
some of its scenes 'Ulysses' is a rather strong draught to ask some sensitive, though normal, persons to take. But my considered opinion, after long reflection, is that, whilst in
many places the effect of 'Ulysses' on the reader undoubtedly is somewhat emetic, nowhere
does it tend to be an aphrodisiac. 'Ulysses' may therefore be admitted into the United
States" (185). One year later, the United States Court of Appeals agreed and concluded its
opinion by stating: "We think that Ulysses is a book of originality and sincerity of treatment and that it has not the effect of promoting lust. Accordingly, it does not fall within
the statute [prohibiting importation of obscene materials], even though it justly may offend
many" (*U.S. v. One Book Entitled Ulysses* 708).

The 1922 burnings of Joyce's *Ulysses* had been preceded ten years earlier with the burning of his *Dubliners.* In a letter dated September 11, 1912, Joyce wrote: "The 1000 copies of
Dubliners which are printed are to be destroyed by fire this morning" (Ellman 319). Several days later, Joyce wrote to W.B. Yeats: "I suppose you will have heard of the fate of my
book *Dubliners.* Roberts refused to publish it and finally agreed to sell me the first edition
for 30 so that I might publish it myself. Then the printer refused to hand over the 1000
copies which he had printed either to me or to anyone else and actually broke up the type
and burned the whole first edition" (Gilbert 71–72). Then again, years later, Joyce wrote in
a letter dated December 19, 1919: "For the publication of *Dubliners* I had to struggle for ten
years. The whole first edition of 1000 copies was burnt at Dublin by fraud; some say it was
the doing of priests, some of enemies, others of the then Viceroy or his consort Countess
Aberdeen" (Gilbert 132).

Three years after *Dubliners* and seven years before *Ulysses* were burned, D.H.
Lawrence's *The Rainbow* was set afire by the English authorities or as one critic put it in
his November 20, 1915, essay on the suppression of the book, "Last Saturday, at Bow Street,
Mr. D.H. Lawrence's new novel *The Rainbow* was brought before the bench and sentenced
to death" (Draper 104). The magistrate, Sir John Dickinson, described the book "as 'utter
filth' and said that he had never read anything more disgusting than this book'" (Draper
105). As reported by de Grazia, "In the *Daily News* Robert Lynd called Lawrence's novel
'windy, tedious, boring, and nauseating' and to boot 'a monstrous wilderness of phallicism'
... The most dangerous notice came from the book critic of the Star. James Douglas: 'These

people are not human beings,' he wrote of *The Rainbow's* characters. 'They are creatures ... immeasurably lower than the lowest animal in the Zoo.' Douglas recommended prosecution, for when literature refuses to 'conform to the ordered laws that govern human society ... it must pay the penalty. The sanitary inspector of literature must notify it and call for its isolation'" (1992 57).

While magistrate Dickinson "agreed with the Solicitor Muskett that the novel was 'just a mass of obscenity of thought, idea, and action throughout,'" there was reason, writes de Grazia, "to suspect, however, that the suppression was related to the wartime atmosphere in England. The book was published in autumn 1915, when the war was not going well.... On the day that *The Rainbow* was ordered burned, Winston Churchill's resignation from the cabinet was announced.... The day's news included a report that not enough unmarried Englishmen had volunteered, and now Lord Derby threatened conscription. Richard Aldington wrote in 1931 that he believed 'the real reason for the attack' on Lawrence's book 'was that he denounced war'" (1992 62).

Others have suggested that while the book's "filth" may have been the reason given for suppressing *The Rainbow,* the magistrate's condemnation of the work may have been based on other matters; Sagar has observed that Dickinson's "son had been killed at the front six weeks earlier. Lawrence was known to be against the war, and to have a German wife. The dedication of *The Rainbow* to Else cannot have helped him. On 15 November *The Times* reported: 'At Bow Street Police Court on Saturday, Mssrs Methuen and Co. [Limited], publishers, Essex Street, Strand, were summoned before Sir John Dickinson to show cause why 1,011 copies of D.H. Lawrence's novel *The Rainbow* should not be destroyed. The defendants expressed regret that the book should have been published, and the magistrate ordered that the copies should be destroyed'" (90). According to Sagar, "The legend is that the confiscated copies were burnt by the public hangman outside the Royal Exchange" (90).

Just as *The Rainbow* was denounced as a "filthy" obscene book because, in part, of the inclusion of references to homosexuality, so too was Radclyffe Hall's "lesbian novel" *The Well of Loneliness* burned thirteen years later. Early in November 1928, the Bow Street Magistrates' Court in London concluded that the *Well of Loneliness* was obscene and ordered it destroyed. The November 17, 1928, *Daily Express* reported: "Two hundred and forty-seven copies of *The Well of Loneliness,* the novel which Mr. James Douglas condemned in the *Sunday Express,* will be flung into the furnace at Scotland Yard to-day" (Brittain 102). Magistrate Chartres Biron declared in his condemnation of the book: "The mere fact that the book deals with unnatural offences between women would not in itself make it an obscene libel. It might even have a strong moral influence. But in the present case there is not one word which suggests that anyone with the horrible tendencies described is in the least degree blameworthy. All the characters are presented as attractive people and put forward with admiration. What is even more serious is that certain acts are described in the most alluring terms" (Brittain 100).

Critic James Douglas, editor of the *Sunday Express* had called for the suppression of *The Well of Loneliness,* just as he had demanded the suppression of Lawrence's *The Rainbow.* In his condemnation of Hall's book, Douglas relied on the usual condemnatory metaphors: pestilence, plague, polluted, contagion, poison:

> In order to prevent the contamination and corruption of English fiction it is the duty of the critic to make it impossible for any other novelist to repeat this outrage....
>
> The consequence is that this pestilence is devastating the younger generation. It is wrecking young lives. It is defiling young souls....

I have seen the plague stalking shamelessly through great social assemblies.... The contagion cannot be escaped....

Perhaps it is a blessing in disguise or a curse in disguise that this novel forced upon our society a disagreeable task which it has hitherto shirked, the task of cleaning itself from the leprosy of these lepers, and making the air clean and wholesome once again....

I would rather give a healthy boy or a healthy girl a phial of prussic acid than this novel. Poison kills the body, but moral poison kills the soul [Brittain 54–57].

Douglas "ended with a demand that the publishers should admit having made a grave mistake, and withdraw the book at once. If they failed to do so, he there and then appealed to the Home Secretary to set the law in motion by instructing the Director of Public Prosecutions to consider whether the book was fit for circulation" (Dickson 149).

The law "was set in motion" and after the Magistrates' Court decided that *The Well of Loneliness* was obscene, "on Friday 14th December, the appeal was heard before Sir Robert Wallace and eleven magistrates sitting at the Quarter Sessions." The verdict was upheld, the court concluding: "The view of this Court, put in a word, is that this is a disgusting book when properly read — a disgusting book — that it is an obscene book and a book prejudicial to the morals of the community. In our view the Order made by the Magistrate was a perfectly correct one and the Appeal will be dismissed" (Dickson 166–167).

While during the first quarter of the twentieth century Americans were conducting their "crusade" against "unclean" books and burning Joyce's "dirty" Ulysses, and the British were reducing to ashes Lawrence's "filthy" *The Rainbow* and Joyce's "leprous" *Ulysses* and *Dubliners,* the Germans were passing "An Act for the Protection of Youth Against Trashy and Smutty Literature" and were setting fire to "trashy" juvenile fiction. The *Schund und Schmutz* bill adopted by the Reichstag provided for "a sort of 'moral censorship' over literature and art" ("German Censorship of 'Literary Trash and Mud'" 28).

Years before the bill was adopted in 1926, German youth groups and churches were campaigning in a "moral crusade" to rid the land of various vices. In her 1922 essay, "The Moral Revolt of Germany's Youth," Lilian Eagle portrayed a positive image of the *Jugenbewegung* which was one of the supporters of the act against trashy and smutty literature; she wrote: "The moral crusade undertaken by the youthful reformers plays an important part in the story of modern reform. The great revolution that followed the World War, instead of proving a cleansing story, has developed more and more into an economic struggle, and as there is no one to protect the young from post-war vices and evils they are determined to do it themselves. Smoking and drinking are tabooed. Shops with unclean postcards and books are boycotted. Flaming protests against immoral performances in theatres and cinemas are posted in all public places.... Even if these efforts have until now remained abortive, they are in a right direction" (Eagle 450–451). The article is illustrated with a photograph of a bonfire of burning books, the caption reading: "Berlin police burning wagon loads of trashy juvenile fiction which school teachers have collected in an effort to suppress the evils of bad literature."

The "Act for the Protection of Youth Against Trashy and Smutty Literature," as Lasker reported in 1927, "had the "backing of the churches, social agencies, organized labor and — a force that does not exist as yet in any other country as an effective political factor — several hundred thousand young people enrolled in self-governing local and national leagues of their own, the so-called Youth Movement. In fact, youth was the originator and the chief protagonist of the measure. Its fight during and since the war [World War I] for moral sanitation inevitably led to a recognition of the evil influences of obscene and trashy literature. Some years ago, when sentiment along this line began to crystallize, the newspapers reported raids on bookshops here and there, and many a cobbled market-place was strangely lit up with a bonfire of collected literary refuse" (622).

Efforts to eradicate the "trash and dirt" included distribution of anti–*Schund* pamphlets and lists of "good books," petitioning the Reichstag, and promoting programs for the *Schundkampfwoche* (Battle against Trashy Literature Week); for example, "The program for the *Schundkampfwoche* in Steele-Ruhr in 1924 included exhibits, lectures, an 'Uraltes Volksgut' (an entertainment described as a remedy for the madnesses of the kitsch-dominated times), and, the piece de resistance, a bonfire on the last evening of the week at which a collection of assorted *Schund* would be symbolically burned" (Stieg 34).

Within a decade, the Nazis provided the world with the most notorious book burnings of the century. While some of the books burned by the Nazis were set afire because they were "un–German," "pacifist," "Jewish," "Marxist," or "subversive," other writings were reduced to ashes because they were "immoral" or "obscene." While the books by Karl Marx, Frederick Engels, Upton Sinclair, Karl Kautsky, Emil Ludwig, Erich Maria Remarque, Lenin, Stalin, Karl Liebknecht, and others were burned in the bonfires all across Germany on May 10, 1933, because they were "socialistic," "pacifist," and "subversive," the books by Theodore Dreiser, Magnus Hirschfeld, and others were burned because they dealt with "low love affairs," homosexuality, and related sexual subjects.

As reported in *The New York Times* on May 11, 1933: "The crusade against the 'un–German spirit,' which has been in progress here [Kiel] for a week, culminated here tonight [May 10] with the public burning of about 2,000 examples of pacifist literature and erotic publications gathered by the students of Kiel University. One of the speakers charged that the Freudian theory undermined the ethics of German sex life and must therefore be stamped out" (12). Lending libraries (private bookstores from which one "rented" a book) became targets of the book burners searching for obscene works being lent by these "literary bordellos." As Hill reports, "On 6 May 'fighting committees' of the two main Nazi student organizations, branches of the Stahlhelm (a right-wing paramilitary organization) at universities, SA troopers, and police collected and seized books from bookstores and especially lending libraries, described by [Nazi librarian official Wolfgang] Hermann, as 'literary bordellos.' His characterization reflected the view of professional librarians that the lending libraries spread a dangerous infection with their immoral, sexually explicit, and trashy books. Some of these books were burned four days later" (14).

Four days before the May 10, 1933, book burnings, the Nazis raided Mangus Hirschfeld's Institute in Berlin gathering books dealing with sexuality, especially homosexuality. As Hill describes: "The Institute studied homosexuality and lesbianism, advocated reform of the criminal code regarding sexuality, prepared briefs for legal cases concerning sexual crimes, and was the first German institution to provide marriage counseling. For three hours the students emptied inkwells onto carpets and broke, or vandalized framed paintings and prints, glass, porcelain, or marble vessels, lights, sculptures, and decorations. They confiscated books, periodicals, photographs, anatomical models, a famous wall tapestry, and a bust of Hirschfeld. After music, speeches, and songs outside at noon they departed but were succeeded at 3:00 P.M. by SA men, who removed 10,000 books from the institute's library. A few days later they carried the bust of Hirschfeld on a pole in a torchlight parade before throwing it on the bonfire with the books from the institute" (15).

English-American author Christopher Isherwood presented much the same account of the Nazi raid on Hirschfeld's institute and the burning of the books: "On May 6, the Institute was raided by a party of about a hundred students. They arrived in trucks, early in the morning, playing a brass band.... They smashed the doors down and rushed into the building. They spent the morning pouring ink over carpets and manuscripts and loading their trucks with books from the Institute's library, including many which had nothing to do with sex: historical works, art journals, etc. In the afternoon, a troop of S.A. men arrived and made a more careful search, evidently knowing what they were looking for.... A few days after the raid, the seized books and papers were publicly burned, along with a bust of Hirschfeld, on the square in front of the Opera House" (128–129). The Nazis then "formally deprived Hirschfeld of his German citizenship. He was living in Nice and planning to reopen the Institute there. But he died before he could do so, on May 15, 1935" (Isherwood 129).

During the same decade the Nazis were burning "un–German," "pacifist," "filthy" books, a massive number of obscene-erotic books were being burned in the United States. As Gertzman has indicated, "Raids engineered by John Sumner [Comstock's successor as Secretary of the New York Society for the Suppression of Vice] during 1935 led to the seizure and burning of $150,000 worth of erotic books and photographs, as well as the plates from which the books were printed. In mid–March Police Commissioner Valentine announced that twenty-five thousand volumes, when burned in the steam-heated headquarters, would produce two days' supply of heat, saving sixty dollars on the department's coal bill. Sumner made his first appearance of this kind of event in November of that year and helped janitorial staff stoke up the fire as cameras flashed.... Indeed, these sorts of book burnings were fairly common in the 1930s" (135). The photograph picturing Sumner throwing the "filthy" publications into the furnace appeared in the *New York Journal American* with the caption: "Obscene Tomes Fed to Police Bonfire." In describing the photograph, Gertzman writes: "Sumner (center, wearing hat) aiding workmen burn pornographic magazines, pamphlets, postcards, and lending-library sex-pulp novels in the furnace of police headquarters. He and two workmen are holding copies of *Jack Ketch the Hangman*" (136).

When in 1939 John Steinbeck's *Grapes of Wrath* was being set afire in California, Illinois, and Oklahoma, the book was denounced not only as "un–American" and "subversive," but also as "filthy," "vile propaganda," and "false sensationalism" (*Look* 15). Steinbeck's novel was condemned especially by large agricultural, anti-labor interests in California who objected to both the "obscenity" in the book and the portrayal of the migrant workers as being mistreated and living in misery and poverty. The president of the Associated Farmers of Kern County, California, denounced the obscenity in the book: "We are angry ... because we were attacked by a book obscene in the extreme sense of the word.... It is so filthy for you to point out its vile propaganda.... Americans have the right to say what they please, but they do not have the right to attack a community in such words that any red-blooded American would refuse to allow his daughter to read them" (*Look* 15).

The fiery annihilation of obscene books continued in the United States into the second half of the twentieth century. In 1953, the public burning in New Jersey of obscene books, films, and photographs was reminiscent of Savanarola's fifteenth century bonfire of the vanities. As reported in *The New York Times*, "More than $100,000 worth of salacious movies, photographs and books went up in flames here today [March 7, 1953] in a demonstration staged by the Newark police and fire departments to 'bring home the menace of pornography.' Forty clergymen, civic leaders and presidents of the Parent-Teachers Associations were guests at the burning, which took place on the municipal dock at the foot of Center Street. Public Safety Director John B. Keenan touched off the blaze, saying, 'I believe it a good idea to show that this stuff was actually destroyed.' Into the fire went 80,000 feet of eight- and sixteen-millimeter film, some in sound and color; 40,000 lewd photographs, 720 colored still negatives used for screen projection, fifty-nine decks of playing cards with lascivious pictures on the back, and fifty-seven books, completely pornographic in language and illustrated with obscene photographs" ("Lewd Seizures Burned" 72).

When in 1973, copies of *Slaughterhouse-Five* were burned in the furnace at North Dakota's Drake High School, the Vonnegut work was condemned not only because it was an "unpatriotic" book, but also because it contained "obscene and vulgar" language and "four letter words." When three years later, *Slaughterhouse-Five* was banned in two high schools in Long Island, New York, the book was condemned along with several other works labeled "anti–American, anti–Catholic, anti–Semitic, and just plain filthy." When this censorship case reached the United States Supreme Court in 1982, some of the "filthy" language that had been condemned by the school board banning such books as *Soul on Ice,* *Go Ask Alice,* and *The Fixer,* was listed by Justice Lewis Powell in an Appendix accompanying his dissenting opinion; Justice Powell included in his listing the "vulgar" language appearing in *Slaughterhouse-Five;* also listed were some "anti–Christian" passages from Vonnegut's novel dealing with the absurdities and tragedies of war. Among the passages cited by Justice Powell were: "Get out of the road, you dumb motherfucker. The last word was still a novelty in the speech of white people in 1944. It was fresh and astonishing to Billy, who had never fucked anybody.... But the Gospels actually taught this: Before you kill somebody, make absolutely sure he isn't well connected.... The flaw in the Christ stories, said the visitor from outer space, was that Christ who didn't look like much, was actually the son of the Most Powerful Being in the Universe. Readers understood that, so, when they came to the crucifixion, they naturally thought ... Oh boy — they sure picked the wrong guy to lynch this time! And that thought had a brother: There are right people to lynch. People not well connected.... The visitor from outer space made a gift to Earth of a new Gospel. In it, Jesus really WAS a nobody, and a pain in the neck to a lot of people with better connections than he had.... Why don't you go fuck yourself? Don't think I haven't tried.... He was going to have revenge, and that revenge was sweet ... It's the sweetest thing there is, said Lazaro. People fuck with me, he said, and Jesus Christ are they ever fucking sorry" (*Board of Education v. Pico* 898–903). While this was the type of "vulgar" language that had thrust *Slaughterhouse-Five* into the school furnace in North Dakota in 1973, the United States Supreme Court ten years later, in a five to four decision, decided against the New York school board that had removed the books from the school library shelves.

In February 1977, the Ku Klux Klan of South Carolina protested the inclusion of John Steinbeck's *Of Mice and Men* and Margaret Walker's *Jubilee* in the school libraries, the Klan asserting that the books included profanity and descriptions of sexual relations. One of the Klan leaders declared: "We ask [everyone], regardless of race, color, creed or political or religious beliefs to stop this means of educating our young.... These books should be destroyed, burnt" (*Newsletter on Intellectual Freedom* May 1977 73). This February 1977 suggestion that *Of Mice and Men* be set afire was put into effect in August 1977 in Oil City, Pennsylvania. The novel by Steinbeck, one of the literary works most often banned in the schools, came under attack in Oil City, with a school board member stating he was "definitely in favor of having the book removed, because of the vulgarity and profanity contained in the book"; the school board "voted six to two to ban the book. According to an employee of the school district, most copies of the work were burned" (*Newsletter on Intellectual Freedom* November 1977 155).

Besides burning the classic works *Ulysses, Grapes of Wrath* and *Slaughterhouse-Five,* Americans were setting fire to less classic writings—comic books. For example, as reported by Wright: "On December 10, 1948, the students of St. Patrick's Parochial School in Binghamton, New York, achieved brief notoriety. Under the auspices of their proud teachers and parents, the students gathered some two thousand comic books into a pile in the school courtyard and torched them. Community leaders staged the event as part of their movement to boycott comic books that 'stressed crime and sex.' Elsewhere in New York, the Bishop of the Albany Catholic Diocese urged all Catholics to boycott dealers who sold comic books with 'sensational details' of crime and sex. Similar comic book bonfires followed at the Peter and Paul Parochial School in Auburn, New York, and at the St. Cyril's Parish School in Chicago" (86).

Fredric Wertham's influential anti–comic book work *Seduction of the Innocent,* in addition to condemning the violence portrayed in the comics, denounced the erotic nature of some of these "perverted" publications being purchased by the youth. Wertham warned: "The short circuit which connects violence with sex is a primitive pattern slumbering in all people. It can easily be released in children if it is drilled into them early enough and long enough. It is to these primitive layers of the undeveloped mind, to this weak spot, that comic books appeal" (179). In the section of the book devoted to a discussion and description of how "comic books stimulate children sexually," Wertham finds it necessary to state: "To describe the morbid aspects of sex as purveyed in stories which have no artistic justification may sound obscene. But it can hardly be objected to in this book for adults since it is the common subject matter of what we give children to read" (174). He then proceeds to give examples of comic book portrayals of women's "headlights," legs, and buttocks and portrayals arousing fear in girls; further, Wertham warns of the homoerotic nature of the comic books: "Just as ordinary crime comic books contribute to the fixation of violent and hostile patterns by suggesting definite forms for their expression, so the Batman type of story helps to fixate homoerotic tendencies by suggesting the form of an adolescent-with-adult or Ganymede-Zeus type of love-relationship" (190).

This concern that comics portray homosexuality sympathetically is expressed by Wertham when he devotes two pages to Batman and Robin's relationship; in part, he writes: "Either Batman or his young boy friend or both are captured, threatened with every imaginable weapon, almost blown to bits, almost crushed to death, almost annihilated. Sometimes Batman ends up in bed injured and young Robin is shown sitting next to him. At home they lead an idyllic life.... They live in sumptuous quarters, with beautiful flowers in large vases, and have a butler, Alfred. Batman is sometimes shown in a dressing gown.... It is like a wish dream of two homosexuals living together. Sometimes they are shown on a couch, Bruce reclining and Dick sitting next to him, jacket off, collar open, and his hand on his friend's arm" (190).

The significance of *Seduction of the Innocent* on comic book bannings and burnings is referred to by Martin Barker: "How could it come about that a man of wide intellect and understanding ... has ended up being remembered for a book which, more than almost any other one can think of, acted as the intellectual justification for a series of censorious laws ... and even book burnings?" (216). Pointing out that Wertham did not criticize the comic book burners, Barker writes: "Nor did he speak out against the book burnings that particularly erupted in 1948–49, at the time of his first well-publicized attacks on the comics. Yet, as a Jew who wrote extensively on the cultural paranoia of Nazism in Germany, should not he have thought of the parallels with the Nazis' organized book burnings?" (217).

Before the century was over, more Savanarola-type bonfires of vanities were reducing to ashes "immoral" books, records, and tapes in various American towns. For example, in 1981, "students at Omaha Christian School watched January 29 as their principal set fire to a pile of books that he labeled distractions which could 'hinder Christian lives.' Thrown into the flames were Batman and Daffy Duck comic books, *National Geographic,* a record album jacket of the defunct rock group The Animals, and a book called *50 True Tales of Terror*. The Rev. Lars Wessberg, principal of the school, said his action was 'symbolic' and that the burned materials had been contributed voluntarily by students. As the books burned, Wessberg read from the Book of Acts: 'And not a few of them that practiced magical arts brought their books together and burned them in the sight of all'" (*Newsletter on Intellectual Freedom* March 1981 42).

Similarly, four months later, Elvis Presley and Willie Nelson recordings were burned in Gastonia, North Carolina, along with other tapes and records and *The Living Bible*. As reported in the *Newsletter on Intellectual Freedom:* "A new twist has been added to the minor epidemic of ritual burnings of Rock music album jackets, currently sweeping churches and church schools in the Midwest and South. Along with Elvis Presley and Willie Nelson, about 150 students at Temple Christian school in Gastonia burned copies of *The Living Bible*. A new and modernized translation of the scriptures, *The Living Bible* has been criticized by fundamentalists as a dangerous corruption of the word of God. School principal Ed Deneve called the book 'a perverted commentary of the King James Version. It's basically somebody's paraphrases.' Deneve also argued that Rock music 'appeals to the flesh' and forces students into immoral activities. 'It causes alcohol and drug problems. It all leads to that, and Rock 'n' Roll is the starter.' In addition to records, tapes, and bibles, the students burned T-shirts and posters promoting popular music heroes" (July 1981 105).

Twelve years later, two books dealing with homosexuality were set afire in Kansas City, Missouri: Nancy Garden's *Annie on My Mind* and Frank Mosca's *All-American Boys*. The former is a novel about two high school girls who develop a lesbian relationship and the latter with a gay relationship between two teen-age boys. The books were burned just as the Kansas City board of education was debating whether to maintain *Annie on My Mind* in the school libraries: "In Kansas City, Missouri, although protesters burned copies of the books [*Annie on My Mind* and *All-American Boys*] on the steps of district headquarters, the district deemed the books acceptable and they are available in all high school libraries" (*Newsletter on Intellectual Freedom* March 1994 52).

While during the second half of the twentieth century Americans were setting fire to the "filthy," "obscene," and "immoral" *Slaughterhouse-Five*, *Of Mice and Men*, records, tapes, and comic books, authorities in other countries were burning some well known works condemned as "sexually exploitative" and "obscene." For example, in Ireland, Edna O'Brien's first book, *The Country Girls*, published in 1960, was burned in her hometown under the supervision of the parish priest. In 1984, *The Paris Review* published an interview with O'Brien in which she was asked: "Is that why they had an auto-da-fé of your first novel in your native village?" She answered: "It was a humble event, as befits a backward place. Two or three people had gone to Limerick and bought *The Country Girls*. The parish priest asked them to hand in the books, which they did, and he burnt them on the grounds of the church. Nevertheless a lot of people read it. My mother was very harsh about it; she thought it was a disgrace. That is the sadness" (O'Brien 1984 40). O'Brien was then asked: "After that small auto-da-fe, did anything else of that kind happened?" She responded: "They used to ban my books, but now when I go there, people are courteous to my face, though rather slanderous behind my back" (40).

In her 1992 essay about O'Brien, Molly McQuade briefly referred to the banning of O'Brien's books and the "ritual burning" of *The Country Girls:* "Despite her mother's known antipathy for books, O'Brien dedicated *The Country Girls* to her. After her mother's death, the writer found a copy of the novel hidden away in her mother's house, with the dedication page ripped out and the rest heavily — perhaps angrily — emended in black ink. Ireland seemed to share Mrs. O'Brien's doubts about the author. *The Country Girls* was banned (so were O'Brien's next six books); the novel's relative candor about women, sex, and religion was considered shocking, and inspired a 'ritual burning' of the book in O'Brien's hometown" (201).

In a 1995 appearance in San Francisco, O'Brien again spoke of the banning and burning of her book: "My first book, 'The Country Girls,' was a simple little tale of two girls who were trying to burst out of their gym frocks and their convent, and their own lives in their own houses, to make it to the big city. It angered a lot of people, including my own family. It was banned; it was called a smear on Irish womanhood. A priest in our parish asked from the altar if anyone who had bought copies would bring them to the chapel grounds. That evening there was a little burning. My mother said women fainted, and I said maybe it was the smoke" (1 *http://www.salon.com/02dec* 1995/departments/litchat.html).

In 1985, the classic *A Thousand and One Nights* was ordered by Egyptian authorities to be burned. In August 1985, *The Index on Censorship* reported: "On 23 April, a judge ruled that a 150-year-old version of *A Thousand and One Nights* was pornographic and ordered it to be seized. The public prosecutor demanded the book be 'burned in a public place' and said that it was the cause of 'a wave of incidents of rape which the country has recently experienced'" (51). Two months later, the *Index* reported: "An Egyptian court has ordered the confiscation of the unexpurgated original edition of *1001 Nights* on the grounds that the 1000 year old Arabic classic posed a threat to the country's morals.... The uncensored version of the book, which is a collection of such stories as 'Ali Baba and the 40 Thieves' and 'Aladdin and his Magic Lamp' was ruled obscene" (October 1985 65).

Four years later, another classic, Henry Miller's *Tropic of Capricorn,* was set afire in Turkey. As reported in the *Newsletter on Intellectual Freedom* in May 1989: "Almost twenty-five years after U.S. censorship of his *Tropic of Capricorn* finally was lifted, Henry Miller's 1939 novel is still a target of the censor. An appeals court in Turkey this winter authorized a public burning of the book as sexually exploitative. Likewise consigned to the flames was *Sudaki Iz* [Shadow on the Water] by popular Istanbul writer Ahmet Altan" (90).

While the obscene books have been set afire because they are seen as obscene, the "dirty," "smutty," and "poisonous" works have been condemned as subversive and threats to the secular and religious authorities. On the surface obscene materials are burned because they lead to "immoral thoughts," arouse "dirty" sexual desires, or encourage "lascivious" images. However, the "leprous," "demonic," "filthy" writings are, at another level seen by fundamentalists, religious and secular, as threats to society, to the stability of government. As Lynn Hunt has pointed out, "From the days of [Pietro] Aretino in the sixteenth century, pornography was clearly linked with political and religious subversion" (35).

When Émile Zola's "obscene" *La Terre* was published in 1887, the book was denounced in England as a threat to the stability of the nation and there were demands that the book be expurgated and banned. One English publication declared: "Zolaism is a disease. It is a study of the putrid. No one can read Zola without moral contamination" (Grazia 1992 43). One member of Parliament asserted that Zola's work was "destroying the whole national life": "Are we to sit still while the country is wholly corrupted by literature of this kind? Are we to wait until the moral fibre of the English race is eaten out, as that of the French is almost? Look what such literature has done for France! It overspread that country like a torrent, and its poison is destroying the whole nation life" (Grazia 1992 43).

Well into the twentieth century, obscene works continued to be condemned as undermining the nation. In 1959, United States Postmaster General Arthur Summerfield, drawing on the now familiar metaphors, saw the pornographic works as leading to a "breakdown of order and decency in this country": "What is likely to happen if we do not rid ourselves of this social cancer? ... The undermining of the moral fiber of the nation's children will spread; with the poisoning of increasing millions of minds. Sex crimes will be a spreading blight on our society, and will become far more prevalent than they are today. And overall, we could expect an ultimate breakdown of order and decency in this country" (Kilpatrick 239). Thus pornography became a political issue since the "cancer" and "poison" contributed to the "breakdown of order in this country."

At the outset of his 1960 work titled *The Smut Peddlers,* Kilpatrick, stated: "There is a social evil in commercial pornography, and I am sympathetic toward the effort to combat it" (v). Mixing his metaphors, Kilpatrick, labels the obscene works "filth," "smut," "dirt," "narcotics," and "sewage." This follows his proclamation in the Foreword that he has "approached the conflict not as a partisan but as a sort of war correspondent" (v). He then proceeds to present his "not as a partisan" approach with the persistent use of the condemnatory metaphors "dirt" and "filth"; "filth" appears at least seven times in the first twelve pages of the book. And finally, the last three words of *The Smut Peddlers* are "merchants of filth" (293). Kilpatrick provided some examples of what he considered pornographic "dirt": "This is the world of paperback pornography; on beyond it, in a realm to be discussed later, lie such erotica as *Fanny Hill,* the memoirs of Frank Harris, and the purulent draining that poured from Henry Miller in *Tropic of Cancer* and *Tropic of Capricorn.* The paperbacks have nothing to do with Ovid, or with Mark Twain, or with Benjamin Franklin, or with any of the works beloved of scholars. This is dirt. This is the sort of pornography D.H. Lawrence denounced so long ago — dirt for dirt's sake, cheap dirt, illiterate dirt, dirt that smells of defecated intelligence, dirt with one excuse for being only — it sells" (33).

The persistent, unrelenting use of such condemnatory metaphors — dirt, filth, poison, sewage, infection, pestilence — to identify and define "obscene" books is misleadingly harmful when determining whether a literary work should be banned and set afire. It has been, however, such language that has contributed to the burnings of "obscene" works now considered classics, from Boccaccio's *Decameron* to Walt Whitman's *Leaves of Grass,* from D.H. Lawrence's *The Rainbow* to James Joyce's *Ulysses,* from John Steinbeck's *Grapes of Wrath* to Radclyffe Hall's *The Well of Loneliness.*

CONCLUSION

Having been immersed in the tragic history of the burnings of books, and sometimes their authors, it strikes one that the indignities, inhumanities, tragedies, and violence have not been captured in the fictional treatments of book burning. One cannot help but conclude that truth has been more enlightening and stranger than fiction. Fictional accounts in short stories, plays, novels, and poetry have fallen short in conveying the atavism, barbarity, and fanaticism of the book burners and fallen short in conveying the fears and cruel punishments of authors whose writings have been blacklisted, banned, burned.

Very seldom has fiction captured the barbarity accompanying the burning of books in China in 213 B.C.E., with hundreds of nonconformist intellectuals being buried alive in trenches; or the tragedy of setting afire in 1240 in Paris twenty wagon-loads of the Talmud and other Hebrew books; or the prolonged punishment of Servetus, having been first found guilty by a civil court for his heretical and immoral life and then tried again by an ecclesiastical court after his death, with a burning of his effigy along with his books; or the brutality of the hanging and quartering of William Thomas in 1554 at the time his *Historie of Italie* was burned, followed with the placing of his head upon London Bridge; or the degradation and indignities imposed on Giordano Bruno—accusations of heresy, the degrading command to recant, the excommunication, the public burning of his book, his death at the stake in 1600; or the violence suffered by William Prynne when his *Histromastix* was burned in 1637 and he was placed in the pillory and his ears cut off and he was branded on both cheeks with the letters S.L. (Schismatical Libeller); or the fanaticism and barbarity of the Nazi book burnings in 1933; or the fear and hysteria leading to book burnings in the United States, reducing to ashes such classics at *Ulysses, Grapes of Wrath,* and *Slaughterhouse-Five;* or the cruelty of the Ayatollah Khomeini's fatwa ordering the killing of Salman Rushdie for the publication of his *The Satanic Verses* which was set afire in 1989 in two English cities; or the religious hatred and fear when in Africa in 2000 Muslims burned Christian works and the Christians retaliated by burning Muslim writings. All this hatred, fear, brutality, atavism — the horror and enormity of the bibliocausts— somehow have not been conveyed successfully in the fictional, satiric, futurist treatments of book burnings.

In the seventeenth century, Cervantes devoted a chapter in *Don Quixote* to the burning of Don Quixote's books because they were seen as contributing to his "nonsensical actions." Don Quixote's niece states: "I should have advised your Worships of my uncle's nonsensical actions so that you could have done something about it by burning those damnable books of his before things came to such a pass; for he has many that ought to be burned as if they were heretics." Whereupon, the priest replied: "I agree with you ... and before tomorrow's sun has set there shall be a public auto-da-fe, and those works shall be condemned to the flames that they may not lead some other who reads them to follow the example of my good friend" (Cervantes 50).

While one may conclude that a detestable book burning is to take place, the rationale for the fiery destruction is to protect a man from committing "nonsensical actions." Of course, there is present the church's, participation in the book burning which in itself is a "nonsensical action," considering the titles chosen to be condemned to the flames. Further, the books have been personified when the niece identified them as "if they were heretics." It should be noted that the seriousness and malice involved in setting the books afire depends to some degree on which of the translations one reads. Some translations have Don Quixote's niece referring to those "damnable books" whereas other translations have her referring to those "unchristian books" and still other translations have her speaking of "these excommunicated books." Further, in one translation the priest declares that "there shall be a public auto-da-fé" while other translations have the priest referring to condemning the books to "the flames." Clearly, the language choice has some impact on how ominous and malicious the book burning is. It is one thing to have a combination of "unchristian books" or "excommunicated books," and "auto-da-fé": it is something else to have a combination of "damnable books" and "condemned to the flames." As despicable as the book burnings may be in this instance, the satiric, comedic context of burning the books to protect Don Quixote from "nonsensical actions" does not fully convey the maliciousness and stupidity of reducing Don Quixote's books to ashes.

In the nineteenth century, Nathaniel Hawthorne devoted his 1844 "Earth's Holocaust" to an auto-da-fé which included the burning of magazines, newspapers, garments, liquor, documents, and finally books. Hawthorne begins his satiric short story with: "Once upon a time — but whether in the time past or time to come, is a matter of little or no moment — this wide world had become so overburdened with an accumulation of worn-out trumpery, that the inhabitants determined to rid themselves of it by a general bonfire" (Hawthorne 362). After the garments, liquor, boxes of tea, legal documents were reduced to ashes, the books were thrown into the bonfire, a bystander exclaiming: "Now we shall have a glorious blaze!" Whereupon a frantic book-seller exclaims: "But what is to become of the Trade?" To which the a bystander replies: "Oh, by all means, let them accompany their merchandize.... It will be a noble funeral pile!" Since the literary works of the past were no longer needed, "a thorough and searching investigation had swept the booksellers' shops, hawkers' stands, public and private libraries, and even the little book-shelf by the country fireside, and had brought the world's entire mass of printed paper, bound or in sheets, to swell the already mountain-bulk of our illustrious bonfire. Thick, heavy folios, containing the labors of lexicographers, commentators, and encyclopedists, were flung in, and, falling among the embers with a leaden thump, smouldered away to ashes, like rotten wood." The books by French, German, and English writers were flung into the fire:

> The small, richly gilt French tomes of the last age, with the hundred volumes of Voltaire among them, went off in a brilliant shower of sparkles, and little jets of flame; while the current literature of the same nation burnt red and blue, and threw an infernal light over the visages of the spectators, converting them all to the aspect of parti-colored fiends. A collection of German stories emitted a scent of brimstone. The English standard authors made excellent fuel, generally exhibiting the properties of sound oak logs ... Milton's works, in particular, sent up a powerful blaze.... From Shakespeare there gushed a flame of such marvelous splendor that men shaded their eyes as against the sun's meridian glory.

While Milton's works "sent up a powerful blaze" and Shakespeare's works "gushed a flame of such marvelous splendor," the writings of the French, such as Voltaire, "threw an infernal light" and the writings of the Germans "emitted a scent of brimstone." In Hawthorne's parable the French and German literature appear to be less worthy, having been identified with hell and damnation, which perhaps deserves to be burned.

As to the burning of religious symbols, the narrator declares: "To my astonishment, the persons who now advanced into the vacant space around the mountain fire, bore surplices and other priestly garments, with which it seemed their purpose to consummate the great Act of Faith." Onto the fire spectators threw crosses, pulpits, and other religious objects. The narrator then states: "Yet I felt that these were but the externals of religion, and might most safely be relinquished by spirits that best knew their deep significance." However, when the Bible was thrown into the flames, the pages, "instead of being blackened into tinder, only assumed a more dazzling whiteness as the finger-marks of human imperfection were purified away. Certain marginal notes and commentaries, it is true, yielded to the intensity of the fiery test, but without detriment to the smallest syllable that had flamed from the pen of inspiration." While Hawthorne appears to be less concerned about the burning of the "externals of religion," he has the Holy Scripture not yielding "to the intensity of the fiery test."

To the "book-worm" who lamented the fiery destruction of the books, the narrator replies: "Is not Nature better than a book?— is not the human heart deeper than any system of philosophy?— is not life replete with more instruction than past observers have found it possible to write down in maxims? Be of good cheer." In the end, in the last paragraph, Hawthorne writes: "The heart — the heart — there was the little yet boundless sphere, wherein existed the original wrong, of which the crime and misery of the outward world were merely types. Purify that inward sphere.... But if we go no deeper than the Intellect, and strive, with merely that feeble instrument, to discern and rectify what is wrong, our whole accomplishment will be a dream; so unsubstantial, that it matters little whether the bonfire, which I have so faithfully described, were what we choose to call a real event, and a flame that would scorch the finger — or only a phosphoric radiance, and a parable of my own brain!"

In Hawthorne's "Earth Holocaust" it does not appear that we get a general condemnation of book burnings. After all, it is not through the Intellect, but through the heart, not through the books of the "book-worm" that we will "rectify what is wrong." Jorge Luis Borges has written: "One of Hawthorne's parables which was almost masterly, but not quite, because a preoccupation with ethics mars it, is 'Earth's Holocaust'" (57). Regarding the "heart — the heart" passage in the last paragraph of the parable, Borges has stated: "Here Hawthorne has allowed himself to be influenced by the Christian, specifically Calvinist, doctrine of the inborn depravation of mankind and does not appear to have noticed that his parable of an illusory destruction of all things can have a philosophical as well as moral interpretation" (58). Similarly Leverenz has observed: "'Earth's Holocaust,' Hawthorne's Bonfire of the Vanities fails where 'The Celestial Railroad' succeeds, partly because it satirizes social reform with a more profoundly uneasy skittishness of tone about the literary marketplace. Yoking tall tale to apocalypse, it swerves to a grotesquely sentimentalized closure celebrating a holy text uncontaminated by readers' fingerprints" (119). In the end, when one has finished reading this parable dealing with a Savonarola-like auto-da-fé in the United States, one does not leave with a sense that this fictional work is a strong indictment of the senseless, hysterical, dangerous fiery destruction of books.

A century later, Sinclair Lewis published *It Can't Happen Here*, a satiric warning of fascism coming to the United States: the arrests of authors, the fear of expressing unorthodox ideas, concentration camps, people "carried off 'under protective arrest,'" citizens "taken away for questioning and not released for weeks, months," and book burnings. The works of such authors as Emerson, Twain, Thoreau, Marx, Shaw, and Tolstoy are prohibited. Vermont newspaper publisher Doremus Jessup, a central character in the novel, removes from his library any books which could be considered radical: "*Das Kapital* and Veblen and all the Russian novels and even Sumner's *Folkways* and Freud's *Civilization and Its Discontents*; Thoreau and other hoary scoundrels..., old files of the *Nation* and *New Republic*" (Lewis 245–246).

Lewis devotes three pages, in a four hundred page novel, to the actual book burning and one gets the impression that this fiery destruction of books is just "another" episode and hence there is an undercutting of the ramifications and horror of the event. Jessup's "thirty-four-volume extra-illustrated edition of Dickens" are confiscated by government officials and Jessup "could not have stayed away from the book-burning. It was like seeing for the last time the face of a dead friend." Among the books thrown into the bonfire were Jessup's own *Martin Chuzzlewit* and he "saw *Alice in Wonderland* and *Omar Khayyam* and Shelley and *The Man Who Was Thursday* and *A Farewell to Arms* burning together, to the greater glory of the Dictator and the greater enlightenment of his people." One can assume that this brief 1935 treatment of a book burning in "fascist" America was partly modeled on the 1933 Nazi book burnings. However, the enormity, the inhumanity of the Nazi book burnings is not captured in *It Can't Happen Here*. Admittedly, Lewis' work is a satire; but a satire must somehow convey the stupidity, barbarity, and serious ramifications of what is being satirized. The book burning in *It Can't Happen Here* is a "feeble" event compared to Lewis' other more poignant, graphic episodes that are part of life in "fascist" America.

During World War II, the Writers' War Board, composed of "writers whose job it is to effect a wartime liaison between government departments and thousands of American writers who wish to help the war effort with their talents" (Bénet v) decided that "May tenth should be commemorated by us in our own way, by a challenge to those [Nazis] who burned the books [on May 10, 1933]. The Board, in co-operation with the Council of Books in Wartime, which is a group of citizens connected with publishing and writing, asked Stephen Vincent Bénet to lend his luminous talents to this end" (Bénet vi). Bénet wrote a radio play titled *They Burned the Books* which was nationally broadcast on May 11, 1942. The cast of characters included a Narrator, a Nazi Voice, Heinrich Heine, Friedrich Schiller, Mark Twain, John Milton, Victor Hugo, and Walt Whitman.

At the outset of the dramatic work, the Narrator states:

Nine! Nine iron years of terror and evil!
Nine years since a fire was lighted in a public square in Berlin.
Nine years since the burning of the books! Do you remember?
Write it down in your calendars, May 10th, 1933. And write it down in red by the light of fire.
[*Crackle of flames, not too big*]
These are people who work by fire.
The Reichstag went up in flames that February
And in March they got their majority and moved in,
The storm-troopers, the heroes of the beer-hall Putsch,
They are all dead and forgotten:
Darius the Persian, Attila the Hun, Alaric the Goth —
All "dust, forgotten dust."

The play ends with the Narrator declaring:

We are waiting, Adolf Hitler.
The books are waiting, Adolf Hitler.
The fire is waiting, Adolf Hitler.
The Lord God of Hosts is waiting, Adolf Hitler.
[*Music up to climax*]
(CURTAIN)

Commendable as it may have been for the American wartime propagandists to attack the Nazi book burners, the play still remained propaganda. It was more an attack on the evil enemy Nazis than on the ritualistic book burning auto-da-fe. Obviously, in such a propagandistic dramatization there was no mention of the book burnings that had been taking place in the first half of the twentieth century in other countries, much less in the United States. To have condemned the practice of book burning would have involved condemning some of our allies and ourselves. As a result, Bénet's *They Burned the Books* lost most of its ethos as a serious work of literature; it lost most of its universality and timelessness.

Ten years later, Ray Bradbury published his dystopian *Fahrenheit 451*, the only novel devoted almost entirely to the subject of book burning. When the book was published in 1953, McCarthyism had led to the banning and burning of some "subversive" books in U.S. overseas libraries and President Eisenhower warned his Dartmouth College audience: "Don't join the book burners." Bradbury's futuristic satire is directed, writes David Mogen, "not at American ideals but at simplistic perversions of them, as well as at the American innocence that assumes totalitarianism can't happen here. However, horror at Hitler inspired the book's original conception, that to burn books is to burn people: 'When Hitler burned a book I felt it as keenly, please forgive me, as burning a human, for in the long sum of history they are one and the same flesh.' And though Hitler is defeated, and McCarthy's era finished, they will always have successors who will keep the firemen at work" (107)— the firemen, in this case, spraying kerosene from their hoses to burn prohibited books. In the end, fireman Guy Montag rebels against this fiery destruction of books, escapes the dictatorial state to an exiled group of people who have taken on the task of memorizing books so that they will not be entirely eliminated. Each member of the group memorized the writings of a particular author; upon arrival Montag is introduced: "I want you to meet Jonathan Swift, the author of that evil political book, *Gulliver's Travels*! And this other fellow is Charles Darwin, and this one is Schopenhauer, and this one is Einstein, and this one here at by elbow is Mr. Albert Schweitzer, a very kind philosopher indeed. Here we all are, Montag, Aristophanes and Mahatma Gandhi and Gautama Buddha and Confucius and Thomas Love Peacock and Thomas Jefferson and Mr. Lincoln, if you please. We are also Matthew, Mark, Luke, and John."

In the world of *Fahrenheit 451* the burning of books is a job performed by firemen, paid to rush to sites, homes, not to put out fires, but to start fires to incinerate the books. While the novel is a warning against tyranny, conformity, and book burning, the sci-fi treatment of book burnings falls short of capturing the participants' attraction to the atavistic, malicious, celebratory fiery violence that is part of the historical and contemporary book burnings.

Shorter literary references to book burnings have appeared in such classic works as Ibsen's *Hedda Gabler* and Orwell's *1984*. Ibsen has Hedda jealously burning the irreplaceable book manuscript of her onetime lover Eilbert Lovborg who is now a competitor with her husband, George Tesman, for a professional position. The manuscript becomes even more important to Hedda when she learns that Mrs. Elvsted (Thea) has worked closely with Lovborg on the preparation of the manuscript. During a visit to "Mademoiselle Diana's parlors" and an encounter with the police, Lovborg loses the manuscript which he pretends he had torn up, devastating Mrs. Elvsted who declares, within hearing of Hedda, "Do you know, Eilert, this thing you've done with the book—for the rest of my life it will seem to me as if you'd killed a little child." Lovborg replies: "You're right, It was like murdering a child." In reality, Tesman has found the lost manuscript and has brought it home where Hedda has locked it in a writing table drawer. At the end of Act Three, out of jealousy and revenge Hedda throws the manuscript sheets into the burning stove and whispers to herself: "Now I'm burning your child, Thea! You, with your curly hair! (*Throwing another sheaf in the stove.*) Your child and Eilert Lovborg's. (*Throwing in the rest.*) Now I'm burning — I'm burning the child."

Hedda's burning of the manuscript is spiteful, dreadful, and tragic; the hate and tragedy is magnified when she personifies the book by whispering, "I'm burning your child." As with book burnings generally, this manuscript burning is rife with symbolism; obviously, more is being incinerated than the manuscript paper pages. Personifying the manuscript into "the child" and burning it transforms the burning of paper pages into something much more devastating. This burning of a human being, "the baby," is simply a variation of Inquisitors burning the "silent heretic." As Milton saw it, to destroy a book was a "kind of homicide."

In a more politically oriented book burning, Orwell briefly refers in *1984* to the "memory holes" into which were sent writings "to be devoured by the flames." In his dystopia, Orwell has Winston Smith working at the Ministry of Truth which housed the "memory holes": "When one knew that any document was due for destruction, or even when one saw a scrap of waste paper lying about, it was an automatic action to lift the flap of the nearest memory hole and drop it in, whereupon it would be whirled away on a current of warm air to the enormous furnaces which were hidden somewhere in the recesses of the building." Winston's job involved a kind of rewriting of history, requiring him to send down the memory hole various writings that did not jibe with official pronouncements and history: "As soon as Winston had dealt with each of the messages, he clipped his speakwritten corrections to the appropriate copy of the *Times* and pushed them into the pneumatic tube. Then, with a movement which was as nearly as possible unconscious, he crumpled up the original message and any notes that he himself had made, and dropped them into the memory hole to be devoured by the flames.... This process of continuous alteration was applied not only to newspapers, but to books, periodicals, pamphlets, posters, leaflets, films, sound tracks, cartoons, photographs— to every kind of literature or documentation which might conceivably hold any political or ideological significance." The incineration of documents, books, and periodicals was a means of destroying memory and history: "All history was a palimpsest, scraped clean and reinscribed exactly as often was necessary. In no case would it have been possible, once the deed was done, to prove that any falsification had taken place" (Orwell 36–37). While the memory hole and the fiery destruction of books, periodicals, and photographs are crucial in the world of *1984,* the barbarity, atavism, and inhumanity of book burnings are not conveyed in the few paragraphs devoted to the mechanized memory hole.

Through the centuries, church and secular authorities have burned books as a means of obtaining and sustaining power by eradicating a history unacceptable to them. In his discussion of censorship, including book burnings, in ancient China, Goodrich has observed that "it is reasonable to suppose, nearly every dynasty has meddled with the records of the ruling house before it" (3). In the sixteenth century, Mayan books and idols were set afire by Spanish invaders and inquisitors attempting to eradicate the Mayan religious-cultural heritage. The Spaniards collected "all the books and ancient writings which the Indians had and in order to erase all the danger and memory of their ancient rites, as many as they were able to find were burned publicly on the day of the auto and at the same time with these (were destroyed) the history of their antiquities" (Tozzer 78). When anti-labor representatives and conservative Americans burned John Steinbeck's *The Grapes of Wrath* they were, in effect, attempting to destroy his history of the mistreatment and dismal working conditions of the farm workers in the west. When the Nazis burned the works of Freud and

Remarque's *All Quiet on the Western Front,* they were intent on depriving the German population of a history unacceptable to the Nazis; one way to cleanse the land of the Jewish-pacifist culture was to burn it. Freud's books were thrown into the bonfires as bystanders heard the Nazis proclaim: "Sigmund Freud—for falsifying our history and degrading its great figures!" Propaganda Minister Joseph Goebbels told the assembled crowd that the book burners had a right to "clean up the debris of the past."

As the twentieth century ended, the book burners continued in their efforts to destroy and rewrite history by incinerating over a million books. During the "ethnic cleansing" that was taking place in the old Yugoslavia, close to two million books were burned in 1992 when the Serbs, dropping incendiary grenades, set fire to Bosnia's National and University Library.

The burning of the library and the books within "is widely considered the largest single act of book burning in modern history" (Bollag A40). The fiery destruction of the books and library containing thousands of rare Muslim and Jewish writings was not simply "collateral damage" that sometimes comes with wartime. In his 1995 article titled "Erasing the Past: The Destruction of Libraries and Archives in Bosnia-Herzegovina," Riedlmayer has pointed out that while the "library was targeted, adjacent buildings stand intact to this day" (7). The library was not a military threat to the Serbs and yet it was specifically targeted; as Bollag has indicated, "the destruction appears to have been part of a wider policy of attacks aimed at erasing Bosnia's multi-ethnic cultural heritage. Across the country, Serbian and sometimes Croatian forces attacked libraries, archives, and houses of worship" (A38). This "largest single act of book burning in modern history" destroyed part of a history; the memories preserved in the books were incinerated.

While the book burners' intent in this case was to erase a cultural-ethnic history, the burning of *any* book—heretical, seditious, obscene—constitutes the destruction of history, for the book is a preserved "record," for better or worse, of memory, the heretical, subversive, obscene, poisonous, cancerous, leprous, dirty, pestilent book included. The book burning becomes especially indefensible when an entire library of a million and a half books is reduced to ashes in one single "bonfire."

The book burners of the twentieth and twenty-first centuries have not been much different from their fellow book burners of centuries past. As the twentieth century ended and the twenty-first began, Christians and Muslims were burning each other's books, Hindus and Muslims were setting fire to each other's writings, Muslim and Jewish works were being reduced to ashes, the Chinese were burning decadent literature, Indonesians were setting fire to works "promoting communism," Egyptians were burning *1001 Nights,* the Turks were burning *Tropic of Capricorn.* As in earlier centuries, the condemned "silent heretics," the "poisonous" pages, the "filthy" fictions have continued to be reduced to ashes by bibliophobes burning books.

BIBLIOGRAPHY

Adler, E.N. "Auto-da-fé and Jews." *The Jewish Quarterly* 13 (1901): 392–437.

Akrigg, G.P. *Jacobean Pageant.* Cambridge, Mass.: Harvard University Press, 1962.

Alden, Raymond. *The Rise of Formal Satire in England.* Hamden, Conn.: Anchor Books, 1961.

Aldington, Richard (trans.). *The Fifteen Joys of Marriage.* London: George Routledge and Sons, n.d.

Alegría, Claribel. "Clash of Cultures." *Index on Censorship* 15 (Sept. 1986): 28–30.

American Libraries 33 (Feb. 2002): 19.

American Library Association Bulletin 35

Ananikian, Mardiros. "Armenian." In *The Mythology of All Races.* Ed. John McCulloch. Vol. 7. Boston: Marshall Jones Co., 1925.

Anastos, Milton. "Porphyry's Attack on the Bible." In *The Classical Tradition.* Ed. Luitpold Wallach. Ithaca, N.Y.: Cornell University Press, 1966. 421–450.

Anaya, Rudolfo. "Take the Tortillas Out of Your Poetry." In *Censored Books: Critical Viewpoints.* Eds. Nicholas Karolides, Lee Buress and John Kean. Metuchen, N.J.: Scarecrow Press, 1993. 25–31.

Andersson, Christiane. "The Censorship of Images in Reformation Germany, 1520–1560." In *Suspended License: Censorship and the Visual Arts.* Ed. Elizabeth C. Childs. Seattle: University of Washington Press, 1997. 32–58.

Andrews, Wayne. *Voltaire.* New York: New Directions Book, 1981.

Arciniegas, German. *Latin America: A Cultural History.* Trans. Joan MacLean. New York: Alfred A. Knopf, 1967.

Article 19 Report, Information Freedom and Censorship. Chicago: American Library Association, 1991

Articles of Impeachment, Exhibited Against Dr. Henry Sacheverell. London, 1710.

Asgill, John. *An Argument Proving, That According to the Covenant of Eternal Life revealed in the Scriptures, Man may be translated from hence into that Eternal Life, without passing through Death, altho the Humane Nature of Christ himself could not be thus translated until he had passed through Death.* London, 1703.

Aspe, Maria-Paz. "Spanish Spirituality's Mid-Sixteenth Century Change of Course." In *The Spanish Inquisition and the Inquisitorial Mind.* Ed. Angel Alcala. Boulder, Colo.: Social Science Monographs, 1987. 421–430.

Augustine, Saint. *Basic Writings of Saint Augustine.* Ed. Whitney Oates. Vol. II. New York: Random House, 1948.

_____. *The Works of Saint Augustine.* Ed. John Rotelle. Vol. 1. Brooklyn: New City Press, 1990.

Avedon, John. *In Exile from the Land of Snows.* New York: Alfred A. Knopf, 1984.

Ayer, Joseph. *A Source Book for Ancient Church History.* New York: Charles Scribner's Sons, 1924.

Babeuf, Gracchus. *The Defence of Gracchus Babeuf Before the High Court of Vendome.* Trans. John A. Scott. Amherst: University of Massachusetts Press, 1967.

Backesheider, Paula R. *Daniel Defoe: His Life.* Baltimore: Johns Hopkins University Press, 1989.

Baddeley, Clair. *Charles III of Naples and Urban VI.* London: William Heinemann, 1894.

Baets, Antoon de. *Censorship of Historical Thought.* Westport, Conn.: Greenwood Press, 2002.

Bainton, Roland. *Hunted Heretic: The Life and Death of Michael Servetus, 1511–1553.* Boston: Beacon Press, 1960.

Bakeless, John. *The Tragical History of Christopher Marlowe.* Vol. II. Cambridge, Mass.: Harvard University Press, 1942.

Baker, J. *Complete History of the Inquisition in Portugal, Italy, the East and West Indies in All Its Branches from the Origin of It in the Year 1163, to Its Present State.* Westminster, 1736.

Bangs, Carl. O. "Arminius and Socinianism." In *Socinianism and Its Role in the Culture of XVIth to XVIIth Centuries.* Ed. Lech Szczucki. Warsaw: PWN-Polish Scientific Publisher, 1983. 81–84.

Baraheni, Reza. "The Perils of Publishing." *Index on Censorship* 7 (Sept./Oct. 1978): 2–17.

Barbour, Philippe. "Breton Language and Culture." In *Censorship: A World Encyclopedia.* Ed. Derek Jones. Vol. I. London: Fitzroy Dearborn, 2001. 294–297.

Barker, Martin. "Frederick Wertham — The Sad

Case of the Unhappy Humanist." In *Pulp Demons*. Ed. John A. Lent. Madison, N.J.: Fairleigh Dickinson University Press, 1999. 215–233.

Barnes, Timothy. *Constantine and Eusebius*. Cambridge, Mass.: Harvard University Press, 1981.

Barnouin, Barbara, and Yu Changgen. *Ten Years of Turbulence*. London: Kegan Paul International, 1993.

Bart, B.F. "Aspects of the Comic in Pulci and Rabelais." *Modern Language Quarterly* 11 (June 1950): 156–163.

Baudot, Georges. *Utopia and History in Mexico: The First Chroniclers of Mexican Civilization, 1520–1569*. Trans. Bernard Ortiz de Montellano and Thelma Ortiz de Montellano. Niwot: University Press of Colorado, 1995.

Beardsley, Monroe. *Thinking Straight*. 2nd ed. Englewood Cliffs, N.J.: Prentice Hall, 1956,

Beauvoir, Simone de. *Must We Burn de Sade?* Trans. Annette Michelson. London: Peter Nevill, 1953.

Beisel, Nicola. *Imperiled Innocents*. Princeton: Princeton University Press, 1997.

Benét, Stephen Vincent. *They Burned the Books*. New York: Farrar and Rinehart, 1942.

Bennett, Verona. "Eastern Promise." *London Times* August 4, 2001: 20c.

Besig v. United States. 208 F.2d 142 (1953).

Besterman, Theodore, ed. *The Complete Works of Voltaire* (Voltaire). Toronto: University of Toronto Press, 1968.

_____.*Voltaire*. Chicago: University of Chicago Press, 1976.

Bett, Henry. *Johannes Scotus Erigena: A Study of Mediaeval Philosophy*. Cambridge: Cambridge University Press, 1925.

Birchall, Fredrick. "Nazi Bookburning Fails to Stir Berlin." *New York Times* May 11, 1933: 12.

Blades, William. *The Enemies of Books*. London, 1888.

Blumenthal. Walter. "American Book Collector." American Book Burnings 6 (Summer, 1956): 13–19.

Board of Education v. Pica. 457 U.S. 853 (1982).

Boas, Frederick. *Christopher Marlow: A Biographical and Critical Study*. Oxford: Clarendon Press, 1940.

Boas, Ralph, and Louise Boas. *Cotton Mather: Keeper of the Puritan Conscience*. Harper and Brothers, 1928.

Bobrick, Benson. *Wide as the Waters*. New York: Simon and Schuster, 2001.

Bocanegra, Mathías de. *Jews and the Inquisition of Mexico: The Great Auto da Fé of 1649*. Trans. Seymour B. Lieberman. Lawrence, Kans.: Coronado Press, 1974.

Boccaccio. Giovanni. *The Life of Dante*. Trans. James R. Smith. In *Yale Studies in English*. Vol. X. New York: Henry Holt, 1901.

Bodde, Derk. *China's First Unifier*. Leiden: E.J. Brill, 1938.

Bodin, Jean. *Six Books of the Commonwealth*. Trans. M.J. Tooley. Oxford: Basil Blackwell, 1955.

Bollag, Burton. "Barely Salvaged in Sarajevo." *The Chronicle of Higher Education* August 15, 2003: A40.

Bonet-Maury, G. "Berquin, Louis de." *The New Schaff-Herzog Encyclopedia of Religious Knowledge*. Ed. Samuel M. Jackson. Vol. II New York: Funk and Wagnalls Co., 1908.

Borges, Charles, and Helmut Feldmann, eds. *Goa and Portugal: Their Cultural Links*. New Delhi: Concept Publishing, 1977.

Borges, Jorge Luis. *Other Inquisitions, 1937–1952*. Trans. Ruth L.C. Simms. Austin: University of Texas Press, 1964.

Borin, Jacqueline. "Embers of the Soul: The Destruction of Jewish Books and Libraries in Poland During World War II." *Libraries and Culture* 28 (Fall 1993): 445–460.

Bosmajian, Haig. *The Language of Oppression*. Lanham, Md.: University Press of America, 1983.

Boulton, James T., ed. *Daniel Defoe*. London: B.T. Batsford, 1965.

Boyer, Paul S. *Purity in Print*. New York: Charles Scribner's Sons, 1968.

Bradbury, Ray. *Fahrenheit 451*. New York: Ballantine Books, 1996.

Brandes, George. *Voltaire*. Vol. II. New York: Tudor Publishing, 1930.

Brittain, Vera. *Radclyffe Hall: A Case Study of Obscenity?* London: Femina Books, 1968.

Brower, Keith, Earl Fitz, Enrique Martinez-Vidal. *Jorge Amado: New Critical Essays*. New York: Routledge, 2001.

Brown, Harold. *Heresies*. Garden City, N.Y.: Doubleday, 1984.

Brown, Heywood, and Margaret Leech. *Anthony Comstock*. New York: Albert and Charles Boni, 1927.

Brown, Horatio. *The Venetian Printing Press*. New York: G.P. Putnam's Sons, 1891.

Buck, Pearl, trans. *All Men Are Brothers* (Shui Hu Chuan). New York: John Da, 1933.

Burkert, Walter. *Greek Religion*. Trans. John Raffan. Cambridge, Mass.: Harvard University Press, 1985.

Burnet, John. *Greek Philosophy: Thales to Plato*. London: Macmillan, 1955.

Burr, David. *Olivi and Franciscan Poverty*. Philadelphia: University of Pennsylvania Press, 1989.

_____. *The Persecution of Peter Olivi*. Philadelphia: The American Philosophical Society, 1976.

Burr, George. *Narratives of the Witchcraft Cases*. New York: Charles Scribner's Sons, 1914.

Burstyn v. Wilson, 343 U.S. 495 (1952).

Bury, J.B. *A History of Freedom of Thought*. London: Oxford University Press, 1952.

_____. *History of the Later Roman Empire*. London: Macmillan, 1923.

Buzas, Ladislaus. *German Library History: 800–1945.* Trans. William D. Boyd. Jefferson, N.C.: McFarland, 1986.

Caistor, Nick. "Cleansing the Teaching Area." *Index on Censorship* 7 (May/June 1978): 18–24.

The Cambridge Ancient History. Eds. J.B. Bury, S.A. Cook, F.E. Adcock. New York: Macmillan, 1927.

Cameron, Keith. *Agrippa D'Aubigne.* Boston: Twayne Publishers, 1997.

Campbell, W.E. *Erasmus, Tyndale and More.* London: Eyre and Spottisoode, 1949.

Capp, Bernard. *English Almanacs, 1500–1800.* Ithaca, N.Y.: Cornell University Press, 1979.

Carlebach, Elisheva. *The Pursuit of Heresy.* New York: Columbia University Press, 1990.

Carmilly-Weinberger, Moshe. *Censorship and Freedom of Expression in Jewish History.* New York: Sepher-Hermon Press, 1977.

Catholic Encyclopedia. Ed. Charles Herberman. Vol. VI. New York: The Encyclopedia Press, 1913.

Censorship. Editor in Chief, Dawn P. Dawson. Vols. 1 and 3. Pasadena, Calif.: Salem Press, 1997.

Cervantes, Miguel de. *Don Quixote.* Trans. Samuel Putnam. New York: Viking Press, 1949.

Chamberlain, Bobby J. *Jorge Amado.* Boston: Twayne Publishers, 1990.

Chandler, Peleg. *American Criminal Trials.* Boston: Timothy H. Carter, 1844.

Chang, Jung. *Wild Swans.* New York: Simon and Schuster, 1991.

Chase, Mary Jane. "Cathedrals: The Continent." *The Oxford Encyclopedia of the Reformation.* Ed. Hans J. Hillerbrand. Vol. I. New York: Oxford University Press, 1996. 282–284.

Chavkin, Samuel. *Storm Over Chile.* Westport, Conn.: Lawrence Hill, 1985.

Chicago Sun Times. November 14, 1973: 40.

Choedon, Dhondub. *Life in the Red Flag People's Commune.* New Delhi: Model Press, 1978.

Christie, Richard. *Etienne Dolet: The Martyr of the Renaissance.* London: Macmillan, 1899.

Chung, Henry. *The Case of Korea.* New York: Fleming H. Revell, 1921.

Cicero. *The Nature of the Gods.* Trans. P.G. Walsh. Oxford: Clarendon Press, 1997.

Clifton, Charles. "Arnold or Brescia." *Encyclopedia of Heresies and Heretics.* Santa Barbara: ABC-CLIO, 1992. 15–16.

Clodd, Edward. *The Story of the Alphabet.* New York: McClure, Phillips, 1904.

Clyde, William M. *The Struggle for the Freedom of the Press: From Caxton to Cromwell.* New York: Burt Franklin, 1970.

Coats, Catharine R. *Subverting the System: D'Aubigne and Calvinists.* Kirkville, Mo.: Sixteenth Century Journal Publishers, 1990.

Cobbett's Parliamentary History of England. Vol. VI. London: T.C. Hansard, 1810.

Cohen, Norman. *The Pursuit of the Millennium.* London: Seeker and Warburg, 1957.

Cohen, Paul. "The Anti-Christian Tradition in China." *The Journal of Asian Studies* 20 (Feb. 1961): 169–180.

Cole, John R. *Pascal: The Man and His Two Loves.* New York: New York University Press, 1995.

Commonwealth of Pennsylvania v. Sharpless. 2 Sergo & R. 91 (1815). In Edward de Grazia. *Censorship Landmarks.* New York: R.R. Bowker, 1969.

Comstock, Anthony. "Vampire Literature." *The North American Review.* Ed. Lloyd Bryce. 153 (Aug. 1891): 160–171.

Conroy, Peter V. *Jean-Jacques Rousseau.* New York: Twayne Publishers, 1998.

Contreras, Jaime. "The Impact of Protestantism in Spain." In *Inquisition and Society in Early Modern Europe.* Trans. Stephen Haliczer. London: Croom Helm, 1987. 47–63.

A Copie of the First Arrest or Decree of the Parlament of Paris, Against the Booke of Santarellus the Jesuit. London, 1634.

Coward, William. *Second Thoughts Concerning the Human Soul.* London, 1702.

Craig, Alec. *The Banned Books of England and Other Countries.* London: George Allen and Unwin, 1962.

Craig, Mary. *Tears of Blood: A Cry for Tibet.* Washington, D.C.: Counterpoint, 1999.

Cramer, F.H. "Book Burning and Censorship in Ancient Rome." *Journal of the History of Ideas* 6 (April 1945): 157–196.

Cranston, Maurice. *The Solitary Self.* Chicago: University of Chicago Press, 1997.

Crawford, William R. *A Century of Latin-American Thought.* Cambridge, Mass.: Harvard University Press, 1944.

Crespo, Virgilio Pinto. "Thought Control in Spain." In *Inquisition and Society in Early Modern Europe.* Trans. Stephen Haliczer. London: Croom Helm 1987. 171–188.

Crocker, Lester. *Embattled Philosopher.* London: Neville Spearman, 1955.

Croke, Brian. "Porphyry's Anti-Christian Chronology." *Journal of Theological Studies* 14 (April 1983): 168–185.

Cross, F.L., ed. *The Oxford Dictionary of the Christian Church.* Oxford: Oxford University Press, 1997.

Crowley, Francis. *Voltaire's Poème sur la loi naturelle.* Berkeley: University of California Press, 1938.

Cumming, Ian. *Helvetius.* London: Routledge and Kegan Paul, 1955.

Cundha, T.B. *Goa's Freedom Struggle.* Bombay: New Age Printing Press, 1961.

Cuthbertson, David. *The Tragedy of the Reformation.* Edinburgh: Oliphant, Anderson and Ferrier, 1912.

Dahl, Svend. *History of the Book.* New York: Scarecrow Press, 1958.

Dante Alighieri. *On World Government (De Monarchia).* Trans. Herbert W. Schneider. Indianapolis: Babbs-Merrill, 1967.

_____. *The Portable Dante.* Ed. Mark Musa. New York: Penguin Books, 1995.

De Grazia, Edward. *Censorship Landmarks.* New York: R.R. Bowker, 1969.

_____. *Girls Lean Back Everywhere: The Law of Obscenity and the Assault on Genius.* New York: Random House, 1992.

DeJean, Joan. "The Politics of Pornography: L'Ecole des Filles." In *The Invention of Pornography.* Ed. Lynn Hunt. New York: Zone Books, 1993. 109–123.

Delgado, Morris. "Uruguay: Against Reason." *Index on Censorship* 8 (Jan/Feb 1979): 49–51.

Deuel, Leo. *Conquistadors Without Swords.* New York: St. Martin's Press, 1967.

Dickinson, Emily. *The Complete Poems of Emily Dickinson.* Ed. Thomas H. Johnson. Boston: Little, Brown, 1960.

Dickson, Lovat. *Radcliffe Hall at the Well of Loneliness.* New York: Charles Scribner's Sons, 1975.

Dictionary of National Biography. Volumes 1, 4, 5, 7, 17, 19, 21. Eds. Leslie Stephen and Sidney Lee. New York: Macmillan, 1908, 1909.

Diefendorf, Barbara. *Beneath the Cross: Catholic and Huguenots in Sixteenth Century Paris.* New York: Oxford University Press, 1991.

Dieguez, Diego. "Spain's Golden Silence." *Index on Censorship* 2 (Spring 1973): 91–99.

Dio. *Dio's Roman History.* Trans. Earnest Cary. Vol. 7. Book 57. London: William Beinemann, 1955.

Ditchfield, P.H. *Books Fatal to Their Authors.* New York: Burt Franklin, 1910.

Dodds, E.R. *The Greeks and the Irrational.* Berkeley: University of California Press, 1951

Donnet, Pierre-Antoine. *Tibet: Survival in Question.* Trans. Tica Broch. Delhi, India: Oxford University Press, 1994.

Draper, R.P., ed. *D.H. Lawrence: The Critical Heritage.* New York: Barnes and Noble, 1970.

Drogin, Marc. *Biblioclasm.* Savage, Md.: Rowman & Littlefield, 1989.

Drummond, William. *The Life of Michael Servetus.* London: John Chapman, 1948.

D'Souza, Bento Graciano. *Goan Society in Transition.* Bombay: Popular Prakashan, 1975.

Dudbridge, Glen. *Lost Books of Medieval China.* London: British Library, 2000.

Dunin, Janusz. "The Tragic Fate of Polish Libraries After 1939." *Solanus* 10 (1996): 5–12.

Duniway, A. *The Development of Freedom of the Press in Massachusetts.* Cambridge, Mass.: Harvard University Press, 1906.

Durant, Will. *The Life of Greece.* New York: Simon and Schuster, 1939.

Duyvendak, J.J.L., trans. *The Book of Lord Shang* (Yang Shang). London: Arthur Probsthain, 1928.

Eagle, Lilian. "The Moral Revolt of Germany's Youth." *Current History* 16 (June 1922): 447–451.

Eaton, Clement. "Censorship of the Southern Mails." *American Historical Review* 48 (Jan. 1943): 266–280.

The Economist 359 (May 26, 2001): 40–41.

Eliot, Charles. *Hinduism and Buddhism.* Vol. 3. London: Edward Arnold, 1921.

Eliot, George. *Middlemarch.* Boston: Houghton Mifflin, 1956.

Ellman, Richard. *James Joyce.* New York: Oxford University Press, 1959.

Encyclopædia Britannica. 14th ed. Vol. 2. London: The Encyclopædia Britannica Co., 1937.

_____. 11th ed. Vol. 3. Cambridge: Cambridge University Press, 1910.

Engel v. Vitale. 370 U.S. 421 (1962).

Epiphanius of Salamis. *The Panarion of Epiphanius of Salamis.* Trans. Frank Williams. Leiden: E.J. Brill, 1994.

Epperson v. Arkansas. 393 U.S. 97 (1968).

Erlanger, Rachel. *The Unarmed Prophet: Savonarola in Florence.* New York: McGraw-Hill, 1988.

Ernst, Morris. *To the Pure: A Study of Obscenity and the Censor.* New York: Viking Press, 1928.

Eusebius. *The Ecclesiastical History.* Trans. J.E.L. Oulton. Cambridge, Mass.: Harvard Press, 1957.

Faison, Seth. "China's Crackdown on Sect More Talk than Action." *New York Times.* August 6, 1999: A8.

_____. "The Followers of Chinese Sect Defend Its Spiritual Gods." *New York Times.* June 30, 1999: A4.

Farrer, James. *Books Condemned to Be Burnt.* London: Elliot Stock, 1892.

Febvre, Lucien, and Henri-Jean Martin. *The Coming of the Book.* Trans. David Gerard. London: N.L.B., 1976.

Fellows, Otis. *Diderot.* Boston: Twayne Publishers, 1989.

Fichtenau, Heinrich. *Heretics and Scholars in the High Middle Ages, 1000–1200.* Trans. Denise Kaiser. University Park: The Pennsylvania State University Press, 1998.

Fichter, Joseph. *Man of Spain: Francis Suarez.* New York: Macmillan, 1940.

Field, Eugene. *Love Affair of a Bibliomaniac.* New York: C. Scribner's Sons, 1916.

Filler, Louis. *The Crusade Against Slavery, 1830–1860.* New York: Harper and Row, 1960.

Fisher, John. *The English Works of John Fisher.* Ed. John E.B. Mayor. Part I. London: Trubner, 1876.

Fitzgerald, Brian. *Daniel Defoe: A Study in Conflict.* London: Seeker and Warburg, 1954.

Flahiff, G.B. "Ecclesiastical Censorship of Books in the Twelfth Century." *Mediaeval Studies* 4 (1942): 1–22.

Florida. R.E. "Voltaire and the Socinians." In *Studies on Voltaire and the Eighteenth Century.* Banbury: Oxfordshire, 1974.

Foe, Anna. *The Jews of Europe After the Black Plague.* Trans. Andrea Grover. Berkeley: University of California Press, 2000.

Forbes, Clarence. "Books for the Burning." *Transactions and Proceedings of the American Philogi-*

cal Association. Vol. 67. Ed. L. Arnold Post. Haverford, Pa.:. American Philological Association, 1936. 114–125.

"A Forgotten Hero of Slavery Days." *The Literary Digest* 38 (April 3, 1909): 569–570.

Foster, David W. *Handbook of Latin American Literature*. 2nd ed. New York: Garland, 1992.

Fox, P. "The Reformation of Poland." In *The Cambridge History of Poland*. Eds. W.F. Reddaway, J.H. Person, O. Halecki. Vol. 1. Cambridge: Cambridge University Press, 1950.

Foxe, John. *The Acts and Monuments of John Foxe*. Vols. 3, 5 and 8. London: R. B. Seeley and W. Burnside, 1837, 1838, 1839.

Fragnito, Gigliola. *Church, Censorship and Culture in Early Modern Italy*. Ed. Gigliola Fragnito. Trans. Adrian Belton. Cambridge: Cambridge University Press, 2001.

Fraina, Louis, ed. *The Proletarian Revolution in Russia*. New York: Communist Press, 1918.

Francesco, Grete de. *The Power of the Charlatan*. New Haven: Yale University Press, 1939.

Frantz, Douglas. "Breaking Old Soviet Ties, Letter by Letter." *New York Times* Sept. 2, 2001: 8.

Frazer, James. G. *The Golden Bough*. Vols. 1, 9, 10. New York: Macmillan, 1935.

Freke, William. *A Dialogue by Way of Question*. London, 1693.

Friedenthal, Richard. *Goethe: His Life and Times*. London: Wiedenfeld and Nicolson, 1963.

Friedman, Jerome. *Michael Servetus: A Case Study in Total Heresy*. Geneva: Droz, 1978.

Friedman, Philip. "The Fate of the Jewish Book During the Nazi Era." In *Jewish Book Annual*. New York: Jewish Book Council, 1997. 81–94.

Friedman, Thomas. "Heard Any Good Jews Lately?" In G. Goshgarian. *Exploring Language*. 8th ed. New York: Addison-Wesley, 1998.

Friedman, Yvonne. "Anti-Talmudic Invective from Peter the Venerable to Nicholas Donin (1144–144)." In *Le Brûlement du Talmud à Paris*. Ed. René-Samuel Sirat. Paris: Les Editions Du Cerf, 1999. 171–189.

Fuller, Thomas. *Church History of Britain: From the Birth of Jesus Christ Until the Year 1648*. Vol. 3. Oxford: Oxford University Press, 1845.

Fulton, John F. *Michael Servetus: Humanist and Martyr*. New York: Herbert Reichner, 1953.

Furbank, P.N. *Diderot: A Critical Biography*. London: Seeker and Warburg, 1992.

Garden, Nancy. *Annie on My Mind*. New York: Farrar, Straus, Giroux, 1982.

Gardner, Alice. *Studies in John the Scot*. London: Oxford University Press, 1900.

Garraty, A., and Mark C. Carnes, eds. *American National Biography*. New York: Oxford University Press, 1999.

Garrison, Wendell, and Francis Garrison. *William Lloyd Garrison, 1805–1879*. Vols. 3 and 4. Boston: Houghton, Mifflin, 1894.

Gaudiani, Claire Lynn. *The Cabaret Poetry of Théophile de Viau*. Turbingen: Gunter Narr Verlag, 1981.

Gebhart, Emile. *Mystics and Heretics in Italy at the End of the Middles Ages*. Trans. Edward Hulme. London: George Allen and Unwin, 1922.

George I of Great Britain. *By the King: A Proclamation*. London, 1660.

Gelb, I.J. *A Study of Writing: The Foundations of Grammatology*. Chicago: University of Chicago Press, 1952.

"German Censorship of 'Literary Trash and Mud.'" *Literary Digest* 92 (Jan. 22, 1927): 28.

Gernet, Jacques. *China and the Christian Impact*. Trans. Janet Lloyd. Cambridge: Cambridge University Press, 1985.

Gershenson, Daniel, and Daniel Greenberg. *Anaxagoras and the Birth of Physics*. New York: Blaisdell, 1964.

Gertzman, Jay A. *Bootleggers and Smuthounds: The Trade in Erotica, 1920–1940*. Philadelphia: University of Pennsylvania Press, 1999.

Gibson, Margaret. *Lanfrance of Bee*. Oxford: Clarendon Press, 1978.

Gilbert, Benjamin. "The Life and Writings of Hinton Rowan Helper." *Register of the Kentucky Historical Society* 53 (January 1955): 58-75.

Gilbert, Stuart, ed. *Letters of James Joyce*. New York: Viking Press, 1957.

Gilchrist, John. "The Perception of Jews in the Cannon Law in the Period of the First Two Crusades." *Jewish History* 3 (Spring 1988): 9–24.

Gillett, Charles. *Burned Books*. New York: Columbia University Press, 1932.

Gillett, E.H. *The Life and Times of John Hus*. Vol. 3. 2nd ed. Boston: Gould and Lincoln, 1864.

Gilmont, Jean-François. "The Border Cities: Antwerp, Strasbourg and Basle." In *The Reformation and the Book*. Ed. Jean-François Gilmont. Aldershot, England: Ashgate Publishing, 1998. 10–20.

Given, James. *Inquisition and Medieval Society*. Ithaca: Cornell University Press, 1997.

Glasse, Cyril. *The New Encyclopedia of Islam*. Walnut Creek: Altamira Press, 2001.

Golden, Samuel. *Jean LeClerc*. New York: Twayne Publishers, 1972.

Goldstone, Lawrence, and Nancy Goldstone. *Out of the Flames*. New York: Broadway Books, 2002.

Goodrich, Luther C. *The Literary Inquisition of Ch'ien-Lung*. Baltimore: Waverly Press, 1935.

Goody, Jack. "Restricted Literacy in Northern Ghana." In *Literacy in Traditional Societies*. Ed. Jack Goody. Cambridge: Cambridge University Press, 1968. 199–264.

G.P. Putnam's Sons v. Calissi. 205 A.2d 913 (1964).

Graetz, H. *History of the Jews*. Vol. 4. Philadelphia: Jewish Publication Society, 1894.

Graham-Yooll, Andrew. "Letter from Argentina." *Index on Censorship* 2 (Summer, 1973): 43–45.

_____ . *The Press in Argentina, 1973–1978.* London: Writers and Scholars Educational Trust, 1979.

_____ . "Twisting the Rules in Argentina." *Index on Censorship* 5 (Winter 1976): 26–30.

Graubard, Mark. *Astrology and Alchemy: Two Fossil Sciences.* New York: Philosophical Library, 1953.

Grayzel, S. Oman. *The Church and the Jews in the XIIIth Century.* New York: Hermon Press, 1966.

Green, F.C. *Jean-Jacques Rousseau: A Critical Study of His Life and Writings.* Cambridge: The University Press, 1955.

Green, Larry. "School Book Protest a Burning Issue." *Los Angeles Times.* June 3, 1978: 1.

Green, V.H.H. *Bishop Reginald Pecock.* Cambridge: Cambridge University Press, 1945.

Greenaway, George W. *Arnold of Brescia.* Cambridge: Cambridge University Press, 1931.

Greenleaf, Richard. "Pastor's Potter Book Fire Inflames N. Mexico Town." *American Libraries* 33 (Feb. 2002): 19.

_____. *Zumarraga and the Mexican Inquisition, 1536–1543.* Washington, D.C.: Academy of American Franciscan History, 1961.

Greg, W.W. *Some Aspects and Problems of London Publishing Between 1550 and 1650.* Oxford: Clarendon Press, 1956.

Grendler, Paul F. "The Destruction of Hebrew Books in Venice." In *American Academy for Jewish Research Proceedings.* Vol. 45. Jerusalem: Central Press, 1978. 103–130.

_____. *The Roman Inquisition and the Venetian Press, 1540–1605.* Princeton: Princeton University Press, 1977.

Griffith, W. *An Exact and True Relation of the Birth and Life of Simon Morin.* London, 1663.

Griffiths, Nicholas. *The Cross and the Serpent.* Norman: University of Oklahoma Press, 1996.

Groot, J.J.M. de. *Sectarianism and Religious Persecution in China.* Amsterdam: J. Miller, 1903–4.

Grossman, Mordecai. *The Philosophy of Helvetius.* New York: Teachers College, Columbia University, 1926.

Grunberger, Richard. *A Social History of the Third Reich.* London: Weidenfeld and Nicolson, 1971.

Guehenno, Jean. *Jean-Jacques Rousseau.* Trans. John and Doreen Weightman. Vol. 2. London: Routledge and Keegan Paul, 1966.

Guthrie, W.K.C. *In the Beginning.* London: Methuen, 1957.

Guy, R. Kent. *The Emperor's Four Treasuries: Scholars and the State in the Late Ch'ien-Lung Era.* Cambridge, Mass.: Harvard University Press, 1987.

Haight, Anne Lyon. *Banned Books.* 3rd ed. New York: R.R. Bowker, 1970.

Haliczer, Stephen, ed. *Inquisition and Society in Early Modern Europe.* London: Croom Helm 1987.

Hall, John W., ed. *The Cambridge History of Japan.* Vol. 4. Cambridge: Cambridge University Press, 1991

Hallewell, L. *Books in Brazil: A History of the Publishing Trade.* Metuchen, N.J.: Scarecrow Press, 1982.

Halperin, David J. *Abraham Miguel Cardozo: Selected Writings.* New York: Paulist Press, 2001.

Halsey v. New York Society for Suppression of Vice. 136 N.E. 219 (1922).

Hamilton, Janet, and Bernard Hamilton, trans. *Christian Dualist Heresies in the Byzantine World.* Manchester: Manchester University Press, 1998.

Han Fei Tzu. *Han Fei Tzu: Basic Writings.* Trans. Burton Watson. New York: Columbia University Press, 1964.

Harrison, G.B. *Skialetheia.* Oxford: Oxford University Press, 1931.

Harrison, Nicholas. *Circles of Censorship.* Oxford: Clarendon Press 1995.

Hart, W.H. *Index Expurgatorius Anglicanus.* New York: Burt Franklin, 1969.

Hauck, A. "Ratramus." In *The New Schaff-Herzog Encyclopedia of Religious Knowledge.* Vol. 9. New York: Funk and Wagnalls, 1911.

Hawthorne, Nathaniel. *Works of Nathaniel Hawthorne.* Vol. 3. New York: Bigelow, Brown, 1923.

Hearn, Lafcadio. *Japan: An Attempt at Interpretation.* New York: Macmillan, 1905.

Heine, Heinrich. *The Complete Poems of Heinrich Heine.* Ed. Hal Draper. Boston: Suhrkamp/Insel Publishers, 1982.

Helper, Hinton R. *The Impending Crisis of the South.* New York: A.B. Burdick, 1860.

Helvetius, C.A. *De L'esprit.* New York: Burt Franklin, 1970.

Hely-Hutchison, John. *The Commercial Restraint of Ireland.* London, 1779.

Hendel, Charles. *Jean-Jacques Rousseau: Moralist.* Vol. 2. London: Oxford University Press, 1934.

Hendrix, Scott. *Luther and the Papacy.* Philadelphia: Fortress Press, 1981.

Hill, Leonidas. "The Nazi Attack on 'Un-German' Literature, 1933–1945." In The *Holocaust and the Book.* Ed. Jonathan Rose. Amherst: University of Massachusetts Press, 2001. 9–46.

Hindus, Milton. *Walt Whitman: The Critical Heritage.* New York: Barnes and Noble, 1971.

Ho, Nguyen. "Erasing Vietnam's Past." *Index on Censorship* 7 (Nov./Dec. 1978): 18–20.

Holbach, Baron. *The System of Nature.* Trans. H.D. Robinson. New York: Burt Franklin, 1970.

Holbrook, Stewart. "Hinton Helper and His Crisis." *American Mercury* 60 (January 1945): 109–113.

Hopf, Constantin. *Martin Bucer and the English Reformation.* Oxford: Basil Blackwell, 1946.

Horrox, Rosemary, ed. *Black Death.* Manchester: Manchester University Press, 1994.

Howe, Marvin. "Chile Seizes a U.S. Professor in Hunt for Leftists." *New York Times* Sept. 25, 1973: 4.

Hsu Ting. *Government Control of the Press in Modern China, 1900–1949.* Cambridge, Mass.: Harvard University Press, 1974.

Hughes, Paul, and James Larkin, eds. *Tudor Royal Proclamations.* Vols. 1 and 2. New Haven: Yale University Press, 1969.

Hughes, Philip. *The Reformation in England.* London: Hollis and Carter, 1956.

Huizinga, Jacob H. *Rousseau: The Self-Made Saint.* New York: Grossman, 1976.

Hulbert, Homer. *History of Korea.* Vol. 1. Ed. Clarence Weems. London: Routledge and Kegan, 1905.

Hunt, Lynn. *The Invention of Pornography.* New York: Zone Books, 1993.

Hus, John. *The Letters of John Hus.* Trans. Matthew Spinka. Manchester: Manchester University Press, 1972.

Ibsen, Henrik. *Four Major Plays.* Trans. Rolf Fjelde. New York: New American Library, 1965.

Imerti, Arthur. *The Triumphant Beast: Geordano Bruno.* New Brunswick, N.J.: American Rutgers University Press, 1964.

In re Worthington. 30 N.Y.S. 361 (1894).

Index on Censorship 2 (Spring, 1973): 3.

_____. 8 (Jan./Feb. 1979): 50.

_____. 14 (August 1985): 51, 65

_____. 17 (Oct. 1988): 40

_____. 19 (March 1990): 26, 28

_____. 19 (June/July 1990): 42

_____. 28 (March/April 1999): 166–167

Isaacs, A.S. "The Talmud in History." In *The Jewish Quarterly Review.* Vol. 13. New York: KTAV Publishing House, 1966. 438–445.

Isherwood, Christopher. *Christopher and His Kind.* New York: Farrar, Straus, Geroux, 1976.

Jackson, Holbrook. *The Fear of Books.* London: Sonino Press, 1932.

Jenkinson, Edward. *Censors in the Classroom: The Mind Benders.* Carbondale: Southern Illinois University Press, 1979.

Jensen, De Lamar. *Confrontation at Worms: Martin Luther and the Diet of Worms.* Provo, Utah: Brigham Young University Press, 1973.

Jewish Encyclopedia. Vol. 5. New York: Funk and Wagnalls, 1903.

John the Scot. *Periphyseon: On the Division of Nature.* Trans. Myra L. Uhlfelder. Indianapolis: Babbs-Merrill, 1976.

Johnson, Jeri. "Introduction." In James Joyce, *Ulysses.* Oxford: Oxford University Press, 1998.

Johnston, Andrew G. "Printing and the Reformation in the Low Countries, 1520–c.1555." In *The Reformation and the Book.* Trans. Karen Maag. Ed. Jean-François Gilmont. Aldershor, England: Ashgate Publishing, 1998. 154–183.

Jones, Ernest. *The Life and Work of Sigmund Freud.* Vol. 3. New York: Basic Books, 1957.

Jourdain, Margaret, ed. and trans. *Diderot's Early Philosophical Works.* Chicago: The Open Court Publishing Co., 1916.

Judgment and Decree of the University of Oxford, Past in Their Convocation, July 21, 1683. Oxford, 1683.

Kamen, Henry. *Inquisition and Society in Spain in the Sixteenth and Seventeenth Centuries.* London: Weidenfeld and Nicolson, 1985.

_____. *The Spanish Inquisition.* New Haven: Yale University Press, 1998.

Karolides, Nicholas. *Banned Books: Literature Suppressed on Political Grounds.* New York: Facts on File, 1998.

_____, Margaret Bald, and Dawn B. Sova. *100 Banned Books.* New York: Checkmark Books, 1999.

"Kashmir Leader Held on Holy Book Burning Protest." http://wwa.cnn.com/2001/WORLD/asiapcf/south/03/16/Kashmir.leader.detained/.

Kawecka-Gryczowa, Alodia, and Janusz Tazbir. "The Book and the Reformation in Poland." In *The Reformation and the Book.* Trans. Karen Maag. Ed. Jean-François Gilmont. Aldershot, England: Ashgate Publishing, 1998.

Kenny, Anthony. "Introduction." In *The Bible as Book: The First Printed Editions.* Eds. Paul Saeger and Kimberly van Kampen. London: British Library, 1990.

Keresztes, Paul. *Imperial Rome and the Christians.* Vol. 2. Lanham, Md.: University Press of America, 1989.

Kernan, Alvin. *The Cankered Muse.* New Haven: Yale University Press, 1959.

Kidder, Robert W. "The Contribution of Daniel Fowle to New Hampshire Printing." Diss. University of Illinois, 1960.

Kilpatrick, James J. *The Smut Peddlers.* Garden City, N.J.: Doubleday, 1960.

Kinder, A. Gordon. "Printing and Reformation Ideas in Spain," In *The Reformation and the Book.* Trans. Karen Maag. Ed. Jean-François Gilmont. Aldershor, England: Ashgate Publishing, 1998. 292–318.

Knapp, Bettina L. *Voltaire Revisited.* New York: Twayne Publishers, 2000.

Kumar, Girja. *The Book on Trial.* New Delhi: Har-Anand Publications, 1997.

Kunitz, Stanley, and Howard Haycraft, eds. *American Authors: 1600–1900.* New York: H.W. Wilson, 138.

Lachenmann, Eugen. "Pascal, Blaise." In *The New Schaff-Herzog Encyclopedia of Religious Knowledge.* Ed. Samuel M. Jackson. New York: Funk and Wagnalls, 1910.

Lacy, Mark. "Fiery Zealotry Leaves Nigeria in Ashes Again." *New York Times* Nov. 29, 2002: A3.

Laertius. *Lives of Eminent Philosophers.* Trans. R.D. Hicks. Vol. 2. London: William Heineman, 1925.

Landa, Diego de. *The Maya.* Ed. and trans. A.R. Pagden. Chicago: J. Philip O'Hara, 1975.

_____. *Relación de las cosas de Yucatan.* Ed. and trans. Alfred Tozzer. Vol. 18. Cambridge, Mass.:

Peabody Museum of American Archaeology and Ethnology, Harvard University, 1941.

La Sale, Antoine de. *The Fifteen Joys of Marriage.* Trans. Brent Pitts. New York: Peter Lang, 1985.

Lasker, Bruno. "Youth Tilts at Smut and Trash." *The Survey* 15 (Feb. 15, 1927): 622.

Lazar, Moshe. "Scorched Parchments and Tortured Memories: The 'Jewishness' of the Anussim Crypto-Jews." In *Cultural Encounters.* Eds. Mary Elizabeth Perry and Anne J. Cruz. Berkeley: University of California Press, 1991. 176–204.

Lea, Henry. *Chapters from the History of Spain.* New York: Burt Franklin, 1967.

_____. *A History of the Inquisition of Spain.* Vols. 2, 3, 4. New York: AMS Press, 1988.

_____. *History of the Inquisition of the Middle Ages.* Vol. 1. New York: Harbor Press, 1955.

Leach, Marjorie. *Guide to the Gods.* Eds. Michael O. Jones and Francis Cattermole-Tally. Santa Barbara: ABC-CLIO, 1992.

Leff, Gordon. *Heresy in the Later Middle Ages.* Manchester: Manchester University Press, 1967.

_____. *Paris and Oxford Universities in the Thirteenth and Fourteenth Centuries.* New York: John Wiley and Sons, 1968.

Legge, James. *The Life and Teachings of Confucius.* Philadelphia: J.B. Lippincott, 1867.

Legman, G. *The Horn Book: Studies in Erotic Folklore and Bibliography.* New York: New York University Books, 1964.

Lehmann-Haupt, Hellmut. *The Book in America.* 2nd ed. New York: R.R. Bowker, 1951.

Lever, Maurice. *Sade: A Biography.* Trans. Arthur Goldhammer. New York: Farrar, Straus and Giroux, 1993.

Leverenz, David. "Historicizing Hell in Hawthorne's Tales." In *New Essays on Hawthorne's Major Tales.* Ed. Millicent Bell. Cambridge: Cambridge University Press, 1993.

Levi, Anthony. *Guide to French Literature.* Detroit: St. James Press, 1994.

Leviero, Anthony. "'Books Burners' Are Assailed by President at Dartmouth; He Asks Courage to End Bias." *New York Times,* June 15, 1953: 1.

Levy, Leanard. *Blasphemy.* New York: Alfred A. Knopf, 1993.

_____. *Treason Against God.* New York: Schocken Books, 1981.

"Lewd Seizures Burned." *New York Times,* March 8, 1953: 72.

Lewis, Bernard. *The Crisis of Islam.* New York: Random House, 2003.

Lewis, Felice F. *Literature, Obscenity and Law.* Carbondale: Southern Illinois University Press, 1978.

Lewis, Sinclair. *It Can't Happen Here.* London: Jonathan Cape, 1936.

Liang Hsiao. "On Shang Yang." In *Shang Yang's Reforms and State Control of China.* Ed. Li Yuning. White Plains, N.Y.: M.E. Sharpe, 1977.

Lidderdale, Jane, and Mary Nicholson. *Dear Miss Weaver.* New York: Viking Press, 1970.

Lilly, William. *Renaissance Types.* London: Fisher Uwin, 1901.

Lindo, E.H. *The History of the Jews of Spain and Portugal.* New York: Burt Franklin, 1970.

Lipp, Solomon. *Three Chilean Writers.* Waterloo, Canada: Wilfred Laurier University Press, 1975.

Livy. *History of Rome.* Trans. George Baker. London: Jones, 1834.

Llorente, J.A. *A Critical History of the Inquisition in Spain.* Williamstown, Mass.: John Lilburne, 1967.

Lloyd, Alan. *Franco.* Garden City, N.J.: Doubleday, 1969.

London Times. August 4, 2001 20C.

Longhurst, John E. *The Age of Torquemada.* 2nd ed. Lawrence, Kans.: Coronado Press, 1964.

Look Magazine. Oct. 24, 1939: 15.

Loserth, Johann. *Wiclif and Hus.* Trans. M.J. Evans. London: Hodder and Stroughton, 1884.

Loth, David. *The Erotic in Literature.* New York: Julian Messner, 1961.

Lounsbury, Thomas. "A Puritan Censor of the State." *The Yale Review* (July 1923): 790–810.

Lowe, N.F. "Why Swift Killed Partridge." *Swift Studies* 6 (1991): 70–82.

Lowenthal, Leo. "Caliban's Legacy." *Cultural Critique* (Winter 1987–88): 5–17.

_____, and Norbert Guterman. *Prophets of Deceit.* Palo Alto, Calif.: Pacific Books, 1970.

Lu, David. *Japan: Documentary History.* Armank, N.Y.: Sharpe, 1997.

Lucas, John. "Catharism." In *Censorship: A World Encyclopedia.* Vol. 1. Ed. Derek Jones. London: Fitzroy Dearborn, 2001. 429–530.

Luciani, V. "Dominis, Marcantonio, de." In *The New Catholic Encyclopedia.* 2nd ed. Vol. 4. Detroit: Thomson/Gale, 2003. 856.

Lusardi, James. "The Career of Robert Barnes." In *The Complete Works of St. Thomas More.* Eds. Louis A. Schuster, et al. Vol. 8. Part 3. New Haven: Yale University Press, 1973. 1367–1415.

Luther, Martin. *Luther's Works.* Vols. 31, 47. Ed. Harold Grimm. Philadelphia: Muhlenberg Press, 1957.

MacDonald, Frederika. *Jean Jacques Rousseau: A New Criticism.* Vol. 2 London: Chapman and Hall, 1906.

MacMullen, Ramsay. *Enemies of the Roman Order.* Cambridge, Mass.: Harvard University Press, 1966.

Madden, R.R. *The Life and Martyrdom of Savonarola.* Vol. I. London: Thomas Newby, 1853.

Manschreck, Clyde. *Melanchthon: The Quiet Reformer.* New York: Abington Press, 1958.

Marcus v. Search Warrant. 367 U.S. 717 (1961).

Margaronis, Maria. "Purgation and Liberation." *Index on Censorship* 28 (March-April 1999): 147–149.

Marshall, Herbert. *The Battleship Potemkin.* New York: Avon Books, 1978.

Mason, Hayden. *Voltaire: A Biography.* London: Granada, 1981.

Mason, John H. *The Irresistible Diderot.* London: Quartet Books, 1982.

Maule, Thomas. *New England Persecutor Mauled.* New York: William Bradford, 1697.

_____. *Truth Held Forth and Maintained.* New York, 1695.

Mayhew, George P. "Swift's Bickerstaff Hoax as an April Fools' Joke." *Modern Philology* 61 (May 1964): 270–280.

Mcquade, Molly. "Edna O'Brien." In *Writing for Your Life, #2.* Ed. Sybil Steinberg. Wainscott, N.Y.: Pushcart Press, 1995. 199–204.

McRae, Jean, trans. *Six Books of the Commonwealth.* Oxford: Basil Blackwell, 1955.

M'Crie, Thomas. *History of the Progress and Suppression of the Reformation in Spain in the Sixteenth Century.* Edinburgh: William Blackstone, 1829.

Melchinger, Siegfried. *Euripides.* New York: Frederick Ungar, 173.

Mendell, Clarence. *Tacitus: The Man and His Work.* New Haven: Yale University Press, 1957.

Metz, Tracy. "The New Crusaders of the USA." *Index on Censorship* 11 (Feb. 1982): 20–22.

Miller, James. *Rousseau: Dreamer of Democracy.* New Haven: Yale University Press, 1984.

Milton, John. *Areopagitica: And, Of Education.* Ed. George H. Sabine. Arlington Heights, Ill.: Harlan Davidson, 1951.

_____. *The Complete Works of John Milton.* IV, Part I. New Haven: Yale University Press, 1966.

_____. *The Prose Works of John Milton.* Vol. 1. London, 1848.

Missouri Rev. Stat., 542.420.

Mogen, David. *Ray Bradbury.* Boston: Twayne Publishers, 1986.

Monster of Monsters. Boston: Zechariah Fowle, 1754.

Montaigne, Michael de. *The Essays of Michael de Montaigne.* Trans. M.S. Screech. London: Allen Lane, 1991.

Moore, R.I. *The Birth of Popular Heresy.* New York: St. Martin's Press, 1975.

_____. *The Formation of a Persecuting Society.* Oxford: Blackwell, 1987.

_____. "Heresy as Disease." In *The Concept of Heresy in the Middle Ages.* Eds. W. Lourdaux and D. Verhelst. The Hague: Martinus Nijhoff, 1976. 1–11.

_____. "Popular Violence and Popular Heresy in Western Europe, c. 1000–1179." In *Persecution and Toleration.* Ed. W.J. Sheils. London: Basil Blackwell, 1984. 43–50.

Moore, Robert. *Daniel Defoe: Citizen of the Modern World.* Chicago: University of Chicago Press, 1958.

More, Thomas. *The Complete Works of St. Thomas More.* Eds. Louis Schuster, et al. Vol. 8, Part 1. New Haven: Yale University Press, 1973.

_____. *The Confutation of Tyndale's Answer.* Eds. Louis Schuster, et al. Vol. 8. New Haven: Yale University Press, 1973.

Mosca, Frank. *All-American Boys.* Boston: Alyson Publications, 1983.

Moulton, Ian. "Printed Abroad and Uncastrated: Marlowe's Elegies with Davies' Epigrams." In *Marlowe, History and Sexuality.* Ed. Paul W. White. New York: AMS Press, 1998. 77–90.

Moura, Clovis. "Climate of Terror." *Index on Censorship* 8 (July-Aug. 1979): 8–10.

Mozley, J.F. *William Tyndale.* New York: Macmillan, 1937.

Mullett, Charles. *The Bubonic Plague and England.* Lexington: University of Kentucky Press, 1956.

Musa, Mark, ed. *The Portable Dante* (Dante Alighieri). New York: Penguin Books, 1995.

National Cyclopedia of American Biography. Vol. 8. New York: James T. White, 1898.

Ndovi, Victor. "Censorship in Malawi." *Index on Censorship* 8 (Jan/Feb 1979): 22–25.

New Catholic Encyclopedia. New York: McGraw-Hill, 1967.

New Oxford Companion to Literature in French. Ed. Peter France. Oxford: Clarendon Press, 1995.

New Schaff-Herzog Encyclopedia of Religious Knowledge. Ed. Samuel Jackson. New York: Funk and Wagnalls, 1909.

New York Times. May 11, 1933: 12.

_____. May 19, 1933: 9.

_____. May 1, 1938: 35.

_____. April 4, 1945: 12.

_____. August 24, 1950: 26.

_____. February 12, 1952: 29.

_____. March 8, 1953: 72.

_____. June 15, 1953: 10.

_____. May 3, 1964: 2.

_____. September 28, 1973: 2.

_____. July 26, 1989: B9.

_____. December 2, 2001: WK 7.

_____. January 1, 2002: A 17.

_____. March 10, 2002: AR 20.

_____. July 12, 2002: A 6.

Newsletter on Intellectual Freedom. 23 (Jan. 1974): 4.

_____. 23 (March 1974): 42.

_____. 26 (May 1977): 73.

_____. 26 (November 1977): 155.

_____. 28 (May 1979): 63.

_____. 30 (March 1981): 42.

_____. 30 (July 1981): 105.

_____. 36 (November 1987): 228.

_____. 38 (May 1989): 90, 107.

_____. 43 (March 1994): 52.

_____. 49 (March 2000): 50.

_____. 50 (January 2001): 11.

_____. 50 (March, 2001): 43.

_____. 53 (July, 2004): 137.

Nicholl, Donald. "Introduction." *Monarchy.* By Dante. London: Weidenfeld and Nicolson, 1954.

Nichols-Pecceu, Martha. "Censorship, Toleration, and Protestant Poetics: The Case of Agrippa d'Aubigne's *Historie universelle.*" *Religion and French Literature* 25 (1998): 41–53.

Niklaus, Robert. *A Literary History of France.* London: Ernest Benn, 1970.

Noble, William. *Bookbanning in America.* Middlebury, Vt.: Paul S. Eriksson, 1990.

Nokes, G.D. *A History of the Crime of Blasphemy.* London: Sweet and Maxwell, 1928.

Noyes, Alfred. *Voltaire.* New York: Sheed and Ward, 1936.

O'Brien, Edna. "The Art of Fiction LXXXII." *The Paris Review* (Sept. 1984): 23–50.

O'Brien, Maureen. "The Rushdie Crisis: A Report from the Front Lines." *Publishers Weekly* 236 (Sept. 29, 1989): 45–48.

O'Brien, T.C., ed. *Corpus Dictionary of Western Churches.* Washington, D.C.: Corpus Publications, 1970.

O'Callaghan, Joseph. *A History of Medieval Spain.* Ithaca: Cornell University Press, 1975.

O'Connor, Eugene, trans. *Hermaphroditus.* Lanham, Md.: Lexington Books, 2001.

Ogilvie, James. *Civil History of the Kingdom of Naples.* London, 1729.

Oliveira, Celso Lemos de. "The Early Jorge Amado." In *Jorge Amado: New Critical Essays.* Eds. Keith H. Brower, Earl E. Fitz, and Enrique Martinez-Vidal. New York: Routledge, 2001. 159–171.

Olmert, Michael. *The Smithsonian Book of Books.* Washington, D.C.: Smithsonian Books, 1992.

Ong, Walter. *Orality and Literacy.* London: Methuen, 1982.

Onishi, Norimitsu. "Two Religions Clashing in Ivory Coast." *New York Times,* Nov. 6, 2000. A 12.

Orieux, Jean. *Voltaire.* Trans. Barbara Bray and Helen Lane. Garden City, N.Y.: Doubleday, 1979.

Orwell, George. *1984.* New York: New American Library, 1961.

Oxford History of Western Philosophy. Ed. Anthony Kenny. Oxford: Oxford University Press, 1994.

Ozguden, Dogan. "The Press Under Martial Law." *Index on Censorship* 2 (Spring 1973): 4–10.

Pagitt, Ephraim. *Heresiography.* London, 1645.

Parton, James. *Life of Voltaire.* Vol. 2. 8th ed. Boston: Houghton, Mifflin, 1895.

Patrouch, Joseph. *Reginald Pecock.* New York: Twayne Publishers, 1970.

Peel, Albert, and Leland Carlson. *The Writings of Robert Harrison and Robert Browne.* London: George Allen and Unwin, 1953.

Peignot, R. *Dictionnaire Critique, Littéraire et Bibliographique.* Paris, 1806.

People v. Fritch. 192 N.E. 2d 713 (1963).

People v. Muller. 96 N.Y. 408 (1884).

Pepys, Samuel. *The Diary of Samuel Pepys.* Trans. Robert Latham and William Matthews. Berkeley: University of California Press, 1976.

Perkins, Michael. *The Secret Record: Modern Erotic Literature.* New York: William Morrow, 1976.

Peter, John. *Complaint and Satire in Early English Literature.* Oxford: Oxford University Press, 1956.

Peter of Vaux-de-Cernay. *The History of the Albigensian Crusade: Peter of Les Vaux-de-Cernay's Historia Albigensis.* Trans. W.A. and M.D. Sibly. Woodbridge, Suffolk: Boydell Press, 1998.

Peters, Edward. *The First Crusade.* 2nd ed. Philadelphia: University of Pennsylvania Press, 1998.

_____. *Heresy and Authority in Medieval Europe.* Philadelphia: University of Pennsylvania Press, 1980.

_____. *Inquisition.* New York: The Free Press, 1988.

Pfeiffer, Rudolf. *History of Classical Scholarship.* Oxford: Clarendon Press, 1968.

Pharr. Clyde, trans. *The Theodosian Code.* Princeton: Princeton University Press, 1952.

Pica v. Bd. of Education, Island Trees Union Free School. 474 F. Supp. 381 (1979).

Plaidy, Jean. *The End of the Spanish Inquisition.* London: Robert Hale, 1961.

_____. *The Spanish Inquisition.* New York: Citadel Press, 1969.

Poole, William. "Witchcraft in Boston." In *The Memorial History of Boston: 1630–1880.* 2 Vols. Ed. Justine Winsor. Ticknor, 1886.

Popper, William. *The Censorship of Hebrew Books.* New York: Burt Franklin, 1968.

Prescott, William. *History of the Reign of Ferdinand and Isabella.* New York: J.B. Alden, 1887.

Prinz, Johannes. *John Wilmot Earl of Rochester: His Life and Writings.* Leipzig: Mayer and Muller, 1927.

Priolkar, Anant K. *The Goa Inquisition.* Bombay: Bombay University Press, 1961.

Publishers Weekly 136 (Nov. 25, 1939): 1994.

_____. 140 (July 5, 1941): 21.

Putnam, George Haven. *Authors and Their Public in Ancient Times.* New York: G.P. Putnam's Sons, 1896.

_____. *The Censorship of the Church of Rome.* 2 Vols. New York: G.P. Putnam's Sons, 1906.

Radishchev, A. *A Journey from St. Petersburg to Moscow.* Trans. Leo Wiener. Ed. Roderick Thaler. Cambridge, Mass.: Harvard University Press, 1958.

Rankin, H.D. *Sophists, Socratics, and Cynics.* London: Croom Helm 1983.

Reece, Jack E. *The Britons Against France.* Chapel Hill: University of North Carolina Press, 1977.

Reischauer, Edwin. *Japan: The Story of a Nation.* 3rd ed. New York: Alfred A. Knopf, 1981.

Rembar, Charles. "The Outrageously Immoral Face." In *Censorship and Freedom of Expression.* Ed. Harry Clor. Chicago: Rand McNally, 1977.

Richards, Michael. *A Time of Silence.* Cambridge: Cambridge University Press, 1998.

Richardson, Robert. "Preface." *The System of Nature*. Vol. 1. By Baron Holbach. New York: Garland, 1984.

Riedlmayer, Andras. "Erasing the Past: The Destruction of Libraries and Archives in Bosnia-Herzegovia." *Middle East Studies Association Bulletin* 19 (July 1995): 7–11.

Riehl, Alois. *Giordano Bruno: A Study in Conscience*. Trans. Agnes Fry. Edinburgh: T.N. Boulis, 1990.

Ritchie, J.M. "The Nazi Book-Burning." *The Modern Language Review* 83 (July 1988): 627–643.

Roeder, Ralph. *Savonarola: A Study in Conscience*. New York: Brentano's Publishers, 1930.

Rolph, C.H. *Books in the Dock*. London: Andre Deutsch, 1969.

Rose, Jonathan, ed. *The Holocaust and the Book*. Amherst: University of Massachusetts Press, 2001.

Rostenberg, Liona. *The Minority Press and the English Crown: A Study in Repression, 1558–1626*. Nieuwkoop, Netherlands: B. DeGraaf, 1971.

Roth v. United States, 354 U.S. 476 (1957).

Rousseau, Jean Jacque. *Emile*. Trans. Barbara Foxley. Ed. J.D. Jimack. London: J.M. Dent, 1992.

Rowdon, Maurice. *The Spanish Terror: Spanish Imperialism in the Sixteenth Century*. London: Constable, 1974.

Rozzo, Ugo. "Italian Literature on the Index." In *Church Censorship and Culture in Early Modern Italy*. Trans. Adrian Belton. Ed. Gigliola Fragnito. Cambridge: Cambridge University Press, 2001. 194–222.

Rugg, Harold. *That Men May Understand*. New York: Doubleday, Doran, 1941.

Rule, William H. *History of the Inquisition*. London: Hamilton, Adams, 1874.

Rushdie, Salman. "The Book Burning." *The New York Review of Books* 36 (March 2, 1989): 26.

Russell, John R. "Libraries Under Fire." *American Library Association Bulletin* 35 (May 1941): 277–281.

Sabatini, Rafael. *Torquemada and the Spanish Inquisition: A History*. Boston: Houghton Mifflin, 1924.

Sade, Marquis de. *Justine, Philosophy in the Bedroom and Other Writings*. Trans. Richard Seaver and Austryn Wainhouse. New York: Grove Weidenfeld, 1965.

_____. *Selected Letters*. Trans. W.J. Strachan. Ed. Margaret Crossland. London: Peter Owen, 1992.

Sa'edi, Gholam Hoseyn. "Iron Under the Party of God." *Index on Censorship* 13 (Feb. 1984): 16–20.

Sagar, Kieth. *The Life of D.H. Lawrence*. New York: Pantheon Books, 1980.

Salmon, J.H.M. "The Abbe Raynal, 1713–96: An Intellectual Odyssey." *History Today* 26 (Feb. 1976): 109–117.

Sanders, Michael. "Book Burning and Brutality." *Index on Censorship* 3 (Spring 1974): 7–13.

Sanford, Robinson Rojas. *The Murder of Allende*. Trans. Andree Conrad. New York: Harper and Row, 1976.

Sansom, G.B. *The Western World and Japan*. New York: Alfred Knopf, 1950.

Sarachek, Joseph. *Faith and Reason*. New York: Hermon Press, 1970.

Savage, W. Sherman. *The Controversy Over the Distribution of Abolition Literature: 1830–1860*. Washington, D.C.: Association for the Study of Negro Life and History, 1938.

Scartazzini, G.N. *A Companion to Dante*. Trans. Arthur J. Butler. London: Macmillan, 1893.

Scase, Wendy. "Reginald Pecock." In *English Writers of the Late Middle Ages*. Ed. M.G. Seymore. Aldershot, England; Ashgate, 1993.

Schiappa, Edward. *Protagoras and Logos*. Columbia: University of South Carolina Press, 1991.

Schlesinger, Stephen, and Stephen Kinzer. *Bitter Fruit: The Story of the American Coup in Guatemala*. Expanded ed. Cambridge, Mass.: Harvard University Press 1999.

Schmid, Wilhelm. *Geschichte der Griechischen Literatur*. Vol. 3. Series 7. Munich: C.H. Hetk'sche Verlagsbuchhandlung, 1940.

Schnur, Harry C. *Mystic Rebels*. New York: Beechhurst Press, 1949.

Schoenhals, Michael, ed. *China's Cultural Revolution, 1966–1969*. Armonk, N.Y.: M.E. Sharpe, 1966.

School Library Journal 48 (Feb. 2002): 27.

Schroeder, Theodore. *Freedom of the Press and "Obscene" Literature*. New York: Free Speech League, 1906.

Scott, Reginald. *The Discoverie of Witchcraft*. Introduction by Montague Summers. London: John Rodker, 1930.

_____. *The Discoverie of Witchcraft*. Introduction by Hugh R. Williamson. Carbondale: Southern University Press, 1964.

Scott, Temple, ed. *The Prose Works of Jonathan Swift*. London: George Bell and Sons, 1907.

Seneca the Elder. *The Elder Seneca*. Trans. M. Winterbottom. Vol. 2. Cambridge, Mass.: Harvard University Press, 1974.

Shaffer, Kenneth. "The Conquest of Books." *Library Journal* 71 (Jan. 15, 1946): 82–86.

Shavit, David. *Hunger for the Printed Word*. Jefferson, N.C.: McFarland, 1997.

Sheridan, Geraldine. *Nicholas Lenglet Dufresnoy and the Literary Underworld of the Ancient Regime*. Oxford: The Voltaire Foundation, 1989.

Shibles, Warren. "The Metaphorical Method." *Journal of Aesthetic Education* 8 (1974): 25–36.

Shui Hu Chuan. *All Men Are Brothers*. Trans. Pearl Buck. New York: John Day, 1933.

Siebert, Fredrick. *Freedom of the Press in England, 1476–1776*. Urbana: University of Illinois Press, 1965.

Sigel, Lisa Z. *Governing Pleasures: Pornography and*

Social Change in England, 1815–1914. New Brunswick, N.J.: Rutgers University Press, 2002.

Smith, D.W. "The Publication of Helvetius's De L'Esprit (1758–9)." *French Studies* 18 (July 1964): 332–344.

Smith, Joseph H., ed. *Colonial Justice in Western Massachusetts: The Pynchon Court Record*. Cambridge, Mass.: Harvard University Press, 1961.

Smith, Preserved. *The Life and Letters of Martin Luther*. New York: Barnes and Noble, 1968.

Smith, William, ed. *Dictionary of Greek and Roman Biography*. Vol. 3. London: John Murray, 1902.

Snow, Edgar. "The Ways of the Chinese Censor." *Current History* 42 (July 1935): 381–386.

Snyder, Louis, ed. *Documents of German History*. New Brunswick, N.J.: Rutgers University Press, 1958.

Sommers, Joseph. *Literature and Ideology: Vargas Llosa's Novelistic Evaluation of Militarism*. New York: New York University Press, 1975.

Sontag, Susan. *Illness as Metaphor*. New York: Farrar, Straus and Giroux, 1977.

Spinka, Matthew. *John Hus at the Council of Constance*. New York Columbia University Press, 1965.

_____. *John Hus' Concept of the Church*. Princeton: Princeton University Press, 1966.

Sroka, Marek. "The University of Cracow Library under Nazi Occupation: 1939–1945." *Libraries and Culture* 34 (Winter 1999): 1–15.

Stainton, Michael. "Sources of the 19th Century Chinese Opposition to the Missionaries and Christianity." *Quarterly Notes on Christianity, and Chinese Religion and Culture* 20 (1977): 130–147.

Starkie, Walter. *Grand Inquisitor*. London: Hodder and Stroughton, 1940.

Stieg, Margaret. "The 1926 German Law to Protect Youth Against Trash and Dirt: Moral Protectionism in a Democracy." *Central European History* 23 (March 1990): 22–56.

_____. *Public Libraries in Nazi Germany*. Tuscaloosa: University of Alabama Press, 1992.

Stone, I.F. *The Trial of Socrates*. New York: Anchor Books, 1988.

Stow, Kenneth R. "The Burning of the Talmud in 1553, in the Light of Sixteenth Century Catholic Attitudes Toward the Talmud." In *Bibliothèque d'Humanisme Renaissance*. Geneva: Librairie Droz S.A., 1972. 435–459.

Suetonius. *The Twelve Caesars*. Trans. Robert Graves. Baltimore, Md.: Penguin Books, 1957.

Summers, Montague. "Introduction." In Reginald Scott. *The Discoverie of Witchcraft*. London: John Rodker, 1930.

Sungolowsky, Joseph. *Beaumarchais*. New York: Twayne Publishers, 1974.

Sweig, Paul. *Walt Whitman: The Making of the Poet*. New York: Basic Books, 1984.

Syme, Ronald. *The Roman Revolution*. Oxford: Clarendon Press, 1939.

Synan, Edward. *The Popes and the Jews in the Middle Ages*. Macmillan, 1965.

Tacitus. *The Annals of Imperial Rome*. Trans. Michael Grant. London: Penguin Books, 1996.

Tallentyre, S.G. *The Life of Voltaire*. New York: Loring and Mussey, 1900.

Tasaburo, Ita. "The Books Burning Policy of the Tokugawa Shognate." In *Act Asiatica: Bulletin of the Institute of Eastern Culture*. Vol. 22. Tokyo: Toho Gaddai, 1972. 36–5l.

Taylor, Larissa J. *Heresy and Orthodoxy in Sixteenth Century Paris*. Leiden: Brill, 1999.

Tazbir, Janusz. *A State Without Stakes*. Trans. A.T. Jordon. Poland: Państwowy Instytut Wydawniczy, 1973.

Tedeschi, John. *The Prosecution of Heresy*. Binghamton, N.Y.: Medieval and Renaissance Texts and Studies, 1991.

Teske, Roland, trans. "Introduction." In *St. Augustine's Arianism and Other Heresies*. Hyde Park, N.Y.: New City Preps, 1995.

Thaddeus, Victor. *Voltaire: Genius of Mockery*. New York: Brentano's Publishers, 1928.

The Theodosian Code. Trans. Clyde Pharr. Princeton: Princeton University Press, 1952.

Thomas, Donald. *A Long Time Burning*. New York: Frederick Praeger, 1969.

_____. *The Marquis de Sade*. Boston: New York Graphic Society, 1976.

Thomas, Hugh. *The Spanish Civil War*. New York: Harper & Row, 1977.

Thomas, William. *A Historie of Italie*. Ed. George B. Parks. Ithaca, N.Y.: Cornell University Press, 1963.

Thorndike, Lynn. *University Records and Life in the Middle Ages*. New York: Octagon Books, 1971.

Tilley, Maureen, trans. *Donatist Martyr Stories: The Church in Roman North Africa*. Liverpool: Liverpool University Press, 1996.

Tindal, Matthew. *The Right of the Christian Church Asserted Against the Romish, and Other Priests*. London, 1706.

Toer, Pramoedya Ananta. *The Mute's Soliloquy*. Trans. William Samuels. New York: Hyperion East, 1999.

Toland, John. *Christianity Not Mysterious*. London, 1696.

Tommaso, Andrea di. "Pulci, Pulci." In *Dictionary of Italian Literature*. Eds. Peter Bondanella and Julia Conaway Bondanella. Westport, Conn.: Greenwood Press, 1979. 422–425.

Topolski, Jerzy. *An Outline History of Poland*. Trans. Olgierd Wojtasiewicz. Warsaw: Interpress Publishers, 1986.

Tozzer, Alfred, ed. and trans. *Relación de las cosas de Yucatan* (Diego de Landa). Vol. 18. Cambridge, Mass.: Peabody Museum of American Archaeology and Ethnology, Harvard University, 1941.

Trebbel, John. *A History of Book Publishing in the United States*. Vol. 4. New York: R.R. Bowker, 1981.

Trevett, Christine. *Montanism*. Cambridge: Cambridge University Press, 1996.

Trevor-Roper, Hugh. "Pietro Giannone and Great Britain." *The Historical Journal* 39 (Sept. 1996): 657–675.

Trobridge, W.R.H. *Cagliostro*. New Hyde Park, N.Y.: University Books, 1961.

Tuberville, A.S. *The Spanish Inquisition*. London: Oxford University Press, 1932.

"Turkey on the Slippery Slope." *Index on Censorship* 3 (Spring 1973):- 2–20.

UNESCO. *Memory of the World: Lost Memory — Libraries and Archives Destroyed in the Twentieth Century*. In *Index on Censorship* 28 (March/April 1999): 166–167.

U.S. News and World Reports 34 (June 26, 1953): 40.

United States Senate. *Hearings Before the Committee on Appropriations*, U.S. Senate. 83rd Congo 1st Sess. on H.R. 6200. 1953.

United States v. Ballard. 322 U.S. 78 (1944).

United States v. One Book Called "Ulysses." 5 F.Supp. 182 (1933).

United States v. One Book Entitled Ulysses. 72 F.2d 705 (1934).

United States v. Paris Adult Theatre I v. Slaton, 413 U.S. 49 (1973).

United States v. 12 200-ft. Reels of Film, 413 U.S. 123 (1973).

Untersteiner, Mario. *The Sophists*. Trans. Kathleen Freeman. New York: Philosophical Library, 1954.

Vanderham, Paul. *James Joyce and Censorship*. London: Macmillan, 1998.

Van Kampen, Kimberly. "Biblical Books and the Circulation of the Psalms in Late-Medieval England." In *The Bible as Book: The First Printed Editions*. Eds. Paul Saenger and Kimberly van Kampen. New Castle, Del.: Oak Knoll Press, 1999. 79–94.

Verbeke, Gerald. "Philosophy and Heresy: Some Conflicts Between Reason and Faith." In *Concept at Heresy in the Middle Ages*. Eds. W. Lourdaux and D. Verhelst. Leuven, Belgium: Leuven University Press, 1976. 172–197.

Voltaire. *The Complete Works of Voltaire*. Ed. Theodore Besterman. Toronto: University of Toronto Press, 1968.

Vonnegut, Kurt. "Books into Ashes." *New York Times* Feb. 7, 1982: E19.

Wakefield, Walter, and Austin Evans, trans. *Heresies of the High Middle Ages*. New York: Columbia University Press, 1991.

Walker, Hugh. *English Satire and Satirists*. London: J.M. Dent and Sons, 1925.

Walker, Lilliston, R. Norris, D. Lotz, R. Handy. A *History of the Christian Church*. 4th ed. New York: Charles Scribner's Sons, 1985.

Watson v. Jones. 13 Wall 679 (1872).

Weaver, May Anne. "A Fugitive from Justice." *New Yorker* 70 (Sept. 12, 1994): 48–60.

Wertenbaker, Thomas. *The Puritan Oligarchy*. New York: Charles Scribner's Sons, 1947.

Wertham, Frederic. *Seduction of the Innocent*. New York: Rinehart, 1954.

West Virginia State Bd. of Ed. v. Barnette. 319 U.S. 624 (1943).

Wheelwright, Philip, ed. *The Presocratics*. New York: Odyssey Press, 1966.

Whitaker, John. *We Cannot Escape History*. New York: Macmillan, 1943.

Whitman, Walt. *Leaves of Grass*. New York: Doubleday, 1997.

Who Was Who in America: Historical Volume, 1607–1896. New Providence, N.J.: Marquis Who's Who, 1963.

Wickwar, William. "Helvetius and Holbach." In *The Social and Political Ideas of Some Great French Thinkers in the Age of Reason*. Ed. F.J.C. Hearnshaw. New York: Barnes and Noble, 1967. 195–216.

Wight, O.W. *The Provincial Letters*. New York: Hurd and Houghton, 1872.

Wild, Laura. *The Romance of the English Bible*. Garden City, N.J.: Doubleday, Doran, 1929.

Wilkinson, Tracy. "Poet of Debate on Victims of Franco." *Seattle Times*, December 12, 2004: A24.

Williams, George. "The Place of the Confesio Fidei of Jonas Schlichting in the Life and Thought of the Minor Church." In *Socinianism and Its Role in the Culture of the XVIth to XVIIth Centuries*. Ed. Lech Szczuki. Warsaw: PWN-Polish Scientific Publisher, 1983.

Williamson, Hugh. "Introduction." In Reginald Scott. *The Discoverie of the Witchcraft*. Carbondale: Southern Illinois University Press, 1964.

_____. *Lorenzo the Magnificent*. New York: G.P. Putnam's Sons, 1964.

Willis, M.D. *Servetus and Calvin*. London: Henry S. King, 1877.

Wilmot, John. *The Works of John Wilmot Earl of Rochester*. Ed. Harold Love. Oxford: Oxford University Press, 1999.

Wilson, Charles. "Shanghai Baby." *New York Times* September 23, 2001: BkRev 24.

Winwar, Francis. *Puritan City: A Story of Salem*. New York: National Travel Club, 1938.

Wood, Anthony. *Anthenae Oxonienses*. Vol. 1. London: 1813.

_____. *Anthenae Oxonienses*. Vol. 4. Oxford, 1820.

_____. *Life and Times of Anthony Wood*. Vol. 3. Oxford, 1898.

Workman, Herbert. *John Wyclif: A Study of the English Medieval Church*. Vol. 2. Oxford: Clarendon Press, 1926.

World Peace Review 48 (August 2001): 38.

Worrall, Arthur J. *Quakers in the Colonial Northeast*. Hanover, N.H.: University Press of New England, 1980.

Worth, Ronald, Jr. *Church, Monarch and Bible in Sixteenth Century England*. Jefferson, N.C.: McFarland, 2000.

Wright, Bradford W. *Comic Book Nation.* Baltimore: John Hopkins University Press, 2001.

Wyclif, John. *Wyclif: Selected English Writings.* Ed. Herbert Winn. London: Humphrey Milford, 1929.

Wylie, A. *Notes on Chinese Literature.* Shanghai: Presbyterian Mission Press, 1922.

Yang Shang. *The Book of Lord Shang.* Trans. J.J.L. Duyvendak. London: Arthur Probsthain, 1928.

Young, John D. *Confucianism and Christianity.* Hong Kong: Hong Kong University Press, 1983.

Yutang, Lin. *A History of the Press and Public Opinion in China.* Shanghai: Kelly and Walsh, 1937.

Zeyl, Donald, ed. *Encyclopedia of Classical Philosophy.* Westport, Conn.: Greenwood Press, 1997.

Zokler, O. "Suarez, Francisco." In *The New Schaff-Herzog Encyclopedia of Religious Knowledge.* Vol. 2. Ed. Samuel Jackson. New York: Funk and Wagnalls, 1911.

Zucotti, Susan. *The Italians and the Holocaust.* New York: Basic Books, 1987.

Zykan v. Warsaw Community School Corp. 621 F.2d 1300 (1980).

INDEX